Albert Einstein's
Theory of
General Relativity

Albert Einstein's Theory of General Relativity

Edited by GERALD E. TAUBER

CROWN PUBLISHERS, INC.
NEW YORK

Printed in the United States of America
Published simultaneously in Canada by
General Publishing Company Limited

Book Design: Shari De Miskey

Library of Congress Cataloging in Publication Data

Main entry under title:

Albert Einstein's theory of general relativity.

Includes bibliographical references and index.
1. General relativity (Physics)
2. Einstein, Albert, 1879–1955.   3. Physicists—
Biography.   I. Tauber, Gerald E.
QC173.6.A4   1979   530.1'1   79-1471
ISBN 0-517-53661-7

Second Printing, August, 1979

May this hour of grateful remembrance serve to strengthen within us the love and esteem in which we hold the treasures of our culture, gained in such bitter struggle. Our fight to preserve those treasures against the present powers of darkness and barbarism cannot then but carry the day.

A. Einstein, New York, 1935

This volume is humbly dedicated to the memory of my parents and the six million victims of the holocaust. May they rest in peace.

CONTENTS

2. EXPOSITION

3. CRITICISMS AND REFUTATIONS

III. EXPERIMENTAL VERIFICATION OF THE GENERAL THEORY
    OF RELATIVITY   114

VIII. GRAVITATION AND THE UNIVERSE 259

IX. CONCLUSION 300

APPENDIXES 315

Wo ich geh und wo ich steh,
Stets ein Bild von mir ich seh,
Auf dem Schreibtisch, an der Wand,
Um den Hals an schwarzem Band.
Männlein, Weiblein, wundersam,
Holen sich ein Autogramm,
Jeder muss ein Kritzel haben
Von dem hochgelehrten Knaben.
Mensch, so frag ich in all dem Glück
Ich im rechten Augenblick,
Bist verrückt du etwa selber
Oder sind die andern Kälber?

Where I go and where I may be,
A picture of myself I always see,
On the desk, hung on a wall,
Around the neck from ribbon fall.
Men and women wonders seeking,
Autographs fetch for safe keeping.
Each must have a little scratch
Which the learned man dispatch.
With good fortune by my side,
Still I ask myself in stride
Is it I in madness heaped
Or are the others merely sheep?

Free translation of "Gelegentliches," Soncino-Gesellschaft, 1929, that appears on the back of a photograph for Mrs. W. Albert Einstein. Reproduced with permission of the Estate of Albert Einstein.

EDITOR'S PREFACE

In 1916 Einstein formulated his General Theory of Relativity, a theory of gravitation, which has withstood the onslaught of time. Recent developments in astrophysics, the discovery of neutron stars and pulsars, a better understanding of the universe in which we live, all these require general relativity for their complete description.

This year, when we are commemorating the centenary of Einstein's birth, it would be most fitting to review the theory of general relativity; to present Einstein's contribution to the scientific thinking of today in non-technical language, to show the additions, confirmations, comparison with newer theories, and the work that has been done on Einstein's unfinished work—this is the aim of this commemorative volume. Most of its content comes from Einstein's own writings, but there are also short contributions from leading scientists on their work in connection with new developments in general relativity, relativistic astrophysics, or cosmology.

In the introduction to this book, Part I, various tributes to Einstein, and some of his responses to them, are gathered. Part II is comprised of articles on the origins and foundations of the general theory of relativity, as well as a non-technical exposition of the theory, criticisms, and refutations—all taken from Einstein's own writings. This is followed by a discussion of experimental tests, both old and new. The fourth part of the book has a collection of several brief essays on the sidelights on relativity. A number of experts describe the important new astrophysical applications in the fifth part. A discussion whether or not gravitational waves exist and whether they can possibly be detected is the subject of the sixth part. Various attempts toward a unified field theory, starting with Einstein's work to present investigations, is the subject of the next part. The story of relativistic cosmology from Einstein's masterful conception until the present is contained in Part VIII. The last part of the book is devoted to the problem of space and future developments. Several appendixes have also been added for the more mathematically inclined reader.

11

It is my special pleasure to express my sincerest appreciation and thanks to the many persons who have given unselfishly of their time and made contributions. In addition, I wish to express my thanks to Dr. Otto Nathan, Trustee of the Estate of Albert Einstein, for permitting us to reprint the many works of Einstein, to Professor Herman M. Schwartz for his masterly translation of the "Dialogue," to Professors John Stachel and Jurgen Ehlers for locating several of Einstein's papers for us, to Professors Gerald Holton and Nathan Rosen for their encouragement, and last but not least to the publisher, Herbert Michelman, for his painstaking editing.

It is our sincere hope that this collection will be not only a tribute to the memory of a great scientist but that the reader will also obtain a better understanding of Einstein's great contribution.

Gerald E. Tauber

Tel Aviv, Israel

PREFACE

The present book is intended, as far as possible, to give an exact insight into the theory of Relativity to those readers who, from a general scientific and philosophical point of view, are interested in the theory, but who are not conversant with the mathematical apparatus of theoretical physics. The work presumes a standard of education corresponding to that of a university matriculation examination, and, despite the shortness of the book, a fair amount of patience and force of will on the part of the reader. The author has spared himself no pains in his endeavour to present the main ideas in the simplest and most intelligible form, and on the whole, in the sequence and connection in which they actually originated. In the interest of clearness, it appeared to me inevitable that I should repeat myself frequently, without paying the slightest attention to the elegance of the presentation. I adhered scrupulously to the precept of that brilliant theoretical physicist L. Boltzmann, according to whom matters of elegance ought to be left to the tailor and to the cobbler. I make no pretence of having withheld from the reader difficulties which are inherent to the subject. On the other hand, I have purposely treated the empirical physical foundations of the theory in a "step-motherly" fashion, so that readers unfamiliar with physics may not feel like the wanderer who was unable to see the forest for trees. May the book bring someone a few happy hours of suggestive thought!

December, 1916   A. EINSTEIN

From A. Einstein, Relativity, *Preface to the first edition, trans. Robert W. Lawson (New York: Crown Publishers,* © *1961). Reprinted by permission of the Estate of Albert Einstein.*

13

I. INTRODUCTION

Albert Einstein does not need an introduction, nor does a book about him or his writings. Nevertheless, we felt it appropriate to add a few words to the tributes paid to Einstein and his responses to these tributes.

In memorial volumes of this kind it is customary to have a biography of the person in whose honor it is written. There already exists a great many biographies of Einstein, so instead of adding to this list, we have reprinted three essays about him. These include an excerpt from *Albert Einstein* by Leopold Infeld, a close collaborator of Einstein's, who paid tribute to Einstein in a few well-chosen sentences. The second contributor is Carl Lanczos, who knew Einstein intimately and describes the significance of Einstein's work in his lecture "The Greatness of Albert Einstein." The third essayist, Gerald Holton, is well acquainted with Einstein's work, having written many critical papers on relativity; in his essay he discusses Einstein's *"Weltbild."*

Einstein received the Nobel Prize in physics; the presentation speech given by S. Arrhenius, chairman of the Nobel Committee for Physics, when the prize was awarded, is included here. Einstein was the guest of honor on many other occasions, but we have limited ourselves here to reprinting only the welcoming address at a luncheon for Einstein in Pasadena, California, by Frederick H. Seares, assistant director of the Mount Wilson Observatory. Among the many other awards and honorary degrees bestowed on Einstein during his lifetime, the one he cherished the most was the degree conferred upon him by the Hebrew University, in Jerusalem; we include this citation here.

When Einstein died in 1955 he was eulogized by many, but probably one of the most sincere expressions came from Niels Bohr, with whom Einstein has carried on a lengthy debate about the validity of quantum mechanics. Bohr's tribute to Einstein is included in this section. I. I. Rabi's tribute to Einstein at the time of his death, which Rabi has updated, is also given here.

Because Albert Einstein was a humble person who did not like to be in the limelight, he limited his addresses to scientific lectures or causes that were close to his heart. Some of his scientific lectures can be found in Part II of this book, but causes—important as they are—do not fit into a volume of this type. Of great interest, however, are Einstein's responses to the honors bestowed upon him, and we have therefore selected three examples of these for inclusion in this book. The first is the Inaugural Address to the Prussian Academy of Sciences, in Berlin, when Einstein was chosen a member of the academy. The second is an address at Max Planck's 70th birthday, when Einstein was presented the Planck Medal by Professor Planck himself. Finally, we also include here Einstein's speech when he received the honorary degree from the Hebrew University, already mentioned.

Much more could be said about Einstein the man and Einstein the scientist, but it is time to stop and let others have their say.

ALBERT EINSTEIN—THE MAN

LEOPOLD INFELD

In seeking to understand Einstein's appeal to the imagination of so many of his fellow men, a strange comparison comes to my mind. In a village in India there is a wise old saint. He sits under a tree and never speaks. The people look at his eyes directed toward heaven. They do not know the thoughts of this old man because he is always silent. But they form their own image of the saint, a picture that comforts them. They sense deep wisdom and kindness in his eyes. They bring food to the tree where the man sits, happy that by this small sacrifice they form a communion with the lofty thoughts of their saint.

In our civilization we do not have primitive villagers and silent, contemplating saints. Yet we see in our newspapers a picture of a man who does not go to the barber, who does not wear a tie or socks, whose eyes seem to be directed away from the little things of our world. He does not toil for personal comfort. He cares little for all the things that mean so much in our lives. If he speaks in defense of a cause he does not do it for his personal glory. It is comforting for us to know that such a man still exists, a man whose thoughts are directed toward the stars. We give him admiration because in admiring him we prove to ourselves that we, too, yearn for the distant stars.

Einstein has become a symbol for many, a monument people have built, a symbol that they need for their own comfort.

From Leopold Infeld, Albert Einstein *(New York: Charles Scribner's Sons, 1950). Reprinted by permission of the publisher.*

And perhaps, in the last analysis, these people are right. Perhaps the real greatness of Einstein lies in the simple fact that, though in his life he has gazed at the stars, yet he also tried to look at his fellow men with kindness and compassion.

THE GREATNESS OF ALBERT EINSTEIN

C. LANCZOS

The emotional state which leads to such achievements
resembles that of the worshipper or the lover;
the daily striving does not arise from a purpose or a programme,
but from an immediate need.
Einstein addressing Max Planck (1918)

Science has become a household world in our days and in the bewildering variety of scientific discoveries we are sometimes apt to lose our bearings and feel the need for a solid resting point in contrast to the ephemeral restlessness of the contemporary scene. Somebody mentions the name Einstein and immediately our reaction is: "This is it. He is the man to whom we should turn."

But why? Why Einstein and not somebody else? Since the end of the last century a whole galaxy of great geniuses have appeared in physics: Here are Marie and Pierre Curie, the discoverers of radium. Here is Max Planck, the discoverer of a new radiation law which initiated an era of physics and became the basis of quantum theory. Here is Ernest Rutherford, who with his ingenious experiments demonstrated the commutability of chemical elements and at the same time paved the way toward a better understanding of the structure of the atom. Here is Niels Bohr, who created the theoretical edifice by which Rutherford's experiments became explainable. Here is Louis de Broglie, the discoverer of the strange "matter waves" which accompany the world of elementary particles. And finally here are the three great founders of the modern theory of matter, called "wave mechanics," or "quantum mechanics": Heisenberg, Schroedinger, and Dirac.

Why then should we single out Einstein as *the* great physicist of our age?

Yet if we should have asked any one of these great physicists which man made the most fundamental contribution to the physics of the twentieth century, they would have answered without hesitation: Albert Einstein. The overwhelming importance of Einstein's physical discoveries and his unique place in the history of science is universally recognized and can hardly be contested.

From Carl Lanczos, "The Place of Albert Einstein in the History of Physics" *lecture series delivered at the University of Michigan, Spring 1962. Reprinted by permission of the University of Michigan.*

Nobody intends to diminish the merits of other great men of science, but there was something in Einstein's mental make-up which distinguished him as a personality without peers. He wrote his name in the annals of science with indelible ink which will not fade as long as men live on earth. There is a finality about his discoveries which cannot be shaken. Theories come, theories go. Einstein did more than formulate theories. He listened with supreme devotion to the silent voices of the universe and wrote down their message with unfailing certainty.

What was so astonishing in his manner of thinking was that he could discover the underlying principle of a physical situation, undeceived by the details, and penetrate straight down to the very core of the problem. Thus he was never deceived by appearances and his findings had to be acknowledged as irrefutable.

What can the educated layman grasp of the phenomenon Einstein? Is it possible that such a deep thinker can be understood only by his technically trained colleagues while the great bulk of humanity is left out in the cold? Is it true that the technical difficulties of the subject are so overwhelming that his findings cannot be put in a language understandable to the large group of people who have a good general education, although they have not been specifically trained in the exact sciences?

It is improbable that the findings of such a deep thinker could not be translated into a universally comprehensible language without losing too much of their substance. This is corroborated by the further circumstance that Einstein was never too much attracted to his technically trained colleagues, who spoke outwardly the same language but had a widely different approach to the deeper exploration of the mysteries of the universe. He considered himself more a philosopher than a professional physicist; he was more at home with visionary people—artists, writers, poets, actors—than with many of his professional associates. They followed the well-trodden path, laid out by the well-established rules of the game. Einstein never played the game according to the traditional rules. To him the universe was important and not the game we play with the universe. This distinction separated him from most of his contemporaries, to whom science is an occupation and not a religion of highest devotion and abandonment.

If we mention the name Einstein anywhere in the world, the response is unmitigated reverence and admiration. "Yes, Einstein, of course, the great physicist and mathematician." But then we ask the question: What do you know of him? What made this Einstein a world figure of such incomparable dimensions that he was held in mystical awe by millions of people as the revered voice of the universe? The answer is usually: "That I cannot tell you. You know, I was never too good in mathematics and to study Einstein you require so much higher mathematics that I am, of course, lost if it comes to really understanding what he has accomplished. I only know that he discovered something very important and that the name of this discovery is relativity."

This answer certainly seems reasonable enough, yet there is a flaw in it. Of course it is impossible to describe in a few sentences what such a great genius accomplished in a long life of ceaseless and devoted meditation. But by spending several hours in serious effort, it is by no means impossible to gain a fairly adequate concept of his achievements. There is so much in the line of general ideas in his investigations which can be stated without any (or with a minimum of) mathematical symbols that one can go a long way in pointing out the specific nature of his reasoning, without being hampered by the technicalities of the mathematical language. This is exactly what the following discussions attempt to do. We shall concentrate on a few fundamental ideas and try to elucidate them from many angles rather than get lost in a multitude of subjects. By this approach something of the scope of Einstein as a physicist will undoubtedly be lost. Einstein was not merely the creator of the theory of relativity. He discovered a host of other basic results in theoretical physics and it has been pointed out more than once that if somebody asked: "Who is the greatest modern physicist after Einstein?" the answer would be: Einstein again. And why? Because, although the theory of relativity in itself would have established his fame forever, had somebody else discovered relativity, his other discoveries would still make him the second greatest physicist of his time.

Nevertheless, it is not an accident that in the popular mind his fame rests on the theory of relativity. His other discoveries could have been made by others. Moreover, they are discoveries which may be modified as science progresses. The theory of relativity, however, was an astonishing discovery which opened an entirely new door in our understanding of the physical universe and it is a door which will never be shut again. Our concepts of space and time have been radically changed by Einstein's first formulation of the principle of relativity, now called "special relativity." This happened when Einstein was only twenty-six years of age. But our most fundamental physical concepts, involving space, time, *and matter,* have been even more radically altered by Einstein's second formulation of the principle of relativity, called "general relativity," which came to its fruition ten years later, during the years 1915–16. Now not only space and time, but *space, time* and *matter* were amalgamated into one fundamental and inseparable unity. His discovery of this unity had a tremendous impact on Einstein's scientific philosophy. From now on he lost interest in the bewildering variety of physical phenomena and focused on one theme only: to find the unifying law which is the basis of all physical events. In the eyes of his colleagues he changed from a "physicist" to a "metaphysicist," a man out for the ultimates—and why should a scientist care for the ultimates?

To Einstein himself it made little difference by what label he was called. For him the watertight conpartments in which we customarily classify our intellectual endeavors did not exist. As a true disciple of Kepler, he too listened to the secret music of the celestial spheres. Is that mathematics, or physics, or alchemy, or astronomy, or philosophy—what does it matter? To his colleagues the difference was that, whereas before he tackled—and how successfully!— all kinds of physical phenomena, now he shut himself up in the half-shadow of his study-room and lost touch with the contemporary problems of science.

Let us examine the phenomenon Einstein at closer range by discussing briefly his astonishing scientific career. He appeared on the scene in 1905, when he had barely finished his university studies. That year saw the appearance of three papers. each one of trailblazing magnitude and each one important for different reasons. The first one, on the so-called "Brownian motion" (named after an English botanist who first observed the phenomenon), dealt with a peculiar phenomenon which is observable in a highly magnifying microscope if we look carefully at an emulsion composed of little particles suspended in a fluid. We observe that these particles do not stand still but make peculiar jerky motions, a kind of dance which becomes the livelier the higher the temperature. If we follow the path of such a particle, we find a highly irregular zig-zag line, apparently without any inner law, as if it were a random phenomenon. Einstein showed that these jerky motions are caused by the many pushes that the suspended particle receives from the still smaller molecules of the fluid which collide with it. It is as if a big punching bag were suspended in the middle of the room and people from all sides were trying their skill on it. That such an apparently random phenomenon should actually satisfy a very definite mathematical law, which can be verified by observations, was surprising to the highest degree. It demonstrated the uncanny ability of Einstein in the line of statistical thinking which accompanied him throughout life and which is little known by those physicists and mathematicians who studied Einstein primarily for his relativistic discoveries.

It now seems hard to believe and yet is a fact that about sixty years ago many people doubted the existence of atoms. Today the atom is public property and the concept of atomic energy a household item in every educated person's thinking. In 1905 one still had the right to assume that the entire atomistic hypothesis was not more than a fake, invented solely to mystify and confuse the minds of physicists. Einstein's paper on the Brownian motion demonstrated almost palpably the correctness of the atomistic hypothesis and many scientists (among them the great physicochemist Wilhelm Ostwald) who before had been on the doubting side were converted to atomism.

The second paper of 1905 dealt with the ideas of space and time and demonstrated that our common notions concerning the existence of an absolute space and an absolute time had to give way to a more flexible approach in which various observers have their own time measurements which do not agree with those of other observers. Few people understood the implications of this profound paper which was destined to play such a fundamental role in the later development of theoretical physics.

The third paper of Einstein also showed a remarkable maturity of scientific thinking. Planck deduced his famous radiation formula in 1900 by assuming that somehow energy is not emitted continuously but in small little packages, called "quanta," thus giving rise to the famous "quantum hypothesis." Einstein showed that Planck's demonstration of his law was in fact inconsistent and required a much more radical change of our concepts than the assumption of a discontinuous emission of energy. We have to assume that light is emitted and absorbed like a localized particle which travels from one point to another as a complete entity. For a hundred years we had learned that light is a wave phenomenon which spreads out on an ever-increasing sphere. To assume now that this was wrong, that light behaves in certain respects like a particle which remains concentrated in a very small volume as it travels from A to B instead of spreading out like a wave, was a strange conclusion indeed, but Einstein demonstrated the soundness and inevitability of such an assumption. This peculiar behavior of radiation, to be a wave from a certain point of view and yet a particle from another, has remained a puzzling mystery of physics up to our day. The first clear-cut formulation of this peculiar dualism —wave on the one side, particle on the other—goes back to Einstein's paper of 1905.

These papers were written in a peculiar style, very characteristic of Einstein's manner of thinking. They did not contain a great deal of mathematical formalism. There was a great deal of text and little in the line of formal manipulations. In the end the startling conclusion was there, obtained apparently with the greatest of ease, and by a reasoning which could not be refuted. Outside sources were hardly ever quoted; it looked as if the author had arrived at his results practically unaided, as if he had conjured up the whole procedure out of thin air, by a wave of his magic wand. This made Einstein suspicious in the eyes of his colleagues. A man who writes so clearly and with so few technicalities cannot be taken too seriously. Something must be wrong with him. It is not proper that he should deduce important results so elegantly, apparently without laborious efforts, and without consulting the opinions of others. And thus it happened that the majority of physicists ignored his work, while a few first-class minds, particularly Planck, Rubens, Nernst, and von Laue, accepted this amazing fledgeling as a full-grown member of their august community, in spite of the fact that he was much younger.

It is thus understandable that as early as 1909 Einstein received a call to a professorship at the University of Zürich. At that time he was employed as a minor consultant at the Swiss Patent Office in Berne. When he announced his resignation because he was going to Zürich as a professor of the university, his boss got red in the face and blurted out: "Now, Mr. Einstein, don't make any silly jokes. Nobody would believe such an absurdity."* Yet the absurdity was true, as were so many of the apparent "absurdities" which were encoun-

*Cf. Carl Seelig: *Albert Einstein* (Europa Verlag, Zürich, 1954), p. 108 (author's translation).

tered in Einstein's theories, and Einstein's fame spread more and more. In 1914 he was called to Berlin as director of the Physics Section of the world-famous Kaiser-Wilhelm-Institut, the highest honor that Germany could bestow on him. In the meantime he pursued his studies concerning the nature of radiation. These profound researches contributed fundamentally toward the development of quantum theory and the deeper understanding of the structure of the atom. Between the years 1905 and 1925 he was the undisputed leader of a whole generation of theoretical physicists. Nobody could compete with him in the depth of comprehension and the uncanny simplicity with which he could derive fundamental results from a few basic experimental results.

In the meantime he was in the grip of a mighty idea which germinated slowly. Almost from the beginning he realized that his space-time theory of 1905 could not be considered as the final solution but only as a first step to something much more comprehensive. After ten years of incessant ponderings which led him to many false leads and cul-de-sacs, he arrived at his "general theory of relativity," which was hailed as his masterpeice and which Einstein himself considered as his most fundamental discovery. This theory showed that our customary ideas concerning geometry do not correspond to the geometry actually realized in the physical universe. The geometry which we have learned in school for thousands of years—it is called "Euclidean geometry," because it was the Greek geometer Euclid who put this geometry in a remarkably exact, scientific system—is in fact *not* the geometry of nature. It is true that Einstein's paper of 1905 had already demonstrated that our traditional ideas about space and time fall down if motions of high velocities are involved. But the mathematician Minkowski succeeded in translating Einstein's physical ideas into the language of geometry by showing that Einstein's theory can be interpreted as a new geometrical theory of the universe in which *space and time together* have to be considered as the proper subject of geometry, and not space alone. In other words, for the physical universe our ordinary space is only part of the picture; the full picture emerges if we add time to space and unify space and time into a world of not three but four dimensions. This new world was still of the Euclidian type; the difference was only that in our ordinary geometrical constructions we stop too soon. We start with a point, which has no extension, then follows a line which extends in length only, then a plane, which extends in length and width, then a space which extends in length, width, and height. Here we usually stop. But, Minkowski argued, we should not stop but go one step further by adding to length, width, and height one further dimension. This is the dimension of *time* which to our senses appears in such completely different garb, so completely incompatible with space, and yet it so happens that for the physical universe it plays exactly the role of an added dimension in a world which is formed out of *space and time.* Minkowski's view did not fundamentally alter our customary Euclidean geometry; it merely added one more dimension to it.

The new discovery of 1915 modified this picture very decisively by showing that the geometry of Euclid, even if extended from three to four dimensions, does not do full justice to the physical world because it pictures it geometrically in the form of a completely *flat* country. In actual fact we should imagine the universe as a *hilly* country with mountains and valleys, instead of as a monotonous plane which extends from infinity to infinity, free of any imperfections. Let us imagine bumps on this plane, like mole-hills which cover a field infested by rodents. What are these mole-hills? They appear to us as *matter.* Whenever we perceive matter at some place in the universe, we actually perceive a mole-hill on a generally flat field. These mole-hills were left out in Euclid's geometry but in fact they are the most important agents of the universe, since anything that happens in the universe is somehow related to the action of matter.

This theory was of tremendous abstraction and tremendous boldness. Never has the human mind perceived such astonishing constructions. We knew, of course, that geometry is important. We all learn geometry in school, even if later we forget almost everything of this truly fascinating subject. And why do we learn geometry? Because it is recognized that the laws of space are important, because, after all, it is this space in which physical action takes place. But notice the extraordinary change which came to our geometrical thinking through the meditations of a single man: Albert Einstein. In Newton's physics we had an empty space like a huge empty box, into which matter is put from the outside. In addition, we had time in which physical action takes place. We thus had three basic entities which were apparently completely independent of each other: space, time, and matter. But Minkowski's interpretation of Einstein's theory of special relativity showed that space and time are not independent of each other but form one inseparable unit, the world of space-time. This four-dimensional space-time world now took over the role of Newton's empty receptacle into which matter was put from the outside.

Then came Einstein's great discovery of 1915 which carried the synthesis to the ultimate. Matter is not put from the outside into an empty box but forms an integral part of geometry. Matter belongs to geometry. What we observe as matter is in fact a hill in a generally flat country. We can measure such a hill by its curvature. Curvature is a strictly geometrical quantity which apparently has nothing to do with physics. For example, we can measure the curvature of our globe by determining the radius of the earth, which is about 4000 miles. Now, if we put a certain amount of matter, such as a lump of steel, on a balance and found that it weighs, let us say, a pound, we would certainly not think that this pound has anything to do with a length. But Einstein's theory has shown that this pound can be converted into length because we can figure out the exact amount by which the generally flat Euclidean world has been indented by the presence of that pound of steel.

But then if time is nothing but length, and mass is nothing but length, what else do we have in physics? Space, time, matter—these are the three basic entities of the physical universe. Time has been absorbed by space as an added dimension. Matter has been absorbed by space as a curvature property of space. What is left? Is it possible that space is everything? Is it possible that if only we understood the proper geometry of space, we would understand *all* physics, since the whole physical universe is nothing but the manifestation of a certain kind of geometry?

This was an intoxicating thought which caught Einstein and never let him go again. Up to the discovery of general relativity he was a sober physicist like anybody else. He accepted the customary rules laid down by the empiricists. After all, what is the role of the theoretical physicist? He follows the lead of the experimental physicist. The experimental physicist finds certain relations on the basis of his measurements. Then comes the theoretical physicist who finds the mathematical equation which fits the measurements. If he is lucky, he may find a rather comprehensive mathematical equation which will fit many particular experiments. But can he ask the question: Why did nature realize this particular equation and not something else? To ask such a question is not becoming to a physicist. He takes the results of observations for granted and if he succeeds with a precise mathematical description of the phenomena, his task as a physicist is ended. Thus, for example, Newton took the astronomical measurements of Kepler and found his famous gravitational theory, by which he could give a perfect description of planetary motion, in harmony with the observed facts. The only assumption he had to make was that between any two masses a force is acting which is proportional to the product of the masses and inversely proportional to the square of their distance. We may be inclined to ask, why the square of the distance and not the cube or some other power? But all such questions are idle because they go beyond the realm of observable facts. The observations verify the law of Newton, and that is enough. What else could happen if the observations were different is a nonsensical question since no such observations exist and we cannot go outside the world of facts which is given to us.

But the amazing thing about Einstein's discovery was that he did not follow the usual sequence. His theory was not motivated by some new gravitational experiments. He started on essentially *speculative* grounds, although on the firm basis of some well-known experimental facts whose correctness could not be doubted. He felt that these facts expressed more than some accidental relations, that in fact they were the emanation of some basic *principles* realized in the physical world. From here, by higher and higher abstractions and by making use of the most advanced tools of mathematics, he came to the formulation of certain equations, the celebrated "Einstein gravitational equations." In the case of Newton it was not so surprising that he arrived at the right law of gravity. He had the observations of Kepler at his disposal and by careful analysis of these observations he established a set of equations which described these observations perfectly. This was in his own time a very great achievement and nobody wants to tarnish to the slightest degree the ingenuity of Newton. The inverse square law of the gravitational force was demanded in order to account for the ellipses in which the planets revolve around the sun, according to the careful observations of Kepler.

Einstein's starting point was completely different. It had something to do with the general properties of space and time and the nature of reference systems which we erect for the purpose of physical measurements. From these very general speculations he suddenly arrived with logical necessity at his equations. This was not according to the established rules of the game. This was black magic more than anything else. To stare in empty air and pull out results from nothing as a result of speculations, as the old Greek philosophers were wont to do, was disdained since the time of Galileo as a nonsensical procedure. One had to experiment first and see what happened. Then one tried to codify these experiments by a mathematical equation. This had been the well-established rule for hundreds of years. And now Einstein dared to challenge this procedure by reverting to the dreams of the ancients who tried to *understand* nature on the basis of logical deductions rather than *describe* it on the basis of carefully conducted experiments. The magical thing about Einstein was, however, that he succeeded where the ancients failed. He had the mighty tools of mathematics at his disposal, developed in a slow evolution of more than two thousand years since the time of Plato and Aristotle. The equations of Einstein, arrived at by purely speculative means, told us that indeed the planets *had* to move around the sun in ellipses and not in something else because our universe is not any mathematical universe, but a marvelously *reasonable* and well-ordered mathematical universe, pervaded by a supreme Cosmic Wisdom.

Not only did the entire Newtonian theory fall out of the bag, but there were a few exceedingly delicate additional effects, not predicted by the Newtonian theory, which could be checked by very careful measurements. One of them involved the bending of light rays by the sun, which demanded a total eclipse of the sun for its verification. It was shortly after the First World War, in 1919, that an expedition organized by some English astronomers was able to check Einstein's prediction. The observations agreed perfectly with the prediction of the theory and it was now that Einstein became world-famous.

But Einstein was not a man who could rest on his laurels. He was too much wedded to the universe to care too much for human recognition. The psychological impact of the success of his theory was quite profound on Einstein himself, because it had shown him that inspired mathematical speculation can soar into heights that mere experimentation could never achieve. The idea that we may not merely *describe* the physical universe but *understand* its inner workings had an intoxicating effect on his thinking. If it was possible to achieve such a speculative victory in the field of gravitation, why should we stop here? Why should we not go further and try to find a similarly reasonable explanantion for the other fundamental phenomena of nature, namely, electricity and the mysterious quantum effects? From 1925 on, his interest in the current affairs of physics begins to slacken. He voluntarily abdicated his leadership as the foremost physicist of his time, and receded more and more into voluntary exile from the laboratory, a state into which only a few of his colleagues were willing to follow. During the last thirty years of his life he became more and more a recluse who lost touch with the contemporary development of physics. His eyes were glued on the universe and the possibility of penetrating to the ultimate core where all secrets would be resolved and understood as the emanation of a single world law. In his great paper of 1916 he showed how the replacement of Euclidean geometry by the more advanced geometry developed by the great German mathematician Riemann—and thus called Riemannian geometry—was able to explain all the gravitational phenomena. But electricity did not seem to find its natural place in this geometry and thus he attempted to give it up in favor of a still more comprehensive form of geometry. Again and again he jubilantly felt that he had found the final answer, but again and again he admitted his defeat, returning to his starting point. In the last ten years of his life he settled for a certain "unified field theory" which he considered the final answer and the true fulfillment of all his hopes. Yet we have good reason to doubt that he truly achieved his goal.

Nor is this point of any importance in the evaluation of Einstein as a man and a scientist. He has given us a new picture of the universe and he has demonstrated the power of inspired abstract thinking. Never before had any human being attained such marvelous insights into the inner heart of the physical universe. Never before would it have been possible even to hope that some day our minds may clearly recognize the master plan according to which the universe is constructed. What he accomplished in a single lifetime is stupendous and a sufficient basis for research for hundreds of years to come. In an era of unprecedented aggressiveness and destruction he held up a mirror to the human mind which demonstrated its greatness and its boundless possibilities if turned toward inspired constructive reasoning. He thus occupies a place in the history of civilization which is unique and may never be duplicated.

DISCUSSION

QUESTION. What was Einstein's relation to mathematics?
ANSWER. Einstein's attitude toward mathematics went through a considerable change during his life. In the early years of his scientific career he was under the influence of the Viennese philosopher and physicist Ernst Mach and consequently displayed a rather sceptical view toward mathematics. Mach was wedded to the view that anything that could be interpreted as "metaphysical" or "absolute" should be expurgated from the domain of science. Hence he was anxious to show that mathematics could not be considered in any way as an absolute necessity in physical research. In his view it was a purely historical accident that the mathematical sciences became so predominant after the Renaissance; under different cultural influences physics could have taken a completely differ-

ent turn. The early Einstein shared with Mach a certain suspicion of mathematics. He was afraid that the elegance of the mathematical mechanism might obscure the the physical problem and give a purely formalistic answer which might smother the deeper essence of the physical situation.

This attitude changed radically with the advent of general relativity. In his search for the general solution of the problem of coordinates he soon realized that without the heavy mechanism of absolute calculus (also called "tensor calculus") no progress of any kind would be conceivable. He soon saw that here was an apparently brittle and uninspiring chapter of mathematics that could be molded into something eminently lively and physical. From then on his predilection for mathematical constructions never left him because he realized that the future progress of theoretical physics would lean more and more on strictly mathematical models which cannot be interpreted in so-called "physical" terms. In fact, in his later years he was occasionally deceived by purely formal analogies which he invoked for the explanation of physical phenomena although they did not possess that clarifying and persuasive feature that the theory of tensors and Riemannian geometry possessed to such a high degree.

QUESTION. Is it not true that special relativity, that is, Einstein's theory of 1905, had a much greater and more lasting effect on physics than his general relativity theory of 1915?

ANSWER. This is true and under the circumstances easily understandable. Special relativity established the unity of space and time and gave a very definite prescription by which all the previous equations of physics had to be modified in order to harmonize with his new geometrical model of the universe which demanded that time should not play a role independent of space. Special relativity thus had repercussions in all branches of physics. General relativity, although of much more fundamental character, is first of all restricted to the phenomenon of universal gravitation, which is a relatively well-investigated chapter of physics in no way comparable in importance to the electric and quantum phenomena. Moreover, up to now general relativity could give no clues concerning the atomistic structure of matter and was thus of no help in the understanding of nuclear phenomena. There is little doubt that in a future, more comprehensive theory of matter Einstein's general relativity will play a leading and decisive role.

ON EINSTEIN'S WELTBILD

BY GERALD HOLTON

Harvard University, Cambridge, Massachusetts

A *Weltbild,* world image or world view, is a constellation of intentions and thoughts which, if sufficiently stable and coherent, can characterize the internal intellectual architecture of a person or a period as recognizably and functionally as does the external style of dress or of buildings. Much has been written on the explicit *Weltbild* of individuals, groups, or periods, e.g., by J. T. Merz, Karl Mannheim, Kurt Lewin, and Erik Erikson. The latter, for example, defines it as follows: "A world view, then, is an all-inclusive conception which, when it is historically viable, integrates a group's imagery. According to our formula, it focuses disciplined attention on a selection of verifiable facts; it liberates a joint vision which enhances a sense of historical reality; and it actualizes a widening fellowship with strong work commitments" (Erik H. Erikson, *Toys and Reasons* [New York: W. W. Norton & Co., Inc., 1977], p. 178). He speaks of this "necessary search for a cosmological order" as a psychological need (op. cit., p. 61).

What takes precedence on this occasion, of course, is Einstein's own views about his own *Weltbild*. In 1934 he published a book of collected essays to which he gave (or allowed it to be given) the title *Mein Weltbild* (edited by Carl Seelig, Querido Verlag, Amsterdam, 1934). The essays are divided into five sections entitled "How I See the World," "Politics and Pacificism," "Fight against National Socialism," "Jewish Problems," and "Scientific Contributions."

What strikes one at once is the wide range over which the components appear to be distributed. As we know also from his letters and other writings, Einstein's world image consisted not only of scientific and epistemological components, but encompassed also attitudes and commitments to peace and pacificism, social democracy, internationalism, a cultural form of Zionism, a religiosity he termed "cosmic religion"—and, correspondingly, opposition to arbitrary absolutes that support sects, tribalism, castes, and nationalism.

At first glance, the variety and spread of components make it difficult to see that they stem from a coherent world image. However, I shall try to show that the elements are much more consistent than they seem, and that in fact they are anchored in the very process of Einstein's thinking and of grasping reality through the construction of theories in science and outside.

First, what does Einstein himself mean by *"Weltbild"*? We can find the answer not in some capsule definition, which he did not provide, but rather in the way he used the word in his writings. One of his earliest mentions appears in the essay "Motive of Research" (1918, republished under the title "Principles of Research"). In this essay, a key passage (in translation) runs as follows:

> Man seeks to form for himself, in whatever manner is suitable for him, a simplified and easy-to-survey [*uebersichtliches*] image of the world [*Bild der Welt*] and so to overcome the world of experience by striving to replace it to some extent by this image. This is what the painter does, and the poet, the speculative philosopher, the natural scientist, each in his own way. Into this image and its formation he transfers the center of gravity of his emotional life in order to seek the peace and steadiness that he cannot find within the too narrow confines of swirling and personal experience.

It is a brilliant and graphic description of a process now known much more widely from psychological studies of young scientists and other scholars

—the creation of one's own world image as an act of integration and self-transcendence through which the world of experience, with all its external pressures, chance, chaos, and unreason, is left behind as one transfers the center of one's being into the sphere above in which rationality and security can be attained.

Einstein goes on to discuss the chief problem with this prescription: the complexity of nature and the limitations of human abilities. And in any case, what place does the *Weltbild* of the theoretical physicist occupy among all these possible images of the world?

To answer the last question, Einstein notes that the physicist has to settle for a theory which in the first instance deals with the "simplest phenomena," at the cost of understanding the complexities and at the cost of "completeness." But then, "Does the product of such a modest effort deserve the proud name '*Weltbild*' "? The answer, Einstein says, is Yes, and for a very specific reason. For the general laws so found can claim to be valid for any natural phenomenon, even the most complex. For from the most general laws, found by attending to the simplest phenomena, it should be possible to find, "by means of pure deduction, a description, that is to say the theory, of every natural process, including life, if this process of deduction does not go beyond the capacity of the human intellect." The renunciation of the physical *Weltbild* with respect to completeness is thus not a renunciation in principle.

And as if to drive in this important point, Einstein immediately repeats it. "The supreme task of the physicist is to seek those most general, elementary laws out of which the *Weltbild* can be achieved through pure deduction." And, referring to an insistent theme to which Einstein devoted a good deal of his epistemological writing, he adds that to these elementary laws there is no "logical path," "but only intuition, supported by being sympathetically in touch with experience." The source for the inexhaustible perseverence and patience necessary for work of this kind, Einstein notes, is the "longing to behold this pre-established harmony" between the world constructed by our theory and the world of experience. The "state of feeling" of one engaged on such a task "is akin to that of the religious person or one who is in love." The work is not a matter of choice but of "immediate necessity."

Already we notice in this brief essay—and there are many passages of the same kind in Einstein's writings—that one glimpses a coherence of different parts in the *Weltbild* he describes: the rational and the intuitive; the phenomena of physical nature which are relatively easily dealt with, and the phenomena of life which are far more difficult but also ultimately become manageable; the emotional base of the motivation of the scientist; the overriding role of key notions such as simplicity (simplification) and necessity; the drive toward completeness and the opposition to the arbitrary; and the function of the *Weltbild* as a task which the individual puts before himself as part of his intellectual growth, rather than the acceptance of current dogma.

When we keep these organizing themes and attitudes in mind, we can begin to detect coherence in some of Einstein's other essays that, if read superficially, seem to put together important but unconnected ideas. Take for example the splendid essay "Wie ich die Welt sehe" [The World as I See It], which is in fact the very first essay in *Mein Weltbild* and which gives the first of the five sections its heading. Published about a dozen years after "Motive of Research," which we have just discussed, it sounds almost like a social-scientific credo developed in "free association." He confesses that he feels the requirement of a frugal, simple existence. He regards class distinctions as unjustified. Without any apparent connection he further confesses that he does not believe in the freedom of will, since one acts not only under external necessity but also in accordince with inner necessity. His life would seem empty, he acknowledges, without a feeling of kinship with persons of like mind and without the occupation with the objective, eternally unreachable in art and science. Without any apparent transition, Einstein then continues to speak of his passionate sense of social justice and social responsibility; his regret not to have felt belonging wholeheartedly to any place or group, his political ideal (democracy: "Let every man be respected as an individual and no man idolized"); his horror of the military system and popular patriotism. And then suddenly, in the last paragraph, he turns to "the most beautiful experience we can have" which is "the mysterious. It is the fundamental emotion which stands at the cradle of true art and true science." He ends with defining "true religiosity" in terms of "a knowledge of the existence of something we cannot penetrate," and confesses himself satisfied with a glimpse of the "reason that manifests itself in nature."

While in this essay only little is said about science, we can see that the main themes that pervaded it are quite parallel to those which organized the essay of 1918 that dealt specifically with scientific research. That is, the main thematic material is concerned with parsimony and simplicity; necessity and determinism; egalitarianism and the refusal of dogmatic absolutes; and the motivating power of the pursuit of rationality, in one's own work and in the *Weltbild* itself.

Writing seventeen years later still, in 1947, Einstein explicitly returned to the concept of *Weltbild* in his Autobiographical Notes, concentrating now on the scientific and philosophical rather than the social aspects. Early in the essay he turns to the *"mechanische Weltbild"* of physics before relativity theory, and begins the discussion by pointing out its "dogmatic rigidity." Much could be handled with the attitude that God had created the Newtonian laws of motion together with the necessary masses and forces, but in fact the attempts to base electromagnetism on this theoretical structure was doomed to failure, leaving physics without a uniform base.

But before going into the details concerning his dissatisfaction with the mechanical world view, Einstein interrupts his critique and asks on what basis one can criticize any physical theory at all (keeping in mind that he is dealing with grand theories whose object is the totality of physical phenomena). In reply, he puts forth two criteria. The first is the requirement that the theory must not be falsified by the empirical fact, the principle of "external validation." The second criterion is necessary in part because one can almost always adjust the failing theory, "ad hoc," by means of artificial additional assumptions that do not go to the heart of the matter. Therefore this second criterion is one of "inner perfection," which he admits he can only "vaguely characterize" as a requirement for "naturalness" or "logical simplicity" of the premises.

With these criteria Einstein returns to his critique of the mechanistic *Weltbild* reigning when he embarked on his earliest work. The mechanistic theories failed on the first criterion; for example, they lacked sound mechanical models to explain optical effects. But more important were the failures with respect to the second criterion, because in advanced theories there is a much greater distance between the basic concepts and axioms on the one hand and what is directly observable on the other, leaving much more room for the quasi-aesthetic criteria to come into play.

On that score, Einstein lists four specific dissatisfactions. Thus it was particularly offensive *("besonders haesslich")* that the inertial systems in Newtonian mechanics are not only infinite in number but also, each of them, specially distinguished over all accelerating systems. Secondly, there was no necessity for the choice of definition of force or potential energy, but a great deal of latitude was available. Third, there was an internal asymmetry in the theory, insofar as inertial mass appears in Newton's laws of motion and the law of gravitational force but not in expressions of, say, the electric force. And lastly, Einstein found it "unnatural" that there are two kinds of energy, potential and kinetic.

Because of these and other faults in the state of physics around 1900, Einstein confesses that by and by he "despaired of the possibilities of discovering the true laws by means of constructive efforts based on known facts." He says he "came to the conviction that only the discovery of a universal formal principle could lead us to assured results"—which is of course just what he accomplished in relativity theory by the postulation of two, apparently contradictory, axiomatic postulates of relativity.

The rewards of doing that were immediate and many, as Einstein explains. The old conceptions of space and of time were deprived of their "absolute" character but became special sub-sets of general spacetime. With the disappearance of the conception of simultaneity of distant events as an absolute, all phenomena had to be conceived of as propagated by continuous functions in space, and the material point-singularity therefore did not appear as a basic concept of the theory. And the laws of conservation of momentum and of energy fused into one principle, with mass eliminated as an independent conception. A huge portion of the world of phenomena and events had become subsumed, in the relativistic *Weltbild,* in a four-dimensional structure, the Parmenidean crystal-universe in which changes, e.g., motions, are as far as possible *aufgehoben* and, instead, the main themata are those of constancy and invariance, causal sequences (determinism and necessity), and the fusion of previously very different portions of physics.

Nevertheless, Einstein knew as early as 1907, and records again in his Autobiographical Notes forty years later, that the magnificent solution was flawed: Relativity theory is left with "two kinds of physical things, i.e., (1) measuring rods and clocks, (2) all other e.g., the electromagnetic field, the material point, etc. This, in a certain sense, is inconsistent; strictly speaking, measuring rods and clocks would have to be represented as solutions of the basic equations. . . ." Therefore, the work of finding those most general, elementary laws, from which by pure deduction the *Weltbild* can be won, had to continue.

From the beginning of his labors, Einstein's view of an adequate *Weltbild* would have destined him to progress from the special theory of relativity to the general theory, and from there to the search for a unified field theory. In his essay "The Fundaments of Theoretical Physics" (*Science,* May 24, 1940), Einstein wrote that "from the very beginning there has always been present the attempt to find a unifying theoretical basis for all these single sciences, consisting of a minimum of concepts and fundamental relationships, from which all the concepts and relationships of the single disciplines might be derived by logical process." I have analyzed in detail in another place* the algorithm which Einstein described as his process for going from the plane of infinitely many, incongruous, or unrelated sense experiences (the world of phenomena) by a leap of the intuitively guided imagination, to an over-arching system of axioms, from which in turn, by pure deduction, consequences are formulated that can then be correlated with the original basic plane of experience. Going through this schema repeatedly is operationally equivalent to the search for a simplified and easy-to-survey image of the world, which can be put in place of the world of experience that is thereby overcome.

We can now understand better what the relation is between Einstein's general *Weltbild* and his work in physics. It is clear from his writings that Einstein did not think of the scientific world image as separated by some boundary from a person's *Weltbild* in the more general sense. Entirely in accord with his typical attitude of refusing to tolerate unnatural and unnecessary boundaries, he thought of the scientific *Weltbild* as a special version of, and embedded in, a person's total *Weltanschauung.* The same continuist point of view was repeatedly stressed in his remarks on thinking itself: e.g., "scientific thought is a development of pre-scientific thought" (in "The Problem of Space, Ether, and the Field in Physics," 1930), or "all this applied as much and in the same manner, to the thinking in daily life as to the more consciously and systematically constructed thinking in the sciences" ("Remarks on Bertrand Russell's Theory of Knowledge," 1944), and "The whole of science is nothing

---

*"Einstein's Model for Constructing a Scientific Theory," in Einstein Centennial volume being published by Vieweg Verlag under the editorship of R. Sexl.

more than a refinement of everyday thinking" (*Physics and Reality,* 1936).

The physical theory is thus one aspect of a more general *Weltbild,* sharing with it the criteria of "inner perfection" and the fundamental themata that have validated themselves in the successful pursuit of the physical world image. Among these themata, which guided Einstein in theory construction, are clearly these: unity (or unification) and cosmological scale (egalitarian applicability of principles throughout the total realm of experience); primacy of formal rather than mechanistic or materialistic explanation; parsimony and necessity; symmetry and reciprocity; simplicity; causality; completeness; and of course constancy and invariance, found in the laws guiding the phenomena, rather than postulated absolutes or dogma, adopted *ab initio.*

The end product of Einstein's schema for attaining a *Weltbild* is a comprehension of reality that can be called cosmological, in the sense of being orderly, harmonious, and systematic. It is a *Weltbild* characterized by six properties:

1. It aims at completeness in dealing with the factual base of experience initially in the physical sense but ultimately encompassing all life. In its completeness, it provides the sense of necessity of what actually happens, whether simple or complex, with no room left for accidental or non-causal elements (as was also the case in Newton's own long-term ambition). The schema tells us why those things that do happen do, and those that do not happen do not.

2. It is a model for the effective rational working of the mind, in science and outside of science, but with the primacy of rationality modified by other, e.g., intuitive, discontinuous processes. It thereby gives a role to both aspects of human reason.

3. The *Weltbild* delimits and tames (i.e., has a place for) the unknowable, the mysterious, which surrounds the knowable. It identifies the human capacity for wonder as a motivation, and finds in the nonderivable but discoverable, insistent rationality of nature itself a place for what Einstein calls cosmic religion.

4. It provides a framework for going beyond strictly scientific thinking, to help achieve a rational and more or less coherent treatment of non-scientific elements of personal life, e.g., questions of ethics (as we shall see below).

5. It is a program for day-to-day actualization of one's life, both the internal life of the mind and its requirements for mental health through the success of one's scientific work (as in finding a way out of the "despair" generated by the contradictions in the mechanistic *Weltbild*), but also of the social life, as members of the community of searchers in the same fields (recall the remark concerning "the sense of kinship with men of like mind," an element without which, Einstein claimed, "life would have seemed to me empty"). This element refers clearly to Erikson's remarks concerning the "joint vision which enhances a sense of historical reality" as well as the role of the world view to "actualize a widening fellowship with strong work commitments."

6. The *Weltbild* defines itself also as a vision with respect to counter-visions, i.e., other world views, and so defines the conflict with them.

Before we turn to this sixth point, let me briefly elaborate on the fourth, to show how his world image in the larger sense works for Einstein in the field outside science.

From among many candidates I choose Einstein's succinct little essay entitled "The Laws of Science and the Laws of Ethics" (1950). It will illustrate that Einstein regarded the same algorithm for reaching a sound scientific *Weltbild* to work also for attaining a sound ethical viewpoint.

While he agrees that scientific statements of facts and relations "cannot produce ethical directives," he points out that these "ethical directives can be made rational and coherent by logical thinking and empirical knowledge. If we can agree on some fundamental ethical propositions, then other ethical propositions can be derived from them, provided that the original premises are stated with sufficient precision. Such ethical premises play a similar role in ethics, to that played by axioms in mathematics." As an example, he considers the question whether or not it is right to tell lies. To find a satisfactory answer he suggests that one has to trace back the ethical directive on lying to some basic premises which can be taken for granted. From the empirical observations that lying destroys confidence, and that without confidence any social cooperation, which is essential to make human life possible and tolerable, is made impossible or at least difficult, he finds that the fundamental ethical premises, from which the rule "Thou shalt not lie" can be traced, are "Human life shall be preserved" and "Pain and sorrow shall be lessened as much as possible."

These ethical premises themselves do not have to be taken tacitly for granted in an arbitrary manner. Rather, we can make use here of the sensitivity of certain persons of "moral genius," some "inspired individuals" who can advance ethical axioms so comprehensive and well founded that other people will "accept them as grounded in the vast mass of the individual emotional experience." There is a complete parallel here with the method by which sound scientific axioms are obtained by persons of sound physical intuition from the wide range of experienced phenomena. Also the method of deriving from these axioms, by deduction, consequences that can be checked back against the ground of experience is quite analogous in both cases. Einstein ends the brief essay with a reiteration of both points: "Ethical axioms are found and tested not very differently from the axioms of science. *Die Wahrheit liegt in der Bewaehrung.* Truth is what stands the test of experience."

Finally, on the sixth point listed above: Any world view defines itself with respect to other world views, and may be antithetical to them. Einstein himself worked consciously against the mechanical *Weltbild,* as he did against militarism and nationalism. It was not entirely surprising that his relativistic *Weltbild,* in the larger sense, gave rise to attacks from antithetical points of view, not only in physics but also in political ideology. For example, as has been

shown by Philipp Frank and others, the scientific and philosophical consequences of relativity theory were vigorously attacked by V. I. Lenin and the
Soviet philosophers who followed him. In Lenin's *Materialism and Empirio-
Criticism* (1909), he demonstrates how the school of recent physics (in which
he lumps E. Mach, H. Poincaré, K. Pearson, Pierre Duhem and Philipp Frank;
Frank had recently published a semi-popular exposition of relativity) are a
danger to materialism (which Lenin called his "Weltanschauung") and threat-
ened to replace it with empirio-criticism (which Lenin calls "a peculiar brand
of agnosticism"). The key problem, in Lenin's view, was that the recent physics
might induce a "denial or doubt of the objective reality given to us in our
sensation and reflected in our scientific theories." Here the school departs from
"materialism" and becomes a "school of idealistic physics." A particular cause
of idealistic physics is singled out to be "the principle of relativity, the relativity
of science, a principle which in a period of bankruptcy of old theories . . . leads
to idealism."

Although it is not clear how much of Lenin's attack was really politically
motivated by the particular Marxism then being advocated by A. Bogdanov
and others, Lenin was undoubtedly correct in smelling out that the *Weltbild*
of relativity theory was at the very least agnostic concerning such postulated
absolutes as the "objective reality of the external world" on which Lenin's
dialectical materialism depended.

Another kind of attack upon Einstein's *Weltbild* was launched by Nazi
scientists, politicians, and philosophers. The basic tenets from which these
attacks were launched were a curious constellation of elements: Mixed with
anti-Jewish and anti-pacifist diatribes was also the view that the true science,
i.e., one characteristic of the "Nordic race," has to be empirical and observational rather than abstract and formalistic, and based on "sound common-
sense" rather than on conceptions so far from the intuitions of the man in the
street or the Newtonian physicist.

This is, of all times, not a proper occasion to look further into that dark
chapter of modern history. But it will serve to remind ourselves of the solemn
fact that Einstein's values, and our own, escaped only quite narrowly from
being overwhelmed by its sinister opponent. Moreover, in the last decades of
his life Einstein kept warning of the persisting danger to the main elements
making up his world view, as he had set them forth in his *Mein Weltbild*.
Whether there shall be anyone left in the future to celebrate Einstein's second
centennial may well depend on how well mankind learns to respect the sanity,
coherence, and wisdom of Einstein's message.

Acknowledgment

I wish to express my indebtedness to Miss Helen Dukas and the Estate
of Albert Einstein for help and for permission to cite from writings of Einstein.
I am happy to acknowledge research support by grants from the National
Science Foundation and the National Endowment for the Humanities.

NOBEL PRIZE FOR PHYSICS—1921

PRESENTATION SPEECH BY PROFESSOR S. ARRHENIUS

Chairman of the Nobel Committee for Physics of the Royal Swedish Academy of Sciences

Your Majesty, Your Royal Highnesses, Ladies and Gentlemen.

There is probably no physicist living today whose name has become so widely known as that of Albert Einstein. Most discussion centres on his theory of relativity. This pertains essentially to epistemology and has therefore been the subject of lively debate in philosophical circles. It will be no secret that the famous philosopher Bergson in Paris has challenged this theory, while other philosophers have acclaimed it wholeheartedly. The theory in question also has astrophysical implications which are being rigorously examined at the present time.

Throughout the first decade of this century the so-called Brownian movement stimulated the keenest interest. In 1905 Einstein founded a kinetic theory to account for this movement by means of which he derived the chief properties of suspensions, i.e. liquids with solid particles suspended in them. This theory, based on classical mechanics, helps to explain the behaviour of what are known as colloidal solutions, a behaviour which has been studied by Svedberg, Perrin, Zsigmondy, and countless other scientists within the context of what has grown into a large branch of science, colloid chemistry.

A third group of studies, for which in particular Einstein has received the Nobel Prize, falls within the domain of the quantum theory founded by Planck in 1900. This theory asserts that radiant energy consists of individual particles, termed "quanta," approximately in the same way as matter is made up of particles, i.e. atoms. This remarkable theory, for which Planck received the Nobel Prize for Physics in 1918, suffered from a variety of drawbacks and about the middle of the first decade of this century it reached a kind of impasse. Then Einstein came forward with his work on specific heat and the photoelectric effect. This latter had been discovered by the famous physicist Hertz in 1887. He found that an electrical spark passing between two spheres does so more readily if its path is illuminated with the light from another electrical discharge. A more exhaustive study of this interesting phenomenon was carried out by Hallwachs who showed that under certain conditions a negatively charged body, e.g. a metal plate, illuminated with light of a particular colour —ultraviolet has the strongest effect—loses its negative charge and ultimately assumes a positive charge. In 1899 Lenard demonstrated the cause to be the emission of electrons at a certain velocity from the negatively charged body. The most extraordinary aspect of this effect was that the electron emission velocity is independent of the intensity of the illuminating light, which is

From Nobel Lectures in Physics (1901–1921) *(Amsterdam: Elsevier Scientific Publishing Co., 1967). Reprinted by permission of the publisher and Nobel Foundation.*

proportional only to the number of electrons, whereas the velocity increases with the frequency of the light. Lenard stressed that this phenomenon was not in good agreement with the then prevailing concepts.

An associated phenomenon is photo-luminescence, i.e. phosphorescence and fluorescence. When light impinges on a substance the latter will occasionally become luminous as a result of phosphorescence or fluorescence. Since the energy of the light quantum increases with the frequency, it will be obvious that a light quantum with a certain frequency can only give rise to the formation of a light quantum of lower or, at most, equal frequency. Otherwise energy would be created. The phosphorescent or fluorescent light hence has a lower frequency than the light inducing the photo-luminescence. This is Stokes' rule which was explained in this way by Einstein by means of the quantum theory.

Similarly, when a quantum of light falls on a metal plate it can at most yield the whole of its energy to an electron there. A part of this energy is consumed in carrying the electron out into the air; the remainder stays with the electron as kinetic energy. This applies to an electron in the surface layer of the metal. From this can be calculated the positive potential to which the metal can be charged by irradiation. Only if the quantum contains sufficient energy for the electron to perform the work of detaching itself from the metal does the electron move out into the air. Consequently, only light having a frequency greater than a certain limit is capable of inducing a photo-electric effect, however high the intensity of the irradiating light. If this limit is exceeded the effect is proportional to the light intensity at constant frequency. Similar behaviour occurs in the ionisation of gas molecules and the so-called ionisation potential may be calculated, provided that the frequency of the light capable of ionising the gas is known.

Einstein's law of the photo-electrical effect has been extremely rigorously tested by the American Millikan and his pupils and passed the test brilliantly. Owing to these studies by Einstein the quantum theory has been perfected to a high degree and an extensive literature grew up in this field whereby the extraordinary value of this theory was proved. Einstein's law has become the basis of quantitative photo-chemistry in the same way as Faraday's law is the basis of electro-chemistry.*

*It is perhaps strange that Einstein received the Nobel Prize not for his theory of relativity, but mainly for his work on the photo-electric effect. It appeared that the Prize committee wanted to avoid any complications which might arise from the opposition Einstein had aroused among some of his colleagues and countrymen. Of course, that work—as the others—was of sufficient importance to get Einstein the Nobel Prize, even if he had never produced the theory of relativity.

EINSTEIN IN PASADENA

The presence here of hundreds of people to greet a distinguished man of science is a part of something without parallel in our American life. When newspapers everywhere continue, day after day, to give front page space to a man whose work does not directly touch the lives of the people, it signifies something unusual. The public itself would first catch the humor of a suggestion that it knows anything about relativity; and yet the warm interest in the man who has given us relativity continues.

Part of this interest is our spontaneous response to a gracious personality, full of modesty and kindness and humanity. For the rest, it means, I think, that our imagination has in some way been touched. We realize that Professor Einstein has done things on the remote frontiers of science where man seems to approach the mystery of his existence; we know that he has changed the space and time we thought a safe framework to which we might tie all our activities; that he has dared to think about the bounds of the universe itself. Those who have seen his work at first hand feel the beauty of its logical structure; others marvel that there could be any new way of thinking about stubborn old realities. And why shouldn't these things stir the imagination?

Nevertheless, Einstein himself would insist on the purely intellectual character of what he has done. He has remarked, "Relativity has nothing to do with the soul; it is a matter only for the head." But what intellectual achievement ever remained wholly detached from human feeling? The work of Copernicus was such an achievement. Yet it precipitated the bitterest of controversies because it tumbled man out from the place of honor in the center of the universe and suggested that he was of less importance than he thought. Again, the painstaking inductions of Darwin put life into the long-dormant doctrine of evolution; and you well know the emotional reactions to that intellectual effort. These are extreme instances; but even the work of Newton, which held no threat for man's cherished beliefs, profoundly influenced his outlook on life as well as his views of the physical world. And so, before such an achievement as relativity, we can not remain passive. Even though we know none of its details, we feel the freshening wind of new thought and find ourselves stirred; and we feel that it is good to be so stirred.

No one at this moment would dare predict how the influences, direct and indirect, of Einstein's investigations are finally to be reckoned. Nevertheless, of their scientific aspect much may be said. We know that his contributions to physics in fields other than relativity would justify an award of the Nobel prize several times over, and we know the importance to both physics and astronomy of relativity itself. From these recognized accomplishments I turn to something that has received little comment.

Remarks on behalf of the Mount Wilson Observatory by its assistant director, Frederick H. Seares, at a luncheon, February 24, 1931. From Science, *73 (April 10, 1931): 379–80. Reprinted by permission of* Science.

In a sense scientific investigation is a game. The physicist must assemble his protons and electrons into a world—not any world, but one which has the properties of the physical world about us. As with all games, there are rules. Some of these are predetermined, for example, the fundamental rules of thinking. Others we choose for ourselves; and in this choice we have astonishing freedom. If I wish to arrange a shuffled pack of cards in sequences according to the four suits, you know a score of solitare games, each with its own set of rules, by which this may be done. But it is not obvious that the game of world building may be played in more than one way. It remained for Einstein to show us that such is the case, and that if we judiciously change the rules we may still win fairly, with a greatly increased score. As a matter of fact, we have unconsciously been revising the rules of the game ever since men began to think in a scientific way; but we didn't realize it until Einstein drove it home in a way not to be ignored.

Thus with our notion of space. It may seem to you queer that space, which doubtless you think of as a great empty void, should have anything to do with rules. I don't know why it is that we so seldom point out to laymen that the space of physics and astronomy is not the void which separates objects from each other. The physicist never thinks of space apart from objects within it; in his mind is always the idea of distance—the distances of objects from each other. When he says that space has certain properties he is talking not about the empty void, but about how he makes measurements to find what these distances are. But you ask: Is he not obliged to measure distance in a definite way? The answer is, No. He may measure in any way he likes, along what we call a straight line for example; or, if he finds reason for so doing, he may measure along some curve connecting two objects and call that result the distance.

The physicist's space is therefore essentially a set of rules for measurement. Those used until Einstein suggested a change were unconsciously adopted by Euclid two thousand years ago. Until less than a century ago no one realized that by accepting one of Euclid's postulates we had committed ourselves to making measurements in a particular way, or that measurements could be made in any other way. Even then we looked upon the matter as a geometrical curiosity without practical significance; and by the time Einstein suggested the advantages of a change and we began to hear about curved space, our long-held ideas had become so fixed that readjustment was hard. For the layman it was even worse. He had in mind the empty void; and how could such a thing as a void be flat or curved? But if we say that curved space means only a new set of rules which require that measurements be made along curved lines, the idea at least makes sense, even though you may not be convinced that such a strange procedure is advantageous. But I assure you that it is, for it enables us to win the game with a score we could not otherwise attain. If that statement brings no illumination, let me ask you, What is the distance from here to New York? Your answer undoubtedly will be the miles measured over the curved surface of the earth, because that is the distance which every-day experience makes it useful to know.

As with our ideas of space, so with a dozen others. Each has been transformed and set before us in new light. Quite apart from the intrinsic importance of the results is the remarkable fact that such momentous changes of view-point could be made. By teaching us that, Einstein has put into our hands new power. The value of this service, it seems to me, can not be set too high.

AN HONORARY DEGREE*—CITATION

At its meeting on the ninth of February, 1949, the Senate of the Hebrew University in Jerusalem had before it the distinguished name of

Professor Albert Einstein

one of the greatest scientists of all time.

By his discovery of the Theory of Relativity and the Theory of Photons Professor Einstein has revolutionized the study of physics and enriched human thought and science by entirely new conceptions. He has been a valiant champion of human liberty and freedom of thought. He has given his support to the Zionist movement, and his wise counsel has been at the service of the Hebrew University since its inception. His life and work have shed lustre on the Jewish people throughout the world.

In token of the gratitude of the Hebrew University to Professor Albert Einstein and of its profound admiration for his great achievements, the Senate has decided to confer on him the degree of

Doctor Philosophiae Honoris Causa
of the Hebrew University

Professor Albert Einstein is hereby invested with all the dignity and privilege appertaining to the Degree of Doctor.

(–) Leon Simon   (–) Simha Assaf
    for President   Rector

The degree was conferred at Princeton, Tuesday afternoon, March 15, 1949. Reprinted by permission of the Hebrew University.

*Albert Einstein received many honours and degrees, but he valued especially the one bestowed by the Hebrew University (as seen by his reply).

ALBERT EINSTEIN: 1879–1955

NIELS BOHR

With the death of Albert Einstein, a life in the service of science and humanity which was rich and fruitful as any in the whole history of our culture has come to an end. Mankind will always be indebted to Einstein for the removal of the obstacles to our outlook which were involved in the primitive notions of absolute space and time. He gave us a world picture with a unity and harmony surpassing the boldest dreams of the past.

Einstein's genius, characterized equally by logical clarity and creative imagination, succeeded in remolding and widening the imposing edifice whose foundations had been laid by Newton's great work. Within the frame of the relativity theory, demanding a formulation of the laws of nature independent of the observer and emphasizing the singular role of the speed of light, gravitational effects lost their isolated position and appeared as an integral part of a general kinematic description, capable of verification by refined astronomical observations. Moreover, Einstein's recognition of the equivalence of mass and energy should prove an invaluable guide in the exploration of atomic phenomena.

Indeed, the breadth of Einstein's views and the openness of his mind found most remarkable expression in the fact that, in the very same years when he gave a widened outlook to classical physics, he thoroughly grasped the fact that Planck's discovery of the universal quantum of action revealed an inherent limitation in such an approach. With unfailing intuition Einstein was led to the introduction of the idea of the photon as the carrier of momentum and energy in individual radiative processes. He thereby provided the starting point for the establishment of consistent quantum theoretical methods which have made it possible to account for an immense amount of experimental evidence concerning the properties of matter and even demanded reconsideration of our most elementary concepts.

The same spirit that characterized Einstein's unique scientific achievements also marked his attitude in all human relations. Notwithstanding the increasing reverence which people everywhere felt for his attainments and character, he behaved with unchanging natural modesty and expressed himself with a subtle and charming humor. He was always prepared to help people in difficulties of any kind, and to him, who himself had experienced the evils of racial prejudice, the promotion of understanding among nations was a foremost endeavor. His earnest admonitions on the responsibility involved in our rapidly growing mastery of the forces of nature will surely help to meet the challenge to civilization in the proper spirit.

To the whole of mankind Albert Einstein's death is a great loss, and to those of us who had the good fortune to enjoy his warm friendship it is a grief that we shall never more be able to see his gentle smile and listen to him. But the memories he has left behind will remain an ever-living source of fortitude and encouragement.

ALBERT EINSTEIN—A TRIBUTE

I. I. RABI

Columbia University, New York

Einstein, more than any other man, set the tone of 20th Century physics. His theories of special and general relativity were the capstones of classical physics and the theory of fields. His theory of light quanta and his later demonstration of the nature of the fluctuations of "black body" radiation raised the paradox of the wave-particle duality, which was partly resolved two decades later in the principle of complementarity of Niels Bohr and Werner Heisenberg. His 1917 paper, introducing the ideas of spontaneous and stimulated emission of radiation, was the first clear statement of the statistical nature of fundamental atomic phenomena. The famous Einstein A and B coefficients led to the quantitative use of the correspondence principle and to the formulation of the Kramers-Heisenberg dispersion formula, which in turn led to Heisenberg's matrix mechanics. Einstein was therefore in a very real sense the founder of the statistical theory of fundamental atomic phenomena.

There is scarcely any important fundamental idea in modern physics whose origin does not trace back at least in part to Einstein. Yet, like many another father, he was not really satisfied with the children of his scientific imagination. He never regarded his mighty contributions to quantum theory as other than provisional suggestions for the ordering of phenomena. The subsequent formulations of quantum mechanics and especially the thoroughgoing statistical interpretations were to him philosophically and esthetically repugnant.

The Einstein-Bose statistics and the Einstein condensation phenomenon were his last important positive contributions to quantum theory. His subsequent role with respect to quantum theory was that of a critic. He applied the force of his great imagination to the construction of imaginary experiments which involved the theory in seemingly paradoxical and contradictory predictions. The resolution of these paradoxes, chiefly through the efforts of Bohr, served to refine and clarify the principle of complementarity but left Einstein unconvinced.

His real love was the theory of fields, which he pursued with unremitting vigor to the very end of his more than 50 years of active scientific life. This

Adapted by Columbia University I. I. Rabi, Professor Emeritus, from a tribute in Scientific American, *192 (June 1955): 32. Reprinted with permission. Copyright © 1955 by Scientific American, Inc. All rights reserved, also by permission of Professor I. I. Rabi.*

preoccupation is to a large degree the key to his scientific personality. The theory of general relativity was constructed on the basis of a physical observation of the equivalence of inertial and gravitational mass under certain simple circumstances. Beyond that, his guiding principles were his esthetic and philosophical urge for simplicity and symmetry. His intuition and taste led him to believe that the equivalence principle was true in general, and that the equations of physics must be covariant in all systems of coordinates. With these guidelines and with the use of mathematical tools already at hand, he built a theory of gravitation and of the structure of the cosmos.

Like a mystic who has had a divine illumination, Einstein in his search for the ideal could be satisfied with nothing less than a theory which would encompass all phenomena—atomic and cosmic. He once remarked to me in a discussion concerning the newly discovered meson: "We already know that the electron is quantized in charge and mass. Should not this be enough empirical information for a theory of matter?" It was a goal of this grandeur that drove him in his search for a unified field theory.

Einstein was a unique personality. He was not attracted by fame or fortune nor swayed by the opinions of the majority. He knew his talent and guarded it jealously against outside interference. Although fearless in support of any cause he considered worthy, he gave only so much of himself and no more. Physics was his life, and he lived it according to his own lights, with complete objectivity and integrity.

He was the prince of physicists, and the imprint of his mighty strides will give direction to his beloved science for generations to come.

INAUGURAL ADDRESS TO THE PRUSSIAN ACADEMY OF SCIENCES (1914)

Gentlemen,

First of all, I have to thank you most heartily for conferring the greatest benefit on me that anybody can confer on a man like myself. By electing me to your Academy you have freed me from the distractions and cares of a professional life and so made it possible for me to devote myself entirely to scientific studies. I beg that you will continue to believe in my gratitude and my industry even when my efforts seem to you to yield but a poor result.

Preussische Akademie der Wissenschaften, Sitzungsberichte, 1914, part 2, pp. 739–42, trans. in The World as I See It *(New York: Covici-Friede, 1934). Also in* Ideas and Opinions *(New York: Crown Publishers, 1954) under the title "Principles of Theoretical Physics." Reprinted by permission of the Estate of Albert Einstein.*

Perhaps I may be allowed à propos of this to make a few general remarks on the relation of my sphere of activity, which is theoretical physics, towards experimental physics. A mathematician friend of mine said to me the other day half in jest: 'The mathematician can do a lot of things, but never what you happen to want him to do just at the moment'. Much the same often applies to the theoretical physicist when the experimental physicist calls him in. What is the reason for this peculiar lack of adaptability?

The theorist's method involves his using as his foundation general postulates or 'principles' from which he can deduce conclusions. His work thus falls into two parts. He must first discover his principles and then draw the conclusions which follow from them. For the second of these tasks he receives an admirable equipment at school. Once, therefore, he has performed the first task in some department, or for some complex of related phenomena, he is certain of success, provided his industry and intelligence are adequate. The first of these tasks, namely, that of establishing the principles which are to serve as the starting point of his deduction, is of an entirely different nature. Here there is no method capable of being learnt and systematically applied so that it leads to the goal. The scientist has to worm these general principles out of nature by perceiving certain general features which permit of precise formulation, amidst large complexes of empirical facts.

Once this formulation is successfully accomplished, inference follows on inference, often revealing relations which extend far beyond the province of the reality from which the principles were drawn. But as long as the principles capable of serving as starting points for the deduction remain undiscovered, the individual fact is of no use to the theorist; indeed he cannot even do anything with isolated empirical generalisations of more or less wide application. No, he has to persist in his helpless attitude towards the separate results of empirical research, until principles which he can make the basis of deductive reasoning have revealed themselves to him.

This is the kind of position in which theory finds itself at present in regard to the laws of heat, radiation, and molecular movement at low temperatures. About fifteen years ago nobody had yet doubted that a correct account of the electrical, optical and thermal properties of bodies was possible on the basis of Galileo-Newtonian mechanics applied to the movement of molecules and of Clerk Maxwell's theory of the electro-magnetic field. Then Planck showed that in order to establish a law of heat radiation consonant with experience, it was necessary to employ a method of calculation the incompatibility of which with the principles of classical physics became clearer and clearer. For with this method of calculation Planck introduced the quantum hypothesis into physics, which has since received brilliant confirmation. With this quantum hypothesis he dethroned classical physics as applied to the case where sufficiently small masses are moved at sufficiently low speeds and high rates of acceleration, so that today the laws of motion propounded by Galileo and

Newton can only be allowed validity as limiting laws. In spite of assiduous efforts, however, the theorists have not yet succeeded in replacing the principles of mechanics by others which fit in with Planck's law of heat radiation or the quantum hypothesis. No matter how definitely it has been proved that heat is to be explained by molecular movement, we have nevertheless to admit today that our position in regard to the fundamental laws of this motion resembles that of astronomers before Newton in regard to the motions of the planets.

I have just now referred to a group of facts for the theoretical treatment of which the principles are lacking. But it may equally well happen that clearly formulated principles lead to conclusions which fall entirely, or almost entirely, outside the sphere of reality at present accessible to our experience. In that case it may need many years of empirical research to ascertain whether the theoretical principles correspond with reality. We have an instance of this in the theory of relativity.

An analysis of the fundamental concepts of space and time has shown us that the principle of the constant velocity of light in empty space, which emerges from the optics of bodies in motion, by no means forces us to accept the theory of a stationary luminiferous ether. On the contrary, there is nothing to prevent our framing a general theory which takes account of the fact that in experiments carried out on the earth we are wholly unconscious of the translatory motion of the earth. This involves using the principle of relativity, which says that the laws of nature do not alter their form when one proceeds from the original (legitimate) system of co-ordinates to a new one which is in uniform translatory motion with respect to it. This theory has received impressive confirmation from experience and has led to a simplification of the theoretical description of groups of facts already connected together.

On the other hand, from the theoretical point of view this theory is not wholly satisfactory, because the principle of relativity just formulated prefers *uniform* motion. If it is true that no absolute significance can be attached to *uniform* motion from the physical point of view, the question arises whether this statement must not also be extended to non-uniform motions. It became clear that one arrives at a quite definite enlargement of the relativity theory if one postulates a principle of relativity in this extended sense. One is led thereby to a general theory of gravitation which includes dynamics. For the present, however, we have not the necessary array of facts to test the legitimacy of our introduction of the postulated principle.

We have ascertained that inductive physics asks questions of deductive, and vice versa, to answer which demands the exertion of all our energies. May we soon succeed in making permanent progress by our united efforts!

ADDRESS TO PROFESSOR PLANCK

How shall I put into words what moves me, as I stand at this moment before the honored master and friend with whom I have been united for so many years through common aspirations. It was twenty-nine years ago when I, as a youth, became enthusiastic about Professor Planck's ingenious derivation of the radiation law, which determined for the first time the exact size of atoms and applied Boltzmann's statistical method in such a novel way. Even at that time you, honored master, realized that behind your newly introduced constant h a fundamental quality of all events is hidden, whose elucidation must be one of the most important goals of future decades. The realization of that program—from a fundamental point of view—forms the content of the most important branch of the new physics.

Was it a wonder that I also was drawn into the sphere of your formulation of the problem? From my first exposure to it I struggled to reach a deeper understanding of the relationship of ideas that came about as a result of your efforts to work with physicists more and more. In particular, there were two ideas around which my fervent efforts grouped themselves: Natural events seem so completely determined that not only is the time sequence connected by laws but also the initial state. I strove to give expression to this idea by the search for the determining systems of equations. The general relativity postulate as well as the unified structure of physical space, i.e. the field, should show the way. This aim yet remains unreached, and there can hardly be found a colleague who does not share my hope in arriving at a deeper understanding of reality in this way. What I discovered in the area of the quantum theory are only occasional insights, or so to speak, splinters that broke off during the fruitless attempts toward solving the large problem. I feel unworthy to receive such a great honor for these.

Although I strongly believe that we shall not stop at subcausality, but will even arrive at overcausality in the indicated sense, I admire very much accomplishments in the name of quantum mechanics of this generation of younger physicists, and believe in the deep truth of that theory; and I think that the limitation of the theory to statistical laws will be only temporary.

Now a word to you, dear and honored Mr. Planck. I know, and I am glad to be able to express to you, that I owe you a great deal for your intellectual

On the occasion of the 50th anniversary of Professor Planck's doctorate, the German Physical Society at Berlin, together with the German Society for Technical Physics, organized a festive meeting on June 28, 1929. At that time the Planck medal, issued in honor of Professor Planck's 70th birthday, was bestowed upon Professor Planck by the chairman of the German Physical Society, Professor Heinrich Konen-Bonn. Thereupon Professor Planck bestowed a second medal to Professor Albert Einstein. The above address was given by Albert Einstein in response to this presentation. From Forschungen und Fortschritte 5 *(1929): 248. Reprinted by permission of the Estate of Albert Einstein.*

stimulation and your humanity. You were one of the most effective stimulants to this developing scientist, and the first who supported the relativity theory. You have decisively contributed to my promotions and have provided working facilities that are given to only a few. In all matters that concerned work and action there was agreement between us. I often had the opportunity to admire the objectivity with which you—not influenced by personal or political motives —always served the cause.

Your ideas will continue to be effective as long as there will be a physics, and I hope the example you set will influence those who follow.

Filled with these thoughts and feelings, I accept happily but also with humility the Planck Medal from your hands.

AN HONORARY DEGREE—ACCEPTANCE

The little that I could do, in a long life favored by external circumstances to deepen our physical knowledge, has brought me so much praise that for a long time I have felt rather more embarrassed than elated. But from you there comes a token of esteem that fills me with pure joy—joy about the great deeds that our Jewish people have accomplished within a few generations, under exceptionally difficult conditions, by itself alone, through boundless courage and immeasurable sacrifices. The University which twenty-seven years ago was nothing but a dream and a faint hope, this University is today a living thing, a home of free learning and teaching and happy brotherly work. There it is, on the soil that our people has liberated under great hardships; there it is, a spiritual center of a flourishing and buoyant community whose accomplishments have finally met with the universal recognition they deserved.

In this last period of the fulfillment of our dreams there was but one thing that weighed heavily upon me: the fact that we were compelled by the adversities of our situation to assert our rights through force of arms; it was the only way to avert complete annihilation. The wisdom and moderation the leaders of the new state have shown gives me confidence, however, that gradually relations will be established with the Arab people which are based on fruitful cooperation and mutual respect and trust. For this is the only means through which both peoples can attain free independence from the outside world.

To all my colleagues of the Hebrew University I extend my heartfelt thanks for this token of their appreciation and kindness.

Remarks upon receiving from the Hebrew University the degree of Doctor Philosophiae Honoris Causa *at Princeton, March 15, 1949. Reprinted by permission of the Hebrew University and the Estate of Albert Einstein.*

II. THE GENERAL THEORY
OF RELATIVITY

It has often been said that only twelve people in the world can understand Einstein's theory of relativity. This may have been true some time ago, but nowadays every graduate student with some knowledge of mathematical formalism can follow the exposition in countless textbooks. A number of popular accounts are also in existence, but none surpasses the one given by Einstein himself in his *Relativity: The Special and General Theory* and faithfully translated by Robert W. Lawson.

The bulk of the material that follows is a reprint of Part II of Einstein's book *Relativity* dealing with the General Theory of Relativity. In order to convey some feelings about the origin and foundations of the theory, several articles, also from the pen of Albert Einstein, accompany these reprints. We begin with "Notes on the Origin of the General Theory of Relativity," which gives us some insight into how Einstein arrived at his theory. This is followed by a lecture delivered to the Nordic Assembly of Naturalists in Gothenburg, which, in effect, may be considered Einstein's Nobel Prize address. Finally, there are two newspaper articles, one from the *Times of London* and the second from the *New York Times,* as well as a lecture delivered at King's College, London. We realize that there may be some duplications, but as Einstein said himself in the Preface to his book this is inevitable in the interest of clearness.

During Einstein's life there were criticisms of his theory, some even with vicious personal attacks on him, but Einstein always managed to keep his cool and confound his critics. We have chosen three typical replies: The first is a reply to Ernst Reichenbächer who maintains that the theory of gravitation can be formulated without the use of general relativity. Einstein agrees, but shows that it is the principle of relativity that provides the necessary ingredient for a simple consistent theory. The second article is a reply to a vicious personal attack by what Einstein calls the "Anti-relativistic Company." The third and last in that series is an imaginary dialogue between a relativist and a critic, written by Einstein and masterfully translated by Hermann M. Schwartz.

The final article is a brief summary of a lecture delivered at Yale University, which opens new avenues, followed by an evaluation of the influence of relativity on scientific thought taken from an address by Sir Arthur S. Eddington.

ORIGINS AND FOUNDATIONS

NOTES ON THE ORIGIN OF THE GENERAL THEORY OF RELATIVITY

I gladly accede to the request that I should say something about the history of my own scientific work. Not that I have an exaggerated notion of the importance of my own efforts, but to write the history of other men's work demands a degree of absorption in other people's ideas which is much more in the line of the trained historian; to throw light on one's own earlier thinking appears incomparably easier. Here one has an immense advantage over everybody else, and one ought not to leave the opportunity unused out of modesty.

When by the special theory of relativity I had arrived at the equivalence of all so-called inertial systems for the formulation of natural laws (1905), the question whether there was not a further equivalence of coordinate systems followed naturally, to say the least of it. To put it in another way, if only a relative meaning can be attached to the concept of velocity, ought we nevertheless to persevere in treating acceleration as an absolute concept?

From the purely kinematic point of view there was no doubt about the relativity of all motions whatever; but physically speaking, the inertial system seemed to occupy a privileged position, which made the use of coordinate systems moving in other ways appear artificial.

I was of course acquainted with Mach's view, according to which it appeared conceivable that what inertial resistance counteracts is not acceleration as such but acceleration with respect to the masses of the other bodies existing in the world. There was something fascinating about this idea to me, but it provided no workable basis for a new theory.

I first came a step nearer to the solution of the problem when I attempted to deal with the law of gravity within the framework of the special theory of relativity. Like most writers at the time, I tried to frame a *field-law* for gravitation, since it was no longer possible, at least in any natural way, to introduce direct action at a distance owing to the abolition of the notion of absolute simultaneity.

From "Mein Weltbild" *(Amsterdam: Querido Verlag, 1934). English translation in* Ideas and Opinions *(New York: Crown Publishers, 1954). Reprinted by permission of the publisher and the Estate of Albert Einstein.*

The simplest thing was, of course, to retain the Laplacian scalar potential of gravity, and to complete the equation of Poisson in an obvious way by a term differentiated with respect to time in such a way that the special theory of relativity was satisfied. The law of motion of the mass point in a gravitational field had also to be adapted to the special theory of relativity. The path was not so unmistakably marked out here, since the inert mass of a body might depend on the gravitational potential. In fact, this was to be expected on account of the principle of the inertia of energy.

These investigations, however, led to a result which raised my strong suspicions. According to classical mechanics, the vertical acceleration of a body in the vertical gravitational field is independent of the horizontal component of its velocity. Hence in such a gravitational field the vertical acceleration of a mechanical system or of its center of gravity works out independently of its internal kinetic energy. But in the theory I advanced, the acceleration of a falling body was not independent of its horizontal velocity or the internal energy of a system.

This did not fit in with the old experimental fact that all bodies have the same acceleration in a gravitational field. This law, which may also be formulated as the law of the equality of inertial and gravitational mass, was now brought home to me in all its significance. I was in the highest degree amazed at its existence and guessed that in it must lie the key to a deeper understanding of inertia and gravitation. I had no serious doubts about its strict validity even without knowing the results of the admirable experiments of Eötvös, which— if my memory is right—I only came to know later. I now abandoned as inadequate the attempt to treat the problem of gravitation, in the manner outlined above, within the framework of the special theory of relativity. It clearly failed to do justice to the most fundamental property of gravitation. The principle of the equality of inertial and gravitational mass could now be formulated quite clearly as follows: In a homogeneous gravitational field all motions take place in the same way as in the absence of a gravitational field in relation to a uniformly accelerated coordinate system. If this principle held good for any events whatever (the "principle of equivalence"), this was an indication that the principle of relativity needed to be extended to coordinate systems in non-uniform motion with respect to each other, if we were to reach a natural theory of the gravitational fields. Such reflections kept me busy from 1908 to 1911, and I attempted to draw special conclusions from them, of which I do not propose to speak here. For the moment the one important thing was the discovery that a reasonable theory of gravitation could only be hoped for from an extension of the principle of relativity.

What was needed, therefore, was to frame a theory whose equations kept their form in the case of non-linear transformations of the coordinates. Whether this was to apply to arbitrary (continuous) transformations of coordinates or only to certain ones, I could not for the moment say.

I soon saw that the inclusion of non-linear transformations, as the principle of equivalence demanded, was inevitably fatal to the simple physical interpretation of the coordinates—i.e., that it could no longer be required that coordinate differences should signify direct results of measurement with ideal scales or clocks. I was much bothered by this piece of knowledge, for it took me a long time to see what coordinates at all meant in physics. I did not find the way out of this dilemma until 1912, and then it came to me as a result of the following consideration:

A new formulation of the law of inertia had to be found which in case of the absence of a "real gravitational field" passed over into Galileo's formulation for the principle of inertia if an inertial system was used as a coordinate system. Galileo's formulation amounts to this: A material point, which is acted on by no force, will be represented in four-dimensional space by a straight line, that is to say, by a shortest line, or more correctly, an extremal line. This concept presupposes that of the length of a line element, that is to say, a metric. In the special theory of relativity, as Minkowski had shown, this metric was a quasi-Euclidean one, i.e., the square of the "length" ds of a line element was a certain quadratic function of the differentials of the coordinates.

If other coordinates are introduced by means of a non-linear transformation, ds^2 remains a homogeneous function of the differentials of the coordinates, but the coefficients of this function ($g_{\mu\nu}$) cease to be constant and become certain functions of the coordinates. In mathematical terms this means that physical (four-dimensional) space has a Riemannian metric. The timelike extremal lines of this metric furnish the law of motion of a material point which is acted on by no force apart from the forces of gravity. The coefficients ($g_{\mu\nu}$) of this metric at the same time describe the gravitational field with reference to the coordinate system selected. A natural formulation of the principle of equivalence had thus been found, the extension of which to any gravitational field whatever formed a perfectly natural hypothesis.

The solution of the above-mentioned dilemma was therefore as follows: A physical significance attaches not to the differentials of the coordinates but only to the Riemannian metric corresponding to them. A workable basis had now been found for the general theory of relativity. Two further problems remained to be solved, however.

1. If a field-law is expressed in terms of the special theory of relativity, how can it be transferred to the case of a Riemannian metric?

2. What are the differential laws which determine the Riemannian metric (i.e., $g_{\mu\nu}$) itself?

I worked on these problems from 1912 to 1914 together with my friend Grossmann. We found that the mathematical methods for solving problem 1 lay ready in our hands in the absolute differential calculus of Ricci and Levi-Civita.

As for problem 2, its solution obviously required the construction (from the $g_{\mu\nu}$) of the differential invariants of the second order. We soon saw that these had already been established by Riemann (the tensor of curvature). We had already considered the right field-equation for gravitation two years before the publication of the general theory of relativity, but we were unable to see how they could be used in physics. On the contrary, I felt sure that they could not do justice to experience. Moreover I believe that I could show on general considerations that a law of gravitation invariant with respect to arbitrary transformations of coordinates was inconsistent with the principle of causality. These were errors of thought which cost me two years of excessively hard work, until I finally recognized them as such at the end of 1915, and after having ruefully returned to the Riemannian curvature, succeeded in linking the theory with the facts of astronomical experience.

In the light of knowledge attained, the happy achievement seems almost a matter of course, and any intelligent student can grasp it without too much trouble. But the years of anxious searching in the dark, with their intense longing, their alternations of confidence and exhaustion and the final emergence into the light—only those who have experienced it can understand that.

FUNDAMENTAL IDEAS AND PROBLEMS
OF THE THEORY OF RELATIVITY

Lecture delivered to the Nordic Assembly of Naturalists at Gothenburg*

If we consider that part of the theory of relativity which may nowadays in a sense be regarded as bona fide scientific knowledge, we note two aspects which have a major bearing on this theory. The whole development of the theory turns on the question of whether there are physically preferred states of motion in Nature (physical relativity problem). Also, concepts and distinctions are only admissible to the extent that observable facts can be assigned to them without ambiguity (stipulation that concepts and distinctions should have meaning). This postulate, pertaining to epistemology, proves to be of fundamental importance.

These two aspects become clear when applied to a special case, e.g. to classical mechanics. Firstly we see that at any point filled with matter there exists a preferred state of motion, namely that of the substance at the point considered. Our problem starts however with the question whether physically preferred states of motion exist in reference to *extensive* regions. From the

From Nobel Lectures in Physics (1901–1921) *(Amsterdam: Elsevier Scientific Publishing Co., 1967). Reprinted by permission of the publisher, Nobel Foundation, and the Estate of Albert Einstein.*

*The Lecture was not delivered on the occasion of the Nobel Prize award, and did not, therefore, concern the discovery of the photoelectric effect. [See also Presentation Speech on the award of Nobel Prize for Physics, 1921, to Einstein.]

viewpoint of classical mechanics the answer is in the affirmative; the physically preferred states of motion from the viewpoint of mechanics are those of the inertial frames.

This assertion, in common with the basis of the whole of mechanics as it generally used to be described before the relativity theory, far from meets the above "stipulation of meaning." Motion can only be conceived as the relative motion of bodies. In mechanics, motion relative to the system of coordinates is implied when merely motion is referred to. Nevertheless this interpretation does not comply with the "stipulation of meaning" if the coordinate system is considered as something purely imaginary. If we turn our attention to experimental physics we see that there the coordinate system is invariably represented by a "practically rigid" body. Furthermore it is assumed that such rigid bodies can be positioned in rest relative to one another in common with the bodies of Euclidian geometry. Insofar as we may think of the rigid measuring body as existing as an object which can be experienced, the "system of coordinates" concept as well as the concept of the motion of matter relative thereto can be accepted in the sense of the "stipulation of meaning." At the same time Euclidian geometry, by this conception, has been adapted to the requirements of the physics of the "stipulation of meaning." The question whether Euclidian geometry is valid becomes physically significant; its validity is assumed in classical physics and also later in the special theory of relativity.

In classical mechanics the inertial frame and time are best defined together by a suitable formulation of the law of inertia: It is possible to fix the time and assign a state of motion to the system of coordinates (inertial frame) such that, with reference to the latter, force-free material points undergo no acceleration; furthermore it is assumed that this time can be measured without disagreement by identical clocks (systems which run down periodically) in any arbitrary state of motion. There are then an infinite number of inertial frames which are in uniform translational motion relative to each other, and hence there is also an infinite number of mutually equivalent, physically preferred states of motion. Time is absolute, i.e. independent of the choice of the particular inertial frame; it is defined by more characteristics than logically necessary, although—as implied by mechanics—this should not lead to contradictions with experience. Note in passing that the logical weakness of this exposition from the point of view of the stipulation of meaning is the lack of an experimental criterion for whether a material point is forcefree or not; therefore the concept of the inertial frame remains rather problematical. This deficiency leads to the general theory of relativity. We shall not consider it for the moment.

The concept of the rigid body (and that of the clock) has a key bearing on the foregoing consideration of the fundamentals of mechanics, a bearing which there is some justification for challenging. The rigid body is only approximately achieved in Nature, not even with desired approximation; this concept does not therefore strictly satisfy the "stipulation of meaning." It is also logically unjustifiable to base all physical consideration on the rigid or solid body and then finally reconstruct that body atomically by means of elementary physical laws which in turn have been determined by means of the rigid measuring body. I am mentioning these deficiencies of method because in the same sense they are also a feature of the relativity theory in the schematic exposition which I am advocating here. Certainly it would be logically more correct to begin with the whole of the laws and to apply the "stipulation of meaning" to this whole first, i.e. to put the unambiguous relation to the world of experience last instead of already fulfilling it in an imperfect form for an artificially isolated part, namely the space-time metric. We are not, however, sufficiently advanced in our knowledge of Nature's elementary laws to adopt this more perfect method without going out of our depth. At the close of our considerations we shall see that in the most recent studies there is an attempt, based on ideas by Levi-Civita, Weyl, and Eddington, to implement that logically purer method.

It more clearly follows from the above what is implied by "preferred states of motion." They are preferred as regards the laws of Nature. States of motion are preferred when, relative to the formulation of the laws of Nature, coordinate systems within them are distinguished in that with respect to them those laws assume a form preferred by simplicity. According to classical mechanics the states of motion of the inertial frames in this sense are physically preferred. Classical mechanics permits a distinction to be made between (absolutely) unaccelerated and accelerated motions; it also claims that velocities have only a relative existence (dependent on the selection of the inertial frame), while accelerations and rotations have an absolute existence (independent of the selection of the inertial frame). This state of affairs can be expressed thus: According to classical mechanics "velocity relativity" exists, but not "acceleration relativity." After these preliminary considerations we can pass to the actual topic of our contemplations, the relativity theory, by characterizing its development so far in terms of principles.

The special theory of relativity is an adaptation of physical principles to Maxwell-Lorentz electrodynamics. From earlier physics it takes the assumption that Euclidean geometry is valid for the laws governing the position of rigid bodies, the inertial frame, and the law of inertia. The postulate of equivalence of inertial frames for the formulation of the laws of Nature is assumed to be valid for the whole of physics (special relativity principle). From Maxwell-Lorentz electrodynamics it takes the postulate of invariance of the velocity of light in a vacuum (light principle).

To harmonize the relativity principle with the light principle, the assumption that an absolute time (agreeing for all inertial frames) exists, had to be abandoned. Thus the hypothesis is abandoned that arbitrarily moved and suitably set identical clocks function in such a way that the times shown by two of them, which meet, agree. A specific time is assigned to each inertial frame; the state of motion and the time of the inertial framework are defined, in accordance with the stipulation of meaning, by the requirement that the light principle should apply to it. The existence of the inertial frame thus defined and the validity of the law of inertia with respect to it are assumed. The time for each inertial frame is measured by identical clocks that are stationary relative to the frame.

The laws of transformation for space coordinates and time for the transition from one inertial frame to another, the Lorentz transformations as they are termed, are unequivocally established by these definitions and the hypotheses concealed in the assumption that they are free from contradiction. Their immediate physical significance lies in the effect of the motion relative to the used inertial frame on the form of rigid bodies (Lorentz contraction) and on the rate of the clocks. According to the special relativity principle the laws of Nature must be covariant relative to Lorentz transformations; the theory thus provides a criterion for general laws of Nature. It leads in particular to a modification of the Newtonian point motion law in which the velocity of light in a vacuum is considered the limiting velocity, and it also leads to the realization that energy and inertial mass are of like nature.

The special relativity theory resulted in appreciable advances. It reconciled mechanics and electrodynamics. It reduced the number of logically independent hypotheses regarding the latter. It enforced the need for a clarification of the fundamental concepts in epistemological terms. It united the momentum and energy principle, and demonstrated the like nature of mass and energy. Yet it was not entirely satisfactory—quite apart from the quantum problems, which all theory so far has been incapable of really solving. In common with classical mechanics the special relativity theory favours certain states of motion—namely those of the inertial frames—to all other states of motion. This was actually more difficult to tolerate than the preference for a single state of motion as in the case of the theory of light with a stationary ether, for this imagined a real reason for the preference, i.e. the light ether. A theory which from the outset prefers no state of motion should appear more satisfactory. Moreover the previously mentioned vagueness in the definition of the inertial frame or in the formulation of the law of inertia raises doubts which obtain their decisive importance, owing to the empirical principle for the equality of the inertial and heavy mass, in the light of the following consideration.

Let K be an inertial frame without a gravitational field, K' a system of coordinates accelerated uniformly relative to K. The behaviour of material points relative to K' is the same as if K' were an inertial frame in respect of which a homogeneous gravitational field exists. On the basis of the empirically known properties of the gravitational field, the definition of the inertial frame thus proves to be weak. The conclusion is obvious that any arbitrarily moved frame of reference is equivalent to any other for the formulation of the laws of Nature, that there are thus no physically preferred states of motion at all in respect of regions of finite extension (general relativity principle).

The implementation of this concept necessitates an even more profound modification of the geometric-kinematical principles than the special relativity theory. The Lorentz contraction, which is derived from the latter, leads to the conclusion that with regard to a system K' arbitrarily moved relative to a (gravity field free) inertial frame K, the laws of Euclidean geometry governing the position of rigid (at rest relative to K') bodies do not apply. Consequently the Cartesian system of coordinates also loses its significance in terms of the stipulation of meaning. Analogous reasoning applies to time; with reference to K' the time can no longer meaningfully be defined by the indication on identical clocks at rest relative to K', nor by the law governing the propagation of light. Generalizing, we arrive at the conclusion that gravitational field and metric are only different manifestations of the same physical field.

We arrive at the formal description of this field by the following consideration. For each infinitesimal point-environment in an arbitrary gravitational field a local frame of coordinates can be given for such a state of motion that relative to this local frame no gravitational field exists (local inertial frame). In terms of this inertial frame we may regard the results of the special relativity theory as correct to a first approximation for this infinitesimally small region. There is an infinite number of such local inertial frames at any space-time point; they are associated by Lorentz transformations. These latter are characterised in that they leave invariant the "distance" ds of two infinitely adjacent point events—defined by the equation:

$$ds^2 = c^2 dt^2 - dx^2 - dy^2 - dz^2$$

which distance can be measured by means of scales and clocks. For, x, y, z, t represent coordinates and time measured with reference to a local inertial frame.

To describe space-time regions of finite extent arbitrary point coordinates in four dimensions are required which serve no other purpose than to provide an unambiguous designation of the space-time points by four numbers each x_1, x_2, x_3 and x_4, which takes account of the continuity of this four-dimensional manifold (Gaussian coordinates). The mathematical expression of the general relativity principle is then, that the systems of equations expressing the general laws of Nature are equal for all such systems of coordinates.

Since the coordinate differentials of the local inertial frame are expressed linearly by the differentials dx_ν of a Gaussian system of coordinates, when the latter is used, for the distance ds of two events an expression of the form

$$ds^2 = \Sigma g_{\mu\nu} \, dx_\mu dx_\nu \; (g_{\mu\nu} = g_{\nu\mu})$$

is obtained. The $g_{\mu\nu}$, which are continuous functions of x_ν, determine the metric in the four-dimensional manifold where ds is defined as an (absolute) parameter measurable by means of rigid scales and clocks. These same parameters $g_{\mu\nu}$ however also describe with reference to the Gaussian system of coordinates the gravitational field which we have previously found to be identical with the physical cause of the metric. The case as to the validity of the special relativity theory for finite regions is characterised in that when the system of coordinates is suitably chosen, the values of $g_{\mu\nu}$ for finite regions are independent of x_ν.

In accordance with the general theory of relativity the law of point motion in the pure gravitational field is expressed by the equation for the geodetic line. Actually the geodetic line is the simplest mathematically which in the special case of constant $g_{\mu\nu}$ becomes rectilinear. Here therefore we are confronted with the transfer of Galileo's law of inertia to the general theory of relativity.

In mathematical terms the search for the field equations amounts to ascertaining the simplest generally covariant differential equations to which the gravitational potentials $g_{\mu\nu}$ can be subjected. By definition these equations should not contain higher derivatives of $g_{\mu\nu}$ with respect to x_ν than the second, and these only linearly, which condition reveals these equations to be a logical transfer of the Poisson field equation of the Newtonian theory of gravity to the general theory of relativity.

The considerations mentioned led to the theory of gravity which yields the Newtonian theory as a first approximation and furthermore it yields the motion of the perihelion of Mercury, the deflection of light by the sun, and the red shift of spectral lines in agreement with experience.*

To complete the basis of the general theory of relativity, the electromagnetic field must still be introduced into it which, according to our present conviction, is also the material from which we must build up the elementary structures of matter. The Maxwellian field equations can readily be adopted into the general theory of relativity. This is a completely unambiguous adoption provided it is assumed that the equations contain no differential quotients of $g_{\mu\nu}$ higher than the first, and that in the customary Maxwellian form they apply in the local inertial frame. It is also easily possible to supplement the gravitational field equations by electromagnetic terms in a manner specified by the Maxwellian equations so that they contain the gravitational effect of the electromagnetic field.

These field equations have not provided a theory of matter. To incorporate the field generating effect of ponderable masses in the theory, matter had therefore (as in classical physics) to be introduced into the theory in an approximate, phenomenological representation.

And that exhausts the direct consequences of the relativity principle. I shall turn to those problems which are related to the development which I have traced. Already Newton recognized that the law of inertia is unsatisfactory in

*As regards the red shift, the agreement with experience is not yet completely assured, however. [See also Part III and, in particular, Displacement of Spectral Lines Towards the Red (ed.)]

a context so far unmentioned in this exposition, namely that it gives no real cause for the special physical position of the states of motion of the inertial frames relative to all other states of motion. It makes the observable material bodies responsible for the gravitational behaviour of a material point, yet indicates no material cause for the inertial behaviour of the material point but devises the cause for it (absolute space or inertial ether). This is not logically inadmissible although it is unsatisfactory. For this reason E. Mach demanded a modification of the law of inertia in the sense that the inertia should be interpreted as an acceleration resistance of the bodies against *one another* and not against "space." This interpretation governs the expectation that accelerated bodies have concordant accelerating action in the same sense on other bodies (acceleration induction).

This interpretation is even more plausible according to general relativity which eliminates the distinction between inertial and gravitational effects. It amounts to stipulating that, apart from the arbitrariness governed by the free choice of coordinates, the $g_{\mu\nu}$-field shall be completely determined by the matter. Mach's stipulation is favoured in general relativity by the circumstance that acceleration induction in accordance with the gravitational field equations really exists, although of such slight intensity that direct detection by mechanical experiments is out of the question.

Mach's stipulation can be accounted for in the general theory of relativity by regarding the world in spatial terms as finite and self-contained. This hypothesis also makes it possible to assume the mean density of matter in the world as *finite,* whereas in a spatially infinite (quasi-Euclidean) world it should disappear. It cannot, however, be concealed that to satisfy Mach's postulate in the manner referred to a term with no experimental basis whatsoever must be introduced into the field equations, which term logically is in no way determined by the other terms in the equations. For this reason this solution of the "cosmological problem" will not be completely satisfactory for the time being.

A second problem which at present is the subject of lively interest is the identity between the gravitational field and the electromagnetic field. The mind striving after unification of the theory cannot be satisfied that two fields should exist which, by their nature, are quite independent. A mathematically unified field theory is sought in which the gravitational field and the electromagnetic field are interpreted only as different components or manifestations of the same uniform field, the field equations where possible no longer consisting of logically mutually independent summands.

The gravitational theory, considered in terms of mathematical formalism, i.e. Riemannian geometry, should be generalized so that it includes the laws of the electromagnetic field. Unfortunately we are unable here to base ourselves on empirical facts as when deriving the gravitational theory (equality of the inertial and heavy mass), but we are restricted to the criterion of mathematical simplicity which is not free from arbitrariness. The attempt which at present appears the most successful is that, based on the ideas of Levi-Civita, Weyl and Eddington, to replace Riemannian metric geometry by the more general theory of affine correlation.

The characteristic assumption of Riemannian geometry is the attribution to two infinitely adjacent points of a "distance" ds, the square of which is a homogeneous second order function of the coordinate differentials. It follows from this that (apart from certain conditions of reality) Euclidean geometry is valid in any infinitely small region. Hence to every line element (or vector) at a point P is assigned a parallel and equal line element (or vector) through any given infinitesimally adjacent point P' (affine correlation). Riemannian metric determines an affine correlation. Conversely, however, when an affine correlation (law of infinitesimal parallel displacement) is mathematically given, generally no Riemannian metric determination exists from which it can be derived.

The most important concept of Riemannian geometry, "space curvature," on which the gravitational equations are also based, is based exclusively on the "affine correlation." If one is given in a continuum, without first proceeding from a metric, it constitutes a generalization of Riemannian geometry but which still retains the most important derived parameters. By seeking the simplest differential equations which can be obeyed by an affine correlation there is reason to hope that a generalization of the gravitation equations will be found which includes the laws of the electromagnetic field. This hope has in fact been fulfilled although I do not know whether the formal connection so derived can really be regarded as an enrichment of physics as long as it does not yield any new physical connections. In particular a field theory can, to my mind, only be satisfactory when it permits the elementary electrical bodies to be represented as solutions free from singularities.

Moreover it should not be forgotten that a theory relating to the elementary electrical structures is inseparable from the quantum theory problems. So far also relativity theory has proved ineffectual in relation to this most profound physical problem of the present time. Should the form of the general equations some day, by the solution of the quantum problem, undergo a change however profound, even if there is a complete change in the parameters by means of which we represent the elementary process, the relativity principle will not be relinquished and the laws previously derived therefrom will at least retain their significance as limiting laws.

ON THE THEORY OF RELATIVITY

It is a particular pleasure to me to have the privilege of speaking in the capital of the country from which the most important fundamental notions of

Lecture at King's College, London, 1921. Published in Mein Weltbild *(Amsterdam: Querido Verlag, 1934). English translation in* Ideas and Opinions *(New York: Crown Publishers, Copyright 1954). Reprinted by permission of the publisher and the Estate of Albert Einstein.*

theoretical physics have issued. I am thinking of the theory of mass motion and gravitation which Newton gave us and the concept of the electromagnetic field, by means of which Faraday and Maxwell put physics on a new basis. The theory of relativity may indeed be said to have put a sort of finishing touch to the mighty intellectual edifice of Maxwell and Lorentz, inasmuch as it seeks to extend field physics to all phenomena, gravitation included.

Turning to the theory of relativity itself, I am anxious to draw attention to the fact that this theory is not speculative in origin; it owes its invention entirely to the desire to make physical theory fit observed fact as well as possible. We have here no revolutionary act but the natural continuation of a line that can be traced through centuries. The abandonment of certain notions connected with space, time, and motion hitherto treated as fundamentals must not be regarded as arbitrary, but only as conditioned by observed facts.

The law of the constant velocity of light in empty space, which has been confirmed by the development of electrodynamics and optics, and the equal legitimacy of all inertial systems (special principle of relativity), which was proved in a particularly incisive manner by Michelson's famous experiment, between them made it necessary, to begin with, that the concept of time should be made relative, each inertial system being given its own special time. As this notion was developed, it became clear that the connection between immediate experience on one side and coordinates and time on the other had hitherto not been thought out with sufficient precision. It is in general one of the essential features of the theory of relativity that it is at pains to work out the relations between general concepts and empirical facts more precisely. The fundamental principle here is that the justification for a physical concept lies exclusively in its clear and unambiguous relation to facts that can be experienced. According to the special theory of relativity, spatial coordinates and time still have an absolute character in so far as they are directly measurable by stationary clocks and bodies. But they are relative in so far as they depend on the state of motion of the selected inertial system. According to the special theory of relativity the four-dimensional continuum formed by the union of space and time (Minkowski) retains the absolute character which, according to the earlier theory, belonged to both space and time separately. The influence of motion (relative to the coordinate system) on the form of bodies and on the motion of clocks, also the equivalence of energy and inert mass, follow from the interpretation of coordinates and time as products of measurement.

The general theory of relativity owes its existence in the first place to the empirical fact of the numerical equality of the inertial and gravitational mass of bodies, for which fundamental fact classical mechanics provided no interpretation. Such an interpretation is arrived at by an extension of the principle of relativity to coordinate systems accelerated relatively to one another. The introduction of coordinate systems accelerated relatively to inertial systems involves the appearance of gravitational fields relative to the latter. As a result of this, the general theory of relativity, which is based on the equality of inertia and weight, provides a theory of the gravitational field.

The introduction of coordinate systems accelerated relatively to each other as equally legitimate systems, such as they appear conditioned by the identity of inertia and weight, leads, in conjunction with the results of the special theory of relativity, to the conclusion that the laws governing the arrangement of solid bodies in space, when gravitational fields are present, do not correspond to the laws of Euclidean geometry. An analogous result follows for the motion of clocks. This brings us to the necessity for yet another generalization of the theory of space and time, because the direct interpretation of spatial and temporal coordinates by means of measurements obtainable with measuring rods and clocks now breaks down. That generalization of metric, which had already been accomplished in the sphere of pure mathematics through the researches of Gauss and Riemann, is essentially based on the fact that the metric of the special theory of relativity can still claim validity for small regions in the general case as well.

The process of development here sketched strips the space-time coordinates of all independent reality. The metrically real is now only given through the combination of the space-time coordinates with the mathematical quantities which describe the gravitational field.

There is yet another factor underlying the evolution of the general theory of relativity. As Ernst Mach insistently pointed out, the Newtonian theory is unsatisfactory in the following respect: If one considers motion from the purely descriptive, not from the causal, point of view, it only exists as relative motion of things with respect to one another. But the acceleration which figures in Newton's equations of motion is unintelligible if one starts with the concept of relative motion. It compelled Newton to invent a physical space in relation to which acceleration was supposed to exist. This introduction *ad hoc* of the concept of absolute space, while logically unexceptionable, nevertheless seems unsatisfactory. Hence Mach's attempt to alter the mechanical equations in such a way that the inertia of bodies is traced back to relative motion on their part not as against absolute space but as against the totality of other ponderable bodies. In the state of knowledge then existing, his attempt was bound to fail.

The posing of the problem seems, however, entirely reasonable. This line of argument imposes itself with considerably enhanced force in relation to the general theory of relativity, since, according to that theory, the physical properties of space are affected by ponderable matter. In my opinion the general theory of relativity can solve this problem satisfactorily only if it regards the world as spatially closed. The mathematical results of the theory force one to this view, if one believes that the mean density of ponderable matter in the world possesses some finite value, however small.

WHAT IS THE THEORY OF RELATIVITY?

I gladly accede to the request of your colleague to write something for *The Times* on relativity. After the lamentable breakdown of the old active intercourse between men of learning, I welcome this opportunity of expressing my feelings of joy and gratitude toward the astronomers and physicists of England. It is thoroughly in keeping with the great and proud traditions of scientific work in your country that eminent scientists should have spent much time and trouble, and your scientific institutions have spared no expense, to test the implications of a theory which was perfected and published during the war in the land of your enemies. Even though the investigation of the influence of the gravitational field of the sun on light rays is a purely objective matter, I cannot forbear to express my personal thanks to my English colleagues for their work; for without it I could hardly have lived to see the most important implication of my theory tested.

We can distinguish various kinds of theories in physics. Most of them are constructive. They attempt to build up a picture of the more complex phenomena out of the materials of a relatively simple formal scheme from which they start out. Thus the kinetic theory of gases seeks to reduce mechanical, thermal, and diffusional processes to movements of molecules—i.e., to build them up out of the hypothesis of molecular motion. When we say that we have succeeded in understanding a group of natural processes, we invariably mean that a constructive theory has been found which covers the processes in question.

Along with this most important class of theories there exists a second, which I will call "principle-theories." These employ the analytic, not the synthetic, method. The elements which form their basis and starting-point are not hypothetically constructed but empirically discovered ones, general characteristics of natural processes, principles that give rise to mathematically formulated criteria which the separate processes or the theoretical representations of them have to satisfy. Thus the science of thermodynamics seeks by analytical means to deduce necessary conditions, which separate events have to satisfy, from the universally experienced fact that perpetual motion is impossible.

The advantages of the constructive theory are completeness, adaptability, and clearness, those of the principle theory are logical perfection and security of the foundations.

The theory of relativity belongs to the latter class. In order to grasp its nature, one needs first of all to become acquainted with the principles on which it is based. Before I go into these, however, I must observe that the theory of relativity resembles a building consisting of two separate stories, the special

Written at the request of the London Times *and published on November 28, 1919. From* Ideas and Opinions *(New York: Crown Publishers, copyright 1954). Reprinted by permission of the publisher and the Estate of Albert Einstein.*

theory and the general theory. The special theory, on which the general theory rests, applies to all physical phenomena with the exception of gravitation; the general theory provides the law of gravitation and its relations to the other forces of nature.

It has, of course, been known since the days of the ancient Greeks that in order to describe the movement of a body, a second body is needed to which the movement of the first is referred. The movement of a vehicle is considered in reference to the earth's surface, that of a planet to the totality of the visible fixed stars. In physics the body to which events are spatially referred is called the coordinate system. The laws of the mechanics of Galileo and Newton, for instance, can only be formulated with the aid of a coordinate system.

The state of motion of the coordinate system may not, however, be arbitrarily chosen, if the laws of mechanics are to be valid (it must be free from rotation and acceleration). A coordinate system which is admitted in mechanics is called an "inertial system." The state of motion of an inertial system is according to mechanics not one that is determined uniquely by nature. On the contrary, the following definition holds good: A coordinate system that is moved uniformly and in a straight line relative to an inertial system is likewise an inertial system. By the "special principle of relativity" is meant the generalization of this definition to include any natural event whatever: Thus, every universal law of nature which is valid in relation to a coordinate system C, must also be valid, as it stands, in relation to a coordinate system C', which is in uniform translatory motion relatively to C.

The second principle, on which the special theory of relativity rests, is the "principle of the constant velocity of light in vacuo." This principle asserts that light in vacuo always has a definite velocity of propagation (independent of the state of motion of the observer or of the source of the light). The confidence which physicists place in this principle springs from the successes achieved by the electrodynamics of Maxwell and Lorentz.

Both the above-mentioned principles are powerfully supported by experience, but appear not to be logically reconcilable. The special theory of relativity finally succeeded in reconciling them logically by a modification of kinematics—i.e., of the doctrine of the laws relating to space and time (from the point of view of physics). It became clear that to speak of the simultaneity of two events had no meaning except in relation to a given coordinate system, and that the shape of measuring devices and the speed at which clocks move depend on their state of motion with respect to the coordinate system.

But the old physics, including the laws of motion of Galileo and Newton, did not fit in with the suggested relativist kinematics. From the latter, general mathematical conditions issued, to which natural laws had to conform, if the above-mentioned two principles were really to apply. To these, physics had to be adapted. In particular, scientists arrived at a new law of motion for (rapidly moving) mass points, which was admirably confirmed in the case of electrically charged particles. The most important upshot of the special theory of relativity concerned the inert masses of corporeal systems. It turned out that the inertia of a system necessarily depends on its energy-content, and this led straight to the notion that inert mass is simply latent energy. The principle of the conservation of mass lost its independence and became fused with that of the conservation of energy.

The special theory of relativity, which was simply a systematic development of the electrodynamics of Maxwell and Lorentz, pointed beyond itself, however. Should the independence of physical laws of the state of motion of the coordinate system be restricted to the uniform translatory motion of coordinate systems in respect to each other? What has nature to do with our coordinate systems and their state of motion? If it is necessary for the purpose of describing nature, to make use of a coordinate system arbitrarily introduced by us, then the choice of its state of motion ought to be subject to no restriction; the laws ought to be entirely independent of this choice (general principle of relativity).

The establishment of this general principle of relativity is made easier by a fact of experience that has long been known, namely, that the weight and the inertia of a body are controlled by the same constant (equality of inertial and gravitational mass). Imagine a coordinate system which is rotating uniformly with respect to an inertial system in the Newtonian manner. The centrifugal forces which manifest themselves in relation to this system must, according to Newton's teaching, be regarded as effects of inertia. But these centrifugal forces are, exactly like the forces of gravity, proportional to the masses of the bodies. Ought it not to be possible in this case to regard the coordinate system as stationary and the centrifugal forces as gravitational forces? This seems the obvious view, but classical mechanics forbid it.

This hasty consideration suggests that a general theory of relativity must supply the laws of gravitation, and the consistent following up of the idea has justified our hopes.

But the path was thornier than one might suppose, because it demanded the abandonment of Euclidean geometry. This is to say, the laws according to which solid bodies may be arranged in space do not completely accord with the spatial laws attributed to bodies by Euclidean geometry. This is what we mean when we talk of the "curvature of space." The fundamental concepts of the "straight line," the "plane," etc., thereby lose their precise significance in physics.

In the general theory of relativity the doctrine of space and time, or kinematics, no longer figures as a fundamental independent of the rest of physics. The geometrical behavior of bodies and the motion of clocks rather depend on gravitational fields, which in their turn are produced by matter.

The new theory of gravitation diverges considerably, as regards principles, from Newton's theory. But its practical results agree so nearly with those of Newton's theory that it is difficult to find criteria for distinguishing them which are accessible to experience. Such have been discovered so far:

1. In the revolution of the ellipses of the planetary orbits round the sun (confirmed in the case of Mercury).

2. In the curving of light rays by the action of gravitational fields (confirmed by the English photographs of eclipses).

3. In a displacement of the spectral lines toward the red end of the spectrum in the case of light transmitted to us from stars of considerable magnitude (unconfirmed so far).*

The chief attraction of the theory lies in its logical completeness. If a single one of the conclusions drawn from it proves wrong, it must be given up; to modify it without destroying the whole structure seems to be impossible.

Let no one suppose, however, that the mighty work of Newton can really be superseded by this or any other theory. His great and lucid ideas will retain their unique significance for all time as the foundation of our whole modern conceptual structure in the sphere of natural philosophy.

Note: Some of the statements in your paper concerning my life and person owe their origin to the lively imagination of the writer. Here is yet another application of the principle of relativity for the delectation of the reader: Today I am described in Germany as a "German savant," and in England as a "Swiss Jew." Should it ever be my fate to be represented as a *bête noire,* I should, on the contrary, become a "Swiss Jew" for the Germans and a "German savant" for the English.

FIELD THEORIES: OLD AND NEW

While physics wandered exclusively in the paths prepared by Newton, the following conception of physical reality prevailed: Matter is real, and matter undergoes only those changes which we conceive as movements in space. Motion, space and also time are real forms. Every attempt to deny the physical reality of space collapses in face of the law of inertia. For if acceleration is to be taken as real, then that space must also be real within which bodies are conceived as accelerated.

Newton saw this with perfect clarity, and consequently he called space "absolute." In his theoretical system there was a third constituent of independent reality—the motive forces acting between material particles, such forces being considered to depend only on the position of the particles. These forces

*This criterion has since been confirmed.

From the New York Times, *February 3, 1929. Reprinted by permission of the Estate of Albert Einstein.*

between particles were regarded as unconditionally associated with the particles themselves and as distributed spatially according to an unchanging law.

The physicists of the nineteenth century considered that there existed two kinds of such matter, namely, ponderable matter and electricity. The particles of ponderable matter were supposed to act on each other by gravitational forces under Newton's law, the particles of electrical matter by Coulomb forces also inversely proportional to the square of the distance. No definite views prevailed regarding the nature of the forces acting between ponderable and electrical particles.

THE OLD THEORY OF SPACE

Mere empty space was not admitted as a carrier for physical changes and processes. It was only, one might say, the stage on which the drama of material happenings was played. Consequently Newton dealt with the fact that light is propagated in empty space by making the hypothesis that light also consists of material particles interacting with ponderable matter through special forces. To this extent Newton's view of nature involved a third type of material particle, though this certainly had to have very different properties from the particles of the other forms of matter. Light particles had, in fact, to be capable of being formed and of disappearing. Moreover, even in the eighteenth century it was already clear from experience that light traveled in empty space with a definite velocity, a fact which obviously fitted badly into Newton's theoretical system, for why on earth should the light particles not be able to move through space with any arbitrary velocity?

It need not, therefore, surprise us that this theoretical system, built up by Newton with his powerful and logical intellect, should have been overthrown precisely by a theory of light. This was brought about by the Huygens-Young-Fresnel wave theory of light which the facts of interference and diffraction forced on stubbornly resisting physicists. The great range of phenomena, which could be calculated and predicted to the finest detail by using this theory, delighted physicists and filled many fat and learned books. No wonder then that the learned men failed to notice the crack which this theory made in the statue of their eternal goddess. For, in fact, this theory upset the view that everything real can be conceived as the motion of particles in space. Light waves were, after all, nothing more than undulatory states of empty space, and space thus gave up its passive role as a mere stage for physical events. The ether hypothesis patched up the crack and made it invisible.

The ether was invented, penetrating everything, filling the whole of space, and was admitted as a new kind of matter. Thus it was overlooked that by this procedure space itself had been brought to life. It is clear that this had really happened, since the ether was considered to be a sort of matter which could nowhere be removed. It was thus to some degree identical with space itself, that is, something necessarily given with space. Light was thus viewed as a dynamical process undergone, as it were, by space itself. In this way the field theory was born as an illegitimate child of Newtonian physics, though it was cleverly passed off at first as legitimate.

To become fully conscious of this change in outlook was a task for a highly original mind whose insight could go straight to essentials, a mind that never got stuck in formulae. Faraday was this favored spirit. His instinct revolted at the idea of forces acting directly at a distance which seemed contrary to every elementary observation. If one electrified body attracts or repels a second body, this was for him brought about not by a direct action from the first body on the second, but through an intermediary action. The first body brings the space immediately around it into a certain condition which spreads itself into more distant parts of space, according to a certain spatio-temporal law of propagation. This condition of space was called "the electric field." The second body experiences a force because it lies in the field of the first, and vice versa. The "field" thus provided a conceptual apparatus which rendered unnecessary the idea of action at a distance. Faraday also had the bold idea that under appropriate circumstances fields might detach themselves from the bodies producing them and speed away through space as free fields; this was his interpretation of light.

Maxwell then discovered the wonderful group of formulae which seems so simple to us nowadays and which finally built the bridge between the theory of electro-magnetism and the theory of light. It appeared that light consists of rapidly oscillating electro-magnetic fields.

After Hertz, in the '80s of the last century, had confirmed the existence of the electro-magnetic waves and displayed their identity with light by means of his wonderful experiments, the great intellectual revolution in physics gradually became complete. People slowly accustomed themselves to the idea that the physical states of space itself were the final physical reality, especially after Lorentz had shown in his penetrating theoretical researches that even inside ponderable bodies the electro-magnetic fields are not to be regarded as states of the matter, but essentially as states of the empty space in which the material atoms are to be considered as loosely distributed.

DISSATISFIED WITH DUAL THEORY

At the turn of the century physicists began to be dissatisfied with the dualism of a theory admitting two kinds of fundamental physical reality: on the one hand the field and on the other hand the material particles. It is only natural that attempts were made to represent the material particles as structures in the field, that is, as places where the fields were exceptionally concentrated. Any such representation of particles on the basis of the field theory would have been a great achievement, but in spite of all efforts of science it has not been accomplished. It must even be admitted that this dualism is today sharper and more troublesome than it was ten years ago. This fact is connected with the latest impetus to developments in quantum theory, where the theory of the continuum (field theory) and the essentially discontinuous interpretation of the elementary structures and processes are fighting for supremacy.

We shall not here discuss questions concerning molecular theory, but shall describe the improvements made in the field theory during this century.

These all arise from the theory of relativity, which has in the last six months entered its third stage of development. Let us briefly examine the chief points of view bringing to these three stages and their relation to field theory.

The first stage, the special theory of relativity, owes its origin principally to Maxwell's theory of the electro-magnetic field. From this, combined with the empirical fact that there does not exist any physically distinguishable state of motion which may be called "absolute rest," arose a new theory of space and time. It is well known that this theory discarded the absolute character of the conception of the simultaneity of two spatially separated events. Well known is also the courage of despair with which some philosophers still defend themselves in a profusion of proud but empty words against this simple theory.

On the other hand, the services rendered by the special theory of relativity to its parent, Maxwell's theory of electro-magnetic field, are less adequately recognized. Up to that time the electric field and the magnetic field were regarded as existing separately even if a close causal correlation between the two types of field was provided by Maxwell's field equations. But the special theory of relativity showed that this causal correlation corresponds to an essential identity of the two types of field. In fact, the same condition of space, which in one coordinate system appears as a pure magnetic field, appears simultaneously in another coordinate system in relative motion as an electric field, and vice versa. Relationship of this kind displaying an identity between different conceptions, which therefore reduce the number of independent hypotheses and concepts of field theory and heighten its logical self-containedness is a characteristic feature of the theory of relativity. For instance, the special theory also indicated the essential identity of the conceptions' inertial mass and energy. This is all generally known and is only mentioned here in order to emphasize the unitary tendency which dominates the whole development of the theory.

THEORY OF GRAVITATION

We now turn to the second stage in the development of the theory of relativity, the so-called general theory of relativity. This theory also starts from a fact of experience which till then had received no satisfactory interpretation: the equality of inertial and gravitational mass, or, in other words, the fact known since the days of Galileo and Newton that all bodies fall with equal acceleration in the earth's gravitational field. The theory uses a special theory as its basis and at the same time modifies it: the recognition that there is no state of motion whatever which is physically privileged—that is, that not only velocity but also acceleration are without absolute significance—forms the starting point of the theory. It then compels a much more profound modification of the conceptions of space and time than were involved in the special theory. For even if the special theory forced us to fuse space and time together to an invisible, four-dimensional continuum, yet the Euclidean character of the continuum remained essentially intact in this theory. In the general theory of relativity this hypothesis regarding the Euclidean character of our space-time continuum had to be abandoned and the latter given the structure of a so-called Riemannian space. Before we attempt to understand what these terms mean let us recall what this theory accomplished.

It furnished an exact field theory of gravitation and brought the latter into a fully determinate relationship to the metrical properties of the continuum. The theory of gravitation, which until then had not advanced beyond Newton, was thus brought within Faraday's conception of the field in a necessary manner; that is, without any essential arbitrariness in the selection of the field laws. At the same time gravitation and inertia were fused into an essential identity. The confirmation which this theory has received in recent years through the measurement of the deflection of light rays in a gravitational field and the spectroscopic examination of binary stars is well known.

The characteristics which especially distinguish the general theory of relativity and even more the new third stage of the theory, the unitary field theory, from other physical theories are the degree of formal speculation, the slender empirical basis, the boldness in theoretical construction and, finally, the fundamental reliance on the uniformity of the secrets of natural law and their accessibility to the speculative intellect. It is this feature which appears as a weakness to physicists who incline toward realism or positivism, but is especially attractive, nay, fascinating, to the speculative mathematical mind. Meyerson in his brilliant studies on the theory of knowledge justly draws a comparison of the intellectual attitude of the relativity theoretician with that of Descartes, or even of Hegel, without thereby implying the censure which a physicist would read into this.

However that may be, in the end experience is the only competent judge.

Yet in the meantime one thing may be said in defense of the theory. Advance in scientific knowledge must bring about the result that an increase in formal simplicity can only be won at the cost of an increased distance or gap between the fundamental hypothesis of the theory on the one hand and the directly observed facts on the other hand. Theory is compelled to pass more and more from the inductive to the deductive method, even though the most important demand to be made of every scientific theory will always remain: that it must fit the facts.

We now reach the difficult task of giving to the reader an idea of the methods used in the mathematical construction which led to the general theory of relativity and to the new unitary field theory.

THE PROBLEM STATED

The general problem is: Which are the simplest formal structures that can be attributed to a four-dimensional continuum and which are the simplest laws that may be conceived to govern these structures? We then look for the mathematical expression of the physical fields in these formal structures and for the field laws of physics—already known to a certain approximation from earlier researches—in the simplest laws governing this structure.

The conceptions which are used in this connection can be explained just as well in a two-dimensional continuum (a surface) as in the four-dimensional continuum of space and time. Imagine a piece of paper ruled in millimeter squares. What does it mean if I say that the printed surface is two-dimensional? If any point P is marked on the paper, one can define its position by using two numbers. Thus, starting from the bottom left-hand corner, move a pointer toward the right until the lower end of the vertical through the point P is reached. Suppose that in doing this one has passed the lower ends of X vertical (millimeter) lines. Then move the pointer up to the point P passing Y horizontal lines. The point P is then described without ambiguity by the numbers X Y (coordinates). If one had used, instead of ruled millimeter paper, a piece which had been stretched or deformed the same determination could still be carried out; but in this case the lines passed would no longer be horizontals or verticals or even straight lines. The same point would then, of course, yield different numbers, but the possibility of determining a point by means of two numbers (Gaussian coordinates) still remains. Moreover, if P and Q are two points which lie very close to one another, then their coordinates differ only very slightly.

When a point can be described by two numbers in this way, we speak of a two-dimensional continuum (surface).

RIEMANNIAN METRIC

Now consider two neighboring points P, Q on the surface and a little way off another pair of points P', Q'. What does it mean to say that the distance PQ is equal to the distance $P'Q'$? This statement only has a clear meaning when we have a small measuring rod which we can take from one pair of points to the other and if the result of the comparison is independent of the particular measuring rod selected. If this is so, the magnitudes of the tracts PQ, $P'Q'$ can be compared. If a continuum is of this kind we say it has a metric. Of course, the distance between the points P, Q must depend on the coordinate differences *(dx, dy)*. But the form of this dependence is not known à priori. If it is of the form:

$$ds^2 = g_{11}dx^2 + 2g_{12}dxdy + g_{22}dy^2$$

then it is called a Riemannian metric.

If it is possible to choose the coordinates so that this expression takes the form: $ds^2 = dx^2 + dy^2$ (Pythagoras' theorem), then the continuum is Euclidean (a plane).

Thus it is clear that the Euclidean continuum is a special case of the Riemannian. Inversely, the Riemannian continuum is a metric continuum which is Euclidean in infinitely small regions, but not in finite regions. The quantities g_{11}, g_{12}, g_{22} describe the metrical properties of the surface: that is, the metrical field.

By making use of empirically known properties of space, especially the law of the propagation of light, it is possible to show that the space-time continuum has a Riemannian metric. The quantities g_{11}, etc., appertaining to it determine not only the metric of the continuum but also the gravitational field. The law governing the gravitational field is found in answer to the question: Which are the simplest mathematical laws to which the metric (that is the g_{11}, etc.) can be subjected? The answer was given by the discovery of the field laws of gravitation, which have proved themselves more accurate than the Newtonian law. This rough outline is intended only to give a general idea of the sense in which I have spoken of the "speculative" methods of the general theory of relativity.

EXPANDING THE THEORY

This theory having brought together the metric and gravitation would have been completely satisfactory if the world had only gravitational fields and no electromagnetic fields. Now it is true that the latter can be included within the general theory of relativity by taking over and appropriately modifying Maxwell's equations of the electro-magnetic field, but they do not then appear like the gravitational fields as structural properties of the space-time continuum, but as logically independent constructions. The two types of field are causally linked in this theory, but still not fused to an identity. It can, however, scarcely be imagined that empty space has conditions or states of two essentially different kinds, and it is natural to suspect that this only appears to be so because the structure of the physical continuum is not completely described by the Riemannian metric.

The new unitary field theory removes this fault by displaying both types of field as manifestations of one comprehensive type of spatial structure in the space-time continuum. The stimulus to the new theory arose from the discovery that there exists a structure between the Riemannian space structure and the Euclidean, which is richer in formal relationships than the former, but poorer than the latter. Consider a two-dimension Riemannian space in the form of the surface of a hen's egg. Since this surface is embedded in our (accurately enough) Euclidean space, it possesses a Riemannian metric. In fact, it has a perfectly definite meaning to speak of the distance of two neighboring points P, Q on the surface. Similarly it has, of course, a meaning to say of two such pairs of points *(PQ) (P'Q')*, at separate parts of the surface of the egg, that the distance PQ is equal to the distance $P'Q'$. On the other hand, it is impossible now to compare the direction PQ with the direction $P'Q'$. In particular it is meaningless to demand that $P'Q'$ shall be chosen parallel to PQ. In the corresponding Euclidean geometry of two dimensions, the Euclidean geometry of the plane, directions can be compared and the relationship of parallelism can exist between lines in regions of the plane at any distance from one another (distant parallelism). To this extent the Euclidean continuum is richer in relationships than the Riemannian.

A MATHEMATICAL DISCOVERY

The new unitary field theory is based on the following mathematical discovery: There are continua with a Riemannian metric and distant parallelism which nevertheless are not Euclidean. It is easy to show, for instance, in the case of three-dimensional space, how such a continuum differs from a Euclidean.

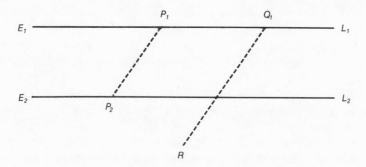

First of all, in such a continuum there are lines whose elements are parallel to one another. We shall call those "straight lines." It also has a definite meaning to speak of two parallel straight lines as in the Euclidean case. Now choose two such parallels: E_1L_1 and E_2L_2 and mark on each a point, P_1, P_2.

On E_1L_1 choose in addition a point Q_1. If we now draw through Q_1 a straight line Q_1R parallel to the straight line P_1P_2, then in Euclidean geometry this will cut the straight line E_2L_2; in the geometry now used the line Q_1R and the line E_2L_2 do not in general cut one another. To this extent the geometry now used is not only a specialization of the Riemannian but also a generalization of the Euclidean geometry. My opinion is that our space-time continuum has a structure of the kind here outlined.

The mathematical problem whose solution, in my view, leads to the correct field laws is to be formulated thus: Which are the simplest and most natural conditions to which a continuum of this kind can be subjected? The answer to this question which I have attempted to give in a new paper yields unitary field laws for gravitation and electro-magnetism.

EXPOSITION

A. SPECIAL AND GENERAL PRINCIPLE OF RELATIVITY

The basal principle, which was the pivot of all our previous considerations, was the *special* principle of relativity, *i.e.* the principle of the physical relativity of all *uniform* motion. Let us once more analyse its meaning carefully.

It was at all times clear that, from the point of view of the idea it conveys to us, every motion must be considered only as a relative motion. Returning to the illustration we have frequently used of the embankment and the railway carriage, we can express the fact of the motion here taking place in the following two forms, both of which are equally justifiable:

(a) The carriage is in motion relative to the embankment.

(b) The embankment is in motion relative to the carriage.

In *(a)* the embankment, in *(b)* the carriage, serves as the body of reference in our statement of the motion taking place. If it is simply a question of detecting or of describing the motion involved, it is in principle immaterial to what reference-body we refer the motion. As already mentioned, this is self-evident, but it must not be confused with the much more comprehensive statement called "the principle of relativity," which we have taken as the basis of our investigations.

The principle we have made use of not only maintains that we may equally well choose the carriage or the embankment as our reference-body for the description of any event (for this, too, is self-evident). Our principle rather asserts what follows: If we formulate the general laws of nature as they are obtained from experience, by making use of

(a) the embankment as reference-body,

(b) the railway carriage as reference-body,

then these general laws of nature *(e.g.* the laws of mechanics or the law of the propagation of light *in vacuo)* have exactly the same form in both cases. This can also be expressed as follows: For the *physical* description of natural processes, neither of the reference-bodies K, K' is unique (lit. "specially marked out") as compared with the other. Unlike the first, this latter statement need not of necessity hold *a priori;* it is not contained in the conceptions of "motion" and "reference-body" and derivable from them; only *experience* can decide as to its correctness or incorrectness.

From Albert Einstein, Relativity, *trans. Robert W. Lawson (New York: Crown Publishers, © 1961), Chapter XVIII. Reprinted by permission of the Estate of Albert Einstein.*

Up to the present, however, we have by no means maintained the equivalence of *all* bodies of reference K in connection with the formulation of natural laws. Our course was more on the following lines. In the first place, we started out from the assumption that there exists a reference-body K, whose condition of motion is such that the Galileian law holds with respect to it: A particle left to itself and sufficiently far removed from all other particles moves uniformly in a straight line. With reference to K (Galileian reference-body) the laws of nature were to be as simple as possible. But in addition to K, all bodies of reference K' should be given preference in this sense, and they should be exactly equivalent to K for the formulation of natural laws, provided that they are in a state of *uniform rectilinear and non-rotary motion* with respect to K; all these bodies of reference are to be regarded as Galileian reference-bodies. The validity of the principle of relativity was assumed only for these reference-bodies, but not for others (*e.g.* those possessing motion of a different kind). In this sense we speak of the *special* principle of relativity, or special theory of relativity.

In contrast to this we wish to understand by the "general principle of relativity" the following statement: All bodies of reference K, K', etc., are equivalent for the description of natural phenomena (formulation of the general laws of nature), whatever may be their state of motion. But before proceeding further, it ought to be pointed out that this formulation must be replaced later by a more abstract one, for reasons which will become evident at a later stage.

Since the introduction of the special principle of relativity has been justified, every intellect which strives after generalisation must feel the temptation to venture the step towards the general principle of relativity. But a simple and apparently quite reliable consideration seems to suggest that, for the present at any rate, there is little hope of success in such an attempt. Let us imagine ourselves transferred to our old friend the railway carriage, which is travelling at a uniform rate. As long as it is moving uniformly, the occupant of the carriage is not sensible of its motion, and it is for this reason that he can without reluctance interpret the facts of the case as indicating that the carriage is at rest, but the embankment in motion. Moreover, according to the special principle of relativity, this interpretation is quite justified also from a physical point of view.

If the motion of the carriage is now changed into a non-uniform motion, as for instance by a powerful application of the brakes, then the occupant of the carriage experiences a correspondingly powerful jerk forwards. The retarded motion is manifested in the mechanical behaviour of bodies relative to the person in the railway carriage. The mechanical behaviour is different from that of the case previously considered, and for this reason it would appear to be impossible that the same mechanical laws hold relatively to the non-uniformly moving carriage, as hold with reference to the carriage when at rest or in uniform motion. At all events it is clear that the Galileian law does not hold with respect to the non-uniformly moving carriage. Because of this, we feel compelled at the present juncture to grant a kind of absolute physical reality to non-uniform motion, in opposition to the general principle of relativity. But in what follows we shall soon see that this conclusion cannot be maintained.

B. THE GRAVITATIONAL FIELD

"If we pick up a stone and then let it go, why does it fall to the ground?" The usual answer to this question is: "Because it is attracted by the earth." Modern physics formulates the answer rather differently for the following reason. As a result of the more careful study of electromagnetic phenomena, we have come to regard action at a distance as a process impossible without the intervention of some intermediary medium. If, for instance, a magnet attracts a piece of iron, we cannot be content to regard this as meaning that the magnet acts directly on the iron through the intermediate empty space, but we are constrained to imagine—after the manner of Faraday—that the magnet always calls into being something physically real in the space around it, that something being what we call a "magnetic field." In its turn this magnetic field operates on the piece of iron, so that the latter strives to move towards the magnet. We shall not discuss here the justification for this incidental conception, which is indeed a somewhat arbitrary one. We shall only mention that with its aid electromagnetic phenomena can be theoretically represented much more satisfactorily than without it, and this applies particularly to the transmission of electromagnetic waves. The effects of gravitation also are regarded in an analogous manner.

The action of the earth on the stone takes place indirectly. The earth produces in its surroundings a gravitational field, which acts on the stone and produces its motion of fall. As we know from experience, the intensity of the action on a body diminishes according to a quite definite law, as we proceed farther and farther away from the earth. From our point of view this means: The law governing the properties of the gravitational field in space must be a perfectly definite one, in order correctly to represent the diminution of gravitational action with the distance from operative bodies. It is something like this: The body (e.g. the earth) produces a field in its immediate neighbourhood directly: the intensity and direction of the field at points farther removed from the body are thence determined by the law which governs the properties in space of the gravitational fields themselves.

In contrast to electric and magnetic fields, the gravitational field exhibits a most remarkable property, which is of fundamental importance for what follows. Bodies which are moving under the sole influence of a gravitational field receive an acceleration, *which does not in the least depend either on the*

From Albert Einstein, Relativity, *trans. Robert W. Lawson (New York: Crown Publishers,* © *1961), Chapter XIX. Reprinted by permission of the Estate of Albert Einstein.*

material or on the physical state of the body. For instance, a piece of lead and a piece of wood fall in exactly the same manner in a gravitational field *(in vacuo),* when they start off from rest or with the same initial velocity. This law, which holds most accurately, can be expressed in a different form in the light of the following consideration.

According to Newton's law of motion, we have

$$(Force) = (inertial\ mass) \times (acceleration),$$

where the "inertial mass" is a characteristic constant of the accelerated body. If now gravitation is the cause of the acceleration, we then have

$$(Force) = (gravitational\ mass) \times (intensity\ of\ the\ gravitational\ field),$$

where the "gravitational mass" is likewise a characteristic constant for the body. From these two relations follows:

$$(acceleration) = \frac{(gravitational\ mass)}{(inertial\ mass)} \times (intensity\ of\ the\ gravitational\ field).$$

If now, as we find from experience, the acceleration is to be independent of the nature and the condition of the body and always the same for a given gravitational field, then the ratio of the gravitational to the inertial mass must likewise be the same for all bodies. By a suitable choice of units we can thus make this ratio equal to unity. We then have the following law: The *gravitational* mass of a body is equal to its *inertial* mass.

It is true that this important law had hitherto been recorded in mechanics, but it had not been *interpreted.* A satisfactory interpretation can be obtained only if we recognise the following fact: *The same* quality of a body manifests itself according to circumstances as "inertia" or as "weight" (lit. "heaviness"). In the following section we shall show to what extent this is actually the case, and how this question is connected with the general postulate of relativity.

C. INERTIAL AND GRAVITATIONAL MASS

We imagine a large portion of empty space, so far removed from stars and other appreciable masses, that we have before us approximately the conditions required by the fundamental law of Galilei. It is then possible to choose a Galileian reference-body for this part of space (world), relative to which points at rest remain at rest and points in motion continue permanently in uniform rectilinear motion. As reference-body let us imagine a spacious chest resembling a room with an observer inside who is equipped with apparatus. Gravitation naturally does not exist for this observer. He must fasten himself with

From Albert Einstein, Relativity, *trans. Robert W. Lawson (New York: Crown Publishers,* © *1961), Chapter XX. Reprinted by permission of the Estate of Albert Einstein.*

strings to the floor, otherwise the slightest impact against the floor will cause him to rise slowly towards the ceiling of the room.

To the middle of the lid of the chest is fixed externally a hook with rope attached, and now a "being" (what kind of a being is immaterial to us) begins pulling at this with a constant force. The chest together with the observer then begin to move "upwards" with a uniformly accelerated motion. In course of time their velocity will reach unheard-of values—provided that we are viewing all this from another reference-body which is not being pulled with a rope.

But how does the man in the chest regard the process? The acceleration of the chest will be transmitted to him by the reaction of the floor of the chest. He must therefore take up this pressure by means of his legs if he does not wish to be laid out full length on the floor. He is then standing in the chest in exactly the same way as anyone stands in a room of a house on our earth. If he releases a body which he previously had in his hand, the acceleration of the chest will no longer be transmitted to this body, and for this reason the body will approach the floor of the chest with an accelerated relative motion. The observer will further convince himself *that the acceleration of the body towards the floor of the chest is always of the same magnitude, whatever kind of body he may happen to use for the experiment.*

Relying on his knowledge of the gravitational field (as it was discussed in the preceding section), the man in the chest will thus come to the conclusion that he and the chest are in a gravitational field which is constant with regard to time. Of course he will be puzzled for a moment as to why the chest does not fall in this gravitational field. Just then, however, he discovers the hook in the middle of the lid of the chest and the rope which is attached to it, and he consequently comes to the conclusion that the chest is suspended at rest in the gravitational field.

Ought we to smile at the man and say that he errs in his conclusion? I do not believe we ought to if we wish to remain consistent; we must rather admit that his mode of grasping the situation violates neither reason nor known mechanical laws. Even though it is being accelerated with respect to the "Galileian space" first considered, we can nevertheless regard the chest as being at rest. We have thus good grounds for extending the principle of relativity to include bodies of reference which are accelerated with respect to each other, and as a result we have gained a powerful argument for a general-ised postulate of relativity.

We must note carefully that the possibility of this mode of interpretation rests on the fundamental property of the gravitational field of giving all bodies the same acceleration, or, what comes to the same thing, on the law of the equality of inertial and gravitational mass. If this natural law did not exist, the man in the accelerated chest would not be able to interpret the behaviour of the bodies around him on the supposition of a gravitational field, and he would not be justified on the grounds of experience in supposing his reference-body to be "at rest."

Suppose that the man in the chest fixes a rope to the inner side of the lid, and that he attaches a body to the free end of the rope. The result of this will be to stretch the rope so that it will hang "vertically" downwards. If we ask for an opinion of the cause of tension in the rope, the man in the chest will say: "The suspended body experiences a downward force in the gravitational field, and this is neutralised by the tension of the rope; what determines the magnitude of the tension of the rope is the *gravitational mass* of the suspended body." On the other hand, an observer who is poised freely in space will interpret the condition of things thus: "The rope must perforce take part in the accelerated motion of the chest, and it transmits this motion to the body attached to it. The tension of the rope is just large enough to effect the acceleration of the body. That which determines the magnitude of the tension of the rope is the *inertial mass* of the body." Guided by this example, we see that our extension of the principle of relativity implies the *necessity* of the law of the equality of inertial and gravitational mass. Thus we have obtained a physical interpretation of this law.

From our consideration of the accelerated chest we see that a general theory of relativity must yield important results on the laws of gravitation. In point of fact, the systematic pursuit of the general idea of relativity has supplied the laws satisfied by the gravitational field. Before proceeding further, however, I must warn the reader against a misconception suggested by these considerations. A gravitational field exists for the man in the chest, despite the fact that there was no such field for the co-ordinate system first chosen. Now we might easily suppose that the existence of a gravitational field is always only an *apparent* one. We might also think that, regardless of the kind of gravitational field which may be present, we could always choose another reference-body such that *no* gravitational field exists with reference to it. This is by no means true for all gravitational fields, but only for those of quite special form. It is, for instance, impossible to choose a body of reference such that, as judged from it, the gravitational field of the earth (in its entirety) vanishes.

We can now appreciate why that argument is not convincing, which we brought forward against the general principle of relativity at the end of Section A. It is certainly true that the observer in the railway carriage experiences a jerk forwards as a result of the application of the brake, and that he recognises in this the non-uniformity of motion (retardation) of the carriage. But he is compelled by nobody to refer to this jerk to a "real" acceleration (retardation) of the carriage. He might also interpret his experience thus: "My body of reference (the carriage) remains permanently at rest. With reference to it, however, there exists (during the period of application of the brakes) a gravitational field which is directed forwards and which is variable with respect to time. Under the influence of this field, the embankment together with the earth moves nonuniformly in such a manner that their original velocity in the backwards direction is continuously reduced."

D. MECHANICS AND RELATIVITY

We have already stated several times that classical mechanics starts out from the following law: Material particles sufficiently far removed from other material particles continue to move uniformly in a straight line or continue in a state of rest. We have also repeatedly emphasised that this fundamental law can only be valid for bodies of reference K which possess certain unique states of motion, and which are in uniform translational motion relative to each other. Relative to other reference-bodies K the law is not valid. Both in classical mechanics and in the special theory of relativity we therefore differentiate between reference-bodies K relative to which the recognised "laws of nature" can be said to hold, and reference-bodies K relative to which these laws do not hold.

But no person whose mode of thought is logical can rest satisfied with this condition of things. He asks: "How does it come that certain reference-bodies (or their states of motion) are given priority over other reference-bodies (or their states of motion)? *What is the reason for this preference?* In order to show clearly what I mean by this question, I shall make use of a comparison.

I am standing in front of a gas range. Standing alongside of each other on the range are two pans so much alike that one may be mistaken for the other. Both are half full of water. I notice that steam is being emitted continuously from the one pan, but not from the other. I am surprised at this, even if I have never seen either a gas range or a pan before. But if I now notice a luminous something of bluish colour under the first pan but not under the other, I cease to be astonished, even if I have never before seen a gas flame. For I can only say that this bluish something will cause the emission of the steam, or at least *possibly* it may do so. If, however, I notice the bluish something in neither case, and if I observe that the one continuously emits steam whilst the other does not, then I shall remain astonished and dissatisfied until I have discovered some circumstance to which I can attribute the different behavior of the two pans.

Analogously, I seek in vain for a real something in classical mechanics (or in the special theory of relativity) to which I can attribute the different behaviour of bodies considered with respect to the reference-systems K and K'.[1] Newton saw this objection and attempted to invalidate it, but without success. But E. Mach recognised it most clearly of all, and because of this objection he claimed that mechanics must be placed on a new basis. It can only be got rid of by means of a physics which is conformable to the general principle of relativity, since the equations of such a theory hold for every body of reference, whatever may be its state of motion.

From Albert Einstein, Relativity, *trans. Robert W. Lawson (New York: Crown Publishers,* © *1961), Chapter XXII. Reprinted by permission of the Estate of Albert Einstein.*
1. The objection is of importance more especially when the state of motion of the reference-body is of such a nature that it does not require any external agency for its maintenance, *e.g.* in the case when the reference-body is rotating uniformly.

E. INFERENCES FROM THE GENERAL PRINCIPLE
OF RELATIVITY

The considerations of Section XX* show that the general principle of relativity puts us in a position to derive properties of the gravitational field in a purely theoretical manner. Let us suppose, for instance, that we know the space-time "course" for any natural process whatsoever, as regards the manner in which it takes place in the Galileian domain relative to a Galileian body of reference K. By means of purely theoretical operations (*i.e.* simply by calculation) we are then able to find how this known natural process appears, as soon from a reference-body K' which is accelerated relatively to K. But since a gravitational field exists with respect to this new body of reference K', our consideration also teaches us how the gravitational field influences the process studied.

For example, we learn that a body which is in a state of uniform rectilinear motion with respect to K (in accordance with the law of Galilei) is executing an accelerated and in general curvilinear motion with respect to the accelerated reference-body K' (chest). This acceleration or curvature corresponds to the influence on the moving body of the gravitational field prevailing relatively to K'. It is known that a gravitational field influences the movement of bodies in this way, so that our consideration supplies us with nothing essentially new.

However, we obtain a new result of fundamental importance when we carry out the analogous consideration for a ray of light. With respect to the Galileian reference-body K, such a ray of light is transmitted rectilinearly with the velocity c. It can easily be shown that the path of the same ray of light is no longer a straight line when we consider it with reference to the accelerated chest (reference-body K'). From this we conclude, *that, in general, rays of light are propagated curvilinearly in gravitational fields.* In two respects this result is of great importance.

In the first place, it can be compared with the reality. Although a detailed examination of the question shows that the curvature of light rays required by the general theory of relativity is only exceedingly small for the gravitational fields at our disposal in practice, its estimated magnitude for light rays passing the sun at grazing incidence is nevertheless 1.7 seconds of arc. This ought to manifest itself in the following way. As seen from the earth, certain fixed stars appear to be in the neighbourhood of the sun, and are thus capable of observation during a total eclipse of the sun. At such times, these stars ought to appear to be displaced outwards from the sun by an amount indicated above, as compared with their apparent position in the sky when the sun is situated at another part of the heavens. The examination of the correctness or otherwise of this deduction is a problem of the greatest importance, the early solution

From Albert Einstein, Relativity, *trans. Robert W. Lawson (New York: Crown Publishers © 1961), Chapter XXI. Reprinted by permission of the Estate of Albert Einstein.*
*[See Section C of this book.]

of which is to be expected of astronomers.[1]

In the second place our result shows that, according to the general theory of relativity, the law of the constancy of the velocity of light *in vacuo,* which constitutes one of the two fundamental assumptions in the special theory of relativity and to which we have already frequently referred, cannot claim any unlimited validity. A curvature of rays of light can only take place when the velocity of propagation of light varies with position. Now we might think that as a consequence of this, the special theory of relativity and with it the whole theory of relativity would be laid in the dust. But in reality this is not the case. We can only conclude that the special theory of relativity cannot claim an unlimited domain of validity; its results hold only so long as we are able to disregard the influences of gravitational fields on the phenomena (*e.g.* of light).

Since it has often been contended by opponents of the theory of relativity that the special theory of relativity is overthrown by the general theory of relativity, it is perhaps advisable to make the facts of the case clearer by means of an appropriate comparison. Before the development of electrodynamics the laws of electrostatics were looked upon as the laws of electricity. At the present time we know that electric fields can be derived correctly from electrostatic considerations only for the case, which is never strictly realised, in which the electrical masses are quite at rest relatively to each other, and to the co-ordinate system. Should we be justified in saying that for this reason electrostatics is overthrown by the field-equations of Maxwell in electrodynamics? Not in the least. Electrostatics is contained in electrodynamics as a limiting case; the laws of the latter lead directly to those of the former for the case in which the fields are invariable with regard to time. No fairer destiny could be alloted to any physical theory, than that it should of itself point out the way to the introduction of a more comprehensive theory, in which it lives on as a limiting case.

In the example of the transmission of light just dealt with, we have seen that the general theory of relativity enables us to derive theoretically the influence of a gravitational field on the course of natural processes, the laws of which are already known when a gravitational field is absent. But the most attractive problem, to the solution of which the general theory of relativity supplies the key, concerns the investigation of the laws satisfied by the gravitational field itself. Let us consider this for a moment.

We are acquainted with space-time domains which behave (approximately) in a "Galilean" fashion under suitable choice of reference-body, *i.e.* domains in which gravitational fields are absent. If we now refer such a domain to a reference-body K' possessing any kind of motion, then relative to K' there exists a gravitational field which is variable with respect to space and time.[2]

---

1. By means of the star photographs of two expeditions equipped by a Joint Committee of the Royal and Royal Astronomical Societies, the existence of the deflection of light demanded by theory was first confirmed during the solar eclipse of 29th May, 1919. [Cf. Part III.]

2. This follows from a generalisation of the discussion in Section XX [Section C of this book].

The character of this field will of course depend on the motion chosen for K'. According to the general theory of relativity, the general law of the gravitational field must be satisfied for all gravitational fields obtainable in this way. Even though by no means all gravitational fields can be produced in this way, yet we may entertain the hope that the general law of gravitation will be derivable from such gravitational fields of a special kind. This hope has been realised in the most beautiful manner. But between the clear vision of this goal and its actual realisation it was necessary to surmount a serious difficulty, and as this lies deep at the root of things, I dare not withhold it from the reader. We require to extend our ideas of the space-time continuum still farther.

F. BEHAVIOUR OF CLOCKS AND MEASURING RODS

Hitherto I have purposely refrained from speaking about the physical interpretation of space- and time-data in the case of the general theory of relativity. As a consequence, I am guilty of a certain slovenliness of treatment, which, as we know from the special theory of relativity, is far from being unimportant and pardonable. It is now high time that we remedy this defect; but I would mention at the outset, that this matter lays no small claims on the patience and on the power of abstraction of the reader.

We start off again from quite special cases, which we have frequently used before. Let us consider a space-time domain in which no gravitational field exists relative to a reference-body K whose state of motion has been suitably chosen. K is then a Galileian reference-body as regards the domain considered, and the results of the special theory of relativity hold relative to K. Let us suppose the same domain referred to a second body of reference K', which is rotating uniformly with respect to K. In order to fix our ideas, we shall imagine K' to be in the form of a plane circular disc, which rotates uniformly in its own plane about its centre. An observer who is sitting eccentrically on the disc K' is sensible of a force which acts outwards in a radial direction, and which would be interpreted as an effect of inertia (centrifugal force) by an observer who was at rest with respect to the original reference-body K. But the observer on the disc may regard his disc as a reference-body which is "at rest"; on the basis of the general principle of relativity he is justified in doing this. The force acting on himself, and in fact on all other bodies which are at rest relative to the disc, he regards as the effect of a gravitational field. Nevertheless, the space-distribution of this gravitational field is of a kind that would not be possible on Newton's theory of gravitation.[1] But since the observer believes in the general theory of relativity, this does not disturb him; he is quite in the right

From Albert Einstein, Relativity, *trans. Robert W. Lawson (New York: Crown Publishers, © 1961), Chapter XXIII. Reprinted by permission of the Estate of Albert Einstein.*

1. The field disappears at the centre of the disc and increases proportionally to the distance from the centre as we proceed outwards.

when he believes that a general law of gravitation can be formulated—a law which not only explains the motion of the stars correctly, but also the field of force experienced by himself.

The observer performs experiments on his circular disc with clocks and measuring-rods. In doing so, it is his intention to arrive at exact definitions for the signification of time- and space-data with reference to the circular disk K', these definitions being based on his observations. What will be his experience in this enterprise?

To start with, he places one of two identically constructed clocks at the centre of the circular disc, and the other on the edge of the disc, so that they are at rest relative to it. We now ask ourselves whether both clocks go at the same rate from the standpoint of the non-rotating Galilean reference-body K. As judged from this body, the clock at the centre of the disc has no velocity, whereas the clock at the edge of the disc is in motion relative to K in consequence of the rotation. As a consequence of a previous result it follows that the latter clock goes at a rate permanently slower than that of the clock at the centre of the circular disc, i.e. as observed from K. It is obvious that the same effect would be noted by an observer whom we will imagine sitting alongside his clock at the centre of the circular disc. Thus on our circular disc, or, to make the case more general, in every gravitational field, a clock will go more quickly or less quickly, according to the position in which the clock is situated (at rest). For this reason it is not possible to obtain a reasonable definition of time with the aid of clocks which are arranged at rest with respect to the body of reference. A similar difficulty presents itself when we attempt to apply our earlier definition of simultaneity in such a case, but I do not wish to go any further into this question.

Moreover, at this stage the definition of the space co-ordinates also presents insurmountable difficulties. If the observer applies his standard measuring-rod (a rod which is short as compared with the radius of the disc) tangentially to the edge of the disc, then, as judged from the Galilean system, the length of this rod will be less than 1, since moving bodies suffer a shortening in the direction of the motion. On the other hand, the measuring-rod will not experience a shortening in length, as judged from K, if it is applied to the disc in the direction of the radius. If, then, the observer first measures the circumference of the disc with his measuring-rod and then the diameter of the disc, on dividing the one by the other, he will not obtain as quotient the familiar number $\pi = 3.14 \ldots$, but a larger number,[1] whereas of course, for a disc which is at rest with respect to K, this operation would yield π exactly. This proves that the propositions of Euclidean geometry cannot hold exactly on the rotating disc, nor in general in a gravitational field, at least if we attribute the length 1 to the rod in all positions and in every orientation. Hence the idea of a

---

1. Throughout this consideration we have to use the Galilean (non-rotating) system K as reference-body, since we may only assume the validity of the results of the special theory of relativity relative to K (relative to K' a gravitational field prevails).

straight line also loses its meaning. We are therefore not in a position to define exactly the co-ordinates x, y, z relative to the disc by means of the method used in discussing the special theory, and as long as the co-ordinates and times of events have not been defined, we cannot assign an exact meaning to the natural laws in which these occur.

Thus all our previous conclusions based on general relativity would appear to be called in question. In reality we must make a subtle detour in order to be able to apply the postulate of general relativity exactly. I shall prepare the reader for this in the following paragraphs.

G. EUCLIDEAN AND NON-EUCLIDEAN CONTINUUM

The surface of a marble table is spread out in front of me. I can get from any one point on this table to any other point by passing continuously from one point to a "neighbouring" one, and repeating this process a (large) number of times, or, in other words, by going from point to point without executing "jumps." I am sure the reader will appreciate with sufficient clearness what I mean here by "neighbouring" and by "jumps" (if he is not too pedantic). We express this property of the surface by describing the latter as a continuum.

Let us now imagine that a large number of little rods of equal length have been made, their lengths being small compared with the dimensions of the marble slab. When I say they are of equal length, I mean that one can be laid on any other without the ends overlapping. We next lay four of these little rods on the marble slab so that they constitute a quadrilateral figure (a square), the diagonals of which are equally long. To ensure the equality of the diagonals, we make use of a little testing-rod. To this square we add similar ones, each of which has one rod in common with the first. We proceed in like manner with each of these squares until finally the whole marble slab is laid out with squares. The arrangement is such, that each side of a square belongs to two squares and each corner to four squares.

It is a veritable wonder that we can carry out this business without getting into the greatest difficulties. We only need to think of the following. If at any moment three squares meet at a corner, then two sides of the fourth square are already laid, and, as a consequence, the arrangement of the remaining two sides of the square is already completely determined. But I am now no longer able to adjust the quadrilateral so that its diagonals may be equal. If they are equal of their own accord, then this is an especial favour of the marble slab and of the little rods, about which I can only be thankfully surprised. We must needs experience many such surprises if the construction is to be successful.

If everything has really gone smoothly, then I say that the points of the marble slab constitute a Euclidean continuum with respect to the little rod, which has been used as a "distance" (line-interval). By choosing one corner

From Albert Einstein, Relativity, *trans. Robert W. Lawson (New York: Crown Publishers, © 1961), Chapter XXIV. Reprinted by permission of the Estate of Albert Einstein.*

of a square as "origin," I can characterise every other corner of a square with reference to this origin by means of two numbers. I only need state how many rods I must pass over when, starting from the origin, I proceed towards the "right" and then "upwards," in order to arrive at the corner of the square under consideration. These two numbers are then the "Cartesian co-ordinates" of this corner with reference to the "Cartesian co-ordinate system" which is determined by the arrangement of little rods.

By making use of the following modification of this abstract experiment, we recognise that there must also be cases in which the experiment would be unsuccessful. We shall suppose that the rods "expand" by an amount proportional to the increase of temperature. We heat the central part of the marble slab, but not the periphery, in which case two of our little rods can still be brought into coincidence at every position on the table. But our construction of squares must necessarily come into disorder during the heating, because the little rods on the central region of the table expand, whereas those on the outer part do not.

With reference to our little rods—defined as unit lengths—the marble slab is no longer a Euclidean continuum, and we are also no longer in the position of defining Cartesian co-ordinates directly with their aid, since the above construction can no longer be carried out. But since there are other things which are not influenced in a similar manner to the little rods (or perhaps not at all) by the temperature of the table, it is possible quite naturally to maintain the point of view that the marble slab is a "Euclidean continuum." This can be done in a satisfactory manner by making a more subtle stipulation about the measurement or the comparison of lengths.

But if rods of every kind (*i.e.* of every material) were to have *in the same way* as regards the influence of temperature when they are on the variably heated marble slab, and if we had no other means of detecting the effect of temperature than the geometrical behaviour of our rods in experiments analogous to the one described above, then our best plan would be to assign the distance *one* to two points on the slab, provided that the ends of one of our rods could be made to coincide with these two points; for how else should we define the distance without our proceeding being in the highest measure grossly arbitrary? The method of Cartesian co-ordinates must then be discarded, and replaced by another which does not assume the validity of Euclidean geometry for rigid bodies.[1] The reader will notice that the situation depicted here corre-

---

1. Mathematicians have been confronted with our problem in the following form. If we are given a surface (*e.g.* an ellipsoid) in Euclidean three-dimensional space, then there exists for this surface a two-dimensional geometry, just as much as for a plane surface. Gauss undertook the task of treating this two-dimensional geometry from first principles, without making use of the fact that the surface belongs to a Euclidean continuum of three dimensions. If we imagine constructions to be made with rigid rods *in the surface* (similar to that above with the marble slab), we should find that different laws hold for these from those resulting on the basis of Euclidean plane geometry. The surface is not a Euclidean continuum with respect to the rods, and we cannot

sponds to the one brought about by the general postulate of relativity (Section XXIII*).

H. GAUSSIAN CO-ORDINATES

According to Gauss, this combined analytical and geometrical mode of handling the problem can be arrived at in the following way. We imagine a system of arbitrary curves (see Fig. 4) drawn on the surface of the table. These we designate as u-curves, and we indicate each of them by means of a number.

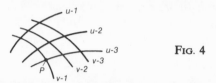

Fig. 4

The curves $u=1$, $u=2$ and $u=3$ are drawn in the diagram. Between the curves $u=1$ and $u=2$ we must imagine an infinitely large number to be drawn, all of which correspond to real numbers lying between 1 and 2. We have then a system of u-curves, and this infinitely dense" system covers the whole surface of the table. These u-curves-must not intersect each other, and through each point of the surface one and only one curve must pass. Thus a perfectly definite value of u belongs to every point on the surface of the marble slab. In like manner we imagine a system of v-curves drawn on the surface. These satisfy the same conditions as the u-curves, they are provided with numbers in a corresponding manner, and they may likewise be of arbitrary shape. It follows that a value of u and a value of v belong to every point on the surface of the table. We call these two numbers the co-ordinates of the surface of the table (Gaussian co-ordinates). For example, the point P in the diagram has the Gaussian co-ordinates $u=3$, $v=1$. Two neighbouring points P and P', on the surface then correspond to the co-ordinates

$$P: \qquad u, v$$
$$P': \qquad u + du, v + dv,$$

where du and dv signify very small numbers. In a similar manner we may indicate the distance (line-interval) between P and P', as measured with a little

---

define Cartesian co-ordinates *in the surface*. Gauss indicated the principles according to which we can treat the geometrical relationships in the surface, and thus pointed out the way to the method of Riemann of treating multi-dimensional, non-Euclidean *continua*. Thus it is that mathematicians long ago solved the formal problems to which we are led by the general postulate of relativity.

*[See Section F of this book.]

From Albert Einstein, Relativity, *trans. Robert W. Lawson (New York: Crown Publishers, © 1961), Chapter XXV. Reprinted by permission of the Estate of Albert Einstein.*

rod, by means of the very small number ds. Then according to Gauss we have

$$ds^2 = g_{11}du^2 + 2g_{12}dudv + g_{22}\,dv^2,$$

where g_{11}, g_{12}, g_{22}, are magnitudes which depend in a perfectly definite way on u and v. The magnitudes g_{11}, g_{12} and g_{22} determine the behaviour of the rods relative to the u-curves and v-curves, and thus also relative to the surface of the table. For the case in which the points of the surface considered form a Euclidean continuum with reference to the measuring-rods, but only in this case, it is possible to draw the u-curves and v-curves and to attach numbers to them, in such a manner, that we simply have:

$$ds^2 = du^2 + dv^2.$$

Under these conditions, the u-curves and v-curves are straight lines in the sense of Euclidean geometry, and they are perpendicular to each other. Here the Gaussian co-ordinates are simply Cartesian ones. It is clear that Gauss co-ordinates are nothing more than an association of two sets of numbers with the points of the surface considered, of such a nature that numerical values differing very slightly from each other are associated with neighbouring points "in space."

So far, these considerations hold for a continuum of two dimensions. But the Gaussian method can be applied also to a continuum of three, four or more dimensions. If, for instance, a continuum of four dimensions be supposed available, we may represent it in the following way. With every point of the continuum we associate arbitrarily four numbers, x_1, x_2, x_3, x_4, which are known as "co-ordinates." Adjacent points correspond to adjacent values of the co-ordinates. If a distance ds is associated with the adjacent points P and P', this distance being measurable and well-defined from a physical point of view, then the following formula holds:

$$ds^2 = g_{11}dx_1{}^2 + 2g_{12}\,dx_1dx_2 \ldots + g_{44}dx_4{}^2,$$

where the magnitudes g_{11}, etc., have values which vary with the position in the continuum. Only when the continuum is a Euclidean one is it possible to associate the co-ordinates $x_1 \ldots x_4$ with the points of the continuum so that we have simply

$$ds^2 = dx_1{}^2 + dx_2{}^2 + dx_3{}^2 + dx_4{}^2.$$

In this case relations hold in the four-dimensional continuum which are analogous to those holding in our three-dimensional measurements.

However, the Gauss treatment for ds^2 which we have given above is not always possible. It is only possible when sufficiently small regions of the continuum under consideration may be regarded as Euclidean continua. For example, this obviously holds in the case of the marble slab of the table and local variation of temperature. The temperature is practically constant for a small part of the slab, and thus the geometrical behaviour of the rods is *almost* as it ought to be according to the rules of Euclidean geometry. Hence the imperfections of the construction of squares in the previous section do not show themselves clearly until this construction is extended over a considerable portion of the surface of the table.

We can sum this up as follows: Gauss invented a method for the mathematical treatment of continua in general, in which "size-relations" ("distances" between neighbouring points) are defined. To every point of a continuum are assigned as many numbers (Gaussian co-ordinates) as the continuum has dimensions. This is done in such a way, that only one meaning can be attached to the assignment, and that numbers (Gaussian co-ordinates) which differ by an indefinitely small amount are assigned to adjacent points. The Gaussian co-ordinate system is a logical generalisation of the Cartesian co-ordinate system. It is also applicable to non-Euclidean continua, but only when, with respect to the defined "size" or "distance," small parts of the continuum under consideration behave more nearly like a Euclidean system, the smaller the part of the continuum under our notice.

I. SPACE-TIME CONTINUUM OF THE SPECIAL THEORY OF RELATIVITY

In accordance with the special theory of relativity, certain co-ordinate systems are given preference for the description of the four-dimensional, space-time continuum. We called these "Galileian co-ordinate systems." For these systems, the four co-ordinates $x, y, z, t,$ which determine an event or—in other words—a point of the four-dimensional continuum, are defined physically in a simple manner, as set forth in detail in the first part of this book. For the transition from one Galileian system to another, which is moving uniformly with reference to the first, the equations of the Lorentz transformation are valid. These last form the basis for the derivation of deductions from the special theory of relativity, and in themselves they are nothing more than the expression of the universal validity of the law of transmission of light for all Galileian systems of reference.

Minkowski found that the Lorentz transformations satisfy the following simple conditions. Let us consider two neighbouring events, the relative position of which in the four-dimensional continuum is given with respect to a Galileian reference-body K by the space co-ordinate differences dx, dy, dz and the time-difference dt. With reference to a second Galileian system we shall

From Albert Einstein, Relativity, *trans. Robert W. Lawson (New York: Crown Publishers, © 1961), Chapter XXVI. Reprinted by permission of the Estate of Albert Einstein.*

suppose that the corresponding differences for these two events are dx', dy', dz', dt'. Then these magnitudes always fulfil the condition

$$dx^2 + dy^2 + dz^2 - c^2 dt^2 = dx'^2 + dy'^2 + dz'^2 - c^2 dt'^2.$$

The validity of the Lorentz transformation follows from this condition. We can express this as follows: The magnitude

$$ds^2 = dx^2 + dy^2 + dz^2 - c^2 dt^2,$$

which belongs to two adjacent points of the four-dimensional space-time continuum, has the same value for all selected (Galileian) reference-bodies. If we replace x, y, z, $\sqrt{-1}\ ct$ by x_1, x_2, x_3, x_4, we also obtain the result that

$$ds^2 = dx_1^2 + dx_2^2 + dx_3^2 + dx_4^2$$

is independent of the choice of the body of reference. We call the magnitude ds the "distance" apart of the two events or four-dimensional points.

Thus, if we choose as time-variable the imaginary variable $\sqrt{-1}\ ct$ instead of the real quantity t, we can regard the space-time continuum—in accordance with the special theory of relativity—as a "Euclidean" four-dimensional continuum, a result which follows from the considerations of the preceding section.

J. SPACE-TIME CONTINUUM OF THE GENERAL THEORY OF RELATIVITY

In the first part of this book* we were able to make use of space-time co-ordinates which allowed of a simple and direct physical interpretation, and which, according to Section XXVI,** can be regarded as four-dimensional Cartesian co-ordinates. This was possible on the basis of the law of the constancy of the velocity of light. But according to Section XXI,[†] the general theory of relativity cannot retain this law. On the contrary, we arrived at the result that according to this latter theory the velocity of light must always depend on the co-ordinates when a gravitational field is present. In connection with a specific illustration in Section XXIII,[††] we found that the presence of

From Albert Einstein, Relativity, trans. Robert W. Lawson (New York: Crown Publishers, © 1961), Chapter XXVII. Reprinted by permission of the Estate of Albert Einstein.

*Ibid., Part I.
**[See Section I of this book.]
[†][See Section D.]
[††][See Section F.]

a gravitational field invalidates the definition of the co-ordinates and the time, which led us to our objective in the special theory of relativity.

In view of the results of these considerations we are led to the conviction that, according to the general principle of relativity, the space-time continuum cannot be regarded as a Euclidean one, but that here we have the general case, corresponding to the marble slab with local variations of temperature, and with which we made acquaintance as an example of a two-dimensional continuum. Just as it was there impossible to construct a Cartesian co-ordinate system from equal rods, so here it is impossible to build up a system (reference-body) from rigid bodies and clocks, which shall be of such a nature that measuring-rods and clocks, arranged rigidly with respect to one another, shall indicate position and time directly. Such was the essence of the difficulty with which we were confronted in Section XXIII.[§]

But the considerations of Sections XXV[§§] and XXVI[#] show us the way to surmount this difficulty. We refer the four-dimensional space-time continuum in an arbitrary manner to Gauss co-ordinates. We assign to every point of the continuum (event) four numbers, x_1, x_2, x_3, x_4 (co-ordinates), which have not the least direct physical significance, but only serve the purpose of numbering the points of the continuum in a definite but arbitrary manner. This arrangement does not even need to be of such a kind that we must regard x_1, x_2, x_3 as "space" co-ordinates and x_4 as a "time" co-ordinate.

The reader may think that such a description of the world would be quite inadequate. What does it mean to assign to an event the particular co-ordinates x_1, x_2, x_3, x_4, if in themselves these co-ordinates have no significance? More careful consideration shows, however, that this anxiety is unfounded. Let us consider, for instance, a material point with any kind of motion. If this point had only a momentary existence without duration, then it would be described in space-time by a single system of values x_1, x_2, x_3, x_4. Thus its permanent existence must be characterised by an infinitely large number of such systems of values, the co-ordinate values of which are so close together as to give continuity: corresponding to the material point, we thus have a (uni-dimensional) line in the four-dimensional continuum. In the same way, any such lines in our continuum correspond to many points in motion. The only statements having regard to these points which can claim a physical existence are in reality the statements about their encounters. In our mathematical treatment, such an encounter is expressed in the fact that the two lines which represent the motions of the points in question have a particular system of co-ordinate values, x_1, x_2 x_3, x_4, in common. After mature consideration the reader will doubtless admit that in reality such encounters constitute the only actual evidence of a time-space nature with which we meet in physical statements.

[§][See Section F.]
[§§][See Section H.]
[#][See Section I.]

When we were describing the motion of a material point relative to a body of reference, we stated nothing more than the encounters of this point with particular points of the reference-body. We can also determine the corresponding values of the time by the observation of encounters of the body with clocks, in conjunction with the observation of the encounter of the hands of clocks with particular points on the dials. It is just the same in the case of space-measurements by means of measuring-rods, as a little consideration will show.

The following statements hold generally: Every physical description resolves itself into a number of statements, each of which refers to the space-time coincidence of two events A and B. In terms of Gaussian co-ordinates, every such statement is expressed by the agreement of their four co-ordinates x_1, x_2, x_3, x_4. Thus in reality, the description of the time-space continuum by means of Gauss co-ordinates completely replaces the description with the aid of a body of reference, without suffering from the defects of the latter mode of description; it is not tied down to the Euclidean character of the continuum which has to be represented.

K. GENERAL PRINCIPLE OF RELATIVITY— AN EXACT FORMULATION

We are now in a position to replace the provisional formulation of the general principle of relativity given in Section XVIII* by an exact formulation. The form there used, "All bodies of reference K, K', etc., are equivalent for the description of natural phenomena (formulation of the general laws of nature), whatever may be their state of motion," cannot be maintained, because the use of rigid reference-bodies, in the sense of the method followed in the special theory of relativity, is in general not possible in space-time description. The Gauss co-ordinate system has to take the place of the body of reference. The following statement corresponds to the fundamental idea of the general principle of relativity: *"All Gaussian co-ordinate systems are essentially equivalent for the formulation of the general laws of nature."*

We can state this general principle of relativity in still another form, which renders it yet more clearly intelligible than it is when in the form of the natural extension of the special principle of relativity. According to the special theory of relativity, the equations which express the general laws of nature pass over into equations of the same form when, by making use of the Lorentz transformation, we replace the space-time variables x, y, z, t, of a (Galileian) reference-body K by the space-time variables x', y', z', t', of a new reference-

From Albert Einstein, Relativity, *trans. Robert W. Lawson (New York: Crown Publishers, © 1961), Chapter XXVIII. Reprinted by permission of the Estate of Albert Einstein.*
*[See Section A.]

body K'. According to the general theory of relativity, on the other hand, by application of *arbitrary substitutions* of the Gauss variables x_1, x_2, x_3, x_4, the equations must pass over into equations of the same form; for every transformation (not only the Lorentz transformation) corresponds to the transition of one Gauss co-ordinate system into another.

If we desire to adhere to our "old-time" three-dimensional view of things, then we can characterise the development which is being undergone by the fundamental idea of the general theory of relativity as follows: The special theory of relativity has reference to Galileian domains, *i.e.* to those in which no gravitational field exists. In this connection a Galileian reference-body serves as body of reference, *i.e.* a rigid body the state of motion of which is so chosen that the Galileian law of the uniform rectilinear motion of "isolated" material points holds relatively to it.

Certain considerations suggest that we should refer the same Galileian domains to *non-Galileian* reference-bodies also. A gravitational field of a special kind is then present with respect to these bodies (cf. Sections XX and XXIII*).

In gravitational fields there are no such things as rigid bodies with Euclidean properties; thus the fictitious rigid body of reference is of no avail in the general theory of relativity. The motion of clocks is also influenced by gravitational fields, and in such a way that a physical definition of time which is made directly with the aid of clocks has by no means the same degree of plausibility as in the special theory of relativity.

For this reason non-rigid reference-bodies are used, which are as a whole not only moving in any way whatsoever, but which also suffer alterations in form *ad lib.* during their motion. Clocks, for which the law of motion is of any kind, however irregular, serve for the definition of time. We have to imagine each of these clocks fixed at a point on the non-rigid reference-body. These clocks satisfy only the one condition, that the "readings" which are observed simultaneously on adjacent clocks (in space) differ from each other by an indefinitely small amount. This non-rigid reference-body, which might appropriately be termed a "reference-mollusc," is in the main equivalent to a Gaussian four-dimensional co-ordinate system chosen arbitrarily. That which gives the "mollusc" a certain comprehensibility as compared with the Gauss co-ordinate system is the (really unjustified) formal retention of the separate existence of the space co-ordinates as opposed to the time co-ordinate. Every point on the mollusc is treated as a space-point, and every material point which is at rest relatively to it as at rest, so long as the mollusc is considered as reference-body. The general principle of relativity requires that all these molluscs can be used as reference-bodies with equal right and equal success in the formulation of the general laws of nature; the laws themselves must be quite independent of the choice of mollusc.

*[See Sections C and E.]

The great power possessed by the general principle of relativity lies in the comprehensive limitation which is imposed on the laws of nature in consequence of what we have seen above.

L. SOLUTION OF THE PROBLEM OF GRAVITATION

If the reader has followed all our previous considerations, he will have no further difficulty in understanding the methods leading to the solution of the problem of gravitation.

We start off from a consideration of a Galileian domain, *i.e.* a domain in which there is no gravitational field relative to the Galileian reference-body *K*. The behaviour of measuring-rods and clocks with reference to *K* is known from the special theory of relativity, likewise the behaviour of "isolated" material points; the latter move uniformly and in straight lines.

Now let us refer this domain to a random Gauss co-ordinate system or to a "mollusc" as reference-body *K'.* Then with respect to *K'* there is a gravitational field *G* (of a particular kind). We learn the behaviour of measuring-rods and clocks and also of freely-moving material points with reference to *K'* simply by mathematical transformation. We interpret this behaviour as the behaviour of measuring-rods, clocks and material points under the influence of the gravitational field *G*. Hereupon we introduce a hypothesis: that the influence of the gravitational field on measuring-rods, clocks and freely-moving material points continues to take place according to the same laws, even in the case where the prevailing gravitational field is *not* derivable from the Galileian special case, simply by means of a transformation of co-ordinates.

The next step is to investigate the space-time behaviour of the gravitational field *G*, which was derived from the Galileian special case simply by transformation of the co-ordinates. This behaviour is formulated in a law, which is always valid, no matter how the reference-body (mollusc) used in the description may be chosen.

This law is not yet the *general* law of the gravitational field, since the gravitational field under consideration is of a special kind. In order to find out the general law-of-field of gravitation we still require to obtain a generalisation of the law as found above. This can be obtained without caprice, however, by taking into consideration the following demands:

(a) The required generalisation must likewise satisfy the general postulate of relativity.

(b) If there is any matter in the domain under consideration, only its inertial mass, and thus only its energy is of importance for its effect in exciting a field.

From Albert Einstein, Relativity, *trans. Robert W. Lawson (New York: Crown Publishers, © 1961), Chapter XXIX. Reprinted by permission of the Estate of Albert Einstein.*

(c) Gravitational field and matter together must satisfy the law of the conservation of energy (and of impulse).

Finally, the general principle of relativity permits us to determine the influence of the gravitational field on the course of all those processes which take place according to known laws when a gravitational field is absent, *i.e.* which have already been fitted into the frame of the special theory of relativity. In this connection we proceed in principle according to the method which has already been explained for measuring-rods, clocks and freely-moving material points.

The theory of gravitation derived in this way from the general postulate of relativity excels not only in its beauty; nor in removing the defect attaching to classical mechanics which was brought to light in Section XXI*; nor in interpreting the empirical law of the equality of inertial and gravitational mass; but it has also already explained a result of observation in astronomy, against which classical mechanics is powerless.

If we confine the application of the theory to the case where the gravitational fields can be regarded as being weak, and in which all masses move with respect to the co-ordinate system with velocities which are small compared with the velocity of light, we then obtain as a first approximation the Newtonian theory. Thus the latter theory is obtained here without any particular assumption, whereas Newton had to introduce the hypothesis that the force of attraction between mutually attracting material points is inversely proportional to the square of the distance between them. If we increase the accuracy of the calculation, deviations from the theory of Newton make their appearance, practically all of which must nevertheless escape the test of observation owing to their smallness.

We must draw attention here to one of these deviations. According to Newton's theory, a planet moves round the sun in an ellipse, which would permanently maintain its position with respect to the fixed stars, if we could disregard the motion of the fixed stars themselves and the action of the other planets under consideration. Thus, if we correct the observed motion of the planets for these two influences, and if Newton's theory be strictly correct, we ought to obtain for the orbit of the planet an ellipse, which is fixed with reference to the fixed stars. This deduction, which can be tested with great accuracy, has been confirmed for all the planets save one, with the precision that is capable of being obtained by the delicacy of observation attainable at the present time. The sole exception is Mercury, the planet which lies nearest the sun. Since the time of Leverrier, it has been known that the ellipse corresponding to the orbit of Mercury, after it has been corrected for the influences mentioned above, is not stationary with respect to the fixed stars, but that it

*[See Section D.]

rotates exceedingly slowly in the plane of the orbit and in the sense of the orbital motion. The value obtained for this rotary movement of the orbital ellipse was 43 seconds of arc per century, an amount ensured to be correct to within a few seconds of arc. This effect can be explained by means of classical mechanics only on the assumption of hypotheses which have little probability, and which were devised solely for this purpose.

On the basis of the general theory of relativity, it is found that the ellipse of every planet round the sun must necessarily rotate in the manner indicated above; that for all the planets, with the exception of Mercury, this rotation is too small to be detected with the delicacy of observation possible at the present time; but that in the case of Mercury it must amount to 43 seconds of arc per century, a result which is strictly in agreement with observation.

Apart from this one, it has hitherto been possible to make only two deductions from the theory which admit of being tested by observation, to wit, the curvature of light rays by the gravitational field of the sun,[1] and a displacement of the spectral lines of light reaching us from large stars, as compared with the corresponding lines for light produced in an analogous manner terrestrially (i.e. by the same kind of atom).[2] These two deductions from the theory have both been confirmed.

CRITICISMS AND REFUTATIONS

TO WHAT EXTENT CAN THE MODERN THEORY OF GRAVITATION BE FORMULATED WITHOUT RELATIVITY?

The question whether the theory of gravitation can be formulated and derived without the principle of relativity is to be answered in principle doubtless with "yes." For what thus the principle of relativity? I answer this to begin with a comparison. Thermodynamics can certainly be developed without the second law; thus for what employ the second law?

1. First observed by Eddington and others in 1919 [cf. Part III, Deflection of Light by a Gravitational Field].
2. Established by Adams in 1924 [cf. Part III, Displacement of Spectral Lines Towards the Red].

The above letter to the editor (Die Naturwissenschaften 8 *[1920]: 1010–1011*) *is an answer to a preceding letter by Ernst Reichenbächer who feels that the opposition to the theory of gravitation is due to the general theory of relativity and wants to formulate gravitation without the use of the principle of relativity. Reprinted by permission of the Estate of Albert Einstein.*

The answer is obvious. Of two theories which do justice to the present totality of known experience in a subject, the one to be preferred is that which requires fewer independent assumptions. Seen from this point of view the principle of relativity is as valuable for electrodynamics and gravitation as the second law is for thermodynamics. Because it requires many independent hypotheses to arrive at the deductions of the theory of relativity without the use of the principle of relativity. This is displayed by all previous attempts which try to avoid the principle of relativity.

In addition, the introduction of the principle of relativity is also justified from a perceptual theoretical point of view. For the coordinate system is only a means of description and has nothing to do with the objects to be described. Only the general covariantly formulated law will do complete justice to this state of affairs, because in any other formulation statements about means of description and statement about the described object are mixed together. I mention the Galilean law of inertia as an example. It states as follows: Material points separated sufficiently from each other move uniformly in a straight line —"provided that the motion is referred to a suitable moving system of coordinates and that the time is suitably defined." Who does not feel the awkwardness of such a formulation? To omit the conditional clause, however, implies an inaccuracy.

I am now passing to the objections to the relativistic theory of the gravitational field. To begin with, Mr. Reichenbächer forgets the decisive argument, namely that the numerical equality of the inertial and gravitational mass has to be traced to an intrinsic equality.[1] This, as is known, is achieved by the principle of equivalence. Against this principle he (as Mr. Kottler) raises the objection that gravitational fields, in general, cannot be transformed away for finite space-times. He thereby overlooks that this does not matter in the least. What does matter is that we are justified in considering the mechanical behaviour of a material point at a given moment at will (depending on the choice of the reference system) due to inertia or gravitation. More is not necessary; to obtain the intrinsic equality of inertia and gravitation it is not necessary that the mechanical behaviour of two or more masses can be interpreted solely as an inertial effect by the choice of the same coordinates. Nobody denies, for example, that the theory of special relativity does justice to the relative nature of uniform motion, although it is not possible to transform all bodies without acceleration to rest at the same time by the choice of one and the same coordinates.

The case of gravitational fields which can be transformed away is only important as a special case, which certainly must satisfy the laws of nature.

1. Instead of "because gravitation expresses its action in acceleration as a force inherent to matter," Mr. Reichenbächer should have said "because the gravitational acceleration is independent of the material and state of the body influenced by the gravitational force." Only through the last property differs, namely the gravitational field from all other force fields.

The second objection is that the fields which exist in a coordinate system rotating with respect to an inertial system (centrifugal fields, Coriolis fields) are only "fictitious" but not "real" fields. This is valid in Newton's theory, because these fields do not satisfy Poisson's differential equation. According to the general theory of relativity, however, they satisfy the differential equations of the field, and are therefore as "real" as the fields in the neighborhood of a ponderable mass with respect to the chosen coordinate system.

The supporters of the relativity theory are not agreed on the question whether these fields can be traced back indirectly to the action of masses or not. I myself am of the first opinion, according to which all masses in the universe, even at large distances, take part in the existence of the gravitational field at every point. I do not have to enter here into this question closely related to the cosmological problem, although it is of fundamental importance. The justification and superiority respectively of the relativity theory can be judged without decision about this far-lying question, which can be decided only by galactic astronomy.

Mr. Reichenbächer has misunderstood my considerations about the two celestial bodies rotating relatively to each other. One body is thought to be rotating according to Newtonian mechanics and, because of the centrifugal action, is flattened at the poles, while the other one is not (rotating). The inhabitants (of these bodies) would note this by the use of measuring rods, inform each other, and then ask about the real cause of the different behaviour of the celestial bodies. (This consideration has nothing do with the Lorentz contraction.) Newton's answer to this was the "reality" of absolute space, with respect to which one of the two bodies is rotating, but not the other one. I, myself, am of the Machian opinion which can be formulated in the language of the relativity theory as follows: All masses in the universe determine the $g_{\mu\nu}$-field; and this is different, as viewed from the first celestial body, from the one viewed by the second one, because, to be sure, the motions of these masses creating the $g_{\mu\nu}$-field are quite different as seen from the two systems. The inertia is, according to my interpretation, an interaction (transmitted) between the masses in the same sense as those actions which the Newtonian theory considers gravitational actions. What Mr. Reichenbächer says about the two-body problem is from this point of view completely incorrect. The fact that one can approximate the action of all other celestial bodies, except the two being considered, by a quasi-constant $g_{\mu\nu}$-field is not to be confused with the statement that these bodies have no influence on the two which are being considered.

How Mr. Reichenbächer in the paragraph beginning "If we consider the state of affairs correctly," after what has been said before, comes to the conclusion that all laws of nature have to be given a generally convariant form is completely unclear to me. If, for instance, the acceleration has an absolute meaning, then all non-accelerated coordinate systems are preferred by nature; i.e., the laws—referred to them—must be other (and simpler) than the ones referred to accelerated coordinate systems. It then is senseless to complicate the formulation of the laws by forcing them into a generally covariant form.

If, on the other hand, the natural laws are so constructed that they do not take a preferred form by the choice of coordinate systems corresponding to particular states of motion, then one would not abandon the condition of general covariance as a means of investigation. Moreover, if one assumes that for infinitesimal measuring systems (in the ∞-small) the special relativity theory is valid, and that the $g_{\mu\nu}$ derived from it described the gravitational field, then one arrives at the basis of the general theory of relativity. Whether this is the case for Mr. Reichenbächer or not I have not been able to deduce from his exposition.

MY ANSWER TO THE ANTI-RELATIVISTIC COMPANY, INC.

Under the imposing name Working Circle of German Natural Philosophers (Arbeitsgemeinschaft deutscher Naturforscher) a motley crew has collected whose present purpose seems to be to disparage the theory of relativity and me its originator in the eyes of the non-physicists. Recently Messrs. Weyland and Gehrke held their first lecture along these lines in the Philharmonic Hall, at which I was also present. I am quite aware that under the circumstance the two speakers do not deserve an answer from me, for I have good reason to believe that this undertaking has motives other than the striving for truth. If I were a German nationalist with or without swastika instead of a Jew whose thinking is unregulated and international, then . . . I answer only because well-meaning parties have asked repeatedly that I make my interpretation known thereto.

First of all, to my knowledge today there is hardly a researcher who has contributed something of importance in theoretical Physics and does not admit that the whole theory of relativity is constructed self-consistent and in agreement with experimental facts (positively proved) at present. The most important physicists—I mention here H. A. Lorentz, M. Planck, Sommerfeld, Laue, Born, Larmor, Eddington, Debye, Langevin, Levi-Civita—support the theory and have made valuable contributions to it. As outspoken opponents of the relativity theory among physicists of international note, I can name only Lenard. I admire Lenard as master of experimental physics but in theoretical physics he has accomplished nothing so far, and his objections to the theory of general relativity are so superficial that until now I did not find it necessary to answer them in detail. I am considering making up for it.

I am reproached for carrying on a tasteless advertisement for the relativity theory. I can, however, say that I have always been a friend of the well-chosen sober word and concise statement. My flesh creeps at high-sounding phrases

From Berliner Tageblatt und Handels-Zeitung, *August 27, 1920. Reprinted by permission of the Estate of Albert Einstein.*

and words, whether they deal with the relativity theory or something else. I have often made fun of effusiveness, for which I am now to blame. However, I willingly leave that pleasure to the gentlemen of the company, inc.

Now to the lectures. Mr. Weyland who does not seem to be any kind of expert (Doctor? Engineer? Politician? I could not find out what he is) has not mentioned anything pertinent. He has indulged in coarse rudeness and vulgar accusations. The second speaker, Mr. Gehrke, is guilty of creating a false impression on the uninformed layman partly by advancing falsehoods and partly by his one-sided choice of material and representation. The following examples may illustrate this:

Mr. Gehrke maintains that the relativity theory leads to solecism, a statement that every expert will greet as a joke. He bases this on the known example of the two clocks (or twins), one of which makes a round trip with respect to the inertial system while the other does not. He asserts—although he has been refuted by the greatest experts of the theory often both orally and in writing—that the theory leads in this case to the really nonsensical result of two clocks lying side by side each losing time with respect to the other. I can consider this only as an attempt intentionally to mislead the lay public.

Mr. Gehrke furthermore alludes to Mr. Lenard's objections, which are mainly concerned with the mechanics of everday life. His objections are thus untenable in light of the fact that I have proved that the results of the theory of general relativity agree, first of all, with those of classical mechanics.

But what Mr. Gehrke has said about the experimental verification of the theory is the most conclusive evidence that he was not concerned with the disclosure of the true state of affairs.

Mr. Gehrke wants to give the impression that the perihelion motion of Mercury can also be explained without the theory of relativity. There exist two possibilities. Either you invent particular interplanetary masses, which are so large and distributed as to give a perihelion motion of the observed amount (this is, of course, an extremely unsatisfactory way compared with the one given by the theory of relativity which yields the perihelion motion of Mercury without any special assumptions); or you use the work of Gerber, who has given the correct formula for the perihelion motion of Mercury before I did. The experts are not only in agreement that Gerber's derivation is wrong through and through, but the formula cannot be obtained as a consequence of the main assumption made by Gerber. Mr. Gerber's work is therefore completely useless, an unsuccessful and erroneous theoretical attempt. I maintain that the theory of general relativity has provided the first real explanation of the perihelion motion of Mercury. I have not mentioned the work by Gerber originally, because I did not know it when I wrote my work on the perihelion motion of Mercury; even if I had been aware of it, I would not have had any reason to mention it. The personal attack made by Messrs. Gehrke and Lenard on me in connection with this circumstance has generally been considered unfair by the real experts. Until now I considered it beneath my dignity to mention it.

Mr. Gehrke in his lecture has made the masterfully executed English measurements of the deflection of light by the sun appear in a bad light by mentioning the three independent groups only one of which, because of aberration of the heliograph mirror, gave erroneous results. He has suppressed the fact that the English astronomers themselves in their official report considered the results as a brilliant confirmation of the theory of general relativity.

In regard to the question of the red shift of spectral lines, Mr. Gehrke has concealed that the hitherto existing determinations still contradict each other, and that a final decision in this matter yet must come. He has brought out the testimony only against the existence of the red shift as predicted by the theory of relativity, but neglected to mention that these former results lost their power of proof because of the most recent experiments by Grebe and Buchem as well as by Perot.

Finally I want to mention that on my initiative a discussion about the relativity theory will be held at the meeting of scientists in Neuheim. There everyone who dares risk appearing before a scientific forum can put forward his objections.

It will make a curious impression abroad, especially on my Dutch and English colleagues H. A. Lorentz and Eddington, both of whom have been occupied intensely with the theory of relativity and have read about it repeatedly, when they see that the theory as well as its originator are slandered in Germany in such a manner.

DIALOGUE ON OBJECTIONS TO THE THEORY
OF RELATIVITY

*Critic:** For some time now my compeers have frequently advanced in journals all sorts of misgivings about the theory of relativity, but only seldom has one of your relativists[1] replied to that. We shall not investigate whether pride, whether a feeling of weakness, or whether laziness has been the reason for this neglect—perhaps it was an especially potent mixture of all these. Perhaps, also, the criticism betrays not infrequently evidence of the critic's manifesting too little knowledge of the subject. Of that—as stated—we shall not speak, but this I must tell you directly: I have sought you out today

From Albert Einstein, "Dialog über Einwände gegen die Relativitätstheorie," Die Natur-wissenschaften 6 (1918): 697–702. Trans. by H. M. Schwartz, University of Arkansas. Reprinted by permission of the Estate of Albert Einstein.

*The original word is "Kritikus," which stands either for the Latin "Criticus" or the Greek "Kritikos," with possible allusion to the Platonic dialogues [ed.].

1. By "relativist" is to be understood here an adherent of the physical theory of relativity, and not of philosophical relativism.

personally, so as to make it impossible for you to avoid answering as at other times. For rest assured, I shall not budge from the place before you have answered all my questions.

But in order that you do not become overly alarmed, nay perhaps even go about the business (which you cannot after all escape) with a certain satisfaction, I also tell you at once something consoling. I am not, as are some of my colleagues, so much permeated with the worth of my guild, that I appear before you as a superior being of unearthly insight and assurance (like a reporter of scientific literature, or even a theater critic). Rather I speak as a mortal human being, particularly since I well know that criticism is frequently the child of the dearth of one's own ideas. Nor do I want—as one of my colleagues recently—to press hard like a public prosecutor, and to reproach you with the theft of intellectual property or with other dishonorable deeds. Only the need to contribute to the clarification of some points on which opinions still widely diverge has provoked my invasion. Indeed I must ask you to permit the publication of this conversation of ours, not least because the scarcity of paper is not the only scarcity which shortens the sleep of my friend, the editor Berolinensis.*

As I perceive your willingness, I proceed directly to the point. Since the establishment of the special theory of relativity, its result concerning the retarding influence of motion on the rate of a clock has always evoked contradiction, and that—as it seems to me—with good reason. Because this result appears to lead necessarily to a contradiction with the foundations of the theory. So that we understand each other perfectly, let me first state this result of the theory sufficiently sharply.

Let K be a Galilean coordinate system in the sense of the special theory of relativity, namely a reference body with respect to which isolated material points move rectilinearly and uniformly. Let, further, U^1 and U^2 be two clocks that are constructed exactly alike and are under no external influence. These run at the same rate when they are placed either in the immediate vicinity of each other, or at an arbitrary distance from each other and at rest relative to K. But if one of the clocks, say U^2, is in a state of uniform translational motion relative to K, then according to the special theory of relativity it should run more slowly, as judged from the system K, than the clock U^1 which is at rest relative to K. This result is already strange in itself. Serious misgivings are introduced by it when one visualizes the following well-known thought-experiment.

Let A and B be two points of the system K at a distance from each other. To fix our ideas let us suppose that A is the origin of K, and B is a point on the positive x-axis. To begin with, suppose that the two clocks rest at A. They run then at the same rate, and we suppose that the setting of their hands is identical. We now impart to the clock U^2 a constant velocity in the direction

*The reference here is to Arnold Berliner [ed.].

of the positive x-axis, so that it moves toward B. We imagine that the velocity is reversed at B, so that U^2 moves back to A. Upon its arrival at A the clock is detained, so that it is now again at rest relative to U^1. Since the change in the setting of U^2 as judged from K, which might have occurred during the change of the velocity of U^2, surely does not exceed a certain amount, and since U^2 runs more slowly than U^1 (as judged from K) during its uniform motion along the path AB, therefore the clock U^2 must upon its return lag behind the clock U^1, if the path AB is sufficiently long.—Do you agree with this conclusion?

Relativist: I agree unconditionally. I have seen regretfully that some authors, who otherwise accept the foundations of the theory of relativity, wish to evade this inevitable result.

Critic: But here is the rub. According to the principle of relativity, the entire process must after all proceed in exactly the same way when it is represented from a coordinate system K^1 which moves with the clock U^2. Relative to K' it is then the clock U^1 which performs the back-and-forth motion, while the clock U^2 has remained continually at rest. It follows then that at the end of the motion, U^1 must lag behind U^2, in contradiction with the above result. But it surely cannot be asserted by the most trusting adherents of the theory that of two adjacent, resting clocks, each lags behind the other.

Relativist: Your last assertion is of course indisputable. However, the entire mode of reasoning is inadmissible, because according to the special theory of relativity the coordinate systems K and K' are not in the least equivalent. Indeed, this theory asserts only the equivalence of all Galilean (nonaccelerated) coordinate systems, i.e., of such coordinate systems with respect to which sufficiently isolated material points move rectilinearly and uniformly. Such a coordinate system is indeed K, but not the system K', which is accelerated at certain times. No contradiction with the foundations of the theory can therefore be constructed from the result that the clock U^2 lags behind U^1 after its back-and-forth motion.

Critic: I perceive that you have thus rendered this objection ineffective, but I must nevertheless say that I feel myself more persuaded than convinced by your argument. Moreover, my objection becomes immediately resurrected, when one assumes the standpoint of the general theory of relativity. For according to this theory coordinate systems of *any* state of motion are allowed, and hence the process considered before can be referred just as well to the system K', co-moving with U^2, as to the system K.

Relativist: It is certainly correct that from the point of view of the general theory of relativity we can just as well use the coordinate system K' as the coordinate system K. However, one perceives easily that the systems K and K' are not at all equivalent with respect to the process under consideration. For while from the system K the process is to be conceived as above, it appears quite differently when considered from K', as shown by the following comparison. [See p. 103.]

It is well to keep in mind that exactly the same process is described in the left and in the right column, only the description at the left is referred to the coordinate system K, and the description at the right to the coordinate system K'. According to both descriptions, at the end of the process under consideration the clock U^2 lags behind the clock U^1 by a definite amount. When referred to the coordinate system K', this behavior is explained as follows. During the intermediate processes 2 and 4 the clock U^1, moving with velocity v, runs indeed slower than the clock U^2 which is at rest. But this lagging behind is overcompensated by a faster running of U^1 during the intermediate process 3. For according to the general theory of relativity a clock runs the faster the higher the gravitational potential at the place where it is situated, and during the intermediate process 3, U^1 is indeed situated at a place of higher gravitational potential than is U^2.* Calculation shows that this running ahead comes out just twice the amount of the lagging behind during the intermediate processes 2 and 4. Through this consideration the paradox introduced by you becomes fully explained.

Critic: I see indeed that you have pulled yourself out of the noose very adroitly, but I would be lying if I declared myself fully satisfied. The stumbling block is not removed, but only shifted to another spot. Your consideration shows me, namely, only the connection between the difficulty just discussed and another difficulty, which has likewise often been raised. You have solved the paradox by taking into consideration the influence upon the clocks of a gravitational field which exists relative to K'. But is not this gravitational field merely something imaginary? Its existence is after all simulated only by the choice of coordinates. Real gravitational fields are after all always generated by masses, and cannot be made to vanish by a suitable choice of coordinates. How could one believe that a merely imaginary field could have an influence on the running of clocks?

Relativist: To begin with I must call attention to the fact that the distinction "real—unreal" can be of little use to us. With respect to K' the gravitational field "exists" in the same sense as any other physical object which can be defined only with respect to a coordinate system, although it does not exist with respect to the system K. In this there is nothing particularly remarkable, as one recognizes readily from the following example taken from classical mechanics. No one doubts the "reality" of kinetic energy, since otherwise one would end up renouncing the reality of energy in general. It is, however, clear that the kinetic energy of a body depends on the state of motion of the coordinate system; by suitable choice of the latter one can obviously make the

---

*Translator's note: The original has U^1 and U^2 interchanged, which is an obvious misprint, or trivial slip of the pen.

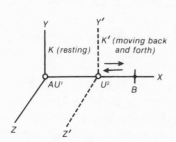 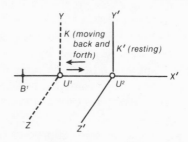

1. The clock U^2 is accelerated in the direction of the positive x-axis by an external force, until it acquires the velocity v. U^1 remains at rest.

2. U^2 moves with the constant velocity v up to the point B of the positive x-axis. U^1 remains at rest.

3. The clock U^2 is accelerated by an external force directed along the negative x-axis, until it acquires the velocity v in the negative x-direction. U^1 remains at rest.

4. U^2 moves back with the constant velocity v in the direction of the negative x-axis, to within the proximity of U^1. U^1 remains at rest.

5. The clock U^2 is brought to rest by an external force.

1. There arises a gravitational field in the direction of the negative x-axis, in which the clock U^1 is accelerated until it acquires the velocity v. An external force acting on the clock U^2 in the direction of the positive x-axis, prevents the clock U^2 from being set in motion by the gravitational field. When the clock U^1 had attained the velocity v, the gravitational field vanishes.

2. U^1 moves with constant velocity v up to the point B' on the negative x-axis. U^2 remains at rest.

3. There arises a homogeneous gravitational field, directed along the positive x-axis, under whose influence the clock U^1 is accelerated in the direction of the positive x-axis until it acquires the velocity v in this direction, whereupon the gravitational field vanishes. An external force acting on the clock U^2 in the direction of the negative x-axis, prevents U^2 from being set in motion by the said gravitational field.

4. U^1 moves with the constant velocity v in the direction of the positive x-axis, to within the proximity of U^2. U^2 remains at rest.

5. There arises a gravitational field, directed along the negative x-axis, which brings the clock U^1 to rest. Then the gravitational field vanishes. U^2 is kept in a state of rest by an external force.

kinetic energy of the progressive motion of a body assume at a given moment any prescribed positive value or the value zero. In the special case that all masses have a velocity of the same direction and magnitude, one can render the total kinetic energy zero by a suitable choice of the coordinate system. The analogy appears to me to be complete.

Instead of differentiating between "real" and "unreal," we shall distinguish more clearly between quantities which belong to the physical system as such (independently of the choice of the coordinate system) and quantities that are dependent on the coordinate system. The obvious thing would have been to require that only quantities of the first kind should be introduced into the laws of physics. It has turned out, however, that this route cannot be realized in practice, as the development of classical mechanics had already clearly shown. One could, for example, contemplate, and one has actually attempted, to introduce into the laws of classical mechanics instead of the coordinates of the material points, only their distances from each other. One could expect a priori that in this manner the goal of the theory of relativity would be attained most simply. But the development of science has not confirmed this conjecture. It cannot dispense with the coordinate system; it must accordingly employ in the coordinates, quantities which cannot be taken as results of definable measurements. According to the general theory of relativity, the four coordinates of the space-time continuum are parameters that can even be chosen completely arbitrarily, and devoid of any independent physical significance. A part of that arbitrariness attaches, however, also to those quantities (field components) with whose help we describe physical reality. Only to certain, in general rather complicated expressions, which are constructed from field components and coordinates, correspond quantities that are measurable independently of the coordinate system (i.e., real quantities). Thus, for instance, there does not correspond to the components of the gravitational field at a space-time point any quantity which is independent of the choice of coordinates; consequently there does not correspond to the gravitational field *at a given place* something "physically real," but rather to this gravitational field in conjunction with other data. One can therefore say that the gravitational field at a given place neither is something "real," nor that it is something "merely fictitious."

The main difficulty encountered in the study of this theory lies indeed in the circumstance that in the general theory of relativity the connection between the quantities that *occur in the equations* and the *measurable* quantities is much more indirect than in the usual theories. Your last objection is based on your not having kept this circumstance consistently in view.

You declared the fields introduced into the clock example to be merely fictitious, also for the reason that the lines of force of *actual* gravitational fields must necessarily be generated by masses; but in the treated example there are no masses which could generate these fields. To this there is a twofold answer. First, it is not a necessary a priori requirement that the conception which is appropriate to the Newtonian theory, according to which every gravitational field can be conceived as generated by masses, be also maintained in the general theory of relativity. This question is once again connected with the aforementioned circumstance that the meaning of the field components is much less directly defined than in the Newtonian theory. Second, however, it cannot be asserted that no masses exist to which one could attribute the production of the field. Of course, the accelerated coordinate systems cannot be brought in as real causes of the field, an opinion which a humorous critic once thought it necessary to ascribe to me. However, all the stars contained in the universe can be thought of as participating in the production of the gravitational field; for during the acceleration stages of the coordinate system K', they are accelerated relative to the latter, and they can thus induce a gravitational field, similarly to the way moving accelerated charges induce an electric field. Approximate integration of the gravitational equations has in fact shown that such induction effects of moving accelerated masses must actually arise. From this reflection it is plain that a complete clarification of the question you have raised can only be obtained when one has formed an idea of the geometric-mechanical constitution of the universe which is compatible with the theory. This I have attempted last year, and have arrived—as it seems to me—at a perfectly satisfactory conception; but to enter into that would lead us too far.*

Critic: According to your last explanations it appears to me that it is in fact impossible to deduce inner contradictions in the theory of relativity from the clock paradox; indeed, it now appears to me not improbable that the theory is in general free from inner contradictions, but from that it does not yet follow that one must give the theory serious consideration. *I do not really see why one must for the sake of an intellectual bias—namely, for the idea of relativity—take upon oneself such horrible complications and calculational difficulties.* That these are not slight, you have yourself shown with sufficient clarity in your last answer. Would it, for instance, enter anyone's mind to utilize the possibility, offered by the theory of relativity, to refer the motions of the celestial bodies of the solar system to a geocentric coordinate system, which participates besides in the rotational motion of the earth? Would one really have to consider this coordinate system, with respect to which the fixed stars whiz around the earth with enormous speeds, as "at rest" and as equally warranted. Does not such a procedure offend against common sense and against the demand for the economy of thought. I cannot refrain from repeating here some drastic words which *Lenard* has recently expressed on the subject. After he reviewed the special theory of relativity, illustrating the "moving" coordinate system by a traveling train, he said: "One supposes now that the imagined train undergoes a distinctly nonuniform motion. If then,

*[cf. A Universe-Finite and yet unbounded (Part VIII).]

through inertial action, everything inside the train is wrecked, while outside everything remains undamaged, then I believe that *no sound mind* would fail to draw the conclusion that it was just the train which changed its motion with a jolt, and not the environment. The general principle of relativity by its simple meaning requires one to admit also in this case that it could possibly have been the environment after all which had experienced the change in velocity, and that the entire misfortune in the train was then only the result of this jolt of the world outside, mediated by a "gravitational action" of the outside world upon the interior of the train. To the question which suggests itself, why then did the church steeple near the train not topple when together with the environment *it* sustained the shock—why do such results of the jolt manifest themselves *so one-sidedly* only in the train, while *nevertheless* no one-sided conclusion about the seat of the change of velocity should be possible—the principle has apparently no answer satisfactory to plain understanding.

Relativist: For many reasons we must take upon ourselves willingly the complications into which the theory leads us. For one thing, it affords a consistently reflecting person great satisfaction to perceive that the concept of absolute motion, to which one cannot assign any kinematic sense, need not be introduced into physics; it cannot be denied that the foundations of physics gain in consistency by the avoidance of this concept. Furthermore, the fact of the equality of the inertia and gravity of bodies calls urgently for an explanation. Aside from that, physics needs some method of arriving at a contiguous action theory of gravitation. Without an effectively restricting principle the theoreticians could hardly venture to tackle this problem, because *too many theories* can be set up, which agree with the fairly limited observations in this area. *Embarras de richesse* is one of the most vicious opponents that embitter the life of the theoretician. By the postulate of relativity the possibilities were so restricted that the course which the theory must follow was marked out. Finally, one had to explain the perihelion motion of the planet Mercury, whose existence has been securely established by the astronomers, and whose explanation on the basis of the Newtonian theory could not be satisfactorily given.

By the assertion of the equivalence of coordinate systems in *principle,* it is not meant that every coordinate system is equally *convenient* for the investigation of a specific physical system; this is already the case in classical mechanics. Strictly speaking, one should not, e.g., say that the earth moves around the sun in an ellipse, since this statement presupposes a coordinate system in which the sun is at rest, whereas classical mechanics does allow also systems relative to which the sun *moves* rectilinearly and uniformly. But as unlikely as it would be to enter anyone's mind to employ a coordinate system of the latter type in the investigation of the motion of the earth, so unlikely would he be to draw from consideration of this example the conclusion that the coordinate systems whose origins lie continually at the center of gravity of the system under consideration, are to be preferred in principle to those other coordinate systems. So is it also with the example you have mentioned. In the investigation of the solar system nobody will employ a coordinate system at rest relative to the terrestrial body, since that would be impractical. But *in principle* such a coordinate system is according to the general theory of relativity fully equivalent to every other system. The fact that the fixed stars circulate with enormous speeds when such a coordinate system underlies our considerations, does not constitute an argument against the *admissibility,* but solely against the usefulness of this choice of coordinates; the same is true of the complicated structure of the gravitational field existing relative to this coordinate system, which would also have, for instance, components corresponding to the centrifugal forces. It is similarly the case with Mr. *Lenard*'s example. In the spirit of the theory of relativity the case must not be conceived in the sense "that it could *possibly* have been after all the environment (of the train), which experienced the change in velocity." It is not a question of two different, mutually exclusive hypotheses about the seat of the motion, but rather about two in-principle equivalent ways of representing the same state of affairs.[1] Only considerations of utility and not of principle can determine which representation one should choose. How little it behooves us, however, to invoke in such matters as so-called "common sense" as arbitrator, is shown by the following counterexample. *Lenard* himself says that no decisive objections had so far been raised against the validity of the *special* principle of relativity (i.e., of the principle of relativity with respect to uniform translational motion of the coordinate systems). The uniformly traveling train could just as well be regarded as "at rest," and the rails along with the entire region as "moving uniformly." Will the "common sense" of the locomotive engineer admit this? He will object that it is after all not *the region* which he has to continually heat and grease, but the locomotive, and that consequently it must be the latter in whose motion the effect of his work may be seen.

Critic: After this conversation I cannot help but admit that the refutation of your conception is not as simple as it appeared to me previously. I do still have some objections in reserve. But I do not want to bother you with that, before I had thought out carefully our conversation of today. Before we part I have another question, which does not concern any objection, but which I rather pose out of sheer curiosity. How is it now with the sick man of theoretical physics, the ether, which some of you have pronounced as conclusively dead?

Relativist: He has behind him a checkered destiny, and one cannot at all

---

1. That the tower does not collapse comes about according to the second mode of representation, because together with the ground and the entire earth it *falls freely* in a gravitational field (existing during the jolt), while the train is prevented from falling freely by external forces (braking forces). A freely falling body behaves with respect to internal processes as a freely floating body removed from all external influences.

say that he is now dead. Before *Lorentz* he existed as an all-penetrating fluid, as a gas-like fluid, and in the most different forms of existence besides, different from author to author. With *Lorentz* it was rigid and it embodied the "resting" coordinate system, a preferred state of motion in the world. According to the special theory of relativity there was no longer any preferred state of motion; this meant denial of the ether in the sense of the previous theories. For if an ether existed, it would have to have at every space-time point a definite state of motion, which would have to play a role in optics. But such a preferred state of motion does not exist, as shown by the special theory of relativity, and therefore there also does not exist any ether in the old sense. The general theory of relativity, as well, knows of no preferred state of motion of a point, which one could possibly interpret as the velocity of an ether. But while according to the special theory of relativity, a portion of space without matter and without an electromagnetic field appears as simply empty, i.e., characterized by no physical quantities whatever, according to the general theory of relativity space that is empty in this sense also has physical qualities, which are characterized mathematically by the components of the gravitational potential, which determine the metric behavior of this portion of space, as well as its gravitational field. One can very well conceive this state of affairs by speaking of an ether, whose state varies continuously from point to point. But one must be on one's guard not to attribute to this "ether" matter-like properties (e.g., a definite velocity at every place).

ON THE PRESENT STATUS OF THE GENERAL RELATIVITY THEORY

I. FUNDAMENTALS

The general relativity theory is based on the following ideas:

(1) As in the earlier theory an attempt is made to construct a model of reality having the characteristics of a four-dimensional continuum, which we shall call "space" for short.

(2) In contrast with the earlier physics, the functions employed for the representation of the material world are required to satisfy those transformation laws of the coördinates, which, *judged from the standpoint of general covariance,* are as simple as possible.

The latter statement expresses the principle of general relativity. This principle represents a purely formal point of view and is not a specific hypothesis concerning nature. For every set of laws, which has any real meaning, may be expressed in general covariant form. Nevertheless this principle is of great

From Albert Einstein, Yale University Library Gazette VI (1932); trans. Professor Leigh Page. Reprinted by permission of the Albert Einstein Estate, the Yale University Library Gazette and Yale University Library, the owner of the original manuscript.

heuristic value. For quite generally non-relativistic theories, although they may appear simple when referred to a particular coördinate system, are actually highly complicated and unnatural when their equations are put in general covariant form. This is true, for example, of Newton's law of gravitation and of his equations of motion. Furthermore, it is evident at once that this principle represents in itself an advance in methodology. For a non-relativistic theory contains not only statements about *things* but also statements which involve the things *and* the *coördinate systems* which serve for their description; such a theory is therefore less satisfactory from the logical standpoint than a relativistic theory, the statements of which are independent of the choice of coördinates.

Regarding (1), I wish to remark that this item of the program is not in accord with the quantum mechanics in its present form; for the latter renounces the possibility of constructing a model of reality. The variables appearing in its equations specify only probabilities, not actualities.

From what has been said it follows that the principle of general relativity *alone* cannot constitute a sufficient formal basis for a theory. The general relativity theory, as developed up to the present, is founded upon the premises:

(3) In (four-dimensional) space an objective significance is attached to a particular Riemann metric

$$ds^2 = g_{\mu\nu}\, dx^\mu\, dx^\nu \ldots (1)$$

This axiom is based directly on the "principle of the constancy of the velocity of light" ($ds = 0$) which finds its origin in the special theory of relativity. It agrees, in fact, with the characteristics of nature in that *congruence* in the infinitesimal appears to be actually realized. (Independence of the equality of elementary bodies, and also of measuring rods, of their past history.)

(4) The question remains, whether the functions appearing in the equations should be everywhere regular (continuous and differentiable), or whether perhaps material particles are to be characterized by singularities. This is an open question. However, I am of the opinion that singularities must be excluded.

II. CRITICAL REMARKS ON THE FORM HERETOFORE GIVEN TO THE GENERAL RELATIVITY THEORY

The variables $g_{\mu\nu}$ suffice to represent both the metric of space (physically interpreted as the content of measurements with measuring rods and clocks) and also the gravitational field. For the description of the electromagnetic field, however, we need new variables ϕ_i, which are introduced most simply by means of the linear form

$$\phi_i\, dx^i \ldots (2)$$

The "gravitational equations" appear as field equations along with the relativistically generalized equations of Maxwell.

$$R_{\mu\nu} = T_{\mu\nu} \ldots (3)$$

The left-hand member of this equation is a "curvature tensor" determined by the $g_{\mu\nu}$ alone, the right-hand member the Maxwell energy tensor. I pass over the favorable features of this theory to proceed at once to a consideration of its defects.

(1) The generalized equations of Maxwell

$$\frac{\partial f^{\mu\nu}}{\partial x^{\nu}} = 0 \ldots (4)$$

as well as the equations (3), which are closely connected with them, exclude the existence of electrical corpuscles free from singularities, as follows from (4) on the basis of Gauss's integral theorem.

(2) The field variables correspond to no unified conception of the structure of the continuum.

(3) The left and right sides of the field equations (3) are related in a logically arbitrary manner (that is to say, without formal necessity). On this account one must look for space structures which contain other structural elements besides the Riemann metric. I shall describe one characteristic of the structure of this kind which I have recently formulated in exact terms.

III. RIEMANN METRIC WITH DISTANT PARALLELISM

A continuum with a Riemann metric may be characterized thus: At every point there is a local orthogonal frame of n-arms (n = number of dimensions), relative to which the Pythagorean theorem holds for infinitesimal regions. These n-armed frames can be rotated independently of one another through an arbitrary angle without thereby altering the Riemann metric represented by them. We shall now assume in addition, that to each direction at the point P there corresponds unambiguously a definite direction at an arbitrary point Q of the continuum, in such a way that orthogonal directions at Q correspond to orthogonal directions at P.

Then the local orthogonal n-armed frames can be so chosen that corresponding arms at all space-points are parallel to one another. Such a space structure may be described by the projections of the arms on a Gaussian coördinate system ($h_s{}^{\nu}$ = ν-component of the s-th arm). If $h_{s\nu}$ are the normalized minors belonging to the $h_s{}^{\nu}$, then the Riemann metric is expressed by the equation

$$g_{\mu\nu} = h_{s\mu} \, h_{s\nu} \ldots (5)$$

The mathematical problem is this: What are the most natural formal laws to which an h-field can be subject? Have these laws any connection with those of physical space?

THE THEORY OF RELATIVITY AND ITS INFLUENCE ON
SCIENTIFIC THOUGHT

ARTHUR STANLEY EDDINGTON

In the days before Copernicus the earth was, so it seemed, an immovable foundation on which the whole structure of the heavens was reared. Man, favourably situated at the hub of the universe, might well expect that to him the scheme of nature would unfold itself in its simplest aspect. But the behaviour of the heavenly bodies was not at all simple; and the planets literally looped the loop in fantastic curves called epicycles. The cosmogonist had to fill the skies with spheres revolving upon spheres to bear the planets in their appointed orbits; and wheels were added to wheels until the music of the spheres seemed wellnigh drowned in a discord of whirling machinery. Then came one of the great revolutions of scientific thought, which swept aside the Ptolemaic system of spheres and epicycles, and revealed the simple plan of the solar system which has endured to this day.

The revolution consisted in changing the view-point from which the phenomena were regarded. As presented to the earth the track of a planet is an elaborate epicycle; but Copernicus bade us transfer ourselves to the sun and look again. Instead of a path with loops and nodes, the orbit is now seen to be one of the most elementary curves—an ellipse. We have to realize that the little planet on which we stand is of no great account in the general scheme of nature; to unravel that scheme we must first disembarrass nature of the distortions arising from a local point of view from which we observe it. The sun, not the earth, is the real centre of the scheme of things—at least of those things in which astronomers at that time had interested themselves—and by transferring our view-point to the sun the simplicity of the planetary system becomes apparent. The need for a cumbrous machinery of spheres and wheels has disappeared.

Every one now admits that the Ptolemaic system, which regarded the earth as the centre of all things belongs to the dark ages. But to our dismay we have discovered that the same *geocentric* outlook still permeates modern physics through and through, unsuspected until recently. It has been left to Einstein to carry forward the revolution begun by Copernicus—to free our conception of nature from the terrestrial bias imported into it by the limitations of our earthbound experience. To achieve a more neutral point of view we have to imagine a visit to some other heavenly body. That is a theme which has attracted the popular novelist, and we often smile at his mistakes when sooner or later he forgets where he is supposed to be and endows his voyagers with some purely terrestrial appanage impossible on the star they are visiting. But

Selections from "The Theory of Relativity and Its Influence on Scientific Thought" *by A. S. Eddington (The Romanes Lecture, 1922), pp. 3–6, 11–12, 31–32. Reprinted by permission of the Oxford University Press.*

scientific men, who have not the novelist's licence, have made the same blunder. When, following Copernicus, they station themselves on the sun, they do not realize that they must leave behind a certain purely terrestrial appanage, namely, *the frame of space and time* in which men on this earth are accustomed to locate the events that happen. It is true that the observer on the sun will still locate his experiences in a frame of space and time, if he uses the same faculties of perception and the same methods of scientific measurement as on the earth; but the solar frame of space and time is not precisely the same as the terrestrial frame, as we shall presently see. . . .

The more closely we examine the processes by which events are assigned to their positions in space and time, the more clearly do we see that our local circumstances play a considerable part in it. We have no more right to expect that the space-time frame on the sun will be identical with our frame on the earth than to expect that the force of gravity will be the same there as here. If there were no experimental evidence in support of Einstein's theory, it would nevertheless have made a notable advance by exposing a fallacy underlying the older mode of thought—the fallacy of attributing unquestioningly a more than local significance to our terrestrial reckoning of space and time. But there is abundant experimental evidence for detecting and determining the difference between the frames of differently circumstanced observers. Much of the evidence is too technical to be discussed here, and I can only refer to the Michelson-Morley experiment. I fear that some of you must be getting rather tired of the Michelson-Morley experiment; but those who go to a performance of Hamlet have to put up with the Prince of Denmark. . . .

It is sometimes complained that Einstein's conclusion that the frame of space and time is different for observers with different motions tends to make a mystery of a phenomenon which is not after all intrinsically strange. We have seen that it depends on a contraction of moving objects which turns out to be quite in accordance with Maxwell's classical theory. But even if we have succeeded in explaining it to ourselves intelligibly, that does not make the statement any the less true! A new result may often be expressed in various ways; one mode of statement may sound less mysterious, but another mode may show more clearly what will be the consequences in amending and extending our knowledge. It is for the latter reason that we emphasize the relativity of space—that lengths and distances differ according to the observer implied. Distance and duration are the most fundamental terms in physics; velocity, acceleration, force, energy, and so on, all depend on them; and we can scarcely make any statement in physics without direct or indirect reference to them. Surely then we can best indicate the revolutionary consequences of what we have learnt by the statement that distance and duration, and all the physical quantities derived from them, do not as hitherto supposed refer to anything absolute in the external world, but are relative quantities which alter when we pass from one observer to another with different motion. The consequence in physics of the discovery that a yard is not an absolute chunk of space, and that what is a yard for one observer may be eighteen inches for another observer, may be compared with the consequences in economics of the discovery that a pound sterling is not an absolute quantity of wealth, and in certain circumstances may "really" be seven and sixpence. The theorist may complain that this last statement tends to make a mystery of phenomena of currency which have really an intelligible explanation; but it is a statement which commends itself to the man who has an eye to the practical applications of currency.

Ptolemy on the earth and Copernicus on the sun are both contemplating the same external universe. But their experiences are different, and it is in the process of experiencing events that they become fitted into the frame of space and time—the frame being different according to the local circumstances of the observer who is experiencing them. That, I take it, is Kant's doctrine, "Space and time are forms of experience." The frame then is not in the world; it is supplied by the observer and depends on him. And those relations of simplicity, which we seek when we try to obtain a comprehension of how the universe functions, must lie in the events themselves before they have been arbitrarily fitted into the frame. The most we can hope for from any frame is that it will not have distorted the simplicity which was originally present; whilst an ill-chosen frame may play havoc with the natural simplicity of things. . . .

If I have succeeded in my object, you will have realized that the present revolution of scientific thought follows in natural sequence on the great revolutions at earlier epochs in the history of science. Einstein's special theory of relativity, which explains the indeterminateness of the frame of space and time, crowns the work of Copernicus who first led us to give up our insistence on a geocentric outlook on nature; Einstein's general theory of relativity, which reveals the curvature of non-Euclidean geometry of space and time, carries forward the rudimentary thought of those earlier astronomers who first contemplated the possibility that their existence lay on something which was not flat. These earlier revolutions are still a source of perplexity in childhood, which we soon outgrow; and a time will come when Einstein's amazing revelations have likewise sunk into the commonplaces of educated thought.

To free our thought from the fetters of space and time is an aspiration of the poet and the mystic, viewed somewhat coldly by the scientist who has too good reason to fear the confusion of loose ideas likely to ensue. If others have had a suspicion of the end to be desired, it has been left to Einstein to show the way to rid ourselves of these "terrestrial adhesions to thought." And in removing our fetters he leaves us, not (as might have been feared) vague generalities for the ecstatic contemplation of the mystic, but a precise scheme of world-structure to engage the mathematical physicist.

III. EXPERIMENTAL VERIFICATION OF THE GENERAL THEORY OF RELATIVITY

In the late 80s Baron von Eötvös carried out a number of experiments in order to test the proportionality of inertia to gravitation. These investigations demonstrated the equality of inertial and gravitational mass, a result which had been assumed to be true, but it took Einstein to show its significance, as we have seen in this book. Since the time of Eötvös these experiments have been repeated several times, and probably the most accurate determination is the one made by R. H. Dicke and his co-workers described here. An even more ambitious project using an earth-orbiting apparatus is discussed by C. W. F. Everitt, among other experiments to be carried out in the future.

The Theory of General Relativity deals with large (heavy) masses and by its nature there are only a number of limited situations in which it plays an important role and can be verified experimentally. Einstein was fully convinced of the correctness of his theory and did not need any experimental proof. Nevertheless, he himself proposed the three so-called "crucial experiments," which for a long time were the only ones known. We give them here, as described in Appendix III of his book *Relativity*.

Einstein's prediction of the deflection of light by the gravitational field (of the sun) was brilliantly confirmed by the solar eclipse experiment of 1919. Since that time several other solar eclipse observations were carried out. Bryce S. deWitt in his article describes the results of the June 30, 1973, expedition which he headed.

For many years the perihelion motion of the planet Mercury had not been accounted for, until Einstein showed that it can be explained by general relativity. The article by G. M. Clemence, reprinted from the *Reviews of*

Modern Physics, shows similar effects for other planets, but it is only Mercury's perihelion motion which is significant enough to be tested.

One of Einstein's predictions was the shift of spectral lines emitted by atoms in strong gravitational fields, say, of massive stars with respect to the same lines emitted by atoms on earth. However, uncertainties in the widths of the spectral lines make these determinations not too reliable. Using resonant absorption of gamma rays, R. V. Pound and G. A. Rebka of Harvard University were able to detect a gravitational red shift even on earth using an internal tower of 22.5 meters. Repetition of the experiments by R. V. Pound and J. L. Snider (also at Harvard) and others confirmed these results, as described by R. V. Pound in his article.

Not only should there be a deflection of light by the gravitational field of the sun, but there should also be a time delay for a light signal propagated from one place to another in the presence of a gravitational field. The development of sensitive radar systems enabled I. I. Shapiro to measure the time taken by a radio signal to travel from earth to Venus and back. Despite great experimental difficulties, described by him here, he was able to carry out the test and confirm Einstein's prediction within experimental error. In the last article C. W. F. Everitt not only discusses these experiments, but describes others, such as the gyroscope experiment, proposed by the late L. I. Schiff, and currently carried out by C. W. F. Everitt and his co-workers. His improved plans for an Eötvös experiment have already been alluded to, but he describes even more ambitious future experimental tests, and "what the next hundred years may bring forth is anyone's guess."

THE EÖTVÖS EXPERIMENT

Nearly four hundred years ago Galileo Galilei demonstrated—by dropping weights of wood and lead from a high tower in Pisa (usually taken to be the famous Leaning Tower)—that apart for the effect of air resistance all bodies fall with the same acceleration. The constancy of gravitational acceleration was tested many times thereafter, culminating in the extraordinary precise experiments made between 1889 and 1908 by the Hungarian physicist Baron Roland von Eötvös.[1]

The date of these experiments has led some physicists to believe that Eötvös' work had a decisive influence on Albert Einstein as he was formulating

Read and approved by Professor R. H. Dicke.

1. Roland v. Eötvös, Desiderius Pekar, and Eugen Fekete, "Beiträge zur Gesetze der Proportionalität von Trägheit und Gravität," *Annalen der Physik* 68 (1922): 11 ff. The paper is based on a prize-winning work for the Bencke Foundation of the University of Göttingen (1909), but was not published earlier, as it was hoped that further experiments would improve the measurements. However, the apparatus was used in the meantime for geophysical work and Eötvös died in 1919, so that his work was published posthumously.

his general theory of relativity between 1908 and 1915. The fact is, as Einstein wrote in 1934, he "had no serious doubts (about the constancy of the gravitational acceleration), even without knowing the results of the admirable experiments of Eötvös, which—if my memory is right—I only came to know later."

When describing the experiment of Galileo it is not always made clear that two fundamental aspects are involved: *(a)* do objects of different mass fall at the same rate? and *(b)* do objects of different composition (but not necessarily different mass) fall at the same rate? One could make a crude Galilean test of the second question by dropping a wooden ball and a hollow lead ball of the same weight and external dimension (to equalize air resistance in both cases). From the experiment one would then learn if carbon and oxygen (the main constituents of wood) respond to gravity in the same fashion as lead, although nuclei of carbon and oxygen atoms contain equal numbers of protons and neutrons, while the nuclei of the lead atoms contain 50 percent more neutrons than protons. If it should turn out—as is indeed the case—that objects accelerate equally regardless of composition, one could then conclude, for example, that nuclear forces, although quantitatively different for light and heavy nuclei have no effect on the gravitational acceleration and neither do electrostatic forces. Although Eötvös made his investigations long before the complex nature of the atom and nucleus was known, he was evidently aware of the importance of testing different substances, since he used brass, glass, cork, snakewood, copper, water and platinum as well as others.

The instrument used by Eötvös consisted basically of a light horizontal beam, 40 centimeters long, suspended by a thin platinum-iridium wire. Attached to the ends of the beam were two weights, one of them suspended 20 centimeters lower than the other. (Although this arrangement was useful for measuring small gravitational gradients in geophysical work, which was Eötvös's main occupation, it made this particular experiment more difficult.)

The principle on which Eötvös based his experiment can be illustrated by considering a weight suspended from a plumb line. In a rotating coordinate system, where the earth appears to be at rest, the mass can be thought of being acted on by two forces: the gravitational attraction causing the mass to fall toward the center of the earth and the centrifugal force—a form of inertial force—tending to throw the mass outward. If weights of different composition are used, the question then is whether the plumb line will always hang precisely along the same direction, thereby indicating a strict proportionality between these two different kinds of force, and correspondingly a strict proportionality (or equality) between gravitational and inertial mass.

In the actual experiment the beam supporting the two masses was lined up facing east and west. Any small difference in the proportionality between gravitational and inertial forces would produce a torque on the beam, making it rotate. Since Eötvös could detect no rotation that could be clearly attributed to a lack of proportionality, regardless of the substance he tested, he reported a null result within the limits of accuracy of his experiment, a remarkable accuracy of five parts in a billion. In order to duplicate Eötvös's accuracy by dropping weights in a tall vacuum chamber having a height equal to that of the Leaning Tower of Pisa, one would have to be able to time the fall of the weights with an accuracy of a hundred-millionth of a second.

A few years ago R. H. Dicke and his co-workers[2] repeated the Eötvös experiment in Princeton in an attempt to improve on the result by using a new and better apparatus. Whereas Eötvös in his work compared the centrifugal acceleration created by the earth's rotation with its gravitational acceleration, the Princeton experiment depended on the acceleration of the earth—and earthbound objects—toward the sun. In this way the experiment contained its own built-in control measurement, which was not the case in Eötvös's work. In principle, two weights are suspended on a beam so that they fall freely toward the sun. Since the rotation of the earth on its axis causes the beam to turn through 360 degrees every 24 hours, any hypothetical difference in gravitational acceleration experienced by the two weights would show up as an oscillation of the beam with a 24-hour period.

The Princeton group designed their apparatus in such a way as to decrease the influence of external effects, thus increasing the sensitivity and accuracy of the measurements. For example, an observer weighing 100 kilograms would have to be 30 meters away if the resulting torque on the instrument were to be less than that of a gravitational anomaly of 10^{-11}. In the Eötvos experiment it must be assumed that the Baron stayed away from the instrument until it had come to rest, and then moved in quickly to read the scale before it could respond to this external force which would create a disturbance 200 times the probable error quoted. In the Princeton experiment this difficulty is avoided by operating the instrument remotely. In addition, the sensitivity to gravitational gradients was reduced by suspending three weights of about the same mass (two copper and one lead chloride) from the vertices of a small equilateral triangle, all three being at the same height. (With a balance of that kind a 100-kilogram man could come as close as 4 meters before a torque equivalent to a 10^{-11} anomaly would occur.) To reduce time-varying disturbances even further the instrument was placed at the bottom of a 12-feet-deep pit not far from the Princeton football stadium and 100 feet from the nearest building, and 1,200 feet from the nearest highway. When an experiment was in progress, the pit was sealed by a four-foot plug of thermal insulation.

Other factors which might affect the sensitivity of the instrument are magnetic impurities which when acted upon by the magnetic field of the earth produce sizable torques, electric fields present in the vacuum chamber surrounding the balance, gas pressure effects, Brownian motion effects, and most important temperature variation effects, as well as other less critical distur-

2. P. G. Roll, R. Krotkov, and R. H. Dicke, "The Equivalence of Inertial and Passive Gravitational Mass," Annals of Physics 26 (1964): 442 ff.

bances. Magnetic disturbances, also encountered by Eötvös, were eliminated by using a quartz suspension fiber and proper heat treatment.

Temperature variation and other similar effects were minimized by using multiple-wall thermal radiation shields and sealing the freely suspended parts of the instrument in a high vacuum. If the correlation between the temperature, its time variation and the balance signal were known, the result could be corrected for temperature variations.

The final limitation on the experiment as performed by Eötvös was optical diffraction in the telescope used to read the scale. The probable error given amounts to a twentieth of a single scale division. As mentioned earlier, the Princeton experiment is controlled remotely and thus the human observer— and with him—any personal bias is eliminated. A combined electro-optical system continuously monitors the rotation angle of the suspended triangle and is able to determine (over an observation period of 10 seconds) any rotation amounting to about 10^{-7} degree of arc. One of the three weights is suspended between two electrodes capable of applying a small torque to cancel any rotation that is detected. In other words, a feedback control system prevents the apparatus from rotating, and the torque required for this purpose is registered on a continuous recorder. Making these and other improvements the Princeton group was able to increase the accuracy of the measurement by a factor of 100, resulting in a sensitivity of three parts in one hundred billions (10^{11}).[3]

It is perhaps remarkable that Eötvös achieved the accuracy he claimed with an instrument which—by the standard of the Princeton one—was much cruder. However, it would be wrong to underestimate the technical skill and experience of a dedicated investigator, such as Eötvös. The new experiment might have shown him in error, but it has not, and consequently Einstein's principle of equivalence has received a firm experimental basis.

THE "CLASSICAL" TESTS

From a systematic theoretical point of view, we may imagine the process of evolution of an empirical science to be a continuous process of induction. Theories are evolved and are expressed in short compass as statements of a large number of individual observations in the form of empirical laws, from which the general laws can be ascertained by comparison. Regarded in this

3. More recently V. B. Braginski and V. I. Papanov, *Zh. Eksp. Teor. Fiz.* 61 (1971): 873–879; translated in *Soviet Physics-J.E.T.P.* 34 (1972): 463–466, using a similar experimental scheme, but a torsion balance in the form of an eight-pointed star with equal masses, four of aluminum and four of platinum, at the points reported a proportionality of gravitational and inertial mass with an accuracy of one part in 10^{12}.

way, the development of a science bears some resemblance to the compilation of a classified catalogue. It is, as it were, a purely empirical enterprise.

But this point of view by no means embraces the whole of the actual process: for it slurs over the important part played by intuition and deductive thought in the development of an exact science. As soon as a science has emerged from its initial stages, theoretical advances are no longer achieved merely by a process of arrangement. Guided by empirical data, the investigator rather develops a system of thought which, in general, is built up logically from a small number of fundamental assumptions, the so-called axioms. We call such a system of thought a *theory*. The theory finds the justification for its existence in the fact that it correlates a large number of single observations, and it is just here that the "truth" of the theory lies.

Corresponding to the same complex of empirical data, there may be several theories, which differ from one another to a considerable extent. But as regards the deductions from the theories which are capable of being tested, the agreement between the theories may be so complete, that it becomes difficult to find any deductions in which the two theories differ from each other. As an example, a case of general interest is available in the province of biology, in the Darwinian theory of the development of species by selection in the struggle for existence, and in the theory of development which is based on the hypothesis of the hereditary transmission of acquired characters.

We have another instance of far-reaching agreement between the deductions from two theories in Newtonian mechanics on the one hand, and the general theory of relativity on the other. This agreement goes so far, that up to the present we have been able to find only a few deductions from the general theory of relativity which are capable of investigation, and to which the physics of pre-relativity days does not also lead, and this despite the profound difference in the fundamental assumptions of the two theories. In what follows, we shall again consider these important deductions, and we shall also discuss the empirical evidence appertaining to them which has hitherto been obtained.

MOTION OF THE PERIHELION OF MERCURY

According to Newtonian mechanics and Newton's law of gravitation, a planet which is revolving round the sun would describe an ellipse round the latter, or, more correctly, round the common centre of gravity of the sun and the planet. In such a system, the sun, or the common centre of gravity, lies in one of the foci of the orbital ellipse in such a manner that, in the course of a planet-year, the distance sun-planet grows from a minimum to a maximum, and then decreases again to a minimum. If instead of Newton's law we insert

From Albert Einstein, Relativity, *trans. Robert W. Lawson (New York: Crown Publishers, © 1961), Appendix III. Reprinted by permission of the Estate of Albert Einstein.*

a somewhat different law of attraction into the calculation, we find that, according to this new law, the motion would still take place in such a manner that the distant sun-planet exhibits periodic variations; but in this case the angle described by the line joining sun and planet during such a period (from perihelion—closest proximity to the sun—to perihelion) would differ from 360°. The line of the orbit would not then be a closed one but in the course of time it would fill up an annular part of the orbital plane, viz. between the circle of least and the circle of greatest distance of the planet from the sun.

According also to the general theory of relativity, which differs of course from the theory of Newton, a small variation from the Newton-Kepler motion of a planet in its orbit should take place, and in such a way, that the angle described by the radius sun-planet between one perihelion and the next should exceed that corresponding to one complete revolution by an amount given by

$$+ \frac{24\pi^3 a^2}{T^2 c^2 (1 - e^2)}.$$

(*N.B.*—One complete revolution corresponds to the angle 2π in the absolute angular measure customary in physics, and the above expression gives the amount by which the radius sun-planet exceeds this angle during the interval between one perihelion and the next. In this expression a represents the major semi-axis of the ellipse, e its eccentricity, c the velocity of light, and T the period of revolution of the planet. Our result may also be stated as follows: According to the general theory of relativity, the major axis of the ellipse rotates round the sun in the same sense as the orbital motion of the planet. Theory requires that this rotation should amount to 43 seconds of arc per century for the planet Mercury, but for the other planets of our solar system its magnitude should be so small that it would necessarily escape detection.[1])

In point of fact, astronomers have found that the theory of Newton does not suffice to calculate the observed motion of Mercury with an exactness corresponding to that of the delicacy of observation attainable at the present time. After taking account of all the disturbing influences exerted on Mercury by the remaining planets, it was found (Leverrier—1859—and Newcomb—1895) that an unexplained perihelial movement of the orbit of Mercury remained over, the amount of which does not differ sensibly from the above-mentioned +43 seconds of arc per century. The uncertainty of the empirical result amounts to a few seconds only.

1. Especially since the next planet Venus has an orbit that is almost an exact circle, which makes it more difficult to locate the perihelion with precision.

DEFLECTION OF LIGHT BY A GRAVITATIONAL FIELD

In Section XXII* it has been already mentioned that according to the general theory of relativity, a ray of light will experience a curvature of its path when passing through a gravitational field, this curvature being similar to that experienced by the path of a body which is projected through a gravitational field. As a result of this theory, we should expect that a ray of light which is passing close to a heavenly body would be deviated towards the latter. For a ray of light which passes the sun at a distance of Δ sun-radii from its centre, the angle of deflection (α) should amount to

$$\alpha = \frac{1.7 \text{ seconds of arc}}{\Delta}$$

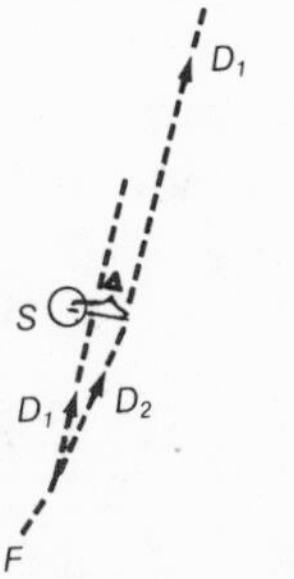

Fig. 5

It may be added that, according to the theory, half of this deflection is produced by the Newtonian field of attraction of the sun, and the other half by the geometrical modification ("curvature") of space caused by the sun.

This result admits of an experimental test by means of the photographic registration of stars during a total eclipse of the sun. The only reason why we must wait for a total eclipse is because at every other time the atmosphere is so strongly illuminated by the light from the sun that the stars situated near the sun's disc are invisible. The predicted effect can be seen clearly from the accompanying diagram. If the sun *(S)* were not present, a star which is practically infinitely distant would be seen in the direction D_1, as observed from the earth. But as a consequence of the deflection of light from the star by the sun, the star will be seen in the direction D_2, *i.e.* at a somewhat greater distance from the centre of the sun than corresponds to its real position.

In practice, the question is tested in the following way. The stars in the neighbourhood of the sun are photographed during a solar eclipse. In addition, a second photograph of the same stars is taken when the sun is situated at another position in the sky, *i.e.* a few months earlier or later. As compared with the standard photograph, the positions of the stars on the eclipse-photograph ought to appear displaced radially outwards (away from the centre of the sun) by an amount corresponding to the angle α.

We are indebted to the Royal Society and to the Royal Astronomical

*From Albert Einstein, Relativity, *trans. Robert W. Lawson (New York: Crown Publishers, © 1961), Appendix III. Reprinted by permission of the Estate of Albert Einstein.*
*[See Part II, section E, Inferences from the General Principle of Relativity.]

Society for the investigation of this important deduction. Undaunted by the war and by difficulties of both a material and a psychological nature aroused by the war, these societies equipped two expeditions—to Sobral (Brazil), and to the island of Principe (West Africa)—and sent several of Britain's most celebrated astronomers (Eddington, Cottingham, Crommelin, Davidson), in order to obtain photographs of the solar eclipse of 29th May, 1919. The relative discrepancies to be expected between the stellar photographs obtained during the eclipse and the comparison photographs amounted to a few hundredths of a millimetre only. Thus great accuracy was necessary in making the adjustments required for the taking of the photographs, and in their subsequent measurement.

The results of the measurements confirmed the theory in a thoroughly satisfactory manner. The rectangular components of the observed and of the calculated deviations of the stars (in seconds of arc) are set forth in the following table of results:

Number of the star	First co-ordinate		Second co-ordinate	
	Observed	Calculated	Observed	Calculated
11	−0.19	−0.22	+0.16	+0.02
5	+0.29	+0.31	−0.46	−0.43
4	+0.11	+0.10	+0.83	+0.74
3	+0.20	+0.12	+1.00	+0.87
6	+0.10	+0.04	+0.57	+0.40
10	−0.08	+0.09	+0.35	+0.32
2	+0.95	+0.85	−0.27	−0.09

TEST OF THE GENERAL RELATIVITY THEORY

According to a telegram from Professor Lorentz to the undersigned, the English expedition under Eddington sent to observe the solar eclipse of May 29 has noted the deflection of light required by the theory of general relativity at the edge of the sun's disk. The provisional value found so far lies between 0.9 and 1.8 seconds of arc. The theory requires 1.7 (seconds of arc).

Berlin, October 9, 1919   A. Einstein

DISPLACEMENT OF SPECTRAL LINES TOWARDS THE RED

In Section XXIII* it has been shown that in a system K' which is in rotation with regard to a Galileian system K, clocks of identical construction,

Letter to the editor, Die Naturwissenschaften 7 (1919): 776. Reproduced by permission of the Estate of Albert Einstein.

From Albert Einstein, Relativity, *trans. Robert W. Lawson (New York: Crown Publishers, © 1961), Appendix III. Reprinted by permission of the Estate of Albert Einstein.*
*[See Part II, Section F, Behaviour of Clocks and Measuring Rods, in this book.]

and which are considered at rest with respect to the rotating reference-body, go at rates which are dependent on the positions of the clocks. We shall now examine this dependence quantitatively. A clock, which is situated at a distance r from the centre of the disc, has a velocity relative to K which is given by

$$v = \omega r,$$

where ω represents the angular velocity of rotation of the disc K' with respect to K. If v_0 represents the number of ticks of the clock per unit time ("rate" of the clock) relative to K when the clock is at rest, then the "rate" of the clock (v) when it is moving relative to K with a velocity v, but at rest with respect to the disc, will, be given by

$$v = v_0 \sqrt{1 - \frac{v^2}{c^2}}$$

or with sufficient accuracy by

$$v = v_0 \left(1 - \tfrac{1}{2}\frac{v^2}{c^2}\right).$$

This expression may also be stated in the following form:

$$v = v_0 \left(1 - \frac{1}{c^2}\frac{\omega^2 r^2}{2}\right).$$

If we represent the difference of potential of the centrifugal force between the position of the clock and the centre of the disc by ϕ, *i.e.* the work, considered negatively, which must be performed on the unit of mass against the centrifugal force in order to transport it from the position of the clock on the rotating disc to the centre of the disc, then we have

$$\phi = -\frac{\omega^2 r^2}{2}.$$

From this it follows that

$$v = v_0 \left(1 + \frac{\phi}{c^2}\right).$$

In the first place, we see from this expression that two clocks of identical construction will go at different rates when situated at different distances from the centre of the disc. This result is also valid from the standpoint of an observer who is rotating with the disc.

Now, as judged from the disc, the latter is in a gravitational field of potential ϕ, hence the result we have obtained will hold quite generally for gravitational fields. Furthermore, we can regard an atom which is emitting spectral lines as a clock, so that the following statement will hold: *An atom absorbs or emits light of a frequency which is dependent on the potential of the gravitational field in which it is situated.*

The frequency of an atom situated on the surface of a heavenly body will be somewhat less than the frequency of an atom of the same element which is situated in free space (or on the surface of a smaller celestial body). Now

$$\phi = -K\frac{M}{r},$$

where K is Newton's constant of gravitation, and M is the mass of the heavenly body. Thus a displacement towards the red ought to take place for spectral lines produced at the surface of stars as compared with the spectral lines of the same element produced at the surface of the earth, the amount of this displacement being

$$\frac{v_0 - v}{v_0} = \frac{K}{c^2}\frac{M}{r}.$$

For the sun, the displacement towards the red predicted by theory amounts to about two millionths of the wave-length. A trustworthy calculation is not possible in the case of the stars, because in general neither the mass M nor the radius r are known.

It is an open question whether or not this effect exists, and at the present time (1920) astronomers are working with great zeal towards the solution. Owing to the smallness of the effect in the case of the sun, it is difficult to form an opinion as to its existence. Whereas Grebe and Bachem (Bonn), as a result of their own measurements and those of Evershed and Schwarzschild on the cyanogen bands, have placed the existence of the effect almost beyond doubt, other investigators, particularly St. John, have been led to the opposite opinion in consequence of their measurements.

Mean displacements of lines towards the less refrangible end of the spectrum are certainly revealed by statistical investigations of the fixed stars: but up to the present the examination of the available data does not allow of any definite decision being arrived at, as to whether or not these displacements are to be referred in reality to the effect of gravitation. The results of observation have been collected together, and discussed in detail from the standpoint of the question which has been engaging our attention here, in a paper by E. Freundlich entitled "Zur Prüfung der allgemeinen Relativitäts-Theorie" (*Die Naturwissenschaften,* 1919, No. 35, p. 520: Julius Springer, Berlin).*

At all events, a definite decision will be reached during the next few years. If the displacement of spectral lines towards the red by the gravitational potential does not exist, then the general theory of relativity will be untenable. On the other hand, if the cause of the displacement of spectral lines be definitely traced to the gravitational potential, then the study of this displacement will furnish us with important information as to the mass of the heavenly bodies.

Note.—The displacement of spectral lines towards the red end of the spectrum was definitely established by Adams in 1924, by observations on the dense companion of Sirius, for which the effect is about thirty times greater than for the sun.   R. W. L.

*[Cf. Terrestrial Measurements of the Gravitational Red Shift later in this book.]

GRAVITATIONAL DEFLECTION OF LIGHT. SOLAR ECLIPSE OF 30 JUNE 1973

BRYCE S. DEWITT

Department of Physics, University of Texas, Austin, Texas

No method for determining the gravitational deflection of light has as simple a concept or as little dependence on secondary parameters as the classical method that makes use of photography during a solar eclipse.[1] The older eclipse observations can be criticized on several grounds, including failure to use identical optics for eclipse and reference exposures, failure to obtain night plates with exactly the same instrumental setup as used for day plates, absence of temperature control, and the unavailability of modern microdensitometric reduction techniques.

The solar eclipse of 30 June 1973 was a member of the "grand cycle" of the twentieth century, which included also the "Eddington eclipse" of 1919 (three saroses earlier and with a rather similar track) during which the first successful photographs of light deflection were made. The 1973 photographs were taken with a telescope mounted in a semipermanent well-insulated building assembled at the oasis of Chinguetti in Mauritania. Electricity in May and June was provided by a logistic support team and in November (when the night plates were exposed) by a gasoline-powered generator.

Technical details of equipment and photography have been described elsewhere.[2] The main advances over previous eclipse expeditions were the following:

1. There was a building that provided complete weather protection for the instruments and a clean working environment for developing the plates.
2. Temperature control for both the telescope and the darkroom was secured by means of air conditioners and special insulation.
3. A loaded tangent-screw drive was used. No manual tracking was attempted at any time.
4. Sensitometric scales to calibrate the nonlinearity of emulsion response were imprinted on the plates just prior to eclipse exposure.
5. Artificial fiducial marks were additionally imprinted. These were used to verify that, with modern plates, emulsion creep has ceased to be a problem.
6. The telescope was left sealed and untouched on site between June and November so as to secure identical optics for eclipse and reference exposures.

At eclipse time over 80% of the stellar light was lost to absorption and scatter by very fine dust driven into the sky by a dust storm in progress. The sky remained unusually bright. Instead of the 1000+ star images that would otherwise have appeared on each plate only 150 measurable ones were obtained.

Both the June and November plates were measured at the Royal Greenwich Observatory, at Herstmonceux, on the Galay II comparator and in Texas on a PDS microphotometer. The plate reductions were made by Burton F. Jones.[3] The final value obtained for the light deflection extrapolated to the solar limb was

$$L = (.95 \pm .11) \times L_E$$

where L_E ($= 1".75$) is Einstein's value.

Although the sky conditions ruined chances for achieving accuracy anywhere near to that obtained with radio interferometry, the fact that valuable data were obtained despite a very bright sky has led to a rethinking of the problem of measuring the light deflection at optical frequencies. Efforts are under way by F. Handler and R. Matzner to see what kind of results may be obtained without waiting for an eclipse! Instead of trying to depend on sophisticated photoelectric devices, they have simply exposed standard good-quality plates to various star fields against a daytime sky background, using the 20-inch astrograph at Lick Observatory with a narrow bandpress. Using optimal instrumental parameters and Mauna Kea Observatory, Hawaii, for purposes of calculation, one finds, with the astrometric data thus far accumulated, that from 75 to 150 plates should provide a determination of the light deflection at optical wavelengths equal to the best published microwave results. A study of results to be expected from photographs taken in an orbiting observatory is also under way.

REFERENCES

1. H. von Klüber, "Determination of Einstein's Light Deflection in the Gravitational Field of the Sun," in *Vistas in Astronomy,* A. Beer, ed. (Pergamon, London, 1960).
2. Texas Mauritanian Eclipse Team, *Astron. J. 81,* 452 (1976).
3. B. F. Jones, *Astron. J. 81,* 455 (1976).

THE RELATIVITY EFFECT IN PLANETARY MOTIONS

G. M. CLEMENCE

U.S. Naval Observatory, Washington, D.C.

INTRODUCTION

It is well known that, according to the general theory of relativity,[1] the elliptical orbit of a planet referred to in a Newtonian frame of reference rotates in its own plane in the same direction as the planet moves, with a speed that is given by

From Reviews of Modern Physics, *19, no. 4 (1947): 361–364. Reprinted by permission of the American Institute of Physics.*

1. See, e.g., A. S. Eddington, *The Mathematical Theory of Relativity* (Cambridge University Press, Teddington, England, 1924), second edition, p. 89.

$$\frac{\delta\bar{\omega}}{\varphi} = \frac{12\pi^2 a^2}{c^2 T^2 (1 - e^2)}.$$

In this formula $\delta\bar{\omega}/\varphi$ is the amount of rotation (commonly called the motion of the perihelion) per revolution of the planet about the sun, a is half the major axis of the ellipse, c is the velocity of light, T is the time required for one revolution of the planet, and e is the eccentricity of the ellipse, if a, c, and T are measured in centimeters and seconds. The fraction of a revolution through which the perihelion advances during one revolution of the planet is represented by $\delta\bar{\omega}/\varphi$, a dimensionless number. For comparison with observations it is convenient to express $\delta\bar{\omega}/\varphi$ in seconds of arc per century. Table I gives the theoretical effects derived from the formula for the five inner planets under the name of $\bar{\omega}'$, based on a value of the solar parallax of 8".790. The last column gives for each planet the motion of the perihelion multiplied by the eccentricity of the orbit; the size of this quantity is a measure of the angular displacement of the planet when it is at perihelion, and hence this is the quantity that fixes the accuracy with which the effect can be determined by analysis of observations.

It is at once evident that the effect can be detected most easily in the motion of Mercury. Indeed, Einstein's announcement of the general theory of relativity in its definitive form[2] was immediately hailed by some astronomers as explaining a previously unaccountable discrepancy between the observed and theoretical motions of this planet. Others were, however, intuitively opposed to relativity, and they directed attention to a small discrepancy yet remaining as evidence that the theory of relativity could not be correct; the relativists contended that the small remaining discrepancy was due to errors either in the observations or in the classical theory of the motion. In justice it should be said that the questions involved are not simple ones, but are complicated by three causes: (1) Observations of Mercury are among the most difficult in positional astronomy. They have to be made in the daytime, near noon, under unfavorable conditions of the atmosphere; and they are subject to large systematic and accidental errors arising both from this cause and from the shape of the visible disk of the planet. (2) The planet's path in Newtonian space is not an ellipse but an exceedingly complicated space-curve due to the disturbing effects of all of the other planets. The calculation of this curve is a difficult and laborious task, and significantly different results have been obtained by different computers. (3) The observations cannot be made in the Newtonian frame of reference. They are referred to the moving equinox, that is, they are affected by the precession of the equinoxes, and the determination of the precessional motion is one of the most difficult problems of positional astronomy, if not the most difficult. In the light of all these hazards it is not

2. A. Einstein, "Die Grundlage der allgemeinen Relativitätstheorie," Ann. d. Physik 49, 769 (1916).

surprising that a difference of opinion could exist regarding the closeness of agreement between the observed and theoretical motions.

I am not aware that relativity is at present regarded by physicists as a theory that may be believed or not, at will. Nevertheless, it may be of some interest to present the most recent evidence on the degree of agreement between the observed and theoretical motions of the planets, which is the object of this article. The evidence is of two kinds: (1) a discussion by the author[3] of observations of Mercury from 1765 to 1937 which was intended to exhaust the useful observational evidence available on the motion of Mercury at that time. In this discussion the relativity effect in the motion of Mercury is confirmed, and some slight evidence of the effect is found in the motion of the earth as well. (2) a discussion by H. R. Morgan[4] of observations of the sun, in which he concludes that the effect is present in the motion of the earth.

In order to render the subject more readily comprehensible, the results are presented here under a different form from that heretofore published and the numerical values have been altered slightly in three ways. Doolittle's calculation[5] of the Newtonian motions, with certain corrections, is used instead of Newcomb's, some new values of the planetary masses are introduced, and Oort's most recent value[6] of the precession is adopted. The observational results remain unchanged. It may be remarked that the effect of the alterations has been to make the agreement between observations and theory slightly worse instead of better, but not significantly so.

THE OBSERVED MOTIONS OF THE PERIHELIA OF MERCURY AND THE EARTH

Unfortunately, the observational material is so extensive and the methods of analysis so complex that it is not practicable here to present any evidence that will enable the reader to form an independent judgment of the errors involved. All that can be done is to give a very brief description of the methods employed, and the numerical results. This is not to minimize the importance

Table I.   Theoretical values of the advance of the perihelia per century

Planet	$\bar{\omega}'$	$e\bar{\omega}'$
Mercury	43".03	8".847
Venus	8.63	0.059
Earth	3.84	0.064
Mars	1.35	0.126
Jupiter	0.06	0.003

3. G. M. Clemence, "The motion of Mercury 1765–1937," Astro. Pap. Am. Ephemeris 11, 1 (1943).

4. H. R. Morgan, "The earth's perihelion motion," Astro. J. 50, 127 (1945).

5. Eric Doolittle, "The secular variations of the elements of the orbits of the four inner planets computed for the epoch 1850.0 G.M.T.," Trans. Am. Phil. Soc. 22, 37 (1925).

6. J. H. Oort, "The constants of precession and of galactic rotation," Bull. Astro. Inst. Netherlands 9, 424 (1943).

of the error estimates, which are, of course, the most critical feature of the entire work; the interested reader will, it is hoped, find a sufficient discussion of the errors in the references.

The term "probable error," whenever it is used in what follows, is not to be understood as meaning the quartile error obtained by multiplying the standard deviation by 0.6745. It is well known that the quartile error measures only the accidental discordances of a set of data, no allowance being made for systematic errors, which in an analysis of a very extended series of observations are likely to be much more important than the accidental discordances. The probable errors given here are in every instance larger than the quartile errors, and they correspond more nearly to what Dorsey[7] has called the "dubiety." I have obtained them by adding to the quartile errors the quantity which, as nearly as I could judge, represents the size of the largest systematic error that could affect the results. It is difficult to define in precise language a quantity that depends on a multiplicity of personal judgments; nevertheless the attempt must be made. By probable error I mean that quantity which, when added to and subtracted from a result, gives a range within which the probability for the inclusion of the true value is one-half; more precisely, the probable error is intended to measure the discordance of all future determinations in addition to those in the past.

The observations of Mercury are of two different kinds: observations of its spherical coordinates on the celestial sphere when it is on the meridian, and observations of the time at which its disk is tangent to the disk of the sun when Mercury crosses the face of the sun. The meridian observations extend from 1765 to 1937 and number about 10,000 in each coordinate. Observations of 17 transits have been used, extending from 1799 to 1940.

The observed coordinates are not discussed directly, but instead the small differences between the observed coordinates and those calculated from a theory of the motions are used. Each of these differences gives rise to an equation of condition, the unknown quantities being corrections to the constants used in the calculated coordinates. These equations are collected into groups extending over about ten years each and solved by the method of least squares. The number of unknown quantities is twelve, one of them being the correction to the assumed, or tabular, position of the perihelion. In principle, a number of corrections at successive epochs to this assumed position of the perihelion are obtained, and the sum of the corrections gives the correction to the assumed *motion* of the perihelion. The procedure followed with the transits of Mercury is much the same, except that the whole series of transits furnishes only two equations of condition because transits can occur only in two narrow regions of Mercury's orbit. These two additional conditions are imposed on the final results of the meridian observations, and another adjustment is made by least squares.

7. N. E. Dorsey, "The velocity of light," Trans. Am. Phil. Soc. **34**, 1 (1944).

Since observations of Mercury do not give the absolute position of the planet in space but only the direction of a line from the planet to the observer, they depend equally on the position of Mercury and the position of the earth, and the motion of the earth's perihelion may be introduced also as an unknown to be determined. Determination of motion made in this way is for several reasons inferior in accuracy to that obtained from observations of the sun, but the determination has some value.

The observations of the sun are more numerous than are those of Mercury, but they extend over about the same length of time. The analysis is simpler because fewer unknowns have to be determined, but the principles involved are the same.

For the total observed rate of motion of Mercury's perihelion at 1850, referred to the moving equinox, I have found, in seconds of arc per Julian century of 36,525 mean solar days, 5599.74±0.41. For the earth I have found from observations of Mercury 6182.0±3.6, and Morgan has obtained from observations of the sun 6183.9±1.2. Weighting the last two determinations in accordance with their assigned probable errors gives, as the definitive result to be used here for the observed motion of the earth's perihelion, 6183.7±1.1.

THE THEORETICAL MOTIONS OF THE PERIHELIA

The theoretical motions of the perihelia, referred to the moving equinox, are obtained by adding together the parts contributed by the gravitational actions of the several planets (and in the case of the earth the portion arising from the non-sphericity of the earth-moon system), the rotational oblateness of the sun, the general precession in longitude, and the relativity effect. The separate contributions are shown in Table II, and for convenience the relativity effect is omitted from the upper part of the table. The discrepancy between the observed motion and the incomplete theory may then be compared directly with the relativity effect, which is given on the last line of the table.

Table II.   Contributions to the motion of the perihelia of Mercury and the earth

Cause			Motion of perihelion	
	m^{-1}		Mercury	Earth
Mercury	6,000,000	± 1,000,000	0".025 ± 0".00	−13".75 ± 2".3
Venus	408,000	± 1,000	277.856 ± 0.68	345.49 ± 0.8
Earth	329,390	± 300	90.038 ± 0.08	
Mars	3,088,000	± 3,000	2.536 ± 0.00	97.69 ± 0.1
Jupiter	1,047.39 ±	0.03	153.584 ± 0.00	696.85 ± 0.0
Saturn	3,499	± 4	7.302 ± 0.01	18.74 ± 0.0
Uranus	22,800	± 300	0.141 ± 0.00	0.57 ± 0.0
Neptune	19,500	± 300	0.042 ± 0.00	0.18 ± 0.0
Solar oblateness			0.010 ± 0.02	0.00 ± 0.0
Moon				7.68 ± 0.0
General precession (Julian century, 1850)			5025.645 ± 0.50	5025.65 ± 0.5
Sum			5557.18 ± 0.85	6179.1 ± 2.5
Observed motion			5599.74 ± 0.41	6183.7 ± 1.1
Difference			42.56 ± 0.94	4.6 ± 2.7
Relativity effect			43.03 ± 0.03	3.8 ± 0.0

The contributions of the planets are directly proportional to their several masses, which are not all known with the desired accuracy. The quantities denoted by m^{-1} are the reciprocals of the adopted masses, the sun's mass being taken as unity, and the attached probable errors give rise to the probable errors associated with the theoretical contributions to the motions. In the case of Mercury each planetary contribution (except that of Mercury itself) is the sum of three parts: the motion of the perihelion in the plane of the orbit, the contribution arising from the motion of the node, and the contribution from the motion of the ecliptic. These last two effects arise from the way in which the longitude of the perihelion is measured; from the equinox along the ecliptic to the node, and then along the orbit of Mercury to the perihelion. The figures given depend on the calculations of Doolittle,[5] but his values of the masses have been altered.

The probable errors of the masses are my own estimates. It is evident from Table II that the uncertainties in the masses of Mercury and Venus contribute most to the uncertainty of the final results; indeed, until these two masses are better determined, the motions of the perihelia of Mercury and the earth can be observed more accurately than they can be calculated. A thorough discussion of meridian observations of Venus would probably give a value of the mass of Mercury with a probable error about fifty percent of that given here. Increased accuracy in the mass of Venus must await the completion of the theory of the motion of Mars now in progress. The most uncertain of the probable errors is that attached to Mercury; de Sitter[8] in 1938 estimated it to be fifty percent larger than the value given here. The estimation of this probable error is a very difficult matter and it may be that de Sitter's guess is better than mine; in this case the penultimate line of the table would read 4".6±3".7 instead of 4".6±2".7.

The effect of the rotational oblateness of the sun is to produce a small additional contribution to the perihelion motions of the planets. The general theory of such effects has been discussed by Brouwer.[9] It is known[10] that if the sun were a homogeneous gas sphere the resulting contribution to the centennial motion of Mercury's perihelion would be 1".2. For the actual sun this value must be multiplied by $4K/3$, K being a dimensionless constant depending on the interior constitution. The value of K is very small for a highly concentrated gas sphere, which the sun is believed to be; Russell[11] has given empirical values deduced from the observed motions of double stars, the more reliable of which range up to 0.02. The latest theoretical determination

8. W. de Sitter, edited and completed by Dirk Brouwer, "On the system of astronomical constants," Bull. Astro. Inst. Netherlands 8, 213 (1938).
9. Dirk Brouwer, "The motion of a particle with negligible mass under the gravitational attraction of a spheroid," Astro. J. 51, 223 (1945).
10. F. Tisserand, Traité de Mécanique Céleste 4, 537 (1896).
11. H. N. Russell, Note on ellipticity in eclipsing binaries, Astrophys. J. 90, 641 (1939).

is that of Motz,[12] who finds 0.006. I adopt the latter value with a probable error of twice its amount, which gives for the centennial perihelion motion of Mercury 0".010±0".02; the probable error is very uncertain. The effect on the earth is much smaller than for Mercury.

The precession is that resulting from Oort's latest discussion;[6] the attached probable error is my estimate.

The probable errors attached to the theoretical relativity-effects correspond to a probable error in the solar parallax of ±0".003.

CONCLUSION

The theoretical relativity effect in the motion of Mercury's perihelion is 43".03±0".03; the value obtained by subtracting all other known effects from the total observed motion is 42".56±0".94. For the earth's perihelion the corresponding figures are 3".8±0".0 and 4".6±2".7. The confirmation by observation of the relativity effect is regarded as satisfactory for both Mercury and the earth.

As soon as the gravitational theory of Mars is placed on a sound basis, the relativity effect in the motion of this planet should be easily detected with higher precision than has been found for the earth.

I am indebted to Professor Schilt and Professor Schwarzschild of Columbia University for valuable aid in connection with this work.

TERRESTRIAL MEASUREMENTS OF THE GRAVITATIONAL RED SHIFT

R. V. POUND

Harvard University, Cambridge, Massachusetts

In the nearly fifty years between 1911 and 1959, astronomers sought to verify by careful observation Einstein's prediction that spectral lines from massive stars should be shifted toward the red, relative to the same lines emitted from atoms in the earthbound laboratory.[1-4] The predicted shift toward the red is exactly that which would result if a photon possessed a gravitating mass related to its energy E as E/c^2, where c is the velocity of light, and, therefore, some of its energy were expended in its escape from the gravitational field of the star. Its remaining energy, and correspondingly, its frequency are reduced and its wavelength increased by a fractional amount $\Delta\Phi/c^2$ where $\Delta\Phi$ is the difference between the gravitational potential at the observer and that at the spectral source. For the best known star, our sun, the fractional red shift should be $\Delta\lambda/\lambda = 2.12 \times 10^{-6}$. Unfortunately almost all solar spectral lines have widths and asymmetrical shapes that render difficult

---

12. Lloyd Motz, "The apsidal motion in binary stars built on a point-source convective-core model with varying guillotine factor," Astrophys. J. **94**, 253 (1941).

the determination of their centers on such a fine scale as this. The predicted shift from stars such as the dense companion of Sirius may be thirty times larger, but the value of $\Delta\Phi$ is relatively uncertain, especially because it depends on the inverse of the uncertain solar radius. As recently as 1959 most astronomers agreed that a convincing quantitative verification of the effect of gravity on frequency, wavelength, or time was still lacking.

The development in the 1950's of improved frequency standards, and their related timekeeping devices known as atomic clocks, raised the hope that sufficient precision would become available to make a test of the prediction in even the very small potential differences available in an earthbound environment. For small elevations h above the earth's surface the gravitational field of the earth should cause a shift toward the blue, or an increase of frequency, amounting to 1.09×10^{-16} per meter. Plans were made to make observations between a mountain top and a valley, but the employment of rocket launched probes and satellites became an even more attractive goal.[5,6] The full effect of the earth, for distances large compared to its radius, should be 7×10^{-10}, fractionally, and atomic clocks had surpassed that level of stability soon after World War II.

In 1958 Rudolf Mössbauer announced an experimental discovery that led to the realization of spectral lines of very high frequency, in fact nuclear γ-rays, that are fractionally many orders of magnitude narrower than any previously available.[7] He developed a technique based on the scattering of low energy γ-rays between nuclei tightly bound to lattice sites in solids, whereby nuclear recoil is avoided. When excited nuclei decay by the emission of γ-rays, they must recoil to provide the momentum E/c imparted to the γ-ray. Similarly, a γ-ray striking and being absorbed by a nucleus delivers that momentum to it, with its associated recoil. If only the nuclear, or atomic, masses absorb these recoils they involve energy losses so large, in comparison with the γ-ray line widths otherwise determined, that the γ-ray emitted from a first excited state and leaving the nucleus in its ground state cannot resonate and excite a similar nucleus already in its ground state to the excited state whereby it would fluoresce. The phenomena of resonant fluorescence and resonant absorption, which had been studied long ago for atomic transitions of much lower energy, with correspondingly small recoil effects, had little utility for γ-rays. Mössbauer discovered that a sharp resonance between emission and absorption did occur at low temperatures in particular for the $129 keV$ γ-ray from a level of ^{191}Ir that lasts for about 5×10^{-10} seconds. He explained the elimination of the energy losses through recoil effects for a small fraction of the events by pointing out that the binding of the nuclei to the lattice allows the recoil momentum of a single event to be shared by a large number of nuclei. Even more significant than the recoil suppression for improved spectral resolution was the absence of broadening of the resonance through the Doppler effects of thermally induced motions. Atomic spectra are usually emitted from gaseous sources and have line widths determined by the first order Doppler effects of their thermal velocities. According to kinetic theory, the r.m.s. component of thermal velocity should be $<v_x^2>^{1/2} = (kT/M)^{1/2}$, where k is Boltzmann's constant, M is the atomic mass and T is the absolute temperature. A fractional r.m.s. line width about 10^{-6}, corresponding to $<v_x^2>^{1/2}/c$ for the fractional Doppler shifts, then would result. In Mössbauer's γ-ray resonance, the same binding to the lattice converts the thermally induced motions to vibrations at the characteristic frequencies of lattice waves. These are mainly such high frequencies that, over the time of emission of the γ-ray, many vibration periods are included. Only the average velocity over that time will determine the center frequency of the line. The spreading is very small because the net displacements are small compared to the wavelength, resulting in little energy being transferred to phase-modulation sidebands. The result is an emission and absorption line of width determined by the decay time of the level and by hyperfine interactions occurring in the solid.

Mössbauer demonstrated the sharp resonant absorption by natural ^{191}Ir in a metal foil of the $129 keV$ γ-ray emitted from the first excited state of ^{191}Ir in a most convincing manner.[8] He mounted a source containing the ^{191}Os parent of the radioactive ^{191}Ir on a turntable to provide motion of the source toward or away from the absorber. The γ-rays of the source transmitted through the absorber were recorded. The line shape of the absorption was determined by varying the speed of the turntable and, thus, of the source relative to the absorber. The Doppler effect introduced by the motion of the source toward or away from the absorber at about one centimeter per second was sufficient to reduce the absorption to one half its maximum value of just over 1% at zero velocity. The fractional line width was thus the remarkably small quantity $\Delta v/c \approx 10^{-10}$, smaller than for any other spectral line then known.

As acquaintance with Mössbauer's discovery spread in late 1959, a project to develop an example of that form of γ-ray resonance with sufficient resolution to allow observation of the effect of gravity in the laboratory was conceived and undertaken independently in several laboratories.[9-14] Attention was focused mainly on two isotopes, of all those to be found in the tables, as being the most promising. These were the $14.4 keV$ transition from a 0.1μ sec first excited state of ^{57}Fe and the $93 keV$ γ-ray from a 9.4μ sec state of ^{67}Zn. The fractional line widths of the resonances ideally should be proportional to the inverse of the product of the γ-ray energy and the lifetime of the state. From these ^{57}Fe should provide a resonance of fractional width just less than 10^{-12} and ^{67}Zn one of 10^{-15}. Longer lived, and in principle narrower, γ-rays can be found, but known perturbations by spin dependent interactions in the solid, as observed in nuclear magnetism, would become important contributors to the line widths. The fraction of the events occurring without recoil or Droppler broadening decreases very rapidly at higher γ-ray energies.

The transition must be fed from a long-lived parent for a practical experiment to be performed. In the case of ^{57}Fe, the parent is ^{57}Co which has a half-life of 270 days and decays by electron capture to a very short lived 136 keV state. Most of the decays from that state emit a $122 keV$ γ-ray, followed by the $14.4 keV$ transition to the ground state. Unfortunately only about 10% of the latter decays produce the desired γ-ray, the others suffering internal conversion leading to the emission of electrons. Cobalt and iron are transition elements which are most often either paramagnetic, ferromagnetic, antiferro-magnetic or ferrimagnetic in the solid state. At the resolution expected, there is as a result the possibility of the splitting up of the levels into hyperfine states as atomic and crystalline fields act upon the 3/2 and ½ spin angular momenta of excited and ground state nuclei. The first reports of successful observation of the ^{57}Fe resonance came from Harvard[15] and from the British Atomic Energy Research Establishment at Harwell.[16] The Harvard experiments stud-ied the resonance of the γ-ray from a ^{57}Co source diffused into iron when it was transmitted through an iron foil absorber that was about one thousandth of an inch thick. The line width between points of half-maximum absorption was about 1.5 times the ideal theoretical value of 0.020 cm/sec based on the lifetime of the excited state; or fractionally 10^{-12}. The low γ-ray energy and the high lattice stiffness resulted in an absorption depth of over 20% at room temperature. Source-absorber velocities well beyond the width of the main line revealed satellite lines confirming for the first example the presence of hy-perfine structure in the γ-ray. Some unsuccessful efforts were carried out by the same group at Harvard to realize the resonance of ^{67}Zn.[17] That resonance was first successfully detected some months later.[18] It was very shallow even though the temperature of liquid helium was employed and the technique did not allow direct observation of the line shape and width. Only many years later did the technique develop to allow realization of that resonance in the pre-dicted form.[19] It still requires liquid helium temperatures and can at best be made only about 1% deep because of the high ($93 keV$) energy and concomi-tant strong recoil. Application to studies such as the gravitational red shift have not yet been carried out with ^{67}Zn.

Although the ^{57}Fe resonance was fractionally 10^{-12} in width, it was felt by the teams at both Harvard and Harwell that it could be utilized to measure the small shift caused by gravity within a laboratory. The basic scheme en-visaged was to separate a source and an absorber by a vertical distance h and determine what velocity of source relative to the absorber would, via its Doppler shift, compensate for the offset produced by gravity. At Harvard, the site chosen was an internal tower, in principle isolated from vibration and noise generated in the building, which was an architectural feature in the design of the Jefferson Physical Laboratory, which was built in 1884. (A previous use of the tower was a study of Coriolis effects in the free fall of objects by Edwin H. Hall in 1903.)[20] The available height h was 22.5 meters, for which the predicted shift was only 2.46×10^{-15}, about 2.5×10^{-3} times the observed line width. It may be noted that the ability to resolve the effect with a source of given strength and absorber of given area, if limited by counting statistics, is independent of h because the linear increase of the effect with h is just offset by the decrease of counting rate, which decreases as the inverse of the square of h. In practice, both groups used a technique that superposed a "modulation" velocity that allowed the transmission to be observed at the sides of the absorption line, where the absorption varies most rapidly with small shifts. In spite of the smallness of the effect compared to the line width, there is an important qualitative difference from the situation for solar spectroscopy. In the laboratory experiment that part of any shift that correlates with changes in the gravitational perturbation can be isolated because the perturbation can be changed at will. The major effort can be made (for example) to allow the whole system to be inverted, whilst leaving all other factors unchanged. This not only doubles the effect sought, but converts the operation to a laboratory experiment, as distinct from an astronomical observation.

The first report of a preliminary result was made in February, 1960, by the Harwell group.[21] They had worked at an outdoor water tower with $h \approx$ 12 meters, taking data for several weeks of that January. Although the result they obtained agreed with expectations at 0.96 times that predicted, with a statistical uncertainty ±0.45, they had not included systematic inversion in their experiment. An oral report by the Harvard group at that time[22] described data accumulated over half-a-dozen inversions, sufficient counts to render the statistical uncertainty less than ±0.10. However, the various runs were inconsistent with such a small statistically based uncertainty and some time was spent in search of a source of inherent instability. As a result, a fundamental, previously overlooked residual effect of temperature was uncovered.[23,24] Although the binding to the lattice site prevents first-order Doppler effects from causing broadening, the well defined mean-squared velocity associated with the lattice vibrations introduces, as derived from special relativity, a time dilation, or isotropic second-order Doppler effect. Accordingly, the frequency of an ^{57}Fe source, or absorber, decreases fractionally by approximately 2.45×10^{-15} per degree Centigrade increase in temperature. In effect its clock slows relative to a laboratory observer as its mean-square thermal velocity increases. Data from a quick experiment fit very nicely with that explanation of the sensitivity to temperature.[23]

With the knowledge of the temperature effect in hand, the Harvard team, by measuring and making corrections for the temperature difference between the source and the absorber, as further resonance data was accumulated derived a result for the red shift in a few days of running.

Their initial published report[25] showed that the effect predicted from the Principle of Equivalence was indeed present and they measured it to be 1.05 ±0.10 times the fraction 4.92×10^{-15} predicted for the difference between the frequencies for the two directions of the travel of the γ-rays. The same equipment was operated for several months after that report and the statistical error reduced to ±0.04.[26] It was very hard to estimate the total uncertainty arising from systematic effects in that first version of the experiment, however.

In order to refine further the precision of the result, the experiment was, with the collaboration of J. L. Snider, redesigned and reconstituted with a new and stronger source, a larger absorber, containing enriched ^{57}Fe, careful temperature control, and several other detailed improvements. In 1964 the new apparatus was employed to extract a result 0.999 ± 0.010 times the predicted result over nearly the same base line. Here the stated uncertainty includes the statistical standard deviation as well as an estimated limit of systematic error.[27] With these two experiments there could remain little doubt about the quantitative validity of the Einstein prediction.

In the same years, two solar spectroscopic experiments of improved accuracy also gave results in agreement with predictions. Brault[28] at Princeton used electronic methods, instead of photographic ones, to measure the line profile of a solar Fraunhofer line of sodium. He obtained a result for the red shift of 1.05 ± 0.05 times that expected. The sodium line had been found by St. John to have little shift from the center to the hub of the solar disk and little asymmetry, probably because it is found high in the solar atmosphere. Blamont and Roddier[29] introduced a novel spectroscopic technique whereby they scattered solar light from a beam of strontium atoms tuned by a Zeeman effect to determine the relative positions of the solar and laboratory strontium spectral lines. In this case they found asymmetries and width changes with position on the sun, but concluded that the data agreed with the predicted shift. More recently, Snider has used the atomic beam scattering technique for a potassium line and reported[30] a red shift 1.01 ± 0.06 times that predicted.

The most recent and by far the most large scale effort devoted to measuring the red shift was carried out by R. F. C. Vessot with collaborators from the Smithsonian Astrophysical Laboratory and the National Aeronautical and Space Administration.[31] This project represents the first use of atomic clocks for relativistic experiments from space vehicles. The clock was a Maser that oscillates at a frequency determined by the hyperfine interval in atomic hydrogen, nominally 1421 MHz. Such clocks have been developed to have drifts as low as a few parts in 10^{15} over some hours in the laboratory. A version was developed by Vessot et al. suitable for use in a small probe that could be projected by a Scout rocket, with provision to monitor its frequency and the probe trajectory from ground stations, as it rose to 10,000 miles altitude and fell back. One of the most difficult problems was from the presence of an ordinary Doppler effect nominally 10^5 times larger than the anticipated effect of gravity on frequency. A special transponder in the probe sent back to the ground a signal sent up from a ground-based atomic clock. That returned signal carried a Doppler shift twice that for the probe clock. By dividing the transponded shift by two and subtracting it from the observed frequency of the clock in the probe, the Doppler effect was cancelled. The rocket probe was launched on June 18, 1976, after many years of planning and development. Preliminary data was reported in the fall of that year.[31] Agreement was found at the level of $\pm 2 \times 10^{-4}$ between the observed and predicted frequency shifts for that part of the run for which orbital data were adequate.

Another, less spectacular, application of modern clocks to measure the effect of the gravity of the earth was carried out by C. O. Alley with the assistance of U.S. naval aircraft.[32] One set of several clocks was kept on the ground while another similar set was carried to altitudes near 10^4 meters in an aircraft for times as long as fifteen hours. Data on the differences in the rates of the two sets were taken during the flights by the use of a communication channel using a laser beam. Integrated differences could be observed after the clocks were brought together on the ground. This experiment confirmed the effects anticipated from the red shift hypothesis with an uncertainty estimated at ± 0.016.

Altogether the effect of gravity on time, frequency and wave length, predicted so long ago by Albert Einstein, has been confirmed by several methods with very good precision. If future tests are envisioned, perhaps they should attempt to measure to such accuracy as to determine the coefficient of a next higher order term in $\Delta\Phi/c^2$. For that it seems clear that only space probes can be employed. The solar gravitational potential in orbit around or on the surface of Mercury, or even closer to the sun, should be large enough and clocks in the forseeable future stable enough to allow determination of the coefficient of a term in the red shift varying as $[\Delta\Phi/c^2]^2$.

1. W. S. Adams, *Proc. Nat. Acad. 11*, 382 (1925).

2. C. E. St. John, *Astrophys. J. 67*, 195 (1928).

3. M. G. Adam, *Mon. Nat. Roy. Astro. Soc. 108*, 446 (1948).

4. E. Finlay-Freundlich, *Ann. Phys.* (Paris) *2*, 765 (1957).

5. S. F. Singer, *Phys. Rev. 104*, 11 (1956).

6. D. Kleppner, R. F. C. Vessot and N. F. Ramsey, *Astrophys. Space Sci. 6*, 13 (1970).

7. R. L. Mössbauer, *Z. Physik 151*, 124 (1958).

8. R. L. Mössbauer, *Naturwissenschaften 45*, 538 (1958).

9. R. V. Pound and G. A. Rebka, Jr., *Phys. Rev. Letters 3*, 439 (1959).

10. T. E. Cranshaw as reported by J. P. Schiffer and W. Marshall, *Phys. Rev. Letters 3*, 556 (1959).

11. S. Ya Barit, M. I. Podgoretskii and F. L. Shapiro, *Zh. Eksperim i Teor. Fiz. 38*, 301 (1960); Soviet Phys.—JETP *11*, 218 (1960).

12. S. Devons, A. J. F. Boyle and D. St. P. Bunbury, private communication, November 17, 1959.

13. R. H. Dicke, private communication, November 12, 1959.

14. Koichi Shimoda, private communication, December 14, 1959.

15. R. V. Pound and G. A. Rebka, Jr., *Phys. Rev. Letters 3*, 554 (1959).

16. J. P. Schiffer and W. Marshall, *Phys. Rev. Letters 3*, 556 (1959).

17. R. V. Pound and G. A. Rebka, Jr., *Phys. Rev. Letters 4*, 397 (1960).

18. P. P. Craig, D. E. Nagle and D. R. F. Cochran, *Phys. Rev. Letters 4*, 561 (1960).

19. G. J. Perlow, W. Potzel, R. M. Kash and H. de Waard, *J. Physique 35*, Colloque C6–197 (1974).

20. Edwin H. Hall, *Phys. Rev.* XVII, 245 (1903).

21. T. E. Cranshaw, J. P. Schiffer and A. B. Whitehead, *Phys. Rev. Letters 4*, 163 (1960).

22. R. V. Pound, *Bull. Am. Phys. Soc. 5*, 72 (1960).

23. R. V. Pound and G. A. Rebka, Jr., *Phys. Rev. Letters 4*, 274 (1960).

24. B. D. Josephson, *Phys. Rev. Letters 4*, 341 (1960).

25. R. V. Pound and G. A. Rebka, Jr., *Phys. Rev. Letters 4*, 337 (1960).

26. R. V. Pound and G. A. Rebka, Jr., *Bull. Am. Phys. Soc. 5*, 428 (1960).

27. R. V. Pound and J. L. Snider, *Phys. Rev. Letters 13*, 539 (1964); *Phys. Rev. 140*, B788, (1965).

28. J. Brault, *Bull. Am. Phys. Soc. 8*, 28 (1963).

29. J. E. Blamont and F. Roddier, *Phys. Rev. Letters 7*, 437 (1961).

30. J. L. Snider, *Phys. Rev. Letters 28*, 853 (1972).

31. R. F. C. Vessot and M. W. Levine, *Gravitazione Sperimentale* Accad. Naz. dei Lincei, Rome p. 371, (1977).

32. C. O. Alley, presented at symposium on Gravitazione Sperimentale, Pavia, Italy, 1976.

THE TIME-DELAY TEST OF GENERAL RELATIVITY

IRWIN I. SHAPIRO

Department of Earth and Planetary Sciences and Department of Physics, Massachusetts Institute of Technology, Cambridge, Massachusetts, October 1978

General relativity predicts that the time delay for a light signal propagating from one place to another will be influenced by the gravitational potential along the path of the signal. This prediction can be tested by measuring the roundtrip, or echo, time delays of signals transmitted from the earth and reflected, say, from another planet. Such a test was not envisioned by Einstein; the means for it did not exist until the 1960's. At that time, it became evident that a test was technically feasible.

Radar systems, developed during the Second World War, had progressed sufficiently by the early 1960's for radar echoes to be obtained from Venus when it was nearest the earth, at so-called inferior conjunction. But for the gravitational potential in the solar system to have a discernible effect on an echo time-delay, the signal must pass near the sun. The predicted increase in the echo time-delay, attributable to the direct gravitational influence of the sun on the propagation, is about 250 microseconds if the signal path just grazes the sun. To test this prediction, it was thus necessary to be able to detect the radar echoes when a planet was on the far side of the sun as viewed from the earth, at so-called superior conjunction. Moreover, the signal-to-noise ratio had to be sufficiently great to allow the echo delay to be timed with an uncertainty small compared with 250 microseconds. Such an achievement was no small feat inasmuch as the echo power decreases with the fourth power of the distance to the target; thus the power in an echo, for example, from Venus at superior conjunction is about one thousandfold weaker than the corresponding echo at inferior conjunction. However, improvements in radar-system sensitivity were being made remarkably rapidly during those years, about a fivefold increase each year. The effects of "compounding" meant that it was possible to carry out the test by the late 1960's, barely six years after the first reliable radar echoes from Venus had been detected.

But other problems still had to be considered. How would one know what the delay should have been had there been no relativistic effect on the echo time-delay? If the orbits of the earth and the target planet were known accurately enough, then one could predict the echo time with adequate precision to distinguish the relativistic from the non-relativistic contribution to the signal delay. Unfortunately, the former is only about 1 part in 10^7 of the latter and the positions of the inner planets were known only to about 1 part in 10^6 from classical optical observations. The radar echo-delay observations, made both near and far from the superior conjunctions of Mercury and Venus, were used both to determine the orbits with adequate precision and to detect the predicted relativistic increase in the signal delay.

The solar corona and planetary topography also had to be dealt with. The corona was a concern because it, too, would be expected to introduce an additional delay in the signal propagation time that increased as the signal path passed closer to the sun. Fortunately, the corona, being a plasma, is dispersive —its effects are frequency-dependent, in a known way. For the cases of interest to us, this coronal delay is inversely proportional to the square of the radio frequency employed in the radar system. Coronal effects can therefore be reduced to negligible levels either by making observations at two, widely different, radio frequencies simultaneously or by using a sufficiently high radio frequency.

The wondrously complicated topography on the inner planets makes the elimination of this potential source of error nearly impossible. However, the topography on these target planets rarely reaches heights (and depths) equivalent to an effect of more than 40 microseconds on the signal delays and, furthermore, can be charted reasonably well with the radar measurements themselves. With echo-delay measurements continued over a long period of time, the orbital, the topographic, and the relativistic effects can all be separated.

The first radar test of this predicted general relativistic effect on echo delays was carried out in 1966–67 and yielded a verification of the predictions to within the estimated experimental uncertainty of ±20%. Later radar measurements, with more sensitive systems, enabled the uncertainty to be reduced fourfold; the result remained in agreement with general relativity. In all these tests, the measurements made near superior conjunctions utilized a single, high (nearly 8000 MHz), radio frequency which ensured that residual coronal effects did not contribute more than a few percent to the total percentage uncertainty in the determination of the relativistic effect.

Most recently, the Viking mission to Mars afforded the opportunity to perform a far more stringent test. Because there were two spacecraft on the surface of Mars, time-delay measurements for signal propagation to these spacecraft were free from the effects of variable topography. Unfortunately, only a single, relatively low (about 2300 MHz), radio frequency was available for these measurements. The effects of the corona, which contributed the largest source of error, were partially eliminated by simultaneous, or near simultaneous, delay measurements to one or the other of the two Viking spacecraft in orbit about Mars. Each of these latter spacecraft contained means for delay measurements at two widely separated (about 2300 and 8400 MHz), radio frequencies on the path from the spacecraft to the earth. Although the data from this 1976–1977 experiment are still being analyzed, preliminary results show agreement with the predictions of general relativity to within the more stringent limit of about 0.2%, representing more than a twentyfold improvement over the earlier radar results.

In the future, significant improvements, by perhaps two or more orders of magnitude, could be achieved in this time-delay test if a spacecraft equipped with a suitable, state-of-the-art, radio system were emplaced on the surface of Mercury or Mars.

EXPERIMENTAL TESTS OF GENERAL RELATIVITY: PAST, PRESENT AND FUTURE

C. W. F. EVERITT

W. W. Hansen Laboratories of Physics, Stanford University, Stanford, California

I. INTRODUCTION

General Relativity—Einstein's theory of gravitation—is at once the most far-reaching and least tested of physical theories. When Einstein advanced it in 1915 he suggested three tests, that is, three effects derived from his equations that were not to be expected on Newton's theory of gravitation.* A fourth consequence of General Relativity, which Einstein recognized but did not like

*[These tests, the anomalous precession of the perihelion of Mercury, the deflection of starlight by the sun, and the gravitational red shift, are described earlier.]

at first, was the concept of an expanding Universe. As is well known, Einstein added a term to his original equation—the cosmological term—to suppress this effect, only to face in 1929 E. Hubble's 1929 discovery of evidence that the Universe is indeed expanding. Einstein then said that this introduction of the cosmological term was the biggest mistake of his life. However, as E. A. Milne pointed out in 1931, a simple non-relativistic interpretation of the expansion of the Universe is also possible. Imagine a shell exploding and sending off shrapnel in all directions. The faster moving pieces will travel faster, and it can be shown that an observer located on any of the flying pieces will see the others receding from him with velocities proportional to distance in exact accord with Hubble's observation.

It seems astonishing that over forty years were to pass before the next feasible test of Einstein's theory was proposed: the experiment with Earth-orbiting gyroscopes to be described in Part III, conceived independently in 1959 by G. E. Pugh and the late Leonard Schiff. Since 1964 other experiments have been suggested or done, utilizing new astronomical observations and techniques of space physics and radar tracking. In this article I outline the history of Einstein's three tests, as well as the new experiments and observations, but first it is instructive to ask why a theory as important as General Relativity should be so hard to check.

Two reasons suggest themselves. One is the unique character of the gravitational interaction; the other may be summed up in the aphorism that Newton was too successful. Not until one hundred and seventy years after the publication of Newton's *Principia* did U. J. J. Leverrier in 1859 discover the first phenomenon—the anomalous precession of Mercury's perihelion—which was inexplicable on Newton's theory. And for many years the significance of Leverrier's result was unclear. The first supposition was that there must be a new planet—Vulcan—perturbing the motions. When the search for Vulcan or a group of smaller planets failed, various ad hoc explanations of the anomaly were suggested. Thus, in the fourth edition of Tait and Steele's *Dynamics of a Particle* (1878) we find the remark, probably due to James Clerk Maxwell, that it could be accounted for by adding a term in $1/r^4$ to the normal inverse square law of gravitation.[1] This, as it turns out, is just what the Einstein correction reduces to in the Newtonian framework, with the crucial difference that Einstein's theory supplies the numerical coefficient for the $1/r^4$ term.

The statement that Newton was too successful may be formalized by examining the magnitudes of general relativistic effects. The focus is sharpened by comparing the very different situations of Einstein's special and general theories of Relativity. Special Relativity describes the behavior of bodies whose relative velocity v approaches the velocity of light c. Effects such as the change of mass and the dilation of time become large as v/c approaches unity and are

1. P. G. Tait and W. J. Steele, *Treatise on the Dynamics of a Particle* (4th edition, London, Macmillan, 1878), p. 383, q. 27.

therefore easy to detect in the lifetimes of swiftly moving elementary particles. General Relativity is another story. The Einstein corrections to Newtonian gravitation are characterized not by the parameter v/c but by GM/c^2R, where G is the gravitational constant, c the velocity of light, M the mass of the source body and R the distance of the observer from it. At the surface of the Sun GM/c^2R is of order 10^{-6}, at the surface of the Earth it is 10^{-9} and at the surface of a ten-ton block of aluminum it is 10^{-22}. The Sun, relativistically speaking, is a small body. For a "black hole"—a gravitationally collapsed star—GM/c^2R is unity, but the experimenter who goes too near a black hole has other problems.

The difficulty of testing General Relativity is compounded by the weakness of the gravitational interaction. To beings like ourselves, whose lives are dominated by gravity, it seems strange that the gravitational interaction is weakest by far of all the forces of Nature, but so it is. The gravitational attraction between two electrons is a factor of 10^{39} smaller than the electrostatic repulsion between them. Even an experiment to measure Newtonian effects, like Henry Cavendish's famous measurement of the gravitational constant G, needs exquisite care to get rid of extraneous disturbances.[2] With the further reduction from the factor GM/c^2R the task of measuring relativistic effects becomes truly formidable.

II. THE STATUS OF EINSTEIN'S THREE TESTS AND OF SHAPIRO'S TIME-DELAY TEST

What is the status of Einstein's three tests? The effect on the orbit of Mercury remains a most impressive test of General Relativity. Its impact in 1915 was dramatic because the predicted motion of 42.9 arc-sec/century so closely matched the observed anomaly, which had been corrected by then from Leverrier's original estimate of 38 arc-sec/century to 43.3 ± 0.3 arc-sec/century. A weak point concerns the influence of the Sun on the orbit of Mercury. If the Sun is oblate—that is, flattened at the poles like the Earth—there will be a Newtonian perturbation of the perihelion motion from it as well as from the planets. Originally any such effect was thought to be less than 0.05 arc-sec/century, but in 1964 R. H. Dicke, following some earlier work with C. Brans on the Jordan scalar-tensor theory of gravitation, suggested that the inside of the Sun might be rotating up to ten times faster than its surface, causing an oblateness large enough to account for 10% of the Leverrier anomaly and a consequent 10% discrepancy with Einstein's theory. Careful measurements by R. H. Dicke and H. M. Goldenberg[3] on the optical shape of the

2. For a critique see C. W. F. Everitt, "Gravitation, Relativity and Precise Experimentation," *Proceedings of the First Marcel Grossman Meeting on General Relativity,* ed. R. Ruffini (Amsterdam: North Holland Publishing Co., 1977), pp. 545–615.

3. R. H. Dicke and H. M. Goldenburg, *Phys. Rev. Letters* **18**, 313 (1967).

Sun in 1968 seemed to confirm this. More recent observations by H. A. Hill and R. T. Stebbins[4] disagree and appear to suggest that the optical shape of the Sun fluctuates with time and cannot be taken as a reliable measure of its mass shape. Without attempting to take sides in this controversy, one may justly remark that the mass distribution of the Sun has never been measured directly, and that the hypothesis that the Sun has a rapidly rotating inner core is an eminently plausible one.

Since 1974 there has been great—and justified—excitement among astrophysicists, following the discovery by J. Taylor and R. Hulse[5] of PSR 1913 + 16, a pulsar in orbit around a massive condensed object (possibly a "black hole"). Strong relativistic effects are expected in this system. The one effect so far measured is the periastron shift, counterpart to the perihelion shift of Mercury, which turns out to be 4.2°/year and is known now to a few tenths of a percent. Although the periastron shift is well determined it fails as a quantitative test of Einstein's theory. Any calculation requires inserting numerical values into a relativistic formula which combines the masses of the pulsar and its companion, both unknown, the orbit parameters, and the angle of the orbit plane to the line of sight, another unknown. Even if the masses were known, allowances would have to be made for the shapes of the two bodies, just as the Sun's shape should be known in computing the perihelion shift of Mercury. The effects are unknown, may be large, and depend on the inclinations of the spin axes of the two bodies to the orbit plane, both unknown. While there is some chance of determining the masses in four years' time when gravitational red shift and periastron data are combined, the other unknowns will remain. Strive as we may we cannot pin much hope on quantitative tests of General Relativity outside the solar system.

In 1968 a new method of measuring starlight deflection* became available through the discovery of radio source 3C279, which lies in the ecliptic plane and is occulted by the Sun during October. The position of 3C279 can be determined with radio interferometers using a second nearby source as reference. It and another set of sources—0111 + 02, 0119 + 11, and 0116 + 08 —have been studied by several observers. Measurements by R. A. Sramek at first differed from the Einstein prediction by 7%, but more recently Formalont and Sramek have confirmed the prediction to within an experimental uncertainty of 1%.[6] Another quite different new technique for measuring starlight deflection, due to H. A. Hill and his colleagues at the University of Arizona,

4. H. A. Hill and R. T. Stebbins, *Astrophys. J.* **200**, 471 (1975).

5. J. H. Taylor, *Ann. N.Y. Acad. Sci.* **262**, 490 (1975); J. H. Taylor, R. A. Hulse, N. A. Fowler, G. E. Gullaborn and J. M. Rankine, *Astrophys. J.* **206**, L53.

*[Space limitations compelled us to omit Everitt's discussion of starlight deflection experiments, which are also discussed in DeWitt's paper.]

6. E. B. Formalont and R. A. Sramek, *Comm. Astrophys.* **7**, 19–33 (1977).

will use a special daytime star detector in the same solar telescope that was applied in the oblateness measurements just mentioned. No results are available yet.

A new test of Einstein's theory, related to the starlight deflection, was suggested in 1964 by I. I. Shapiro,[7] who pointed out that a relativistic delay may be expected in the round-trip travel time of radar ranging signals to planets or spacecraft passing behind the Sun. The delay adds a bump to the apparent orbit. The effect was first observed to about 10% accuracy in radar ranging to Venus during 1967. It has since been studied in data from the Mariner 6 and 7 spacecraft and most recently in ranging to the Viking orbiters and landers on Mars. Many corrections have to be applied to take out subsidiary effects. The best data are from the Viking landers, which agree with the relativistic prediction to 0.3%, the most accurate of all the tests of General Relativity to date except for the gravitational red shift.

Gravitational red shifts are observed in stars. They are mixed up with other effects which limit the accuracy of astronomical checks of the effect to about 20%. Unlike the starlight deflection and ranging experiments, a red shift measurement does not test General Relativity per se, but only Einstein's extended principle of equivalence—though that, of course, is one of the most important hypotheses underlying the theory. A good check only became possible in 1959 when R. V. Pound and G. A. Rebka[8] developed laboratory techniques to measure the red shift by means of the Mössbauer effect. In 1965 Pound and J. L. Snyder[9] confirmed the red shift formula to 1%. A further advance, and one of the most beautiful gravitational experiments done hitherto, has been the sub-orbital Scout launch in June 1976 of a hydrogen maser clock performed by R. F. C. Vessot and M. W. Levine of the Smithsonian Astrophysical Observatory in cooperation with NASA Marshall Center. The results confirm Einstein's extended principle of equivalence to 1 part in 10^4; further analysis may reduce the uncertainties to 50 parts per million.[10]

Thus the gravitational red shift is verified to 1 part in 10^4, the deflection of starlight and time-delay effects to 0.3–1.0%, and the relativistic motion of the perihelion of Mercury to 1%, except for the uncertainty about Newtonian effects from the Sun.

III. THE RELATIVITY GYROSCOPE EXPERIMENT

Tests of General Relativity may be divided into two classes: those checking effects on the motions of massive bodies and those checking effects on electromagnetic radiation (light or radar waves). So far the only effects seen

7. I. I. Shapiro, *Phys. Rev. Letters* **13**, 789–791 (1964).
8. R. V. Pound and G. A. Rebka, Jr., *Phys. Rev. Letters* **4**, 337–341 (1960).
9. R. V. Pound and J. L. Snyder, *Phys. Rev.* **140B**, 788–803 (1965).
10. R. F. C. Vessot and M. W. Levine, *Proceedings of the Second Frequency Standards and Metrology Symposium,* ed. M. Hellwig (National Bureau of Standards, Boulder), pp. 659–688.

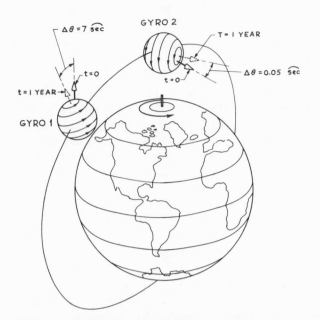

Figure 1: Relativistic Drifts of Gyroscopes in Earth-Orbit

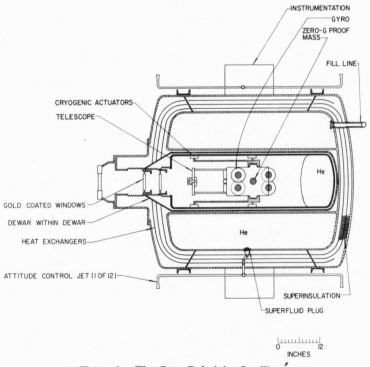

Figure 2: The Gyro Relativity Satellite

on massive bodies have been the perihelion shift of Mercury and its counter-
part the periastron shift of the Taylor-Hulse binary pulsar. Two new terms
come into view when we consider the motions of spinning bodies in a gravitational field. These were first worked out in detail by L. I. Schiff[11] in 1959,
though one had been discussed as early as 1921 by A. D. Fokker,[12] who
proposed looking for a change in direction of the Earth's axis due to its motion
around the Sun. The Fokker effect has never been measured: its predicted value
is 0.018 arc-seconds per year, a factor of four below current uncertainties in
the Earth's rotation and polar wobble.

Figure 1 illustrates the effects calculated by Schiff for ideal gyroscopes in
orbit over the Earth's poles. After one year a gyroscope with its axis parallel
to the Earth's becomes tilted in the plane of the orbit by about 6.9 arc-sec due
to its motion through the gravitational field (the *geodetic* effect). A gyroscope
with its axis at right angles to the Earth's is dragged around through 0.05
arc-sec by the rotation of the Earth (the *motional* effect). Both effects are
defined in the framework of the fixed stars. An experiment to measure them
requires exceedingly accurate gyroscopes and an accurate reference telescope
pointing at a suitable star. Existing gyroscopes operating on Earth have a
limiting performance about six orders of magnitude worse than that needed
for the experiment, but an analysis of gyro errors[13] discloses that *in space*
present-day technology is capable of making a mechanical gyroscope having
a limited drift-rate below 10^{-16} radians/sec, or rather better than 0.001 arc-
sec/year. However, to reach this limit the gyroscope has to operate at a
temperature a few degrees above the absolute zero in order to make use of the
special properties of materials at low temperatures, in particular, superconductivity. At temperatures a few degrees above the absolute zero certain metals
—tin, lead and niobium, for example—lose all electrical resistance. One result
is that a closed sphere or box of superconductor becomes a perfect magnetic
shield, so that a gyroscope placed inside it is completely shielded from changes
in the external magnetic field. Another, to be discussed in a moment, is that
superconductivity provides a new method of reading the direction of the gyro
spin axis.

An experiment to measure the effects predicted by Schiff has been under
development jointly between the Physics and Aeronautics Departments at
Stanford University with NASA support since 1964.[14] Figure 2 illustrates the

11. L. I. Schiff, *Proc. Nat. Acad. Sci.* **46**, 871 (1900). See also G. E. Pugh, WSEG Research
Memorandum No. 11, Weapons System Evaluation Group, the Pentagon, Washington, D.C. 25
(November 1959).

12. A. D. Fokker, *Proc. Kon. Amst. Ak* **23**, 729 (1921).

13. C. W. F. Everitt, in *Experimental Gravitation,* ed. B. Bertotti (New York: Academic
Press, 1974), pp. 331–360.

14. Present members of the Stanford research team include J. T. Anderson, B. Cabrera, D.
B. DeBra, C. W. F. Everitt, W. M. Fairbank, B. C. Leslie, J. A. Lipa, G. J. Siddall and R. A.

experimental package comprising a telescope, four gyroscopes and a proof mass for a drag-compensation system. For mechanical stability the parts are all made from fused quartz, held together in "optical contact" (that is, by molecular adhesion of the quartz surfaces) and maintained at a uniform low temperature. The apparatus is mounted in an evacuated chamber inside a vessel containing 800 liters of liquid helium, designed to maintain a temperature 1.6° above the absolute zero for about two years. Drifts in the gyro and telescope outputs, as well as some other errors, are eliminated by continuously rolling the spacecraft about the line of sight to the star. The roll period is about ten minutes. An interesting feature of the experiment is that the boil-off gas from the liquid helium is used in pointing control of the spacecraft. The boil-off gas is also used in the drag-compensation system, which reduces the accelerations of the spacecraft due to air drag and other sources from their normal level of 10^{-7}g (where g is the acceleration at the Earth's surface) to about 10^{-10}g, by forcing the vehicle to follow the shielded proof mass at its center. The reduction in average acceleration leads to a corresponding improvement in gyro performance.

The gyroscope consists of a ball of optically selected fused quartz 4 centimers in diameter (the size of a Ping-Pong ball), coated with a thin film of superconductor. The ball is electrically suspended by applying voltages to three mutually perpendicular pairs of saucer-shaped plates inside the gyro housing. It is spun up initially to a speed of 12,000 revolutions per minute by gas jets,[15] after which the gas is pumped out and the ball is allowed to run freely in a vacuum. On Earth a potential difference across the gap of about 2,000 volts is needed to lift the ball. In space the potential difference is less than 0.5 volts. Since drift errors from this source are proportional to the square of the voltage, operation in space allows an enormous improvement in gyro performance. Even so, the gyro has to be spherical to about 0.4 millionths of an inch and homogeneous to 1 part in a million.

These constraints on sphericity and homogeneity pose a problem in reading the direction of the gyro spin axis. In conventional electrically suspended gyroscopes the ball is spun up about a known axis and its orientation is read out either optically, by observing a surface pattern, or electrically, from signals generated in the suspension system by the unbalanced ball. Neither method is satisfactory with a homogeneous ball. The solution is to exploit another special property of superconductors—the "London moment"—a magnetic moment

Van Patten. Former contributors include T. D. Bracken, J. Bull, R. R. Clappier, P. Selzer, F. J. van Kann and the late J. R. Nikirk. We have also benefited especially from collaboration with D. E. Davidson.

15. T. D. Bracken and C. W. F. Everitt, *Adv. Cryo. Eng. 13*, 168 (1968); J. A. Lipa, J. R. Nikirk, J. T. Anderson and R. R. Clappier in *Low Temperature Physics LT 14*, ed. M. Crusius and M. Vuorio (Amsterdam: North Holland Publishing Co., 1975), vol. 4, p. 250.

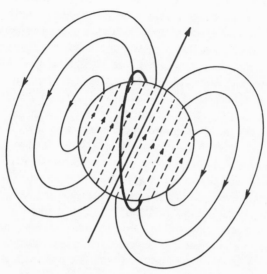

LONDON – MOMENT FIELD $H = 10^{-7}\omega$ GAUSS

Figure 3: Principle of London Moment Readout

developed in a spinning superconductor parallel to the spin axis. Figure 3 illustrates the principle. The gyro rotor is surrounded by a superconducting loop. As it spins it becomes in effect a small magnet. Any change in direction of the spin axis changes the magnetic field through the loop, and this change can be measured by connecting the loop to a very sensitive SQUID (*S*uperconducting *QU*antum *I*nterface *D*evice) magnetometer. With existing magnetometers the new readout can measure a change in direction of 0.001 arc-seconds in 80 hours of observation time.[16]

Low temperature operation of a laboratory gyroscope began at Stanford in 1973. To date we have logged about 1,000 hours of gyro run time at 4° above the absolute zero and more at higher temperatures. Spin speeds of over 6,000 revolutions per minute have been achieved in separate tests at NASA Marshall Center. The work has proceeded in two stages. Up to the end of 1973 we used a large helium vessel, surrounded by two conventional magnetic shields made from "Mu-metal," to develop the gyroscope and operate it in a magnetic field of 10^{-5} gauss (five orders of magnitude below the Earth's field), this being about the lowest field attainable with such shields. Principal credit for this work,

16. B. Cabrera and J. T. Anderson, "Signal Detection in 1/f Noise of a SQUID Magnetometer," *Conference on Future Trends in Superconductive Electronics,* Charlottesville, Va., 1978, AIP Conference Series (in preparation).

which culminated in the first observations of the London moment in the spinning gyroscope, belongs to J. A. Lipa and J. R. Nikirk, with support from J. T. Anderson, R. R. Clappier and J. J. Gilderoy, Jr. The second stage has been to reduce the magnetic fields by two additional orders of magnitude. In parallel with the gyro research B. Cabrera[17] has developed a technique for creating ultra-low magnetic field regions by cooling and expanding a series of superconducting lead bags, one inside the next. Shields up to 8 inches diameter and 30 inches long have been made and kept for 18 months with no fields greater than 5×10^{-8} gauss (seven orders of magnitude below the Earth's field). During 1976 and 1977 we build an apparatus to hold the gyro in an ultra-low field region, and began high-precision gyro readout tests. Recently we completed the first of a new generation of gyro housings and rotors meeting all the tolerances established for the flight experiment.

Many other aspects of the experiment have been worked on. We have built and tested the reference telescope and a nearly full-scale laboratory version of the long hold-time helium vessel for space. To control the flow of liquid helium under zero-gravity conditions a porous plug device was invented[18] which has since been tested in a rocket flight by the Jet Propulsion Laboratory in cooperation with NASA Marshall Center, and has been adopted for the Infra-Red Astronomy Satellite (IRAS) and other low-temperature missions proposed for space. A laboratory simulation of the satellite pointing control system has been completed. In 1972 the DISCOS (a drag-compensation system designed and built by members of the Stanford Department of Aeronautics and Astronautics) was launched in the U.S. Navy's TRIAD I Transit Navigation Satellite; it operated successfully at control levels down to 5×10^{-12} g—more than an order of magnitude better than the requirement for the Relativity Gyroscope experiment.[19]

Almost every test of General Relativity so far done or proposed depends on separating a small relativistic term from other much larger non-relativistic effects. The Einstein contribution to the precession of the perihelion motion of Mercury is about 0.8% of the sum of the known Newtonian terms. Radar time-delay measurements involve corrections for and fitting of 16 to 20 other parameters. The Vessot-Levine gravitational red shift experiment involves highly sophisticated procedures in removing errors from atmospheric disturbances. Modern computing techniques do allow remarkable success in unravelling complex data, but it is a telling point in favour of the Gyroscope

17. B. Cabrera, Ph.D. thesis, Stanford University (1975); B. Cabrera and F. J. van Kann, *Acta Astronautica 5*, 125 (1978).

18. P. M. Selzer, W. M. Fairbank and C. W. F. Everitt, *Adv. Cryo. Eng. 16*, 277 (1970).

19. Staff of the Space Department of the Johns Hopkins Applied Physics Laboratory and Staff of the Guidance and Control Laboratory, Stanford University, *Journal of Spacecraft and Rockets 2*, 631 (1974).

experiment that in it the disturbances are much smaller than the effect to be measured and the limitations come not from external constraints, such as solar corona effects or uncertainties in the figure and rotation of the Earth, but only from manufacturing tolerances on a laboratory instrument. Furthermore the experiment has built-in redundancy: the four gyroscopes are arranged to give a triple check on each effect. At the level of accuracy expected, the geodetic term from the Earth will be measured to 1 part in 10^4 and the motional term to 1%. Also detectable are the Fokker geodetic term from the Sun, which can be measured to 3%, and two other effects: a relativistic coupling between the gyroscope and the Earth's oblateness and the deflection of starlight by the Sun. The starlight deflection appears because there is always one season of the year when the line of sight to the star passes near the Sun. During this time one can turn the experiment round and use the gyroscopes as references for the telescope. With Rigel (the most likely star) the accuracy is likely to be about 1%, though more would be possible with a telescope specially adapted to this purpose. The accuracy in measuring the oblateness term is about 5%.

Neither geodetic nor motional effects have been measured before. The geodetic measurement is nearly two orders of magnitude more precise than any relativistic experiment done so far, apart from Vessot and Levine's clock experiment, which is, as already remarked, a test of Einstein's equivalence principle rather than of General Relativity per se. The motional measurement is even more important since it will detect for the first time gravitation effects from the rotation of the source body (the Earth). It is the gravitational counter-part of observing the magnetic action of an electric current.

IV. TESTING THE EQUIVALENCE OF GRAVITATIONAL AND INERTIAL MASS

The equivalence of gravitational and inertial mass, epitomized in the equal acceleration of balls of different materials dropped from the Leaning Tower of Pisa, is fundamental to General Relativity.*

Several people have argued that an experiment in Earth-orbit could do better than the Earth-based experiment. Operation in space has two advantages. It avoids the seismic disturbances which plagued Roll, Krotkov and Dicke, and allows one to use the gravitational acceleration of the Earth rather than the Sun as the driving acceleration, gaining three orders of magnitude in the effect to be measured. During the past six years P. W. Worden, Jr., and I,[20] with other colleagues at Stanford, have been designing an orbital test of

---

*A description of the Eötvös experiment, the improved Roll, Krotkov and Dicke experiment, as well as earlier and later results using a torsion balance on earth, will be found in the article by R. H. Dicke.

20. P. W. Worden, Jr. and C. W. F. Everitt in *Experimental Gravitation*, ed. B. Bertotti (New York, Academic Press), pp. 387–402.

152

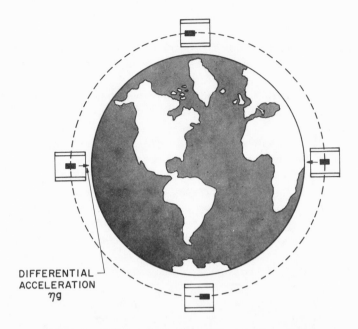

DIFFERENTIAL
ACCELERATION
ηg

Figure 4:   Orbiting Equivalence Principle Experiment

the equivalence of gravitational and inertial mass, employing cryogenic techniques closely related to those used in the Gyroscope experiment. A preliminary laboratory experiment now in progress should reach an accuracy on Earth of 3 parts in 10^{14}, three orders of magnitude below Roll, Krotkov and Dicke's limit.

Merely putting a torsion balance in space is not enough. The difficulty is the gradient in the Earth's gravitational field. Consider two masses at opposite ends of a bar a few centimetres long, lying in the plane of the orbit. Being at different distances from the centre of the Earth, they will experience different gravitational attractions and as a result the balance will be deflected. This disturbance is of much greater significance in an experiment using the Earth as source than is the corresponding disturbance from the Sun in Roll, Krotkov and Dicke's experiment, because the effect is inversely proportional to the cube of the distance from the source body. In fact, while the acceleration acting on any departure from equivalence increases by three orders of magnitude in an orbiting experiment, the gradient effect increases by eight orders of magnitude. A disturbance that was negligible on Earth becomes overwhelming.

The answer is to abandon the time-honoured torsion balance in favour of an apparatus measuring the relative linear displacement of two independently suspended concentric test bodies. Figure 4 illustrates the principle. Two masses, one a 1 cm X 1 cm rod, the other a 6 cm long X 5 cm diameter concentric hollow cylinder, orbit the Earth in a drag-free satellite, and are held oriented in a fixed direction in space within separate, very accurately made, superconducting support cradles. The two bodies are free to move along their common axis; their locations are measured to 10^{-11}cm by a superconducting detector based on principles similar to those used in reading the gyro angle in the Relativity Gyroscope experiment. Any departure from equivalence creates a relative acceleration between the two masses causing them to oscillate back and forth at orbital period. For free-floating masses with a deviation of 1 part in 10^{18} from perfect equivalence the amplitude of relative displacement is 10^{-9} cm.

Historically we have come full circle. Newton's experiment superseded Galileo's by being less susceptible to air drag and giving more precise timing measurements. Eötvös's superseded Newton's by avoiding the uncertainties from flexure in the support and changes in the lengths of the pendulum. The new experiment may be viewed as a return from Eötvös to Galileo, the two orbiting masses being in free fall toward the Earth as were the two balls dropped from the Leaning Tower of Pisa. The advantages over Galileo and his friends lie in having a periodic rather than a constant acceleration, a more accurate position detector, a longer time to make the observations in, and, of course, much lower air drag through operation in high vacuum (though the coupling of spacecraft motions to the test masses by gas molecules is a critical limitation on the experiment). The advantage over Eötvös is that gravity gradient effects are minimized by making the mass-centres of the test bodies coincide. Criteria on centring are discussed elsewhere.[21] Probably the experiment can be done with the mass-centres coincident to 10^{-5} cm, but there are advantages in having them as close as 10^{-8} cm. One might think that inhomogeneities in the test bodies would make precise centring impossible. However, since the main component in the gravity gradient effect acts at twice the orbital frequency of the satellite it can be separated from the signal of interest and used to control a servomechanism which drives the mass-centres into coincidence. With proper design the centring accuracy should reach the measurement limit of 10^{-11} cm; there is a large margin.

A ground-based version of the experiment can use either the Sun's attraction or the Earth's centrifugal acceleration as source, since the apparatus is not limited as Eötvös's was by an imperfectly elastic suspension fibre. In an experiment driven by the Earth's centrifugal acceleration the apparatus is mounted on a very smooth air- or oil-bearing turntable rotating about the vertical with a period of 30 minutes to an hour. It has several advantages. Although Roll, Krotkov and Dicke escaped one difficulty by using the Sun as source they ran into others, because disturbances from Earth-tides, temperature variations and people entering and leaving the building, all have the same 24 hour period as the effect to be measured. These are eliminated in the rotating experiment, and

21. P. W. Worden, Jr., "A Cryogenic Test of the Equivalence Principle," Ph.D. thesis (Stanford University, March 1976), pp. 32ff.

the driving acceleration is larger. With either source the apparatus is appreciably less sensitive to seismic noise than a torsion balance.

We began building the laboratory apparatus in 1973 and have now brought it into operation. It has required the development of new high-precision superconducting magnetic bearings, completed this year, position readouts and a sophisticated controller and data encoder to keep the test masses centred and process the signals. Some equivalence principle data have already been obtained; we expect to improve it considerably during 1979 but need at least three years before reaching the limiting accuracy of 3 parts in 10^{14} on Earth. Since we have not yet mounted the apparatus on a turntable we are limited at present to using the Sun as source. The orbital experiment has been identified in the current NASA Five Year Plan as a possible candidate for flight mission status.

One other exceptionally interesting test of equivalence is the study of the "Nordvedt effect" by laser ranging measurement between the Earth and the Moon. The Earth, being held together by gravitational forces, has a gravitational self-energy corresponding to 1 part in 10^9 of its mass. In 1968, K. Nordvedt[22] discovered that in certain gravitational theories which satisfy equivalence in the ordinary sense, the Earth-Moon system will show an apparent violation due to the Earth's gravitational self-energy such that there will be a twice-monthly oscillation in distance between the two bodies as they rotate in the field of the Sun. For the Brans-Dicke theory, in the form favoured by Dicke, the expected oscillation was quite large, about ten metres. Accurate laser ranging to the Moon has been possible for seven years now through the use of reflectors planted by the Apollo astronauts and in one of the Russian landings. Results of a search for the Norvedt effect were announced in 1977.[23] Nothing was visible at the 30 cm limit of the measurement; the equivalence of gravitational and inertial mass for the different materials of Earth and Moon was verified to a few parts in 10^{11}, the level reached by Roll, Krotkov and Dicke for gold and aluminum test masses.

V. SOME OTHER EXPERIMENTS ON GENERAL RELATIVITY

Of other experiments on General Relativity the most important is the search for gravitational waves. According to the theory, gravitational action can propagate as waves with properties similar to but not quite identical with radio waves. Einstein derived the propagation equations as early as 1916, but not until the pioneering work of J. Weber, begun in 1959, was there any attempt to detect gravitational radiation experimentally.*

22. K. Nordvedt, *Phys. Rev. Letters, 170,* 1186–1187 (1968).
23. J. G. Williams et al., "The New Test of the Equivalence Principle from Lunar Laser Ranging," preprint from JPL, Pasadena and other institutions.
    *[A discussion of gravitational waves and a description of Weber's apparatus and experiments are given in Part VI.]

Weber's observations started a flood of theoretical and experimental research. Seven experimental groups have operated gravitational antennas similar to Weber's, and more are on the way, but none has confirmed the original discovery. Theorists have balked at finding sources for the pulses which would require the annihilation each year from the galaxy of material amounting to a hundred times the mass of the Sun. On the other hand appreciable amounts of gravitational radiation should be released through the collapse of stars and capture of steller material by black holes and neutron stars. The ideal would be to correlate gravitational wave observations with visible supernovae following the collapse of a star. Observations on 408 galaxies over the past thirty or so years give an estimated average of 3.2 events per year detectable in an apparatus having a sensitivity six orders of magnitude higher than Weber's bar.

Various ideas, more or less exotic, have been put forward for better detectors. Research teams at Stanford, Louisiana State University and the University of Rome are building experiments with large aluminum bars similar to Weber's, cooled to liquid helium temperatures, and superconducting position detectors having much in common with those used in the Relativity Gyroscope and orbiting equivalence principle experiments. Research teams at Moscow State University, the University of Rochester, New York, and the University of Regina, Saskatchewan, plan to use large single crystals of quartz or sapphire, which though smaller than the aluminum bars have better mechanical properties. The choice between aluminum and single crystal bars depends on technical considerations of which the most important is converting the mechanical signal into an electrical signal and matching it into a low noise amplifier.

The Weber bar has an inherent shortcoming in that it is poorly matched to the incoming gravitational radiation. Its sensitivity is proportional to the ratio $v_s{}^2/c^2$ where c is the velocity of light and v_s the velocity of sound in the bar, and v_s/c is a very small number—about 10^{-5}. Much higher sensitivity might be achieved by having two separate massive bodies between which the distance is measured by optical or radio means so that the ratio v_s/c is replaced by 1. One suggestion, first investigated by R. Weiss, is to measure the distance between two bodies on the Earth with a laser interferometer. Several groups have worked on laser detectors; the problem is isolation of two independently suspended masses from ground vibrations, a far more difficult task than isolating Weber's bar. Another suggestion, due to A. J. Anderson[24] is to search for gravity waves of very low frequency by radar ranging to spacecraft. The distance measurement is many orders of magnitude less accurate than in laser interferometry between laboratory objects, but this is compensated for by the enormous increase in working distance. A. J. Anderson searched unsuccessfully for gravitational wave effects in data from Mariner 9; since then, the analysis has been carried further by J. D. Anderson, F. Estabrook and

24. A. J. Anderson, *Nature 229*, 547 (1971).

H. Wahlquist from the Jet Propulsion Laboratory, and more experiments are planned.

Gravitational radiation is more a consequence than a test of General Relativity. Some possibility does exist for applying it to distinguish different theories of gravity through the state of polarization of the waves, but its chief interest, if detected, will be in opening a new window on the heavens. Of other new ideas the most ambitious are a series of proposals by V. B. Braginsky, C. M. Caves and K. S. Thorne[25] for generating and detecting relativistic effects in the laboratory in experiments with torsion balances, large crystals and superconducting cavities. One is based on measuring the force between a spinning body suspended from a torsion balance and a rapidly rotating one-ton flywheel. According to General Relativity two bodies rotating in opposite senses experience an attraction over and above the ordinary Newtonian attraction between them. The effect is exceedingly small, about fourteen orders of magnitude smaller than the Newtonian force, but Braginsky, Caves and Thorne have conceived an ingenious way of enhancing it by making the driving force resonate with the natural period of oscillation of the torsion balance. Another experiment briefly discussed by the same authors, and more thoroughly by R. L. Ritter,[26] is to apply a torsion balance to look for changes in the gravitational constant with time. According to a hypothesis advanced in 1935 by P. A. M. Dirac the gravitational attraction between two bodies varies universally with the age of the Universe and should therefore decrease by about 1 part in 10^{11} per year. In General Relativity the gravitational constant is independent of time, but Dirac recently has shown how his hypothesis and Einstein's theory may be made compatible.[27]

In my view, despite the ingenuity of Braginsky, Caves and Thorne's suggestions, the effects they discuss remain many orders of magnitude beyond the limit of present-day laboratory experimentation. Seismic noise is devastating. The relativistic contribution to the acceleration between the flywheel and the suspended spinning body is 10^{-22}g. Roll, Krotkov and Dicke were in deep trouble applying a torsion balance to measure accelerations of 10^{-14}g, and although the new equivalence principle experiment described earlier appears capable of discriminating 10^{-17}g that still leaves five orders of magnitude to go.

More promising are experiments in space. One that seems feasible is a measurement of the relativistic drag of the rotating Earth on the plane of a satellite in orbit over the poles. This effect, first investigated by J. Lense and M. Thirring[28] in 1918, causes a westward drift of the orbit plane as measured at the Earth's surface amounting to a displacement of 5.9 metres per year. It

25. V. B. Braginsky, C. M. Caves and K. S. Thorne, *Phys. Rev. D. 15*, 2047–2068 (1977).

26. R. L. Ritter, *On the Measurement of Cosmological Variations at the Gravitational Constant*, ed. L. Halpern (Gainesville, University Presses of Florida, 1978), pp. 29–70.

27. P. A. M. Dirac, Ibid., pp. 3–20.

28. J. Lense and M. Thirring, *Phys. Zeits. 19*, 156 (1918).

cannot be detected with a single satellite because the perturbations from the Sun and Moon, as well as from irregularities in the Earth's shape, cause displacements of several thousands of metres with uncertainties considerably larger than the effect to be measured. However, R. A. Van Patten and I,[29] in collaboration with J. V. Breakwell and D. Schaechter, have shown that the disturbances can be largely computed out in an experiment with two satellites in nearly equal and opposite polar orbits if the distance between the two satellites is measured each time they pass by Doppler ranging techniques.

Another experiment, even more interesting, would be to look for the spin-spin attraction between two bodies, not by rotating a flywheel in the laboratory as Braginsky, Caves and Thorne suggest, but by using the Earth as the rotating source body.[30] It would use an apparatus similar to the equivalence principle experiment of Figure 4, but with the two test bodies aligned with their common axis parallel to the Earth's axis and spinning at high speed in opposite senses. One would be attracted, the other repelled, and the experiment could consist in looking for a differential motion between them at orbit period. Working in space gets rid of seismic noise and also cancels the large Newtonian acceleration which is such an awkward factor in the Earth-based experiment. The magnitude of the effect depends on the size and speed of the bodies; for an object 50 centimeters across it could be as high as $10^{-17}g$, corresponding to an apparent violation of equivalence at 1 part in 10^{17}.

We may reflect that it was not until 1798, one hundred and fifty-six years after Newton's birth and one hundred and eleven years after the publication of his *Principia,* that Henry Cavendish measured the gravitational attraction between two bodies in the laboratory in what I have described elsewhere as "the first modern physics experiment."[31] Today, one hundred years after Einstein's birth and sixty-four years after the publication of his theory of gravity, experimenters are just beginning to come to grips with the tasks he set before them. What the next hundred years may bring forth is anyone's guess.

29. R. A. Van Patten and C. W. F. Everitt, *Cel. Mech. 13,* 429–447 (1976).

30. C. W. F. Everitt, *Proceedings of the International School on General Relativistic Effects in Physics and Astrophysics: Experiments and Theory,* ed. J. Ehlers (Munich: Max Planck Institut, 1977): pp. 104–120.

31. C. W. F. Everitt, "Gravitation, Relativity and Precise Experimentation," p. 546. (See n 2.)

IV. SIDELIGHTS ON RELATIVITY

The following parts will be devoted to various applications of relativity and its generalization, but we also want to bring together here some sidelights which cannot be classified readily. The first of these is a lecture delivered by Einstein before the Prussian Academy of Science showing the close connection between geometry and relativity. This is followed by the foreword written for Max Jammer's book *Concept of Space*. The famous article "Space-Time" from the *Encyclopaedia Britannica* shows the fundamental change brought by the theory of relativity in the conception of space-time. Not so well known is Einstein and Rosen's discussion of the particle problem in the general theory of relativity. In this excerpt from an article in the *Journal of the Franklin Institute* Einstein tries to show that singularity-free solutions of the field equations can be interpreted as particles. Although this hope was not fulfilled, the solutions found were important in interpreting the so-called Schwarzschild singularity.

On a lighter note we include "Mercer Street and Other Memories," edited by J. A. Wheeler, consisting of various impressions of a visit to Einstein in 1953 by Wheeler and some of his students, as well as an imaginary conversation with Albert Einstein. This part is closed most fittingly by some personal observations of Professor John L. Synge, doyen of the general relativity theory.

GEOMETRY AND EXPERIENCE

One reason why mathematics enjoys special esteem, above all other sciences, is that its propositions are absolutely certain and indisputable, while

Lecture before the Prussian Academy of Science, January 27, 1921. The last part appeared first in a reprint by Springer, Berlin, 1921. English translation from Ideas and Opinions, *(New York: Crown Publishers, 1954). Reprinted by permission of the publisher and the Estate of Albert Einstein.*

those of all other sciences are to some extent debatable and in constant danger of being overthrown by newly discovered facts. In spite of this, the investigator in another department of science would not need to envy the mathematician if the propositions of mathematics referred to objects of our mere imagination, and not to objects of reality. For it cannot occasion surprise that different persons should arrive at the same logical conclusions when they have already agreed upon the fundamental propositions (axioms), as well as the methods by which other propositions are to be deduced therefrom. But there is another reason for the high repute of mathematics, in that it is mathematics which affords the exact natural sciences a certain measure of certainty, to which without mathematics they could not attain.

At this point an enigma presents itself which in all ages has agitated inquiring minds. How can it be that mathematics, being after all a product of human thought which is independent of experience, is so admirably appropriate to the objects of reality? Is human reason, then, without experience, merely by taking thought, able to fathom the properties of real things?

In my opinion the answer to this question is, briefly, this: as far as the propositions of mathematics refer to reality, they are not certain; and as far as they are certain, they do not refer to reality. It seems to me that complete clarity as to this state of things became common property only through that trend in mathematics which is known by the name of "axiomatics." The progress achieved by axiomatics consists in its having neatly separated the logical-formal from its objective or intuitive content; according to axiomatics the logical-formal alone forms the subject matter of mathematics, which is not concerned with the intuitive or other content associated with the logical-formal.

Let us for a moment consider from this point of view any axiom of geometry, for instance, the following: through two points in space there always passes one and only one straight line. How is this axiom to be interpreted in the older sense and in the more modern sense?

The older interpretation: everyone knows what a straight line is, and what a point is. Whether this knowledge springs from an ability of the human mind or from experience, from some cooperation of the two or from some other source, is not for the mathematician to decide. He leaves the question to the philosopher. Being based upon this knowledge, which precedes all mathematics, the axiom stated above is, like all other axioms, self-evident; that is, it is the expression of a part of this *a priori* knowledge.

The more modern interpretation: geometry treats of objects which are denoted by the words straight line, point, etc. No knowledge or intuition of these objects is assumed but only the validity of the axioms, such as the one stated above, which are to be taken in a purely formal sense, i.e., as void of all content of intuition or experience. These axioms are free creations of the human mind. All other propositions of geometry are logical inferences from the axioms (which are to be taken in the nominalistic sense only). The axioms *define* the objects of which geometry treats. Schlick in his book on epistemology has therefore characterized axioms very aptly as "implicit definitions."

This view of axioms, advocated by modern axiomatics, purges mathematics of all extraneous elements, and thus dispels the mystic obscurity which formerly surrounded the basis of mathematics. But such an expurgated exposition of mathematics makes it also evident that mathematics as such cannot predicate anything about objects of our intuition or real objects. In axiomatic geometry the words "point," "straight line," etc., stand only for empty conceptual schemata. That which gives them content is not relevant to mathematics.

Yet on the other hand it is certain that mathematics generally, and particularly geometry, owes its existence to the need which was felt of learning something about the behavior of real objects. The very word geometry, which, of course, means earth-measuring, proves this. For earth-measuring has to do with the possibilities of the disposition of certain natural objects with respect to one another, namely, with parts of the earth, measuring-lines, measuring-wands, etc. It is clear that the system of concepts of axiomatic geometry alone cannot make any assertions as to the behavior of real objects of this kind, which we will call practically-rigid bodies. To be able to make such assertions, geometry must be stripped of its merely logical-formal character by the coordination of real objects of experience with the empty conceptual schemata of axiomatic geometry. To accomplish this, we need only add the proposition: solid bodies are related, with respect to their possible dispositions, as are bodies in Euclidean geometry of three dimensions. Then the propositions of Euclid contain affirmations as to the behavior of practically-rigid bodies.

Geometry thus completed is evidently a natural science; we may in fact regard it as the most ancient branch of physics. Its affirmations rest essentially on induction from experience, but not on logical inferences only. We will call this completed geometry "practical geometry," and shall distinguish it in what follows from "purely axiomatic geometry." The question whether the practical geometry of the universe is Euclidean or not has a clear meaning, and its answer can only be furnished by experience. All length-measurements in physics constitute practical geometry in this sense; so, too, do geodetic and astronomical length measurements, if one utilizes the empirical law that light is propagated in a straight line, and indeed in a straight line in the sense of practical geometry.

I attach special importance to the view of geometry which I have just set forth, because without it I should have been unable to formulate the theory of relativity. Without it the following reflection would have been impossible: in a system of reference rotating relatively to an inertial system, the laws of disposition of rigid bodies do not correspond to the rules of Euclidean geometry on account of the Lorentz contraction; thus if we admit non-inertial systems on an equal footing, we must abandon Euclidean geometry. Without the above interpretation the decisive step in the transition to generally covariant equations would certainly not have been taken. If we reject the relation between the body of axiomatic Euclidean geometry and the practically-rigid body of reality, we readily arrive at the following view, which was entertained by that acute and profound thinker, H. Poincaré: Euclidean geometry is distinguished above all other conceivable axiomatic geometries by its simplicity. Now since axiomatic geometry by itself contains no assertions as to the reality which can be experienced, but can do so only in combination with physical laws, it should be possible and reasonable—whatever may be the nature of reality—to retain Euclidean geometry. For if contradictions between theory and experience manifest themselves, we should rather decide to change physical laws than to change axiomatic Euclidean geometry. If we reject the relation between the practically-rigid body and geometry, we shall indeed not easily free ourselves from the convention that Euclidean geometry is to be retained as the simplest.

Why is the equivalence of the practically-rigid body and the body of geometry—which suggests itself so readily—rejected by Poincaré and other investigators? Simply because under closer inspection the real solid bodies in nature are not rigid, because their geometrical behavior, that is, their possibilities of relative disposition, depend upon temperature, external forces, etc. Thus the original, immediate relation between geometry and physical reality appears destroyed, and we feel impelled toward the following more general view, which characterizes Poincaré's standpoint. Geometry (G) predicates nothing about the behavior of real things, but only geometry together with the totality (P) of physical laws can do so. Using symbols, we may say that only the sum of (G) + (P) is subject to experimental verification. Thus (G) may be chosen arbitrarily, and also parts of (P); all these laws are conventions. All that is necessary to avoid contradictions is to choose the remainder of (P) so that (G) and the whole of (P) are together in accord with experience. Envisaged in this way, axiomatic geometry and the part of natural law which has been given a conventional status appear as epistemologically equivalent.

Sub specie acterni. Poincaré, in my opinion, is right. The idea of the measuring-rod and the idea of the clock coordinated with it in the theory of relativity do not find their exact correspondence in the real world. It is also clear that the solid body and the clock do not in the conceptual edifice of physics play the part of irreducible elements, but that of composite structures, which must not play any independent part in theoretical physics. But it is my conviction that in the present stage of development of theoretical physics these concepts must still be employed as independent concepts; for we are still far from possessing such certain knowledge of the theoretical principles of atomic structure as to be able to construct solid bodies and clocks theoretically from elementary concepts.

Further, as to the objection that there are no really rigid bodies in nature, and that therefore the properties predicated for rigid bodies do not apply to physical reality—this objection is by no means so radical as might appear from a hasty examination. For it is not a difficult task to determine the physical state of a measuring-body so accurately that its behavior relative to other measuring-bodies shall be sufficiently free from ambiguity to allow it to be substituted for the "rigid" body. It is to measuring-bodies of this kind that statements about rigid bodies must be referred.

All practical geometry is based upon a principle which is accessible to experience, and which we will now try to realize. Suppose two marks have been put upon a practically-rigid body. A pair of two such marks we shall call a tract. We imagine two practically-rigid bodies, each with a tract marked out on it. These two tracts are said to be "equal to one another" if the marks of the one tract can be brought to coincide permanently with the marks of the other. We now assume that:

If two tracts are found to be equal once and anywhere, they are equal always and everywhere.

Not only the practical geometry of Euclid, but also its nearest generalization, the practical geometry of Riemann, and therewith the general theory of relativity, rest upon this assumption. Of the experimental reasons which warrant this assumption I will mention only one. The phenomenon of the propagation of light in empty space assigns a tract, namely, the appropriate path of light, to each interval of local time, and conversely. Thence it follows that the above assumption for tracts must also hold good for intervals of clock-time in the theory of relativity. Consequently it may be formulated as follows: if two ideal clocks are going at the same rate at any time and at any place (being then in immediate proximity to each other), they will always go at the same rate, no matter where and when they are again compared with each other at one place. If this law were not valid for natural clocks, the proper frequencies for the separate atoms of the same chemical element would not be in such exact agreement as experience demonstrates. The existence of sharp spectral lines is a convincing experimental proof of the above-mentioned principle of practical geometry. This, in the last analysis, is the reason which enables us to speak meaningfully of a Riemannian metric of the four-dimensional space-time continuum.

According to the view advocated here, the question whether this continuum has a Euclidean, Riemannian, or any other structure is a question of physics proper which must be answered by experience, and not a question of a convention to be chosen on grounds of mere expediency. Riemann's geometry will hold if the laws of disposition of practically-rigid bodies approach those of Euclidean geometry the more closely the smaller the dimensions of the region of space-time under consideration.

It is true that this proposed physical interpretation of geometry breaks down when applied immediately to spaces of submolecular order of magnitude. But nevertheless, even in questions as to the constitution of elementary particles, it retains part of its significance. For even when it is a question of describing the electrical elementary particles constituting matter, the attempt may still be made to ascribe physical meaning to those field concepts which have been physically defined for the purpose of describing the geometrical behavior of bodies which are large as compared with the molecule. Success alone can decide as to the justification of such an attempt, which postulates physical reality for the fundamental principles of Riemann's geometry outside of the domain of their physical definitions. It might possibly turn out that this extrapolation has no better warrant than the extrapolation of the concept of temperature to parts of a body of molecular order of magnitude.

It appears less problematical to extend the concepts of practical geometry to spaces of cosmic order of magnitude. It might, of course, be objected that a construction composed of solid rods departs the more from ideal rigidity the greater its spatial extent. But it will hardly be possible, I think, to assign fundamental significance to this objection. Therefore the question whether the universe is spatially finite or not seems to me an entirely meaningful question in the sense of practical geometry. I do not even consider it impossible that this question will be answered before long by astronomy. Let us call to mind what the general theory of relativity teaches in this respect. It offers two possibilities:

1. The universe is spatially infinite. This is possible only if in the universe the average spatial density of matter, concentrated in the stars, vanishes, i.e., if the ratio of the total mass of the stars to the volume of the space through which they are scattered indefinitely approaches zero as greater and greater volumes are considered.

2. The universe is spatially finite. This must be so, if there exists an average density of the ponderable matter in the universe which is different from zero. The smaller that average density, the greater is the volume of the universe.

I must not fail to mention that a theoretical argument can be adduced in favor of the hypothesis of a finite universe. The general theory of relativity teaches that the inertia of a given body is greater as there are more ponderable masses in proximity to it; thus it seems very natural to reduce the total inertia of a body to interaction between it and the other bodies in the universe, as indeed, ever since Newton's time, gravity has been completely reduced to interaction between bodies. From the equations of the general theory of relativity it can be deduced that this total reduction of inertia to interaction between masses—as demanded by E. Mach, for example—is possible only if the universe is spatially finite.

Many physicists and astronomers are not impressed by this argument. In the last analysis, experience alone can decide which of the two possibilities is realized in nature. How can experience furnish an answer? At first it might seem possible to determine the average density of matter by observation of that part of the universe which is accessible to our observation. This hope is illusory. The distribution of the visible stars is extremely irregular, so that we on no account may venture to set the average density of star-matter in the universe equal to, let us say, the average density in the Galaxy. In any case, however great the space examined may be, we could not feel convinced that there were any more stars beyond that space. So it seems impossible to estimate the average density.

But there is another road, which seems to me more practicable, although it also presents great difficulties. For if we inquire into the deviations of the consequences of the general theory of relativity which are accessible to experience, from the consequences of the Newtonian theory, we first of all find a deviation which manifests itself in close proximity to gravitating mass, and has been confirmed in the case of the planet Mercury. But if the universe is spatially finite, there is a second deviation from the Newtonian theory, which, in the language of the Newtonian theory, may be expressed thus: the gravitational field is such as if it were produced, not only by the ponderable masses, but in addition by a mass-density of negative sign, distributed uniformly throughout space. Since this fictitious mass-density would have to be extremely small, it would be noticeable only in very extensive gravitating systems.

Assuming that we know, let us say, the statistical distribution and the masses of the stars in the Galaxy, then by Newton's law we can calculate the gravitational field and the average velocities which the stars must have, so that the Galaxy should not collapse under the mutual attraction of its stars, but should maintain its actual extent. Now if the actual velocities of the stars—which can be measured—were smaller than the calculated velocities, we should have a proof that the actual attractions at great distances are smaller than by Newton's law. From such a deviation it could be proved indirectly that the universe is finite. It would even be possible to estimate its spatial dimensions.

Can we visualize a three-dimensional universe which is finite, yet unbounded?

The usual answer to this question is "No," but that is not the right answer. The purpose of the following remarks is to show that the answer should be "Yes." I want to show that without any extraordinary difficulty we can illustrate the theory of a finite universe by means of a mental picture to which, with some practice, we shall soon grow accustomed.

First of all, an observation of epistemological nature. A geometrical-physical theory as such is incapable of being directly pictured, being merely a system of concepts. But these concepts serve the purpose of bringing a multiplicity of real or imaginary sensory experiences into connection in the mind. To "visualize" a theory therefore means to bring to mind that abundance of sensible experiences for which the theory supplies the schematic arrangement. In the present case we have to ask ourselves how we can represent that behavior of solid bodies with respect to their mutual disposition (contact) which corresponds to the theory of a finite universe. There is really nothing new in what I have to say about this; but innumerable questions addressed to me prove that the curiosity of those who are interested in these matters has not yet been completely satisfied. So, will the initiated please pardon me, in that part of what I shall say has long been known?

What do we wish to express when we say that our space is infinite? Nothing more than that we might lay any number of bodies of equal sizes side by side without ever filling space. Suppose that we are provided with a great many cubic boxes all of the same size. In accordance with Euclidean geometry we can place them above, beside, and behind one another so as to fill an arbitrarily large part of space; but this construction would never be finished; we could go on adding more and more cubes without ever finding that there was no more room. That is what we wish to express when we say that space is infinite. It would be better to say that space is infinite in relation to practically-rigid bodies, assuming that the laws of disposition for these bodies are given by Euclidean geometry.

Another example of an infinite continuum is the plane. On a plane surface we may lay squares of cardboard so that each side of any square has the side of another square adjacent to it. The construction is never finished; we can always go on laying squares—if their laws of disposition correspond to those of plane figures of Euclidean geometry. The plane is therefore infinite in relation to the cardboard squares. Accordingly we say that the plane is an infinite continuum of two dimensions, and space an infinite continuum of three dimensions. What is here meant by the number of dimensions, I think I may assume to be known.

Now we take an example of a two-dimensional continuum which is finite, but unbounded. We imagine the surface of a large globe and a quantity of small paper discs, all of the same size. We place one of the discs anywhere on the surface of the globe. If we move the disc about, anywhere we like, on the surface of the globe, we do not come upon a boundary anywhere on the journey. Therefore we say that the spherical surface of the globe is an unbounded continuum. Moreover, the spherical surface is a finite continuum. For if we stick the paper discs on the globe, so that no disc overlaps another, the surface of the globe will finally become so full that there is no room for another disc. This means exactly that the spherical surface of the globe is finite in relation to the paper discs. Further, the spherical surface is a non-Euclidean continuum of two dimensions, that is to say, the laws of disposition for the rigid figures lying in it do not agree with those of the Euclidean plane. This can be shown in the following way. Take a disc and surround it in a circle by six more discs, each of which is to be surrounded in turn by six discs, and so on. If this construction is made on a plane surface, we obtain an uninterrupted arrangement in which there are six discs touching every disc except those which lie on the outside. On the spherical surface the construction also seems to promise success at the outset, and the smaller the radius of the disc in proportion to that of the sphere, the more promising it seems. But as the construction progresses it becomes more and more patent that the arrangement of the discs in the manner indicated, without interruption, is not possible, as it should be possible by the Euclidean geometry of the plane. In this way creatures which cannot leave the spherical surface, and cannot even peep out from the spherical surface into three-dimensional space, might discover, merely by experimenting with discs, that their two-dimensional "space" is not Euclidean, but spherical space.

From the latest results of the theory of relativity it is probable that our three-dimensional space is also approximately spherical, that is, that the laws of disposition of rigid bodies in it are not given by Euclidean geometry, but approximately by spherical geometry, if only we consider parts of space which are sufficiently extended. Now this is the place where the reader's imagination boggles. "Nobody can imagine this thing," he cries indignantly. "It can be said, but cannot be thought. I can imagine a spherical surface well enough, but nothing analogous to it in three dimensions."

We must try to surmount this barrier in the mind, and the patient reader will see that it is by no means a particularly difficult task. For this purpose we will first give our attention once more to the geometry of two-dimensional spherical surfaces. In the adjoining figure let K be the spherical surface, touched at S by a plane, E, which, for facility of presentation, is shown in the drawing as a bounded surface. Let L be a disc on the spherical surface. Now

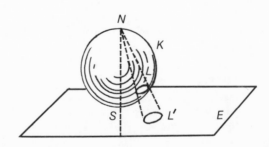

let us imagine that at the point N of the spherical surface, diametrically opposite to S, there is a luminous point, throwing a shadow L' of the disc L upon the plane E. Every point on the sphere has its shadow on the plane. If the disc on the sphere K is moved, its shadow L' on the plane E also moves. When the disc L is at S, it almost exactly coincides with its shadow. If it moves on the spherical surface away from S upwards, the disc shadow L' on the plane also moves away from S on the plane outwards, growing bigger and bigger.

As the disc L approaches the luminous point N, the shadow moves off to infinity, and becomes infinitely great.

Now we put the question: What are the laws of disposition of the disc-shadows L' on the plane E? Evidently they are exactly the same as the laws of disposition of the discs L on the spherical surface. For to each original figure on K there is a corresponding shadow figure on E. If two discs on K are touching, their shadows on E also touch. The shadow-geometry on the plane agrees with the disc-geometry on the sphere. If we call the disc-shadows rigid figures, then spherical geometry holds good on the plane E with respect to these rigid figures. In particular, the plane is finite with respect to the disc-shadows, since only a finite number of the shadows can find room on the plane.

At this point somebody will say, "That is nonsense. The disc-shadows are *not* rigid figures. We have only to move a two-foot rule about on the plane E to convince ourselves that the shadows constantly increase in size as they move away from S on the plane toward infinity." But what if the two-foot rule were to behave on the plane E in the same way as the disc-shadows L'? It would then be impossible to show that the shadows increase in size as they move away from S; such an assertion would then no longer have any meaning whatever. In fact the only objective assertion that can be made about the disc-shadows is just this, that they are related in exactly the same way as are the rigid discs on the spherical surface in the sense of Euclidean geometry.

We must carefully bear in mind that our statement as to the growth of the disc-shadows, as they move away from S toward infinity, has in itself no objective meaning, as long as we are unable to compare the disc-shadows with Euclidean rigid bodies which can be moved about on the plane E. In respect of the laws of disposition of the shadows L', the point S has no special privileges on the plane any more than on the spherical surface.

The representation given above of spherical geometry on the plane is important for us, because it readily allows itself to be transferred to the three-dimensional case.

Let us imagine a point S of our space, and a great number of small spheres, L', which can all be brought to coincide with one another. But these spheres are not to be rigid in the sense of Euclidean geometry; their radius is to increase (in the sense of Euclidean geometry) when they are moved away from S toward infinity; it is to increase according to the same law as the radii of the disc-shadows L' on the plane.

After having gained a vivid mental image of the geometrical behavior of our L' spheres, let us assume that in our space there are no rigid bodies at all in the sense of Euclidean geometry, but only bodies having the behavior of our L' spheres. Then we shall have a clear picture of three-dimensional spherical space, or, rather of three-dimensional spherical geometry. Here our spheres must be called "rigid" spheres. Their increase in size as they depart from S is not to be detected by measuring with measuring-rods, any more than in the case of the disc-shadows on E, because the standards of measurement behave in the same way as the spheres. Space is homogeneous, that is to say, the same spherical configurations are possible in the neighborhood of every point.* Our space is finite, because, in consequence of the "growth" of the spheres, only a finite number of them can find room in space.

In this way, by using as a crutch the practice in thinking and visualization which Euclidean geometry gives us, we have acquired a mental picture of spherical geometry. We may without difficulty impart more depth and vigor to these ideas by carrying out special imaginary constructions. Nor would it be difficult to represent the case of what is called elliptical geometry in an analogous manner. My only aim today has been to show that the human faculty of visualization is by no means bound to capitulate to non-Euclidean geometry.

CONCEPT OF SPACE

In order to appreciate fully the importance of investigations such as the present work of Dr. Jammer one should consider the following points. The eyes of the scientist are directed upon those phenomena which are accessible to observation, upon their apperception and conceptual formulation. In the attempt to achieve a conceptual formulation of the confusingly immense body of observational data, the scientist makes use of a whole arsenal of concepts which he imbibed practically with his mother's milk; and seldom if ever is he aware of the eternally problematic character of his concepts. He uses this conceptual material, or, speaking more exactly, these conceptual tools of thought, as something obviously, immutably given; something having an objective value of truth which is hardly ever, and in any case not seriously, to be doubted. How could he do otherwise? How would the ascent of a mountain be possible, if the use of hands, legs, and tools had to be sanctioned step by step on the basis of the science of mechanics? And yet in the interests of science it is necessary over and over again to engage in the critique of these fundamental concepts, in order that we may not unconsciously be ruled by them. This becomes evident especially in those situations involving development of ideas in which the consistent use of the traditional fundamental concepts leads us to paradoxes difficult to resolve.

Aside from the doubt arising as to the justification for the use of the concepts, that is to say, even in cases where this doubt is not in the foreground of our interest, there is a purely historical interest in the origins or the roots of the fundamental concepts. Such investigations, although purely in the field

*This is intelligible without calculation—but only for the two-dimensional case—if we revert once more to the case of the disc on the surface of the sphere.

From Einstein's foreword to "Concept of Space" by M. Jammer (Cambridge: Harvard University Press, 1954). Reprinted by permission of the Estate of Albert Einstein.

of history of thought, are nevertheless in principle not independent of attempts at a logical and psychological analysis of the basic concepts. But the limitations to the abilities and working capacity of the individual are such that we but rarely find a person who has the philological and historical training required for critical interpretation and comparison of the source material, which is spread over centuries, and who at the same time can evaluate the significance of the concepts under discussion for science as a whole. I have the impression that Dr. Jammer, through his work, has demonstrated that in his case these conditions are in great measure satisfied.

In the main he has limited himself—wisely, it seems to me—to the historical investigation of the concept of *space*. If two different authors use the words "red," "hard," or "disappointed," no one doubts that they mean approximately the same thing, because these words are connected with elementary experiences in a manner which is difficult to misinterpret. But in the case of words such as "place" or "space," whose relation with psychological experience is less direct, there exists a far-reaching uncertainty of interpretation. The historian attempts to overcome such uncertainty by comparison of the texts, and by taking into account the picture, constructed from literature, of the cultural stock of the epoch in question. The scientist of the present, however, is not primarily trained or oriented as a historian; he is not capable of forming nor willing to form his views on the origin of the fundamental concepts in this manner. He is more inclined to allow his views on the manner in which the relevant concepts might have been formed, to arise intuitively from his rudimentary knowledge of the achievements of science in the different epochs of history. He will, however, be grateful to the historian if the latter can convincingly correct such views of purely intuitive origin.

Now as to the concept of space, it seems that this was preceded by the psychologically simpler concept of place. Place is first of all a (small) portion of the earth's surface identified by a name. The thing whose "place" is being specified is a "material object" or body. Simple analysis shows "place" also to be a group of material objects. Does the word "place" have a meaning independent of this one, or can one assign such a meaning to it? If one has to give a negative answer to this question, then one is led to the view that space (or place) is a sort of order of material objects and nothing else. If the concept of space is formed and limited in this fashion, then to speak of empty space has no meaning. And because the formation of concepts has always been ruled by instinctive striving for economy, one is led quite naturally to reject the concept of empty space.

It is also possible, however, to think in a different way. Into a certain box we can place a definite number of grains of rice or of cherries, etc. It is here a question of a property of the material object "box," which property must be considered "real" in the same sense as the box itself. One can call this property the "space" of the box. There may be other boxes which in this sense have an equally large "space." This concept "space" thus achieves a meaning which is freed from any connection with a particular material object. In this way by a natural extension of "box space" one can arrive at the concept of an independent (absolute) space, unlimited in extent, in which all material objects are contained. Then a material object not situated in space is simply inconceivable; on the other hand, in the framework of this concept formation it is quite conceivable that an empty space may exist.

These two concepts of space may be contrasted as follows: *(a)* space as positional quality of the world of material objects; *(b)* space as container of all material objects. In case *(a)*, space without a material object is inconceivable. In case *(b)*, a material object can only be conceived as existing in space; space then appears as a reality which in a certain sense is superior to the material world. Both space concepts are free creations of the human imagination, means devised for easier comprehension of our sense experience.

These schematic considerations concern the nature of space from the geometric and from the kinematic point of view, respectively. They are in a sense reconciled with each other by Descartes' introduction of the coördinate system, although this already presupposes the logically more daring space concept *(b)*.

The concept of space was enriched and complicated by Galileo and Newton, in that space must be introduced as the independent cause of the inertial behavior of bodies if one wishes to give the classical principle of inertia (and therewith the classical law of motion) an exact meaning. To have realized this fully and clearly is in my opinion one of Newton's greatest achievements. In contrast with Leibniz and Huygens, it was clear to Newton that the space concept *(a)* was not sufficient to serve as the foundation for the inertia principle and the law of motion. He came to this decision even though he actively shared the uneasiness which was the cause of the opposition of the other two: space is not only introduced as an independent thing apart from material objects, but also is assigned an absolute role in the whole causal structure of the theory. This role is absolute in the sense that space (as an inertial system) acts on all material objects, while these do not in turn exert any reaction on space.

The fruitfulness of Newton's system silenced these scruples for several centuries. Space of type *(b)* was generally accepted by scientists in the precise form of the inertial system, encompassing time as well. Today one would say about that memorable discussion: Newton's decision was, in the contemporary state of science, the only possible one, and particularly the only fruitful one. But the subsequent development of the problems, proceeding in a roundabout way which no one then could possibly foresee, has shown that the resistance of Leibniz and Huygens, intuitively well founded but supported by inadequate arguments, was actually justified.

It required a severe struggle to arrive at the concept of independent and absolute space, indispensable for the development of theory. It has required no less strenuous exertions subsequently to overcome this concept—a process which is probably by no means as yet completed.

Dr. Jammer's book is greatly concerned with the investigation of the status of the concept of space in ancient times and in the Middle Ages. On the basis of his studies, he is inclined toward the view that the modern concept of space of type *(b)*, that is, space as container of all material objects, was not developed until after the Renaissance. It seems to me that the atomic theory of the ancients, with its atoms existing separately from each other, necessarily presupposed a space of type *(b)*, while the more influential Aristotelian school tried to get along without the concept of independent (absolute) space. Dr. Jammer's views concerning theological influences on the development of the concept of space, which lie outside the range of my judgment, will certainly arouse the interest of those who are concerned with the problem of space primarily from the historical point of view.

The victory over the concept of absolute space or over that of the inertial system became possible only because the concept of the material object was gradually replaced as the fundamental concept of physics by that of the field. Under the influence of the ideas of Faraday and Maxwell the notion developed that the whole of physical reality could perhaps be represented as a field whose components depend on four space-time parameters. If the laws of this field are in general covariant, that is, are not dependent on a particular choice of coördinate system, then the introduction of an independent (absolute) space is no longer necessary. That which constitutes the spatial character of reality is then simply the four-dimensionality of the field. There is then no "empty" space, that is, there is no space without a field. Dr. Jammer's presentation also deals with the memorable roundabout way in which the difficulties of this problem were overcome, at least to a great extent. Up to the present time no one has found any method of avoiding the inertial system other than by way of the field theory.

Princeton, New Jersey   ALBERT EINSTEIN
1953

SPACE-TIME

The theory of relativity has brought about a fundamental change in the scientific conception of space and time, described in a famous saying of Hermann Minkowski—"Henceforth space in itself and time in itself sink to mere shadows, and only a kind of union of the two preserves an independent existence." This union is called space-time.

From Encyclopaedia Britannica, *14th ed., (1929), vol. 21, pp. 103–106. Reprinted by permission of Encyclopaedia Britannica, 14th edition, © 1929–1973 by Encyclopaedia Britannica, Inc., and the Estate of Albert Einstein.*

All our thoughts and concepts are called up by sense-experiences and have a meaning only in reference to these sense-experiences. On the other hand, however, they are products of the spontaneous activity of our minds; they are thus in no wise logical consequences of the contents of these sense-experiences. If, therefore, we wish to grasp the essence of a complex of abstract notions we must for the one part investigate the mutual relationships between the concepts and the assertions made about them; for the other, we must investigate how they are related to the experiences.

So far as the way is concerned in which concepts are connected with one another and with the experiences there is no difference of principle between the concept-systems of science and those of daily life. The concept-systems of science have grown out of those of daily life and have been modified and completed according to the objects and purposes of the science in question.

The more universal a concept is, the more frequently it enters into our thinking; and the more indirect its relation to sense-experience, the more difficult it is for us to comprehend its meaning; this is particularly the case with prescientific concepts that we have been accustomed to using since childhood. Consider the concepts referred to in the words "where," "when," "why," "being," to the elucidation of which innumerable volumes of philosophy have been devoted. We fare no better in our speculations than a fish trying to learn the composition of water.

SPACE

In the present article we are concerned with the meaning of "where," that is, of space. It appears that there is no quality contained in our individual primitive sense-experiences that may be designated as spatial. Rather, what is spatial appears to be a sort of order of the material objects of experience. The concept "material object" must therefore be available if concepts concerning space are to be possible. It is the logically primary concept. This is easily seen if we analyze the spatial concepts, for example, "next to," "touch," and so forth; that is, if we strive to become aware of their equivalents in experience. The concept "object" is a means of taking into account the persistence in time or the continuity, respectively, of certain groups of experience-complexes. The existence of objects is thus of a conceptual nature, and the meaning of the concepts of objects depends wholly on their being connected (intuitively) with groups of elementary sense-experiences. This connection is the basis of the illusion which makes primitive experience appear to inform us directly about the relation of material bodies (which exist, after all, only insofar as they are thought).

In the sense thus indicated we have the (indirect) experience of the contact of two bodies. We need do no more than call attention to this, as we gain nothing for our present purpose by singling out the individual experiences to which this assertion alludes. Many bodies can be brought into permanent contact with one another in manifold ways. We speak in this sense of the position-relationships of bodies *(Lagenbeziehungen)*. The general laws of such position-relationships are essentially the concern of geometry. This holds, at least, if we do not wish to restrict ourselves to regarding the propositions that occur in this branch of knowledge merely as relationships between empty words that have been set up according to certain principles.

PRESCIENTIFIC THOUGHT

Now, what is the meaning of the concept "space" which we also encounter in prescientific thought? The concept of space in prescientific thought is characterized by the sentence "We can think away things but not the space which they occupy." It is as if, without having had experience of any sort, we had a concept, nay, even a presentation, of space; and as if we ordered our sense-experiences with the help of this concept, present a priori. On the other hand, space appears as a physical reality, as a thing which exists independently of our thought, like material objects. Under the influence of this view of space the fundamental concepts of geometry, the point, the straight line, the plane, were even regarded as having a self-evident character. The fundamental principles that deal with these configurations were regarded as being necessarily valid and as having at the same time an objective content. No scruples were felt about ascribing an objective meaning to such statements as "three empirically given bodies (practically infinitely small) lie on one straight line," without demanding a physical definition for such an assertion. This blind faith in evidence and in the immediately real meaning of the concepts and propositions of geometry became uncertain only after non-Euclidean geometry had been introduced.

REFERENCE TO THE EARTH

If we start from the view that all spatial concepts are related to contact-experiences of solid bodies, it is easy to understand how the concept "space" originated, namely, how a thing independent of bodies and yet embodying their position-possibilities *(Lagerungsmöglichkeiten)* was posited. If we have a system of bodies in contact and at rest relatively to one another, some can be replaced by others. This property of allowing substitution is interpreted as "available space." Space denotes the property in virtue of which rigid bodies can occupy different positions. The view that space is something with a unity of its own is perhaps due to the circumstance that in prescientific thought all positions of bodies were referred to one body (reference body), namely the earth. In scientific thought the earth is represented by the co-ordinate system. The assertion that it would be possible to place an unlimited number of bodies next to one another denotes that space is infinite. In prescientific thought the concepts "space" and "time" and "body of reference" are scarcely differentiated at all. A place or point in space is always taken to mean a material point on a body of reference.

EUCLIDEAN GEOMETRY

If we consider Euclidean geometry we clearly discern that it refers to the laws regulating the positions of rigid bodies. It provides the ingenious thought of tracing back all relations concerning bodies and their relative positions to the very simple concept "distance" *(Strecke)*. Distance denotes a rigid body on which two material points (marks) have been specified. The concept of the equality of distances (and angles) refers to experiments involving coincidences; the same remarks apply to the theorems on congruence. Now, Euclidean geometry, in the form in which it has been handed down to us from Euclid, uses the fundamental concepts "straight line" and "plane," which do not appear to correspond, or at any rate, not so directly, with experiences concerning the position of rigid bodies. (On this it must be remarked that the concept of the straight line may be reduced to that of the distance. A hint of this is contained in the theorem: "The straight line is the shortest connection between two points." This theorem served well as a definition of the straight line, although the definition played no part in the logical texture of the deductions.) Moreover, geometricians were less concerned with bringing out the relation of their fundamental concepts to experience than with deducing logically the geometrical propositions from a few axioms enunciated at the outset.

Let us outline briefly how perhaps the basis of Euclidean geometry may be gained from the concepts of distance. We start from the equality of distances (axiom of the equality of distances). Suppose that of two unequal distances one is always greater than the other. The same axioms are to hold for the inequality of distances as hold for the inequality of number. Three distances $\overline{AB'}$, $\overline{BC'}$, $\overline{CA'}$ may, if CA' be suitably chosen, have their marks BB', CC', AA' superposed on one another in such a way that a triangle ABC results. The distance CA' has an upper limit for which this construction is still just possible. The points A, (BB') and C then lie in a "straight line" (definition). This leads to the concepts of producing a distance by an amount equal to itself; dividing a distance into equal parts; expressing a distance in terms of a number by means of a measuring-rod (definition of the space-interval between two points).

When the concept of the interval between two points or the length of a distance has been gained in this way we require only the following axiom (Pythagoras' theorem) in order to arrive at Euclidean geometry analytically. To every point of space (body of reference) three numbers (co-ordinates), x, y, z, may be assigned—and conversely—in such a way that for each pair of points A (x_1, y_1, z_1) and $B(x_2, y_2, z_2)$ the theorem holds:

measure-number: $AB = \sqrt{(x_2 - x_1)^2 + (y_2 - y_1)^2 + (z_2 - z_1)^2}$

All further concepts and propositions of Euclidean geometry can then be built up purely logically on this basis, in particular also the propositions about the straight line and the plane. These remarks are not, of course, intended to replace the strictly axiomatic construction of Euclidean geometry. We merely wish to indicate plausibly how all conceptions of geometry may be traced back to that of distance. We might equally well have epitomized the whole basis of Euclidean geometry in the last theorem above. The relation to the foundations of experience would then be furnished by means of a supplementary theorem. The co-ordinate may and *must* be chosen so that two pairs of points separated by equal intervals, as calculated with the help of Pythagoras' theorem, may be made to coincide with one and the same suitably chosen distance (on a solid). The concepts and propositions of Euclidean geometry may be derived from Pythagoras' proposition without the introduction of rigid bodies; but these concepts and propositions would not then have contents that could be tested. They are not "true" propositions but only logically correct propositions of purely formal content.

Difficulties—A serious difficulty is encountered in the above represented interpretation of geometry in that the rigid body of experience does not correspond *exactly* with the geometrical body. There are no absolutely definite marks, and, moreover, temperature, pressure and other circumstances modify the laws relating to position. It is also to be recollected that the structural constituents of matter (such as atom and electron, *q.v.*) assumed by physics are not in principle commensurate with rigid bodies, but that nevertheless the concepts of geometry are applied to them and to their parts. For this reason consistent thinkers have been disinclined to allow real contents of facts *(reale Tatsachenbestände)* to correspond to geometry alone. They considered it preferable to allow the content of experience *(Erfahrungsbestände)* to correspond to geometry and physics conjointly.

This view is certainly less open to attack than the one represented above: As opposed to the atomic theory it is the only one that can be consistently carried through. Nevertheless it would not be advisable to give up the first view, from which geometry derives its origin. This connection is essentially founded on the belief that the ideal rigid body is an abstraction that is well rooted in the laws of nature.

FOUNDATIONS OF GEOMETRY

We now come to the question: What is a priori certain or necessary, respectively in geometry (doctrine of space) or its foundations? Formerly we thought everything; nowadays we think—nothing. Already the distance—concept is logically arbitrary; there need be no things that correspond to it, even approximately. Something similar may be said of the concepts straight line, plane, of three-dimensionality and of the validity of Pythagoras' theorem. Even the continuum-doctrine is in no wise given the nature of human thought, so that from the epistemological point of view no greater authority attaches to the purely topological relations than to the others.

EARLIER PHYSICAL CONCEPTS

We have yet to deal with those modifications in the space-concept which have accompanied the advent of the theory of relativity. For this purpose we must consider the space-concept of the earlier physics from a point of view different from that above. If we apply the theorem of Pythagoras to infinitely near points, it reads

$$ds^2 = dx^2 + dy^2 + dz^2$$

where ds denotes the measurable interval between them. For an empirically given ds the co-ordinate system is not yet fully determined for every combination of points by this equation. Besides being translated, a co-ordinate system may also be rotated. This signifies analytically: The relations of Euclidean geometry are covariant with respect to linear orthogonal transformations of the co-ordinates.

In applying Euclidean geometry to prerelativistic mechanics a further indeterminateness enters through the choice of the co-ordinate system: the state of motion of the co-ordinate system is arbitrary to a certain degree, namely, in that substitutions of the co-ordinates of the form

$$x' = x - vt$$
$$y' = y$$
$$z' = z$$

also appear possible. On the other hand, earlier mechanics did not allow co-ordinate systems to be applied of which the states of motion were different from those expressed in these equations. In this sense we speak of "inertial systems." In these favoured inertial systems we are confronted with a new property of space so far as geometrical relations are concerned. Regarded more accurately, this is not a property of space alone but of the four-dimensional continuum consisting of time and space conjointly.

APPEARANCE OF TIME

At this point time enters explicitly into our discussion for the first time. In their applications, space (place) and time always occur together. Every event that happens in the world is determined by the space co-ordinates x, y, z, and the time co-ordinate t. Thus the physical description was four-dimensional right from the beginning. But this four-dimensional continuum seemed to resolve itself into the three-dimensional continuum of space and the one-dimensional continuum of time. This apparent resolution owed its origin to the illusion that the meaning of the concept "simultaneity" is self-evident and this illusion arises from the fact that we receive news of near events almost instantaneously owing to the agency of light.

This faith in the absolute significance of simultaneity was destroyed by the law regulating the propagation of light in empty space, or, respectively, by the Maxwell-Lorentz electrodynamics. Two infinitely near points can be connected by means of a light-signal if the relation

$$ds^2 = c^2 dt^2 - dx^2 - dy^2 - dz^2 = 0$$

holds for them. It further follows that ds has a value which, for arbitrarily chosen infinitely near space-time points, is independent of the particular inertial system selected. In agreement with this we find that for passing from one inertial system to another, linear equations of transformation hold which do not in general leave the time-values of the events unchanged. It thus became manifest that the four-dimensional continuum of space cannot be split up into a time continuum and a space continuum except in an arbitrary way. This invariant quantity ds may be measured by means of measuring-rods and clocks.

FOUR-DIMENSIONAL GEOMETRY

On the invariant ds a four-dimensional geometry may be built up which is in a large measure analogous to Euclidean geometry in three dimensions. In this way physics becomes a sort of statics in a four-dimensional continuum. Apart from the difference in the number of dimensions the latter continuum is distinguished from that of Euclidean geometry in that ds^2 may be greater or less than zero. Corresponding to this we differentiate between timelike and spacelike line-elements. The boundary between them is marked out by the element of the "light-cone" $ds^2 = 0$ which starts out from every point. If we consider only elements which belong to the same time-value, we have

$$-ds^2 = dx^2 + dy^2 + dz^2$$

These elements ds may have real counterparts in distances at rest and, as before, Euclidean geometry holds for these elements.

EFFECT OF RELATIVITY, SPECIAL AND GENERAL

This is the modification which the doctrine of space and time has undergone through the restricted theory of relativity. The doctrine of space has been still further modified by the general theory of relativity, because this theory denies that the three-dimensional spatial section of the space-time continuum is Euclidean in character. Therefore it asserts that Euclidean geometry does not hold for the relative positions of bodies that are continuously in contact.

For the empirical law of the equality of inertial and gravitational mass led us to interpret the state of the continuum, in so far as it manifests itself with reference to a noninertial system, as a gravitational field, and to treat noninertial systems as equivalent to inertial systems. Referred to such a system, which is connected with the inertial system by a nonlinear transformation of the co-ordinates, the metrical invariant ds^2 assumes the general form:

$$ds^2 = \sum_{\mu\nu} g_{\mu\nu}\, dx_\mu dx_\nu$$

where the $g_{\mu\nu}$'s are functions of the co-ordinates and where the sum is to be taken over the indices for all combinations $11, 12, \ldots, 44$. The variability of the $g_{\mu\nu}$'s is equivalent to the existence of a gravitational field. If the gravitational field is sufficiently general it is not possible at all to find an inertial system, that is, a co-ordinate system with reference to which ds^2 may be expressed in the simple form given above:

$$ds^2 = c^2 dt^2 - dx^2 - dy^2 - dz^2$$

but in this case, too, there is in the infinitesimal neighbourhood of a space-time point a local system of reference for which the last-mentioned simple form for ds holds. This state of the facts leads to a type of geometry which Riemann's genius created more than half a century before the advent of the General Theory of Relativity of which Riemann divined the high importance for physics.

RIEMANN'S GEOMETRY

Riemann's geometry of an n-dimensional space bears the same relation to Euclidean geometry of an n-dimensional space as the general geometry of curved surfaces bears to the geometry of the plane. For the infinitesimal neighbourhood of a point on a curved surface there is a local co-ordinate system in which the distance ds between two infinitely near points is given by the equation

$$ds^2 = dx^2 + dy^2$$

For any arbitrary (Gaussian) co-ordinate system, however, an expression of the form

$$ds^2 = g_{11} dx^2 + 2g_{12} dx_1 dx_2 + g_{22} dx_2{}^2$$

holds in a finite region of the curved surface. If the $g_{\mu\nu}$'s are given as functions of x_1 and x_2 the surface is then fully determined geometrically. For from this formula we can calculate for every combination of two infinitely near points on the surface the length ds of the minute rod connecting them; and with the help of this formula all networks that can be constructed on the surface with these little rods can be calculated. In particular, the "curvature" at every point of the surface can be calculated; this is the quantity that expresses to what extent and in what way the laws regulating the positions of the minute rods in the immediate vicinity of the point under consideration deviate from those of the geometry of the plane.

This theory of surfaces by Gauss has been extended by Riemann to continua of any arbitrary number of dimensions and has thus paved the way for the general theory of relativity. For it was shown above that corresponding to two infinitely near space-time points there is a number ds which can be obtained by measurement with rigid measuring-rods and clocks (in the case of timelike elements, indeed, with a clock alone). This quantity occurs in the mathematical theory in place of the length of the minute rods in three-dimensional geometry. The curves for which $\int ds$ has stationary values determine the paths of material points and rays of light in the gravitational field, and the "curvature" of space is dependent on the matter distributed over space.

Just as in Euclidean geometry the space-concept refers to the position-possibilities of rigid bodies, so in the General Theory of Relativity the space-time concept refers to the behaviour of rigid bodies and clocks. The space-time continuum, however, differs from the space continuum in that the laws regulating the behaviour of these objects (clocks and measuring-rods) depend on where they happen to be. The continuum (or the quantities that describe it) enters explicitly into the laws of nature, and conversely these properties of the continuum are determined by physical factors. The relations that connect space and time can no longer be kept distinct from physics proper. Nothing certain is known of what the properties of the space-time continuum may be as a whole. Through the General Theory of Relativity, however, the view that the continuum is infinite in its timelike extent but finite in its spacelike extent has gained in probability.

TIME

The physical time-concept answers to the time-concept of the extrascientific mind. Now, the latter has its root in the time-order of the experiences of the individual, and this order we must accept as something primarily given. One experiences the moment "now," or, expressed more accurately, the present sense-experience *(Sinnen-Erlebnis)* combined with the recollection of (earlier) sense-experiences. That is why the sense-experiences seem to form a series, namely the time-series indicated by "earlier" and "later." The experience-series is thought of as a one-dimensional continuum. Experience-series can repeat themselves and can then be recognized. They can also be repeated inexactly, wherein some events are replaced by others without the character of the repetition becoming lost for us. In this way we form the time-concept as a one-dimensional frame which can be filled in by experiences in various ways. The same series of experiences answer to the same subjective time-intervals.

The transition from this "subjective" time *(Ich-Zeit)* to the time-concept of prescientific thought is connected with the formation of the idea that there is a real external world independent of the subject. In this sense the (objective) event is made to correspond with the subjective experience. In the same sense there is attributed to the "subjective" time of the experience a "time" of the corresponding "objective" event. In contrast with experiences external events and their order in time claim validity for all subjects.

This process of objectification would encounter no difficulties were the time-order of the experiences corresponding to a series of external events the same for all individuals. In the case of the immediate visual perceptions of our daily lives, this correspondence is exact. That is why the idea that there is an objective time-order became established to an extraordinary extent. In working out the idea of an objective world of external events in greater detail, it was found necessary to make events and experiences depend on each other in a more complicated way. This was at first done by means of rules and modes of thought instinctively gained, in which the conception of space plays a particularly prominent part. This process of refinement leads ultimately to natural science.

The measurement of time is effected by means of clocks. A clock is a thing which automatically passes in succession through a (practically) equal series of events (period). The number of periods (clock-time) elapsed serves as a measure of time. The meaning of this definition is at once clear if the event occurs in the immediate vicinity of the clock in space; for all observers then observe the same clock-time simultaneously with the event (by means of the eye) independently of their position. Until the theory of relativity was propounded it was assumed that the conception of simultaneity had an absolute objective meaning also for events separated in space.

This assumption was demolished by the discovery of the law of propagation of light. For if the velocity of light in empty space is to be a quantity that is independent of the choice (or, respectively, of the state of motion) of the inertial system to which it is referred, no absolute meaning can be assigned to the conception of the simultaneity of events that occur at points separated by a distance in space. Rather, a special time must be allocated to every inertial system. If no co-ordinate system (inertial system) is used as a basis of reference there is no sense in asserting that events at different points in space occur simultaneously. It is in consequence of this that space and time are welded together into a uniform four-dimensional continuum.

RELATIVITY THEORY AND CORPUSCLES

I shall now show that, according to the general theory of relativity, there exist singularity-free solutions of field equations which can be interpreted as representing corpuscles. I restrict myself here to neutral particles because, in another recent publication in collaboration with Dr. Rosen,* I have treated this question in detail, and because the essentials of the problem can be completely exhibited in this case.

The gravitational field is entirely described by the tensor $g_{\mu\nu}$. In the three-index symbols $\Gamma^\sigma_{\mu\nu}$, there appear also the contravariant $g^{\mu\nu}$ which are defined as the minors of the $g_{\mu\nu}$ divided by the determinant $g(=|g_{\alpha\beta}|)$. In order that the $R_{\iota k}$ shall be defined and finite, it is not sufficient that there shall be, in the neighborhood of every point of the continuum, a system of coordinates in which the $g_{\mu\nu}$ and their first differential quotients are continuous and differentiable, but it is also necessary that the determinant g shall nowhere

From "Physics and Reality," Albert Einstein, Journal of the Franklin Institute 221, no. 3 (March 1936). Reprinted from Ideas and Opinions (New York: Crown Publishers, © 1954) by permission of the publisher and the Estate of Albert Einstein.

*A. Einstein and N. Rosen, "The Particle Problem in the General Theory of Relativity," Physical Review (July 1, 1935) 48, 73–77.

vanish. This last restriction disappears, however, if one replaces the differential equations $R_{\iota k}=0$ by $g^2R_{\iota k}=0$, the left-hand sides of which are *whole* rational functions of the $g_{\iota k}$ and of their derivatives.

These equations have the centrally symmetrical solution given by Schwarzschild

$$ds^2 = -\frac{1}{1-2m/r}dr^2 - r^2(d\theta^2 + \sin^2\theta d\varphi^2) + \left(1-\frac{2m}{r}\right)dt^2$$

This solution has a singularity at $r=2m$, since the coefficient of dr^2 (i.e., g_{11}) becomes infinite on this hypersurface. If, however, we replace the variable r by ρ defined by the equation

$$\rho^2 = r - 2m$$

we obtain

$$ds^2 = -4(2m+\rho^2)d\rho^2 - (2m+\rho^2)^2(d\theta^2 + \sin^2\theta d\varphi^2) + \frac{\rho^2}{2m+\rho^2}dt^2$$

This solution behaves regularly for all values of ρ. The vanishing of the coefficient of dt^2 (i.e., g_{44}) for $\rho=0$ results, it is true, in the consequence that the determinant g vanishes for this value; but, with the methods of writing the field equations actually adopted, this does not constitute a singularity.

If ρ varies from $-\infty$ to $+\infty$, then r varies from $+\infty$ to $r=2m$ and then back to $+\infty$, while for such values of r as correspond to $r < 2m$ there are no corresponding real values of ρ. Hence the Schwarzschild solution becomes a regular solution by representing the physical space as consisting of two identical "sheets" in contact along the hypersurface $\rho=0$ (i.e., $r=2m$), on which the determinant g vanishes. Let us call such a connection between the two (identical) sheets a "bridge." Hence the existence of such a bridge between the two sheets in the finite realm corresponds to the existence of a material neutral particle which is described in a manner free from singularities.

The solution of the problem of the motion of neutral particles evidently amounts to the discovery of such solutions of the gravitational equations (written free of denominators), as contain several bridges.

The conception sketched above corresponds, *a priori*, to the atomistic structure of matter in so far as the "bridge" is by its nature a discrete element. Moreover, we see that the mass constant m of the neutral particles must necessarily be positive, since no solution free of singularities can correspond to the Schwarzschild solution for a negative value of m. Only the examination of the several-bridge-problem can show whether or not this theoretical method furnishes an explanation of the empirically demonstrated equality of the masses of the particles found in nature, and whether it takes into account the facts which the quantum mechanics has so wonderfully comprehended.

In an analogous manner, it is possible to demonstrate that the combined equations of gravitation and electricity (with appropriate choice of the sign of the electrical member in the gravitational equations) produce a singularity-free bridge-representation of the electric corpuscle. The simplest solution of this kind is that for an electrical particle without gravitational mass.

So long as the considerable mathematical difficulties concerned with the solution of the several-bridge-problem are not overcome, nothing can be said concerning the usefulness of the theory from the physicist's point of view. However, it constitutes, as a matter of fact, the first attempt toward the consistent elaboration of a field theory which presents a possibility of explaining the properties of matter. In favor of this attempt one should also add that it is based on the simplest possible relativistic field equations known today.

MERCER STREET AND OTHER MEMORIES

Gathered by

JOHN ARCHIBALD WHEELER

Center for Theoretical Physics, Department of Physics, University of Texas, Austin, Texas

The famous 1950 film *Rashomon* recounts a dramatic episode three times over in the very different versions perceived by three of those who took part. The account of a May 16, 1953, visit to Einstein given here differs in that there are four versions supplied respectively by John Wheeler, Marcel Wellner, Arthur Komar and O. W. Greenberg. The editor (J. A. W.) expresses his appreciation to them for the permission to quote them, and to the Albert Einstein Estate for permission to quote brief passages from Einstein's writings.

MERCER STREET AND OTHER MEMORIES

JOHN ARCHIBALD WHEELER

My first chance to see and hear Albert Einstein came one afternoon in the academic year 1933–34. I was in my first year of postdoctoral work with Gregory Breit in New York. He told me that there would be a quiet, small, unannounced seminar by Einstein that afternoon. We took the train to Princeton and walked to Fine Hall. Unified field theory was to be the topic, it became clear, when Einstein entered the room and began to speak. His English, though a little accented, was beautifully clear and slow. His delivery was spontaneous and serious with every now and then a touch of humor. I was not familiar with his subjects at that time but I could sense that he had his doubts about the particular version of unified field theory he was then discussing. I had been accustomed before this to seminars in physics where equations were taken up one at a time or, if I may say so, dealt with as in retail trade. Here for the first time I saw equations dealt with wholesale. One counted the number of unknowns and the number of supplementary conditions and compared them with the number of equations and the number of coordinate degrees of freedom. The idea was not to solve the equations but rather to decide whether they possessed a solution and whether it was unique. It was clear on this first encounter that Einstein was following very much his own line, independent of the interest in nuclear physics then at high tide in the United States.

In 1938 I moved to Princeton and at infrequent intervals called on Einstein at his house at 112 Mercer Street, climbing the stairs to his second floor study that looked out on the Graduate College. Once discussing with him my hopes some day to understand radiation damping in terms of the interaction between the source and the absorber, he told me about his debate with W. Ritz.[1] The two men joined to write up their contrasting points of view in a joint paper. In it Ritz argued that the elementary interaction is responsible for the irreversibility. In contrast Einstein favored the view that elementary interactions are time symmetric and that any irreversibility is caused by asymmetry in time of the initial conditions. He also made reference to a fascinating paper of Tetrode[2] on the same question.

Especially vivid in my mind is a call I made in 1941 to explain the "sum over histories" approach to quantum mechanics then being developed by Richard Feynman,[3] whom I was fortunate enough to have as a graduate student. I had gone to see Einstein with the hope of persuading him of the naturalness of quantum theory when seen in this new light, connected so closely and so beautifully with the variation principle of classical mechanics. He listened to me patiently for twenty minutes until I finished. At the end he repeated that familiar remark of his, "I still cannot believe that the good Lord plays dice."[4] And then he went on to add again in his beautifully slow, clear, well-modulated and humorous way, "Of course I may be wrong; but perhaps I have earned the right to make my mistakes."

In the fall of 1952 I gave for the first time the course in relativity, general and special, from which I was to learn so much from my students over the years. On May 16, 1953, not quite two years before he died, Einstein was kind enough to invite me to bring the eight to ten students in the course around to his house for tea. [The recollections kindly provided by three of them follow: Arthur Komar, Marcel Wellner and O. W. Greenberg.] Margot Einstein and Helen Dukas served tea as we sat around the dining room table. The students asked questions about everything from the nature of electricity and unified field theory to the expanding universe and his position on quantum theory, and Einstein responded at length and fascinatingly. Finally one student outdid the others in the boldness of his question: "Professor Einstein, what will become of this house when you are no longer living?" Einstein's face took on that humorous smile and again he spoke in that beautiful, slow, slightly accented English that could have been converted immediately into printer's type, "This house will never become a place of pilgrimage where the pilgrims come to look at the bones of the saint." And so it is today. The tourist buses drive up. The pilgrims climb out to photograph the house—but they don't go in.

A further encounter was my last. We persuaded him to give a seminar to a restricted group. In it the quantum was a central topic. No one can forget how he expressed his discomfort about the role of the observer. "When a person such as a mouse observes the universe, does that change the state of the universe?"

In all the history of human thought there is no greater dialogue than that which took place over the years between Niels Bohr and Albert Einstein about the meaning of the quantum. Their discussion has already been depicted in sculpture and surely will be described some day in pictures and words. Nobody can forget Einstein's letter to the young Bohr when first he met him: "I am studying your great works and—when I get stuck anywhere—now have the pleasure of seeing your friendly young face before me smiling and explaining."[5] There is no greater monument to the dialogue than Bohr's summary of it in Paul Arthur Schilpp, editor, *Albert Einstein: Philosopher-Scientist.*[6]

REFERENCES:

1. Ritz, W., and A. Einstein, "Zum gegenwartigen Stand des Strahlungsproblems," *Physik. Zeits. 10,* 323–324 (1909).

2. Tetrode, H., "Über den Wirkungszusammenhang der Welt. Ein erweiterung der dlassischen Dynamik," *Zeits. f. Physik. 10,* 317–328 (1922).

3. Feynman, R. P., "The Principle of Least Action in Quantum Mechanics," doctoral dissertation, Princeton University, 1942; unpublished; available from University Microfilms, Inc., Ann Arbor, Michigan 48106.

4. Einstein, A., letter to Max Born, December 12, 1926.

5. Einstein, A., letter to Niels Bohr, May 2, 1920.

6. Schilpp, P. A., ed., *Albert Einstein: Philosopher-Scientist,* Library of Living Philosophers, Evanston, Illinois, 1949, and subsequent paperback editions elsewhere.

ARTHUR KOMAR'S REMEMBRANCES

There were about eight of us. We sat down and had tea. Miss Dukas brought the tea. Einstein said he was so pleased to have some contact with young people. John Wheeler asked him about the Einstein-Rosen bridge. Why did he first introduce it, then drop it? Einstein said he originally thought of it as a unique structure reaching across two nearly flat sheets. However, when he realized it was not unique, the bridge seemed to him unwieldy, unattractive, and offering too many possibilities. It was not clear what to do with them all.

Arthur Komar's version of the May 16, 1953, visit of Class in Relativity to Einstein's residence at 112 Mercer Street, Princeton, as told to John A. Wheeler, August 8, 1977.

Arthur Komar asked what he thought of the idea of Eddington for getting the dimensionless constants. Einstein replied that he was much interested in finding a theory or an understanding of the dimensionless constants; but he felt that there was no solution of real interest available at that time. Komar did not remember questions about the expanding universe or gravitational radiation or the nature of electricity. He did recall that vivid phrase at the end "This house will never become a place of pilgrimage where the pilgrims come to look at the bones of the saint." The whole encounter was in English. Komar also remembered Einstein's coming to Palmer Physical Laboratory and giving a talk containing two striking comments: (1) The laws of physics should be simple. Someone in the audience asked, "But what if they are not simple?" "Then I would not be interested in them." (2) Einstein was asked why he rejected quantum mechanics. He said he could not accept the concept of a priori probability. Someone in the audience said, "But you were the one who introduced a priori probability, in the A and B coefficients." "Yes, I know that and have regretted it ever since; but when one is doing physics one should not let one's left hand know what one's right hand is doing." At the end of this lecture he sat down, leaned back, sighed and said, "This is my last examination."

EXCERPTS FROM A 10 SEPTEMBER 1977 LETTER FROM MARCEL WELLNER TO JOHN A. WHEELER

"My memory of our meeting with Einstein [May 16, 1953] is still fairly vivid. I seem to recall that most of us were too intimidated to ask him very much, and you had to be our spokesman. This was in spite of the fact that we were pretty well prepared. I am enclosing [see below] a copy of a problem assignment which you gave us shortly before that, and which reflects our preoccupations during the course you were teaching at the time. Your questions 1 and 2 seem particularly relevant here.

"At Einstein's you asked on our behalf what were his thoughts on Mach's principle. This must have been somewhat removed from his own concerns at the time, because you had to repeat the word 'Mach' in its German pronunciation to clarify the question. (As you can see, my memory is mainly of an auditory kind.)

"His answer was somewhat disappointing—at least to me. He said he no longer held to his earlier views about Mach's principle, and that perhaps there wasn't in nature anything corresponding to Mach's principle after all."

PROBLEMS: [For class in relativity in May 1953, a few days before the hoped-for visit with Einstein.]

1. Present Mach's principle in a form as eloquent and clear as possible, and independent of any reference to Einstein's theory. At the end of the presen-

tation, give a brief summary of the points still to be investigated in order that this principle should have a satisfactory and logically sound mathematical formulation.

2. List three questions that you would like to put up to Einstein, with a one paragraph elaboration of each.

3. Treat the problem of an infinitesimal test particle started from rest from an arbitrary point in the Schwarzschild field.

4. Derive the Schwarzschild values for a and b in
$(ds)^2 = -a\,(dr)^2 - r^2[(d\theta)^2 + (\sin\,\theta\,\,d\psi)^2] + b(dt)^2$ from the variation principle $\delta\int\int\int\int Rd(\text{vol}) = 0$.

MERCER STREET

A spring afternoon,
A line of nine walk through the town,
A musty house, the shutters drawn,
A sage lives within.

His key turned the lock
For twenty years, to unify
Electric field, magnetic field,
Space-time, matter, too.

A calm beyond time,
A humble man, received his guests.
To talk, to feel the breath of youth,
To hand them the key.

The day turned to dusk.
The parting time. Advice was sought
For these young men who start the path
He lost long ago.

He shrugged, scratched his head.
Discomforted, at sea, he sent
Them out with "Who am I to say?"
Cool air cleared their heads.

OSCAR WALLACE GREENBERG

187

EINSTEIN'S LAST LECTURE

Quantum theory: In which sense is it not final? "Classical" quantum theory—founded on Hamiltonian equations, similar to electrodynamics founded on Maxwell equations. How did I become a heretic? Radiation raises system to a higher state. One can weaken the field indefinitely. The system is raised more and more rarely to the higher state. The probability becomes infinitely small to produce a finite effect. One cannot of course formulate this situation satisfactorily in any mathematical scheme. Therefore, one is led to a probabilistic description. One finds himself saying that probability is a definite part of reality. It is an advantage that the law of Coulomb can be used in the new scheme, by translation from classical theory. I am a heretic. If radiation causes jumps, it must have a granular character like matter.

What is really the meaning of ψ? Can't believe that the state in quantum theory provides a complete representation of the physical situation. Consider a sphere 1 mm in diameter. One can see it with the eye. It can go to and fro between two planes, ideally elastic. One can forget the internal coordinates of the sphere. Consider a state of fixed energy (Fig. 1). If one neglects the fine structure, all places have the same probability. More accurately, there are some places where the thing can never be. This is contrary to the ordinary Newtonian idea of motion. There is no question that this is true; it certainly corresponds to reality. Fourier analysis shows there is a probability of 1/2 for $v = v_0$, and 1/2 for $v = -v_0$.

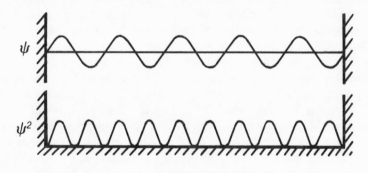

Fig. 1

It is difficult to believe that this description is complete. It seems to make the world quite nebulous unless somebody, like a mouse, is looking at it. The problem is to understand that one can observe the particle with a lantern.

The scheme is of very great practical value as long as we have nothing better, and makes good use of the concepts such as mass and change with

From Einstein's lecture at the J. A. Wheeler relativity seminar, introduced by O. W. Greenberg, in Room 307, Palmer Physical Laboratory, Princeton University, April 14, 1954. [Notes taken by J. A. W. at the time.]

which physics started in the earliest days. But one has to mistrust it if one believes in a deeper scheme.

The Maxwellian scheme is marvellously effective in explaining many things, particularly macroscopic. But it runs into trouble on radiation. Fluctuations are bigger on Planck's law than they are on Maxwellian theory.

I knew in constructing special relativity that it was not complete. So is everything that we do in our time: with one hand we believe; with the other, we doubt. I once thought temperature a basic concept. I feel the same way about Maxwellian theory. But I am now convinced there is no cheap way out. If there are too many hypothetical elements one cannot believe one is on the right track. Thus I came to logical simplicity, a desperate [man's] way to get on the right track. But one event in my life convinced me of the usefulness of logical simplicity. That was general relativity.

It can be looked at as a theory which makes us independent of the inertial system. The concept of inertial system was regarded by the founder himself, and his scientific enemy, Huygens, and Leibniz, as exceedingly unclear. For Galileo, acceleration is the fundamental concept on which mechanics is founded. But what is acceleration? Newton invented the infinitesimal calculus. But this really doesn't provide an answer. There are coordinate systems that are inertial and others that are not. A coordinate system is satisfactory if in it the equations of motion hold. In classical theory there are three independent concepts: space, time, material points. The behavior of material points is determined by the inertial system. But this is like God Almighty, unaffected by anything else. Newton recognized very clearly it was very hard to regard space as something absolute. This is not the direct way I found the theory of gravitation. The real way is a very strange story.

I had to write a paper about the content of special relativity. Then I came to the question how to handle gravity. The object falls with a different acceleration if it is moving than if it is not moving (Fig. 2). Thus a gas falls with another acceleration if heated than if not heated. I felt this is not true. Came out that acceleration is independent of *quality* of matter: pendulum experiments.

Change coordinate system? Then change acceleration. Then I came to a real understanding of the equivalence of gravitational and inertial mass. *No* inertial system can be preferred. That was not so clear to me at that time. But Mach had the same idea, not the relation of gravitational and inertial mass, but that "inertial system" was a very vicious concept. Inertia come from the presence of other bodies? How possible? *Relative* acceleration and against this a resistance. Quite a nice idea. But if you give up space, you have an enormous number of distances, and unhandy consistency relations. Mach not aware of time concept. Great thing that Mach, centuries after Newton, felt that there was something important about this concept of avoiding an inertial system. Need absolute covariance.

Not yet so clear in Riemann's concept of space. His curvature is abso-

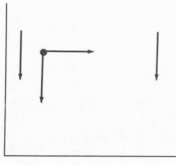

Fig. 2

lutely covariant. But this was not so clear at the time this work was presented by Riemann and his successors. The first to see this clearly was Levi-Civita: absolute parallelism and a way to differentiate. Recognized that possibility to avoid inertial system depended on existence of a Γ-field that described parallelism in the infinitesimally small. This was a great advance. It made it possible to see how to generalize relativity to include electromagnetism.

The representation of matter by a tensor was only a fill-in to make it possible to do something temporarily, a wooden nose in a snow man. The theory wasn't complete, because we know the world is not limited to gravitation. After decades I came to the idea to generalize by using unsymmetric g_{ij}'s, the method of logical consistency gone mad. I was very conscious of this objection. Γ is a field. Without this there is no hope to express things in general relativity.

Present quantum theory based on special relativity is horribly complicated. For most people special relativity, electromagnetism and gravitation are unimportant, to be added in at the end after everything else has been done. On the contrary, we have to take them into account from the beginning. Otherwise it is as if one did a classical problem and put in the law of conservation of energy at the end. Expect to describe a system only by quantum numbers. There is much reasonable in this. But a field theory seems to present us with an infinite number of quantum numbers. There is much reason to be attracted to a theory with no space, no time. But nobody has an idea how to build it up. Of course, to quantize space and time is a childish idea. This is my excuse for feeling so strongly. It is pedagogic to insist that if one has a field theory, one must demand solutions without singularity. If a singularity is allowed, there are too many arbitrary assumptions, and too much arbitrariness.

QUESTIONS

Greenberg: Do you have a different interpretation of deBroglie waves?

Einstein: I consider them almost comparable in reality to light waves, but not quite. There are so many fields as there are masses; and then the trouble of higher ... [word missed].

Callaway: The equivalence principle says it is reasonable to absorb *gravitation* in the metric. But no such principle is known for electromagnetic theory.

Einstein: I believe that the concept of motion has no place in a unified theory; that "geodesic lines" are only a provisory concept, a stopgap. Also it is against the whole idea of quantum theory.

Greenberg: Is there anything in gravitation theory corresponding to radiation?

Einstein: This is a headache. Why not expect also gravitational quanta? But this is hard to include in field theory. Perhaps this is an objection to any field theory that has to do with gravitation. Electromagnetic waves can be put into a container, but gravitational waves cannot—there are two signs of charge for the one; only one for the other. Thus there is a difference in kind between the two theories. This gives the feeling that gravitation is not more true than any classical theory. There is an infinity of constants in a field theory. Only way to overcome: if the condition of nonexistence of singularities in a very unenigmatic way fixed up quantum numbers.

Carlson: What do you think of Bohm's theory?

Einstein: It is clever, but I don't believe it. It is outrageous to believe that the particle between walls does not move.

Komar: Why is unified theory simpler than projective theory?

Einstein: The most basic thing in relativity is the replacement of a field by something like a Γ. In gravitation we have to symmetrize. So we can think unified theory is a simplification of gravitation theory. But gravitation theory is a field theory, and may have difficulties.

Callaway: What do you think of Mach's principle?

Einstein: Mach assumes matter may be permanent. Therefore, why separate the rest of the field from the gravitational field? We have a satisfactory description in conformity with Mach's principle if we have a theory without boundary conditions. I once thought to take the universe roughly static and closed in space. Then came the cosmological λ. But it was a sin against mathematical simplicity. If the world is expanding, it is hopeless. Time is essential. A boundary is unthinkable. Your question is related to the role of matter.

Mozeley: Must a field theory be deterministic?

Einstein: [first few words missed] It is the negative part of determinism that probability should not intervene, because it is not a quality of the system.

THE BLACK HOLE: AN IMAGINARY CONVERSATION WITH ALBERT EINSTEIN

JOHN ARCHIBALD WHEELER

Center for Theoretical Physics, Department of Physics, University of Texas, Austin, Texas

Wheeler: Professor Einstein? Professor Einstein! Oh how wonderful to see you here!

Einstein: Yes, I thought I would surprise you, Mr. Wheeler. But you know I like the sea shore and the waves as much as you do.

Wheeler: But the biggest miracle of all is not our picking the same prospect over sea and distant islands; it is that you should be here at all. What wonderful fortune!

Einstein: Yes, I thought you would be surprised. I am too. Could it have anything to do with those old stories that one is permitted to come back to Earth again for a single hour on one's hundredth birthday? Do you remember Niels Bohr's story about why hang up a horseshoe over your desk?

Wheeler: No, I don't think I heard that one.

Einstein: He used to say, "I don't believe in miracles at all—and especially not in horseshoes. But you know that people who do tell me that it doesn't hurt your luck if you don't believe."[1] That must be the general idea of how come I am here now.

Wheeler: Less than a hour left and that I rejoice in all this beauty. No wonder you don't want to ask questions but only look and smile and close your eyes and look again. But while you look could I ask you some questions? So many colleagues have regretted with me all the questions, great and important questions, that we failed to ask you before you left our midst.

Einstein: But yes. Still you must not consider me an expert. When I was young I made so much trouble for authority that in later life, in punishment, the Lord made me an authority myself[2]; but I am no more.

Wheeler: Why did you not say more about what we today call the "black hole"?

Einstein: Yes, I know what you mean: a completely collapsed star. It was not so easy to discuss such questions in my time. What after all is one to take for the equation of state of the matter of the star? That is not so easy.

Wheeler: Then I'm sure you'll rejoice in the theorems of today that a sufficiently massive collection of cold matter has no escape from gravitational collapse.

Einstein: Of course it is much simpler to stay away from all special assumptions about the relation between density and pressure. That is why in my 1939 paper[3] I considered a collection of well-separated point masses in orbit about their mutual center of gravitation. One discovers that the cluster of mutually gravitating particles is unstable.

Wheeler: Stimulating that was to us all as a beginning. The future will surely see that work continued from the initial stages of instability to the final stages of collapse. But did you never feel an urgency about an extension of these ideas to real stars and an astrophysical search for real black holes?

Einstein: Yes, that is an interesting point. But, no, for me that was an unimportant question of detail. One has only to apply the general relativity theory itself to come to some somewhat reliable conclusions about collapse.

Wheeler: How do you feel about Kerr's exact solution for the geometry around a rotating black hole, consequences of Kerr's and Schild's early mathematical investigations of algebraically special solutions of your gravitational field equation?

Einstein: That is really beautiful! I would never have dared to hope for an exact and simple solution of a problem so difficult.

Wheeler: And how do you react to the work of Carter[4,5] and others?

Einstein: How wonderful it is that they can show that the geometry around a collapsing object, no matter how contorted and asymmetric and violently fluctuating it is, in the end always tends smoothly to an absolutely standard final state depending only on the mass and electric charge and angular momentum of the black hole. Of course, that is outside. But, after all, the critical place is inside. That's where the predicted singularity is. That's where the problem is. It is impossible to believe a prediction that is a singularity.

Wheeler: I and my colleagues have to confess that we have made only a bare beginning at studying the approach to singularity both in cosmology and in black hole physics.

Einstein: To understand that approach is really important.

Wheeler: Our Soviet colleagues propose fascinating physical insights as to what goes on in the final stages of collapse, but not convincing mathematical methodology. Colleagues in the West have the mathematical methodology but so far it has not sufficed to provide the insight that we all want.

Einstein: This is an old story in physics. We know in the end everything comes together in a new and better and larger unity.

Wheeler: Gamow says that you called it "the greatest blunder of my life."[6] The 1929 observation of Hubble[7] revealed that you need not have added an artificial "cosmological term" to your standard 1915 general relativity theory to secure a reasonable account of cosmology. Also it was Friedmann,[8] not you, who in 1922 first worked out that even today standard and simple cosmology from your field equation. I and many colleagues want to ask you how this came about. Was it because[9] you had taken very seriously in your younger days the idea of Spinoza that the universe endures from everlasting to everlasting?[10] Did any contrary conclusion seem to you philosophically unreasonable? In your autobiographical notes[11] you speak of the influence of Spinoza on your outlook. It has been said that "Spinoza rejected the idea of an external Creator suddenly and apparently capriciously creating the world at one particular time rather than another and creating it out of nothing."[10] Do you feel that Spinoza indeed so powerfully influenced what you did and did not do in the field of cosmology?

Einstein: That is very hard to say. Even today we do not know the right way to think about these questions.

Wheeler: Do you envisage a "before" before the big bang and an "after" after the big crunch?

Einstein: One can hold many views on these questions and they all deserve consideration.

Wheeler: This is an exciting time in astrophysics. Some colleagues are inclined to believe that the universe contains less than a tenth of the mass energy that would be required to curve it up into closure. Others, following the lead of other evidence, find indications that the amount of mass energy may be close to what you predicted. What is your view on the question whether the universe is closed?

Einstein: "[We] may present the following arguments against the conception of a space-infinite, and for the conception of a space-bounded, universe: (1) From the standpoint of the theory of relativity, the condition for a closed surface is very much simpler than the corresponding boundary condition at infinity of the quasi-Euclidean structure of the universe. (2) The idea that Mach expressed, that inertia depends upon the mutual action of bodies, is contained, to a first approximation, in the equations of the theory of relativity; ... But this idea of Mach's corresponds only to a finite universe, bounded in space, and not to a quasi-Euclidean infinite universe."[12] "In my opinion the general theory of relativity can only solve this problem [of inertia] satisfactorily if it regards the world as spatially self-enclosed."[13]

Wheeler: I don't have to tell you that there is still a non-negligible body of our colleagues who think that an asymptotically flat universe is more natural than a closed universe.

Einstein: But that view takes the geometry of faraway space out of physics and makes it part of theology, to be discovered by reading Euclid's bible. It puts us back to the days before Riemann, days when space was still for physicists, "a rigid homogeneous something, susceptible of no change or conditions. Only the genius of Riemann, solitary and uncomprehended, had already won its way by the middle of the last century to a new conception of space, in which space was deprived of its rigidity, and in which its power to take part in physical events was recognized as possible."[14]

Wheeler: Space, a new participant in dynamics—that's what you gave us in your equations! Élie Cartan recognized that your geometrodynamics requires initial value data just as does any other dynamics.[15,16] How did you react to his investigations?

Einstein: Yes, Cartan saw into the mathematics deeper than anyone. Yes, I recognized the importance of his work. Yes, I told Helen Dukas, "Don't file Cartan's papers away as you do other papers; keep them out separate so I can study them." Cartan understood things more clearly than anyone.

Still there are two sides to the initial value problem. One is their consequences. They we know in a general way how to calculate. The other is their origin. We still have not the faintest idea of what considerations fix the initial conditions. Your Peebles at Princeton and his colleagues[17] have studied the initial conditions for cosmology more fully than anyone. They show that things in the beginning were not quite so arbitrary as one might have thought. They also find indications that the density is of the same order as what the general theory predicts. That result seems to me a natural one.

Wheeler: Do you then feel that gravitational collapse of the universe is similar in principle to gravitational collapse of a star to a black hole?

Einstein: To think of both processes as equally inescapable is reasonable. I confess it was a surprise to me about the big bang. But once we have to accept that, it seems to me only consistent that we should also accept gravitational collapse, both for stars and for the universe. Yes, that is quite contrary to the idea that Spinoza taught that the universe goes on forever. You mentioned his argument against an original creation. How could nothingness, deprived of all possibility of knowing time, know when to give birth to the universe? How are we to answer this objection today? It must be that time is not so primordial a concept as we take it to be. It must first then come into being when the universe itself begins. That diminished status for time may not be so unreasonable.

Wheeler: But if time is not truly basic, can geometry itself be truly basic? And in that case what happens to your vision of all the forces of nature taking their origin, one way or another, in geometry?

Einstein: The workers of today have a wider understanding of what geometry is and means than was current in my lifetime. Gauge theories—what are they but a new and deeper version of geometry? Even spinor fields nowadays have the "geometry hat" clapped upon their heads, I am told.

Wheeler: But whether you call particles geometry or something else, does it not trouble you that collapse should mean their end?

Einstein: To me the problem of collapse is no greater than the problem of the big bang. Both are a warning that the universe presents deeper issues than we ever realized. That to me is the lesson of the black hole. Alas, I can say no more. I feel myself being carried away, not to return for another hundred years. But let me leave you hope for the work of all your colleagues. "All of these endeavors are based on the belief that existence should have a completely harmonious structure. Today we have less ground than ever before for allowing ourselves to be forced away from this wonderful belief."[18]

REFERENCES

1. Weber, R. L. *A Random Walk in Science* (Institute of Physics, London), 1973, p. 14.

2. Einstein, A. As quoted in B. Hoffmann, *Albert Einstein: Creator and Rebel* (Viking, New York), 1972, p. 24.

3. Einstein, A. "On a stationary system with spherical symmetry consisting of many gravitating masses," *Ann. Math. (U.S.A.) 40*, 922–936 (1939).

4. Carter, B. "An axisymmetric black hole has only two degrees of freedom," *Phys. Rev. Lett. 26*, 331–333 (1970).

5. Carter, B. "Properties of the Kerr metric," in *Black Holes,* Proceedings of 1972 sessions of École d'été de physique théorique, C. DeWitt and B. S. DeWitt, eds. (Gordon and Breach, New York), 1973.

6. Gamow, G. *My World Line* (Viking Press, New York), 1970.

7. Hubble, E. P. "A relation between distance and radial velocity among extragalactic nebulae," *Proc. Nat. Acad. Sci. U.S. 15*, 169–173 (1929).

8. Friedmann, A. "Uber die Krümmung des Raumes," *Z. Phys. 10*, 377–386.

9. The importance of Spinoza's philosophy for Einstein's outlook was kindly emphasized to me by Hans Küng at Tübingen, 12 June 1978.

10. Wolf, A. "Spinoza," *Encyclopaedia Britannica,* Chicago, 1956, vol. 21, p. 235.

11. Schilpp, P. A., ed. *Albert Einstein: Philosopher-Scientist* (Library of Living Philosophers, Evanston, Ill.), 1949.

12. Einstein, A. *The Meaning of Relativity,* 3rd edition (Princeton University Press, Princeton, N.J.), 1950, pp. 107–108.

13. Einstein, A. *Essays in Science* (Philosophical Library, New York), 1934. Translated from *Mein Weltbild* (Querido Verlag, Amsterdam), 1933, p. 55.

14. *Ibid.,* p. 68.

15. Cartan, É. "Sur les equations de la gravitation de Einstein," *J. Math. Pures Appl. 1*, 141–203 (1922).

16. Cartan, É. "La théorie des groupes et les recherches récentes de géométrie differentielle," *Conference Proceedings International Congress of Mathematicians, Toronto (1924), L'Enseign. math. t. 24*, 1–18 (1925).

17. Davis, M., E. J. Groth and P. J. E. Peebles. "Study of galaxy correlations: Evidence for the gravitational instability picture in a dense universe," *Astrophys. J. 212:* L107–L111 (1977).

18. Einstein, A. *Essays in Science* (Philosophical Library, New York), 1934. Translated from *Mein Weltbild* (Querido Verlag, Amsterdam), 1933, p. xx.

MY RELATIVISTIC MILESTONES

J. L. SYNGE

Dublin Institute for Advanced Studies

The mile as a unit of distance will disappear before long, and the word "milestone" is already archaic. So, for the benefit of future generations, let me explain that milestones were blocks of stone set beside highways to tell the weary (or enthusiastic) traveller how many miles he was from his destination. I here recall some milestones I passed in pursuit of relativity.

In 1919, I graduated as a B.A. at Trinity College, Dublin, with a good training in Newtonian mechanics, my favourite subject, and some slight knowledge of electromagnetic theory. The theory of relativity was for me only a matter of vague gossip until in 1920 I bought a book recently translated into English by R. W. Lawson; it was by Albert Einstein and entitled *Relativity: The Special and General Theory: A Popular Exposition.* In the Preface Einstein asserted that he "adhered scrupulously to the precept of that brilliant theoretical physicist, L. Boltzmann, according to whom matters of elegance ought to be left to the tailor and to the cobbler." But "elegance" is a relative term and, although I could not at that time make much out of the general theory, I found the book fascinating. It was my *first milestone,* opening my mind to the possibility (indeed the probability, even the inevitability) that Newton's views about space and time were incorrect.

In that book Einstein devoted a brief chapter to Minkowski's Four-Dimensional Space, remarking (p. 57) that without the important idea contributed by Minkowski, "the general theory of relativity . . . would perhaps have got no farther than its long clothes." Unfortunately for a would-be relativist, I had chosen Greek instead of German at school, and Minkowski's famous paper was not translated until 1923. But with the help of a dictionary and the pictures of space-time in the paper, I reached my *second milestone.* Not only did Minkowski free me from having to wonder why Einstein used the word "relativity"—what was relative to what?—he actually had the rudeness to say that the term "relativity-postulate" seemed to him "very feeble" *(sehr matt)* and proposed instead "the postulate of the absolute world (or briefly, the world-postulate)." His precedent gave me permission to draw my own pictures of space-time, without which I easily got lost in formulae. Mysteries associated with Fitzgerald—Lorentz contractions and retarded clocks vanished when one drew a space-time diagram, although the indefinite line-element took some getting used to.

With the special theory thus under control (at least so I thought), I felt ready to attack the general theory. But I knew nothing of tensor calculus, an essential prerequisite. I have before me the yellowing pages of a copy of Einstein's 1916 paper, with many pencillings indicating my poor knowledge of German—it was not translated until 1923. In linguistic despair, I made a wise decision: I would dip into Einstein's paper for guidance, but I would reconstruct for myself the essentials of tensor calculus, emphasising the geometry. His "summation convention" delighted me as a stroke of genius (how simple!) and in due course I felt (rather presumptuously) that I had a mastery over tensor calculus, applying it not only in relativity but also in classical mechanics. This was my *third milestone*. From that period of self-education, if I may call it that, I still retain prejudices—I squirm when writers continue to write ds^2 for an indefinite quadratic form instead of inserting a factor ± 1 to take care of both timelike and spacelike displacements, a simple trick which Eisenhart used in his *Riemannian Geometry* (1926).

I was now able to carry out formal work in general relativity, but did not feel at ease. Later I read with approval what P. W. Bridgman wrote in the collection entitled *Albert Einstein: Philosopher-Scientist* (Evanston, Illinois, 1949): he accused Einstein of abandoning the operational method, used so successfully in the special theory. In this method the concepts are defined in terms of thought-experiments, and of course you cannot carry out such experiments without thought-apparatus. There was really nothing new about this idea; it is as old as Euclid and Archimedes, and the student of Newtonian mechanics would see (with his mind's eye) the planets moving around the sun. Apart from a clock which registered absolute time, the most essential piece of thought-apparatus with a rigid measuring rod could be used (mentally) to measure the distances between the planets and the sun, and also to measure the planets and the sun to verify that they were themselves rigid bodies, luckily so nearly spherical that they behaved gravitationally as if their masses were concentrated at their centres. Fantastic as this thought-apparatus may seem, it is still the basis of celestial mechanics as practiced by astronomers, for whom "relativistic effects" are merely a small correction, almost negligible compared with Newtonian perturbations.

I knew very well that the thought-apparatus admissible in relativity must not include that master-clock registering absolute time. Einstein had made that very clear, and I was prepared to use instead "proper time" measured by a standard clock as it traversed its world line in space-time. But I had seen no danger sign warning me about rigidity and it was some time before I found that, even in special relativity, the concept of a rigid body must be abandoned; away back in 1909 Born had given a relativisitc definition of rigidity, but admitting fewer degrees of freedom that the classical rigid body of Euler, and not really of much use. Einstein must surely have realised that in his great role as destroyer-and-creator he had killed the rigid body, and yet we find him referring to rigid rods in *The Meaning of Relativity* (Princeton, 1955), p. 91.

Gyroscopic theory is one of the most fascinating chapters in Newtonian mechanics, but it is tied up with the concept of rigidity, and with a heavy heart I realised that I must let it go if I was to conduct thought-experiments in relativity. I should of course make it clear that *in reality* there are no rigid bodies. The point is that the *concept* of rigidity is consistent with the basic concepts of Newtonian mechanics, but inconsistent with those of relativity, unless someone succeeds in defining rigidity in a more sophisticated way. The loss of rigidity worried me so much that I count as my *fourth milestone* a firm determination not to bother about it any more.

Well, then, what is left in the way of thought-apparatus in relativity? The standard clock of course, but there must be some way to communicate between the clocks: why not use photons, which as far as this idealisation is concerned, are merely "particles" with null geodesics for their world lines? This step may seem a small way from the last, but I regard it as my *fifth milestone*—nothing but standard clocks and photons are admitted as the basic apparatus for thought-experiments, and that goes for both special and general relativity.

But of course that is only the background to a subject which is of great mathematical complexity. It has been said that in 1905 the time was ripe for special relativity, and that it would have emerged even if Einstein had never been born. After all, what is special relativity but elaboration of the fact that Maxwell's equations are invariant under Lorentz-Poincaré transformations? But I have never heard it suggested the Einstein's field equations of general relativity were not the product of his own genius.

Dropping tensorial indices and omitting a constant factor, those field equations may be written $G = T$; here G is the Einstein tensor, a complicated expression involving the metric tensor *(g)* and its partial derivatives of the first and second order; T is the energy tensor, representing matter. Now it has been a well-established custom in mathematics, when one seeks to find unknown quantities in terms of known quantities, to put the unknown on the *left* hand side of the equations and the known on the *right*. Thus, when a mathematician sees the equations $G = T$ he is inclined to regard them as a set of partial differential equations in which T is known and g is to be found. But it is not as simple as that. From its very structure, the Einstein tensor G is divergence-free: therefore T must be divergence-free; but the conditions that T should be divergence-free involve the metric tensor g, the very thing we are trying to find!

Thus the situation is indeed complicated, even without mentioning the "coordinate conditions" looming in the background. I count as my *sixth milestone* a remark of W. H. McCrea: the field equations may be written the other way around, in the form $T = G$. This suggests that we should regard the metric tensor g as given; from it the Einstein tensor can be calculated merely by differentiation and some algebraic processes, and since G is automatically divergence-free, so the energy tensor T given by $T = G$ is also divergence-free. The only restriction on g is that it should have the correct signature and be smooth enough to permit the required differentiations. To present the essential idea by a simple analogue, imagine a rather dull (or rather bright!) schoolboy who is asked to solve the quadratic equation

$$x^2 + 3x + 2 = y.$$

He writes it in the form

$$y = x^2 + 3x + 2,$$

and says that, if $x = 1$, then $y = 6$.

I spent a couple of years in the vicinity of that sixth milestone. At first the prospect was dazzling: one could create universe after universe, each one an exact solution of Einstein's field equations. But when one examined the energy tensors thus obtained, they failed to satisfy the physical condition that the density of matter must be positive or zero. And yet if, by an inspired guess, one had thought of the Schwarzschild metric (interior and exterior), the energy tensor would of course have come out right. Nevertheless, one can use the idea to test for possible errors in proposed solutions of the field equations and indeed estimate errors in approximate solutions, particularly in relation to equations of motion.

Do I believe in the theory of relativity, special and general? Much as I dislike the name (I would much prefer to follow Minkowski, but is is now too late), my immediate answer is "Yes," but there are second thoughts, and I count as my *seventh milestone* the fact that I permit myself to have second thoughts. In saying this, I do not wish to associate myself with that small but persistent group of people convinced that the theory contains some essential error against which they protest but which they seem unable to make clear. I take the view, probably shared by many today, that no mathematical theory can possibly account accurately for all physical phenomena. Improvements in the techniques of experiment and observation are bound to reveal inadequacies in all theories, which, when patched up to fit the facts, lose their intellectual appeal. We are concerned with mathematical structures which have, in the words of Leopold Infeld, links with reality. Without those links, all so-called physical theories would merely be elegant pieces of pure mathematics with suggestive physical words thrown in to catch the attention of physicists.

In my younger days, long before I had reached this seventh milestone, I thought that in due course all Newtonian physics would be converted into relativistic form. That has not happened. In recent books on celestial mechanics, I find Newtonian theory, except for an ad hoc insert, to deal with the matter of Mercury. As an incurable relativist I keep wondering relative to what the perihelion of Mercury is rotating.

V. GRAVITATION–THE DESTINY OF THE STARS, OR RELATIVISTIC ASTROPHYSICS

Until fairly recently it had not been thought that relativity—and especially general relativity—played an important role in astrophysics, the physics of stars and other celestial objects. The discovery of quasars with their immense energy output and pulsars, which were shown to be rapidly rotating neutron stars, defied standard explanations, and it was realized that these are large or very dense masses where relativity does play a significant part. This discovery gave rise to a new branch of astrophysics, relativistic astrophysics, and some of its achievements will be described here.

It was S. Chandrasekhar who first pointed out that the equation of state for degenerate matter, such as is present in white dwarfs, must be modified to take into account effects arising from special relativity. In his lecture, reprinted here, he goes much further and traces the evolution of stars to their ultimate demise into white dwarfs, neutron stars, and even into black holes. The limiting mass above which instability sets in is 1.44 solar masses, but at the same time the critical radius is zero. However, general relativistic effects, both in the stresses and space-time, lead directly to the existence of a minimum radius for white dwarf stars.[1] A realistic description of white dwarfs, including their red shift, has been given in an article by Giora Shaviv in this volume.

When J. R. Oppenheimer and G. M. Volkoff developed a completely general relativistic treatment of massive neutron cores,[2] this seemed more a mathematical exercise than a description of actual objects, since neutron stars were unknown. When pulsars, radio sources emitting rapid but regularly timed "pulses," were detected, and clamored for an explanation, the neutron star came into its own. As described so vividly by Jeremiah P. Ostriker here, stars of radii of the order of 10 kilometers and masses approximately the mass of the sun—neutron stars—must exist, since the pulsar that supplies the energy of the Crab Nebula has exactly these properties. Since that time more observational evidence was obtained, and there is now little doubt that neutron stars are a reality.

1. Cf. J. W. Weinberg and G. E. Tauber, "Gravitational Stability of Large Masses," First Prize Essay Award, Gravity Research Foundation, 1963. It had even been suggested that the correlated distribution of masses and radii of stars of this kind might provide an additional experimental test of general relativity, since the empty lower left corner of the H-R diagram indicates the absence of such stars below the critical radius. (However, competing processes, such as inverse beta decay, which are of the same order as general relativistic effects, let those stars evolve to neutron assemblies even before they have reached the limiting mass and radius, thus invalidating any clear identification.)

2. J. R. Oppenheimer and G. M. Volkoff, "On Massive Neutron Cores," *Physical Review* 55 (1939), p. 374. Only the rather technical nature of this classical paper induced us not to include it in this anthology.

Quasars (Quasi Stellar Radio Sources) still await a complete explanation. Their unusually large red shift makes them either extremely distant from the earth or, if the red shift is gravitational in nature, makes them tremendously heavy objects. Their large output of energy gives rise to speculation that ranges from their being supermassive stars to lagging cores of the original expansion of the universe. As Martin J. Rees points out in his Halley Lecture of 1978, excerpts of which are reprinted here, a tenable and widely accepted hypothesis now is that quasars are optically hyperactive galactic nuclei. Eventually massive star clusters and other objects, both of which have been proposed as models for active galactic nuclei, will end as accreting black holes, which may turn out to be a more efficient power source than any conceivable progenitor.

In conclusion, a black hole can be created in any of several ways. It can be a result of fluctuations in the early universe, a gravitational collapse of ordinary stars, supermassive stars, galactic nuclei, or massive star clusters. J. C. Miller and Dennis W. Sciama limit their investigations here to tracing the formation of black holes by gravitational collapse of ordinary stars. So far the existence of black holes is mainly speculative and no definite evidence has been found, but their presence would be another triumph for general relativity.

WHY ARE THE STARS AS THEY ARE?

S. CHANDRASEKHAR

University of Chicago, Chicago, Illinois

This lecture recalls some considerations of forty and more years ago which may have some relevance to the current topics which are the concern of this session of the International School of Physics.

1. EDDINGTON'S PARABLE

Domains of natural phenomena are often circumscribed by well-defined scales, and theories concerning them are successful only to the extent that these scales emerge naturally in them. Thus, to the question "Why are the atoms as they are?", the answer "Because the Bohr radius—$h^2/(4\pi^2 m_e e^2)$~~ $0.5 \cdot 10^{-8}$ cm—provides a correct measure of their dimensions" is apposite. In a similar vein, we may ask "Why are the stars as they are?", intending by such a question to seek the basic reason why modern theories of stellar structure and stellar evolution prevail. EDDINGTON [1] effectively posed this question to himself and answered it in his parable of a physicist on a cloud-bound planet. His parable as he told it is the following.

"The outward flowing radiation may be compared to a wind blowing through the star and helping to distend it against gravity. The formulae to be

From Astrophysics of Neutron Stars and Black Holes, *edited by R. Giacconi and R. Ruffini. Enrico Fermi Course 65 (Amsterdam: North Holland Publishing Co., 1978). Reprinted by permission of the authors, editors, and the Italian Physical Society.*

developed later (eq. [42] in sect. 5 below) enable us to calculate what proportion of the weight of the material is borne by this wind, the remainder being supported by the gas pressure. To a first approximation the proportion is the same at all parts of the star. It does not depend on the density nor on the opacity of the star. It depends only on the mass and molecular weight. Moreover, the physical constants employed in the calculation have all been measured in the laboratory, and no astronomical data are required. We can imagine a physicist on a cloud-bound planet who has never heard tell of the stars calculating the ratio of radiation pressure to gas pressure for a series of globes of gas of various sizes, starting, say, with a globe of mass 10 g, then 100 g, 1000 g and so on, so that his n-th globe contains 10^n g. *Table I* shows the more interesting part of his results.

Table I.

No. of globe	Radiation pressure	Gas pressure	No. of globe	Radiation pressure	Gas pressure
32	0.0016	0.9984	36	0.951	0.049
33	0.106	0.894	37	0.984	0.016
34	0.570	0.430	38	0.9951	0.0049
35	0.850	0.150	39	0.9984	0.0016

"The rest of the table would consist mainly of long strings of 9's and 0's. Just for the particular range of mass about the 33rd to 35th globes the table becomes interesting, and then lapses back into 9's and 0's again. Regarded as a tussle between matter and aether (gas pressure and radiation pressure) the contest is overwhelmingly one-sided except between numbers 33–35, where we may expect something to happen.

"What 'happens' is the stars.

"We draw aside the veil of cloud beneath which our physicist has been working and let him look up at the sky. There he will find a thousand million globes of gas nearly all of mass between his 33rd and 35th globes—that is to say, between ½ and 50 times the Sun's mass. The lightest known star is about $3 \cdot 10^{32}$ g and the heaviest about 2.10^{35} g. The majority are between 10^{33} and 10^{34} g, where the serious challenge of radiation pressure to compete with gas pressure is beginning."

2. THE $(1—\beta_*)$-THEOREM AND THE COMBINATION $(hc/G)^{3/2}H^{-2}$

There are two curious aspects to Eddington's parable. The first is that, while a combination of natural constants of the dimensions of a mass and of stellar magnitude is clearly implied by the calculation, it is not explicitly isolated—a surprising omission in view of Eddington's later propensities. The second is the logical lacuna in the argument: why is the relative extent to which radiation pressure provides support against gravity a relevant factor to the "happening" of stars (*)? The omission is easily rectified and the argument at least ameliorated.

Consider an enclosure containing matter and radiation. Let the matter be in a state of a perfect gas (in the classical Maxwellian sense) so that the pressure due to it is given by

(1)
$$p_{\text{gas}} = \frac{k}{\mu H} \varrho T,$$

where k denotes the Boltzmann constant, H the mass of the hydrogen atom, μ the mean molecular weight, ϱ the density and T the temperature. The pressure due to radiation, in the same enclosure, is given by

(2)
$$p_{\text{rad}} = \frac{1}{3} aT^4,$$

where a denotes Stefan's constant. Consequently, if radiation pressure contributes a fraction $1-\beta$ to the total pressure P, then

(3)
$$P = \frac{1}{1-\beta} \frac{1}{3} aT^4 = \frac{1}{\beta} \frac{k}{\mu H} \varrho T.$$

We may eliminate T from these relations and express P in terms of $\bar{\varrho}$ and β instead of ϱ and T. Thus

(4)
$$T = \left(\frac{k}{\mu H} \frac{3}{a} \frac{1-\beta}{\beta} \right)^{\frac{1}{3}} \varrho^{\frac{1}{3}}$$

and

(5)
$$P = \left[\left(\frac{k}{\mu H} \right)^4 \frac{3}{a} \frac{1-\beta}{\beta^4} \right]^{\frac{1}{3}} \varrho^{\frac{4}{3}} = C(\beta) \varrho^{\frac{4}{3}} \quad \text{(say)}.$$

Now there is a general theorem (CHANDRASEKHAR [2]) which states that the pressure P_c at the center of a star of mass M, in hydrostatic equilibrium and in which the density $\varrho(r)$ at any point r does not exceed the mean density $\bar{\varrho}(r)$ interior to that point r, must satisfy the inequality

(6)
$$\frac{1}{2} G(\tfrac{4}{3}\pi)^{\frac{1}{3}} \bar{\varrho}^{\frac{4}{3}} M^{\frac{2}{3}} \leqslant P_c \leqslant \frac{1}{2} G(\tfrac{4}{3}\pi)^{\frac{1}{3}} \varrho_c^{\frac{4}{3}} M^{\frac{2}{3}},$$

where $\bar{\varrho}$ denotes the mean density of the star and ϱ_c its density at the center. The content of this theorem is no more than the assertion that the actual pressure at the center of a star must be intermediate between those at the centers of two configurations of uniform density, one at a density equal to the mean density $\bar{\varrho}$ of the star and the other at a density equal to the density ϱ_c at the center. If the inequality (6) should be violated, then there must be some

(*)Besides, the values listed in table I are based on the unlikely value of a mean molecular weight $\mu=4$. On this least point, see Eddington's [1] own discussion.

regions in the star in which adverse density gradients prevail; and the occurrence of such adverse density gradients will lead to instabilities. In other words, *we may consider conformity with the inequality* (6) *as a necessary condition for the stable existence of a star.*

The right-hand part of the inequality (6) together with P_c given by eq. (5) requires, as a condition for the existence of a stable star,

$$(7) \qquad \left[\left(\frac{k}{\mu H} \right)^4 \frac{3}{a} \frac{1 - \beta_c}{\beta_c^4} \right]^{\frac{1}{3}} \leqslant \left(\frac{\pi}{6} \right)^{\frac{1}{3}} G M^{\frac{2}{3}} ,$$

or, equivalently,

$$(8) \qquad M \geqslant \left(\frac{6}{\pi} \right)^{\frac{1}{2}} \left[\left(\frac{k}{\mu H} \right)^4 \frac{3}{a} \frac{1 - \beta_c}{\beta_c^4} \right]^{\frac{1}{2}} \frac{1}{G^{\frac{3}{2}}} ,$$

where in the foregoing inequalities β_c is the value of β at the center of the star. Now, Stefan's constant (by virtue of Planck's law) has the value

$$(9) \qquad a = \frac{8\pi^5 k^4}{15 h^3 c^3} .$$

Inserting this value of a in the inequality (8), we obtain

$$(10) \qquad \mu^2 M \left(\frac{\beta_c^4}{1 - \beta_c} \right)^{\frac{1}{2}} \geqslant \frac{(135)^{\frac{1}{2}}}{2\pi^3} \left(\frac{hc}{G} \right)^{\frac{3}{2}} \frac{1}{H^2} = 0.1873 \left(\frac{hc}{G} \right)^{\frac{3}{2}} \frac{1}{H^2} .$$

First we observe that the inequality (10) has isolated the following combination of natural constants of the dimensions of a mass and of stellar magnitude (cf. CHANDRASEKHAR [3]):

$$(11) \qquad \left(\frac{hc}{G} \right)^{\frac{3}{2}} \frac{1}{H^2} \simeq 29.2 \odot .$$

Returning to the inequality (8), we can express it as providing an *upper bound* to $1 - \beta_c$; thus

$$(12) \qquad 1 - \beta_c \leqslant 1 - \beta_* ,$$

where $1 - \beta_*$ is uniquely determined by the mass M and the mean molecular weight μ by the quartic equation

$$(13) \qquad \frac{\mu^2 M}{\odot} = 5.48 \left(\frac{1 - \beta_*}{\beta_*^4} \right)^{\frac{1}{2}} .$$

We may suppose that the following tabulation of $1 - \beta_*$ was made by Eddington's physicist on the cloud-bound planet, who, after isolating the combination of natural constants (11), had concluded, from its existence, a reason for the "happening" of stars.

Table II.

$(M/\odot)\mu^2$	$1-\beta_*$	$(M/\odot)\mu^2$	$1-\beta_*$
0.56	0.01	15.49	0.50
1.01	0.03	26.52	0.60
2.14	0.10	50.92	0.70
3.83	0.20	122.5	0.80
6.12	0.30	224.4	0.85
9.62	0.40	519.6	0.90

3. "HAVE THE STARS ENOUGH ENERGY TO COOL?": EDDINGTON'S PARADOX AND FOWLER'S RESOLUTION

The same combination of natural constants (11) emerged soon afterwards in the context of resolving a paradox EDDINGTON [4] had formulated in the form of one of his famous aphorisms: *"a star will need energy to cool."* The paradox arose while considering the ultimate fate of gaseous stars in the light of the then new knowledge that stars, such as the companion of Sirius, exist which have mean densities in the range $10^5 \div 10^6$) g cm^{-3}. As EDDINGTON stated, "I do not see how a star which has once got into this compressed condition is ever going to get out of it. . . . It would seem that the star will be in an awkward predicament when its supply of subatomic energy fails." Or, as FOWLER [5] stated: "The stellar material will have radiated so much energy that it has less energy than the same matter in normal atoms expanded at the absolute zero of temperature. If part of it were removed from the star and the pressure taken off, what could it do?" Quantitatively, the question arises in the following way.

An estimate of the electrostatic energy E_v per unit volume of an assembly of atoms of atomic number Z ionized down to their bare nuclei is given by

$$(14) \qquad E_v = 1.32 \cdot 10^{11} Z^2 \varrho^{\frac{4}{3}},$$

whereas the kinetic energy E_{kin} per unit of volume of the free particles, under the assumption that they are free as in a perfect gas at a density ϱ and a temperature T, is given by

$$(15) \qquad E_{kin} = \frac{3}{2} \frac{k}{\mu H} \varrho T = \frac{1.24 \cdot 10^8}{\mu} \varrho T.$$

Now, if such matter were released of the pressure to which it is subject, it can resume the state of ordinary normal atoms only if

$$(16) \qquad E_{kin} > E_v,$$

or, according to eqs. (14) and (15), only if

$$(17) \qquad \varrho < (0.94 \cdot 10^{-3} \, T/\mu Z^2)^3 .$$

This inequality will be clearly violated if the density is sufficiently high. This is the essence of Eddington's paradox (though at a later time he disclaimed to this formulation). FOWLER [5] resolved this paradox in 1926 in a paper entitled

"Dense matter"—one of the great landmark papers in the entire subject of stellar structure and stellar evolution: for, in it the notions of Fermi statistics and electron degeneracy are introduced into astrophysics for the first time.

In a completely degenerate electron gas, all the available parts of the phase space, with momenta less than a certain threshold value p_0, are occupied consistently with Pauli's exclusion principle. If $(p)\mathrm{d}p$ denotes the number of electrons, per unit volume, with momenta between p and $p + \mathrm{d}p$, then the assumption of complete degeneracy is equivalent to the assertion

$$(18) \qquad n\,(p) = \begin{cases} \dfrac{8\pi}{h^3}\,p^2 & (p \leqslant p_0), \\[2mm] 0 & (p > p_0). \end{cases}$$

The threshold momentum p_0 is determined by the normalizing condition

$$(19) \qquad n = \int_0^{p_0} n(p)\,\mathrm{d}p = \frac{8\pi}{3h^3}\,p_0^3 \,,$$

where n denotes the number of electrons per unit volume.

For the distribution given in eq. (18), the pressure P and the kinetic energy E_{kin} of the electrons (per unit volume) are given by

$$(20) \qquad P = \frac{8\pi}{3h^3} \int_0^{p_0} p^3 v_p \,\mathrm{d}p$$

and

$$(21) \qquad E_{\text{kin}} = \frac{8\pi}{h^3} \int_0^{p_0} p^2 T_p \,\mathrm{d}p \,,$$

where v_p and T_p are the velocity and the kinetic energy of an electron having a momentum p. If we set

$$(22) \qquad v_p = p/m \quad \text{and} \quad T_p = p^2/2m$$

(appropriate for nonrelativistic velocities) in eqs. (20) and (21), we find

$$(23) \qquad P = \frac{8\pi}{15h^3 m}\,p_0^5 = \frac{1}{20}\left(\frac{3}{\pi}\right)^{\frac{2}{3}} \frac{h^2}{2m}\,n^{\frac{5}{3}}$$

and

$$(24) \qquad E_{\text{kin}} = \frac{8\pi}{10h^3 m}\,p_0^5 = \frac{3}{40}\left(\frac{3}{\pi}\right)^{\frac{2}{3}} \frac{h^2}{2m}\,n^{\frac{5}{3}} \,.$$

Fowler's resolution of Eddington's paradox consists in this. At the temperature and densities that may be expected to prevail in the interiors of the white-dwarf stars, the electrons will be highly degenerate and E_{kin} should be evaluated in accordance with eq. (24), not in accordance with eq. (15); and eq. (24) gives

(25)
$$E_{kin} = \frac{1.39 \cdot 10^{13}}{\mu^{\frac{5}{3}}} \, \varrho^{\frac{5}{3}} \, .$$

A comparison of eqs. (14) and (25) now shows that for sufficiently high densities $E_{kin} > E_v$; and Eddington's paradox does not arise. FOWLER concluded his paper with the following perceptive statement:

> "The black-dwarf material is best likened to a single gigantic molecule in its lowest quantum state. On the Fermi-Dirac statistics, its high density can be achieved in one and only one way, in virtue of a correspondingly great energy content. But this energy can no more be expended in radiation than the energy of a normal atom or molecule. The only difference between black-dwarf matter and a normal molecule is that the molecule can exist in a free state while the black-dwarf matter can only so exist under very high external pressure."

4. THE THEORY OF DEGENERATE CONFIGURATIONS: THE LIMITING MASS

The internal energy ($=3P/2$) of a degenerate electron gas that is associated with a pressure P is *zero-point energy*; and the essential content of Fowler's paper is that this zero-point energy is so great that we may expect a star to eventually settle down to a state in which all of its energy is of this form. Fowler's argument can be formulated more explicitly in the following manner.

According to the expression for the pressure given in eq. (23), we have the relation

(26)
$$P = K_1 \varrho^{\frac{5}{3}}, \quad \text{where} \quad K_1 = \frac{1}{20} \left(\frac{3}{\pi} \right)^{\frac{2}{3}} \frac{h^2}{(\mu_e H)^{\frac{5}{3}}},$$

and μ_e is the mean molecular weight per electron. Equilibrium configurations in which the pressure is a monomial of the density are the polytropes of Emden and an equilibrium configuration in which the relation (26) obtains is a polytrope of index 3/2. And the theory of polytropes directly leads to the relation (CHANDRASEKHAR [6])

(27)
$$K_1 = 0.424 \, GM^3 \, R \, ,$$

or, numerically,

(28)
$$\log (R/R_\odot) = -\tfrac{1}{3} \log (M/\odot) - \tfrac{5}{3} \log \mu_e - 1.40.$$

For a mass equal to the solar mass and $\mu_e = 2$, the relation (28) predicts a radius $R = 1.3 \cdot 10^{-2} \, R_\odot$ and a mean density of $7 \cdot 10^5$ g cm^{-3}. These values are precisely of the order of the radii and mean densities which are encountered in white-dwarf stars. Moreover, according to eqs. (27) and (28) *finite equilib-rium configurations are predicted for all masses.* On these accounts, it came to be accepted that *the white dwarfs, rather than the "black dwarfs"* in Fowler's terminology, *represent the last stages in the evolution of all stars.* And it seemed for a time that one could rest with the comfortable assurance that "all stars have the necessary energy to cool." But this assurance was shattered when it was realized soon afterwards (CHANDRASEKHAR [7, 8]) that the electrons in the centers of degenerate configurations following the mass-radius relation (27) begin to have momenta comparable to mc; and that therefore the equation of state for degenerate matter must be modified to take into account effects arising from special relativity.

The required modifications of eqs. (23) and (24) allowing for the effects of special relativity are readily made. We have only to insert in eqs. (20) and (21) the relations

$$(29) \qquad v_p = \frac{p}{m(1 + p^2/m^2c^2)^{\frac{1}{2}}} \quad \text{and} \quad T_p = mc^2 \left[(1 + p^2/m^2c^2)^{\frac{1}{2}} - 1 \right]$$

in place of the nonrelativistic relations (22). We find that the resulting equation of state can be expressed, parametrically, in the form (CHANDRASEKHAR [9, 10])

$$(30) \qquad P = A f(x), \quad \varrho = Bx^3,$$

where

$$(31) \qquad A = \frac{\pi m^4 c^5}{3h^3}, \quad B = \frac{8\pi m^3 c^3 \mu_e H}{3h^3}$$

and

$$(32) \qquad f(x) = x(x^2 + 1)^{\frac{1}{2}} (2x^2 - 3) + 3 \sinh^{-1} x.$$

According to eqs. (31) and (32), the pressure approximates the relation (23) for low enough electron concentrations, but for increasing electron con-centrations it tends to (cf. CHANDRASEKHAR [7])

$$(33) \qquad P = \frac{1}{8} \left(\frac{3}{\pi} \right)^{\frac{1}{3}} hcn^{\frac{4}{3}}.$$

This limiting form of the relation can be obtained by simply setting $v_p = c$ in eq. (20); then

$$(34) \qquad P = \frac{8\pi c}{3h^3} \int_0^{p_0} p^3 \, dp = \frac{2\pi c}{3h^3} p_0^4;$$

and the elimination of p_0 with the aid of eq. (19) directly leads to the relation (33).

While the modification of the equation of state required by special relativity appears harmless enough, it has a dramatic effect on the predicted mass-radius relation for degenerate configurations.

The relation between P and ϱ corresponding to the limiting form (33) is

$$(35) \qquad P = K_2\, \varrho^{\frac{4}{3}}, \quad \text{where} \quad K_2 = \frac{1}{8}\left(\frac{3}{\pi}\right)^{\frac{1}{3}} \frac{hc}{(\mu_e H)^{\frac{4}{3}}}.$$

In this limit the configuration is therefore a polytrope of index 3. It is well known that, when the the index is 3, the mass is uniquely determined by the constant of proportionality in the pressure-density relation. The theory gives

$$(36) \qquad M_{\text{limit}} = 4\pi \left(\frac{K_2}{\pi G}\right)^{\frac{3}{2}} 6.89 = 0.197 \left(\frac{hc}{G}\right)^{\frac{3}{2}} \frac{1}{(\mu_e H)^2} = 5.76 \mu_e^{-2} \odot.$$

(In eq. (36), 6.89 is a numerical constant derived from the explicit solution of the appropriate Emden's equation.) We observe that eq. (36) isolates once again the same combination of natural constants that we encountered earlier in sect. 2.

A detailed consideration of equilibrium configurations (CHANDRASEKHAR [8–10]) built on the equation of state given by eqs. (30) and (32)

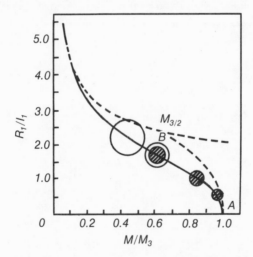

Fig. 1.   The full-line curve represents the exact (mass-radius) relation for completely degenerate configurations. The mass, along the abscissa, is measured in units of the limiting mass (denoted by M_3) and the radius, along the ordinate, is measured in the unit $l_1 = 7.72\mu^{-1\cdot}10^8$ cm. The dashed curve represents the relation that follows from the equation of state (26); at the point B along this curve, the threshold momentum p_0 of the electrons at the center of the configuration is exactly equal to mc. Along the exact curve, at the point where a full circle (with no shaded part) is drawn, p_0 (at the center) is again equal to mc; the shaded parts of the other circles represent the regions in these configurations where the electrons may be considered to be relativistic ($p_0 \gg mc$) (This illustration is reproduced from CHANDRASEKHAR [10].)

shows that the mass-radius relation for these objects, while it approximates eq. (27) for $M \to 0$, predicts that *the radius tends to zero for $M \to M_{\text{limit}}$* (see fig. 1). Therefore, *finite degenerate equilibrium configurations exist only for $M < M_{\text{limit}}$; and stars more massive than M_{limit} "do not have the necessary energy to cool."*

5. A CRITERION WHEN STARS CAN DEVELOP DEGENERATE CORES

Once the existence of the limiting mass was established, the question that required resolution was how one was to relate its existence to the evolution of stars from their gaseous state. If a star has a mass less than M_{limit}, the assumption that it will eventually evolve towards the completely degenerate state and become a black dwarf appears eminently reasonable. But, what if its mass is larger than M_{limit}? Clues as to what might then happen were sought in terms of the equations and inequalities of sect. 2 and 4 (CHANDRASEKHAR [11]).

The first question that had to be resolved was the conditions under which a star, initially gaseous, can develop a degenerate core. A key to the solution of this question was provided by a comparison of eq. (35) with an expression for the electron pressure (as given by the classical perfect-gas equation of state) expressed in terms of a parameter β_e and ϱ as in eq. (5). Thus, with the definition

$$(37) \qquad p_e = \frac{k}{\mu_e H} \varrho T = \frac{\beta_e}{1 - \beta_e} \frac{1}{3} a T^4$$

(where p_e now denotes the electron pressure), we can write

$$(38) \qquad p_e = \left[\left(\frac{k}{\mu_e H} \right)^4 \frac{3}{a} \frac{1 - \beta_e}{\beta_e} \right]^{\frac{1}{3}} \varrho^{\frac{4}{3}} .$$

Comparing this equation with eq. (35), we conclude that, if

$$(39) \qquad \left[\left(\frac{k}{\mu_e H} \right)^4 \frac{3}{a} \frac{1 - \beta_e}{\beta_e} \right]^{\frac{1}{3}} > K_2 = \frac{1}{8} \left(\frac{3}{\pi} \right)^{\frac{1}{3}} \frac{hc}{(\mu_e H)^{\frac{4}{3}}} ,$$

the pressure p_e given by the classical perfect-gas equation is greater than that given by the equation if degeneracy prevailed—not only for the prescribed ϱ and T, but also for all ϱ and T having the same β_e. Inserting for a its value (9), we find that the inequality (39) reduces to (CHANDRASEKHAR [11])

$$(40) \qquad \frac{960}{\pi^4} \frac{1 - \beta_e}{\beta_e} > 1 ,$$

or

(41) $$1 - \beta_e > 0.0921 = 1 - \beta_\omega \quad \text{(say)}.$$

For our present purposes, the principal content of the inequality (41) is the criterion that, for a star to develop degeneracy, it is necessary that the radiation pressure be less than 9.2 percent of the total pressure. As we shall presently show, this requirement effectively excludes massive stars. This last inference is so central to all current schemes of stellar evolution that the directness and the simplicity of the early arguments is perhaps worth repeating.

The two principal elements of the early arguments were these: *first,* that radiation pressure becomes increasingly dominant as the mass of a star increases; and, *second,* that electron degeneracy is possible only so long as radiation pressure is not a significant factor—indeed, as we have seen, it must not exceed 9.2 percent of the total pressure. The second of these elements is a direct and an elementary consequence of the physics of degeneracy; but the first requires some amplification.

That radiation pressure must play an increasingly dominant role as the mass of a star increases in one of the earliest results established in the study of stellar structure; it is, in fact, implicit in the calculation of Eddington's cloud-bound physicist. A quantitative expression to this fact was given by Eddington's *standard model,* which lay at the base of many of the early studies in stellar structure during the twenties and thirties. In this model, the fraction β (=gas pressure/total pressure) introduced in sect. 2 is assumed to be a constant through the star. It follows from eq. (5) that, under this assumption, stars are polytropes of index 3 and that we have the relation (cf. eq. (36))

(42) $$M = 4\pi \left(\frac{C(\beta)}{\pi G} \right)^{\frac{3}{2}} 6.89 ,$$

where $C(\beta)$ has the value given in eq. (5). Equation (42) provides a quartic equation for β similar to eq. (13) for β_*. (The values of $1-\beta$ and β given in table I are in fact derived from eq. (42) with the unlikely value $\mu=4$.)

Equation (42) gives the mass

(43) $$M = 0.197\, \beta_\omega^{-\frac{3}{2}} \left(\frac{hc}{G} \right)^{\frac{3}{2}} \frac{1}{H^2\,\mu^2} = 0.228 \left(\frac{hc}{G} \right)^{\frac{3}{2}} \frac{1}{H^2\,\mu^2} = 6.65\,\mu^{-2}\, \odot$$

for a star in which $\beta=\beta\omega=0.908$. In the standard model, then, stars with masses exceeding $6.65\,\mu^{-2}\odot$ will have radiation pressures that will exceed 9.2 percent of the total pressures. Consequently, stars with masses greater than $6.6\,\mu^{-2}$ cannot, during the course of their evolution, develop degeneracy in the interiors; and, accordingly, an eventual white-dwarf state is impossible for them without a substantial ejection of mass.

The standard model is, of course, only a model. Nevertheless, all of our experience with stellar models for normal stars has confirmed the general (qualitative) correctness of the inferences that were drawn on the basis of the standard model. In particular, the principal conclusion that radiation pressure plays an increasingly dominant role as the mass of the star increases has stood the test of time; and the corollary that stars with masses exceeding 7 or 8$\odot$ cannot develop degeneracy in their interiors has been sustained. These conclusions to which one arrived forty and more years ago appeared so convincing that confident assertions such as the following were made (CHANDRASEKHAR [9, 11]):

> *Given an enclosure containing electrons and atomic nuclei (total charge zero), what happens if we go on compressing the material indefinitely?* (1932)

"The life history of a star of small mass must be essentially different from the life history of a star of large mass. For a star of small mass the natural white-dwarf stage is an initial step towards complete extinction. A star of large mass cannot pass into the white-dwarf stage and one is left speculating on other possibilities." (1934)

While EDDINGTON [12] would not accede to these conclusions, he, nevertheless, very clearly recognized that the existence of an upper limit to the mass of completely degenerate configurations, *if accepted*—he, himself, denied its existence (*) —implied, inevitably, the occurrence of black holes as the end products of the evolution of massive stars. He thus stated:

> "The star apparently has to go on radiating and radiating and contracting and contracting until, I suppose, it gets down to a few kilometers radius when gravity becomes strong enough to hold the radiation and the star can at last find peace. I felt driven to the conclusion that this was almost a *reductio ad absurdum* of the relativistic degeneracy formula. Various accidents may intervene to save the star, but I want more protection than that. I think that there should be a law of Nature to prevent the star from behaving in this absurd way." (1935)

(*) As did MILNE [13]; he wrote; "If the consequences of quantum mechanics contradict very obvious, much more immediate, considerations, then something must be wrong with the principles underlying the equation-of-state derivation. Kelvin's gravitational age-of-the-Sun calculation was perfectly sound; but it contradicted other considerations which had not then been realized. To me it is clear that matter cannot behave as you predict. . . . A theory must not be used to *compel* belief. . . . Eddington is nearly always wrong in his work in the long run, and I am quite prepared to believe that he is wrong here, in his details. But I hold by my general consideration." (1935)

The principal conclusion of the foregoing discussion, namely that stars with masses exceeding a certain lower limit cannot develop degenerate cores during their evolution, implies, conversely, that there exist stars with masses in a range in which when they do develop degeneracy, they do so under conditions in which the degeneracy is extremely relativistic. Under these same conditions, the masses of the degenerate cores cannot exceed $5.76 \cdot (0.5)^2 \odot \sim 1.4\odot$; and, moreover, the density and the radius of the core will be extremely sensitive to the precise conditions—e.g. the exact density—when the degeneracy becomes incipient. It is clear from these general considerations that the evolutionary sequences that stars, with masses in this critical range, will follow will manifest a great variety of possibilities. The detailed and specific calculations on stellar evolution and nucleosynthesis summarized by ARNETT seem to confirm these early expectations—though the concrete calculations and results are, of course, quite beyond anything that could have been anticipated forty years ago.

6. THE MINIMUM MASS FOR GRAVITATIONAL COLLAPSE TO BE POSSIBLE

Finally, there is one further conclusion, of a converse character, that can be drawn from the inequality (6) and the limiting form (33) of the degenerate equation of state. Combining them, we have the inequality

$$(44) \qquad \tfrac{1}{2} G \left(\tfrac{4}{3}\pi\right)^{\frac{1}{3}} \varrho_c^{\frac{4}{3}} M^{\frac{2}{3}} \geqslant P_c = K_2 \varrho_c^{\frac{4}{3}} .$$

This inequality, on simplification, gives (CHANDRASEKHAR [14])

$$(45) \qquad M \geqslant \frac{3}{16\pi} \left(\frac{hc}{G}\right)^{\frac{3}{2}} \frac{1}{H^2 \mu_e^2} = 1.74 \mu_e^{-2} \odot.$$

The meaning of this inequality is this: for a star with a mass less than $1.74\mu_e^{-2}\odot$, the right-hand side of the inequality (6) together with the exact equation of state (30) will enable us to set an *upper limit* to its central density; and this upper limit to the central density, as it is necessarily derived from less than extreme relativistic degeneracy, will be in the range $(10^5 \div 10^9)$ g cm^{-3} (except when the mass is *exactly* equal to $1.74\mu_e^{-2}\odot$). In other words, stars with masses less than $1.74\mu_e^{-2}\odot$ cannot be expected to gravitationally collapse to form neutron stars or black holes: the secular contraction they will undergo during their last phases of evolution will be arrested when they reach white-dwarf densities. It would follow, then, that we can set a lower limit of $0.43\odot$ for neutron stars and black holes that can form under the present conditions in the astronomical universe.

The various facets of stellar structure and stellar evolution we have considered do suggest that *"the stars are as they are, because $(hc/G)3/2H^{-2}$ ($\sim 29.2\odot$) provides a correct measure for their masses."*

REFERENCES

Since this lecture is strictly an account of "considerations of forty and more years ago," there are no references to papers published after the middle thirties. And except in one or two minor instances, no account is taken of ideas developed since those years.

[1] A. S. EDDINGTON: *The Internal Constitution of the Stars* (Cambridge, 1926), p. 15.

[2] S. CHANDRASEKHAR: *Mont. Not. Roy. Astr. Soc.*, **96**, 644 (1936); also *Observatory, 59, 47 (1936).*

[3] S. CHANDRASEKHAR: *Nature*, **139**, 757 (1937).

[4] A. S. EDDINGTON: *The Internal Constitution of the Stars* (Cambridge, 1926), p. 172.

[5] R. H. FOWLER: *Mont. Not. Roy. Astr. Soc.*, **87**, 114 (1926).

[6] S. CHANDRASEKHAR: *Phil. Mag.*, **11**, 592 (1931).

[7] S. CHANDRASEKHAR: *Astrophys. Journ.*, **74**, 81 (1931).

[8] S. CHANDRASEKHAR: *Mont. Not. Roy. Astr. Soc.*, **91**, 456 (1931).

[9] S. CHANDRASEKHAR: *Observatory*, **57**, 373 (1934).

[10] S. CHANDRASEKHAR: *Mont. Not. Roy. Astr. Soc.*, **95**, 207 (1935).

[11] S. CHANDRASEKHAR: *Zeits. Astrophys.*, **5**, 321 (1932).

[12] A. S. EDDINGTON: *Observatory*, **58**, 38 (1935).

[13] E. A. MILNE: from a personal letter dated February 24, 1935; also *Observatory*, **58**, 52 (1935).

[14] S. CHANDRASEKHAR: *Observatory*, **57**, 93 (1934).

RELATIVISTIC EFFECTS IN WHITE DWARFS

GIORA SHAVIV

Department of Physics and Astronomy, Tel Aviv University, Ramat Aviv, Israel

The White Dwarfs (WD) were discovered astronomically as objects that occupy a certain region in two parameter diagrams of stars. Two parameter diagrams are diagrams in which two observed properties of stars are plotted one against the other. The most famous is the Russel-Hertzprung diagram, in which the luminosity is plotted against spectral type. The WD appear in the HR diagram as stars fainter than the main sequence stars of the same spectral type. For example, an AO main sequence (MS) star is about 10 magnitudes brighter than an AO WD. On the other hand, the WD are found in the mass versus radius plane again below the MS stars of the same mass; namely, in comparing a MS star with a WD of the same mass, the WD is found to have a radius smaller by about two orders of magnitude. Consequently, the average density of a WD is about 10^6 times greater than the average density of a MS star. The average density of MS stars is of the order of unity and hence we arrive at the most important feature of WD, namely, extremely high densities. The WD are compact objects. The intrinsic low luminosity of WD hinders their discovery, so the first ones to be discovered were very hot, namely, high effective temperature. This is the reason for the name White Dwarfs. Later, when detailed surveys were carried out it was found that WD of various effective temperatures exist. Thus, there are red dwarfs, green dwarfs, etc. The name WD is still used as a general name for all objects.

The spectroscopic analysis of WD shows that the WD can be classified according to composition of the outer layers. The greatest class, type DA, are WD which show hydrogen lines but no He lines. The second class is type DB and these are WD which show strong He lines, but no H lines. The rest of the types do not have many known members and these are DC, stars with a continuous spectra and no lines deeper than 10%, DG—stars with CaII, and, FeI, lines but no H, DF—stars with CaII and no H, DO—stars with strong HeII lines with HeI or H lines and few single examples. The source for the difference in the surface composition is not yet clear. As will be shown later, hydrogen cannot survive the great densities which exist in WD and hence the hydrogen on the surface must be a very small layer.

Stars in general can be classified from a physical point of view according to the relevant equation of state. The matter in practically all stars is fully ionized either by the high temperature or by the high density (pressure ionization) except for a very small layer near the surface where it can be partly recombined. The pressure inside a star is therefore the sum of radiation, P_{rad} ions, P_{ion} and electronic P_e pressures. The state of WD can be classified as

$$P_e \gg P_{ion} \gg P_{rad}$$

namely, the electrons contribute most of the pressure, the ions have a very small contribution and the radiation pressure is completely negligible.

The electrons obey a Fermi-Dirac distribution since they are fermions. At the typical densities of MS stars there is enough phase space for the electrons, so that they behave as an ideal gas. At high densities, the available space decreases and the electrons are pushed to high energy (and momentum) states.

From the properties of the Fermi-Dirac integrals it follows that the electrons become degenerate if

$$\frac{2.97 \times 10^5}{T} \left(\frac{\rho}{\mu_e} \right)^{\frac{2}{3}} \gg 1$$

where μ_e is the mean molecular weight per electron of the material. When the density is high and the temperature is low, the fermions are degenerate. The degeneracy follows from Pauli principle which does not allow for more than two electrons to occupy the same phase space volume element. Consequently, as the density increases, the electrons are pushed towards higher and higher energies. The maximal energy of the electrons, called the fermi energy, rises. When the density becomes of the order of 10^6 μ_e gm cm^{-3}, the fermi energy is so high that the kinetic energy of the electrons becomes special relativistic. The higher the density the more ideal is the gas of electrons for the following reason. When two electrons scatter from each other, or an electron scattered by an ion, they find in most cases that the final states are occupied and hence no scattering can take place. The electrons can pass very long distances without any scattering. In other words, the degenerate matter is an excellent heat and electrical conductor—exactly like a perfect metal. The energy transport in MS stars is controlled by radiative or convective transfer. In WD the energy transport is dominated completely by the electron conductivity. As a result, the WD are practically isothermal and they can conduct outward any flux.

The central temperatures of MS stars are of the order of $(1–5) \times 10^7$ °K. The radiation field at this high temperature corresponds to X-rays. The extensive envelope of the star, which comprises 50–60% of the total mass acts as a convertor of the invisible X-rays flux to visible photons. This transformation is performed by photon diffusion during which the average energy of the photon, but not the total flux, degrades.

In the case of WD, we find that the star has a very small skin (envelope) in which the heat flux transferred by electron conduction is gradually converted into a heat flux transported by photon diffusion. The difference, however, is that in the case of a WD the mass of the envelope is $10^{-6} - 10^{-10}$ M$_\Theta$. This is roughly the region where electron degeneracy disappears. The reason for the small envelope is the extremely high gravity. On the surface of WD $g = 10^8$ cm sec^{-2}, while on the surface of MS stars g$\sim 10^4$ cm sec^{-2}.

The energy of WD was a puzzle for some time and the source of famous controversies. Today, it is clear that WD are cooling dying stars. The WD are the remnants of the hot cores of massive stars that underwent mass-loss of the whole extended envelope. The hot exposed cores moved quickly from low effective temperatures to high ones. They reached maximal surface temperatures and started to cool at practically constant radius. The internal energy of the WD is made of electronic and ionic contributions. Since the density is already very high, it is impossible for the star to extract energy from the electrons. The ions on the other hand, contribute very little to the total pressure, but still have their internal energy. Upon cooling, the ions lose their internal energy. When the temperature is sufficiently low the ions will crystallize and release the latent heat of crystallization. As discussed above, it is very difficult to perturb the electrons and consequently, the ions crystallize inside a background of a uniform sea of electrons.

White Dwarfs are stars in the state of very high density and low temperature. Actually, the temperature is so low that the pressure of the matter depends only on the density and practically not at all on the temperature. Hence, we can consider the WD as bodies at zero temperatures although the real temperatures may be as high as 10^8 °K. Moreover, at very high densities, the electrons are relativistic and behave correspondingly. The energy density P/ρ is then proportional to $\rho^{\frac{1}{3}}$ so that the pressure of the gas increases with density as $\rho^{4/3}$. Landau was the first to guess the existence of a limiting mass and Chandrasekhar was the first to calculate its value and properties. Due to the fact that the pressure of the gas increases only as a low power of the density, there is a limit to the total mass of such a star. When the mass increases, the density increases, the radius decreases and the gravitational pressure, the pressure of the outer layers increases. Chandrasekhar found that for $M_{CH} =$ 1.44 $\left(\dfrac{2}{\mu_e}\right)^2 M_\Theta$, known today as the Chandrasekhar limiting mass, the density tends to infinity and the radius to zero. There are no WD with masses greater than M_{CH}.

However, real WD cannot reach such high masses because of several reasons. Let us discuss the general relativistic effect first. As the density tends to infinity, the gravitational potential on the surface of the star becomes very high and general relativistic corrections cannot be ignored. The effects of GR are usually small, yet in this case they are quite significant. The major effect of GR is to increase the effective gravity since the inertia of the internal energy adds to the gravitational force. Consequently, the competition between the pressure of the material on one hand and the gravitational pressure of the outer layers ends earlier. Hence, all masses above $M_{GR} = M_{CH} -\epsilon$ are unstable, no infinite densities are obtained and the maximal density is of the order of 10^{10} gm/cm^3.

The value of ϵ depends on the rotational energy of the star. The maximal mass for a WD is now:

$$M = M_{CH}\left[1 + 9/2 \left(\frac{E_{kin}}{E_{grav}} - 1.438\, M_{CH}^{2/3}\, \rho_c^{1/3}\right)\right]$$

and the central density ρ_c is given by

$$\frac{\rho_c}{\rho_0} = 1.750\, \frac{m_e\, M_c^{-\frac{4}{3}}\, \rho_0^{-2/3}}{m_p\, \mu_e}\left(1 - 1.311\frac{J^2}{M_{CH}^4}\right)^{-1}$$

where $\rho_0 = 0.981 \times 10^6\, \mu_e$. The symbols have the following meaning: m_e and m_p—the masses of the electron and proton respectively, μ_e is the mean molecular weight per electron, J is the total angular momentum assuming uniform rotation and E_{grav} is the Newtonian gravitational energy.

The gravitational redshift from a surface of a star depends on the gravitational potential namely on M/R. While the Newtonian limit of M/R is infinity, GR effect gives rise to a finite M/R and hence to a finite redshift which is

$$\frac{M}{R} = 571 \left(\frac{2}{\mu_e}\right)^{2/3} / \left(1 - 1.311 \frac{J^2}{M_{CH}^4}\right)^{1/3} \text{ km/sec.}$$

In most cases even this "modest" redshift is not reached; the reason is the following: As the density of the matter increases, the electrons are shifted to higher and higher energies. Eventually, the fermi energy of the electrons becomes sufficiently high to make inverse β-decays energetically favorable, i.e., the reaction

$$p + e^- \rightarrow n + \gamma$$

occurring inside the nucleons. The critical fermi energy of C^{12} is 13 MeV and it is reached at log $\rho = 10.6$. Iron is less tightly bound and you need only 3.7 MeV to make the inverse β-decay possible. Consequently, Fe^{56} will inverse decay at log $\rho = 9.1$.

The WD are held by electron pressure balancing the gravitational one. When the density increases and inverse β-decay start, the number of electrons decreases and the ions become neutron rich. Consequently, the molecular weight increases and the critical mass decreases. Most of the WD are made of C^{12} and O^{16} which are stable nuclei and have high threshold energy for inverse β-decays. It so happens that the critical density for the inverse β-decay is very close to the critical density for GR and the two effects yield the same maximal mass. However, in WD of other compositions this is not true and generally the limit set by the inverse β-decays is lower than the limit set by GR.

Several attempts to discover the redshift in WD were made. The observations are extremely difficult because the lines observed are heavily pressure broadened. Moreover, the WD may be fast rotators and hence the lines can be Doppler broadened as well. One has to look carefully for the center of the line and measure any redshift. The measured redshift is now the sum of the gravitational shift and a velocity shift. The spatial motion of the WD is not known and it is impossible to deduce from the total observed shift the Doppler part.

The only way to approach the problem is by statistical means, namely, assume that all WD have roughly the same mass, and hence the same redshift and that their velocities are evenly distributed. Fortunately, the spatial velocities of WD's are small. Moreover, for a reason not yet clear, most of the WD's are slow rotators. Following the above basic idea, Greenstein and Trimble analyzed many WD's and found a statistical redshift of the order of 40 ± 10 km/sec. This redshift is way below the upper limit. There might well be a physical reason for it. The majority of the observed WD are single. Several authors have found a correlation between the mass of the core of an evolved star and the total luminosity. When the mass of the core reaches ~ 0.8 M$_\Theta$

the luminosity approaches the Eddington limit and extensive mass loss is expected. The star starts to lose its mass and leaves behind a core that evolves towards the WD. The correlation explains why most WD have log g = 10^8 cm/sec^2 on their surface, namely $M \simeq 0.8\ M_\Theta$.

Hence, most WD have relatively low masses and we have not yet found WD with masses that approach the critical ones.

The situation may be different for WD in binary system. It is clear that the evolution of the stars in binary system is different from that of single stars. The different evolution may explain why the companion of Sirius has a mass of 0.98 M_Θ, which is the highest mass measured directly for a WD.

NEUTRON STARS AND PULSARS IN ASTROPHYSICS

JEREMIAH P. OSTRIKER

Princeton University Observatory

It is doubtful that Einstein ever realized there might exist in Nature objects for which General Relativistic effects were not merely corrections at the 10^{-5} level but were important or even dominant. Neutron Stars are just such objects and their discovery in our galaxy is one of the most exciting stories of modern astrophysics.

In February 1968, a group of radio astronomers at the University of Cambridge announced that a strange new class of radio-emitting objects had been found. The objects were pointlike sources that showed negligible transverse motion and hence were definitely outside the solar system. What was strange about them was that they emitted periodic bursts of radio "noise" in our direction. As a result, they were quickly nicknamed "pulsars" and, although the name misleadingly connotes a pulsating (expanding and contracting) object, it has become the standard term.

The bursts of radio waves from these sources are so accurately timed that any of the four originally discovered pulsars could have been used as a clock accurate to one part per 100 million. This in itself was not so surprising, since terrestrial time has been kept for millennia by means of comparable accurate astronomical clocks based on the spin and orbital motions of the earth. The "tick" periods for the first pulsars discovered, however, ranged from .25 second to 1.3 seconds, far shorter than for any known periodic astronomical phenomenon. What were the objects? The newspapers carried speculations that "little green men" might be trying to communicate with us by means of a radar-like code.

In the next two years new observations and new theories followed one another in rapid succession. The pace has slowed somewhat, and astrophysicists now largely agree on the nature of pulsars; they appear to be neutron stars. The possible existence of neutron stars had been predicted as early as the 1930's, but before they were actually observed they had seemed almost too strange to be credible.

The first indication of something unusual was noticed late 1967 by Jocelyn Bell, then a graduate student at Cambridge, who was investigating the effects on radio observations of the irregular clouds of plasma, or ionized gas, that stream outward from the sun through interplanetary space. Small radio sources are known to scintillate, or twinkle, characteristically as a result of the passage of their rays through this "solar wind." One such scintillating object, however, was observed to cross overhead near midnight, when the effects of the solar wind should have been negligible. Further examination showed that the variations in the radio waves were not caused by passage through the solar wind but were periodic and hence intrinsic to the source itself.

Soon, many more such objects were identified and their pulses studied. Of the first four found, one designated CP 0950 (Cambridge Pulsar at 09 hours 50 minutes right ascension), had a period of only .25 seconds and a pulse width of only 20 milli-seconds. Although the period and pulses were quite regular, their amplitudes were uneven.

From certain properties of the radio pulses it was possible to estimate the distances of the first pulsars to be in the range of tens to hundreds of light years from the earth, roughly the distance range of the visually brightest stars. However, searches at the locations indicated by the radio signals revealed no optically visible objects—at least up to the 21st magnitude. Since they are comparatively close this implies that they must be faint in the optical region. Nevertheless, the objects are intrinsically much brighter radio sources than the sun! At this point the first rudimentary requirements of a theory could be perceived, and it was already possible to say that no known type of astronomical object was likely to be the source of the observed radio emissions.

The big question, of course, was to explain the nature of the pulsars and the mechanism which produces the pulses. The short duration of the pulses and their faintness indicate that they must be either small or cold or both. There are two possible candidates which fulfill these conditions: the "white dwarfs" and "neutron stars." In the former the electrons form a degenerate gas packing them into sizes of the order of the earth with densities up to hundred tons per cubic centimeter. In the latter—the density being a million times as large—the nuclei themselves form a degenerate gas having combined with the electrons into a neutron gas. The repulsive forces between the neutrons are still able to balance the immense gravitational forces, resulting in stable configurations—neutron stars. If white dwarfs resemble giant atoms, the neutron stars would behave like giant nuclei with densities of the order of billions tons per cubic centimeter. Either white dwarfs or neutron stars would be small enough to escape being detected optically.

The gravitational forces associated with a neutron star would be so large that Newtonian physics is inadequate to describe them; general relativity must be used, and the relativistic effects are large. For example, general relativity predicts that a light ray will be bent as it passes by a massive object. This effect, a deflection of a few ten-thousandths of a degree for a ray passing our sun, has been measured and provides one of the principal experimental tests of Einstein's theory. In contrast, a light ray following a "straight line" as it passed through relativistically curved space on a path grazing a neutron star with a mass equal to that of the sun would be deflected by about 30 degrees as seen by a distant observer.

The precise timing of the pulses could be due to one of three causes: A single star can expand and contract regularly, a pair of stars can orbit around each other causing periodic eclipses, and a spinning star can be seen by a distant observer to vary regularly if its surface is not uniformly bright.

Pulsations of white dwarfs had to be ruled out, since none of them could have periods as short as ¼ seconds (the observed period of CP 0950). On the other hand, neutron stars would pulsate with much shorter periods than those required. Clearly, then, pulsars are not pulsating stars in the strict sense of the word. The second possibility that they are binary systems revolving around each other also had to be ruled out. Two white dwarfs orbiting about each other would have a period of nearly two seconds, while two neutron stars—being immensely dense objects—could get close together to have a sufficiently short period, but they would radiate energy in the form of gravitational-waves and as a result spiral closer and closer to each other decreasing the orbital periods much faster than permitted by observation. Thus, by a process of elimination one arrives at a possible model—a rotating white dwarf or rotating neutron star.

Of course arguing by elimination is always a dangerous undertaking. The pulsars might have been a totally new phenomenon, but scientists are conservative and prefer to explore familiar territory (if neutron stars can be considered familiar) before venturing into the unknown. It was possible to consider a white dwarf or a neutron star with some type of searchlight beam fixed to its surface. Once each period the beam would sweep by the observer, who would see a "pulse." If the beam were circular in cross section, it could easily miss a randomly placed observer, so that, if this "lighthouse theory" were correct, there would be many more pulsars emitting than terrestrial viewers could ever observe.

On the basis of these arguments I suggested in mid-1968 a version of the lighthouse theory with a white dwarf as the seat of the phenomenon, arguing on the too conservative grounds that white dwarfs were common (although rapidly rotating white dwarfs were not), whereas the neutron star was, like Thurber's Unicorn, a "mythical beast." Rotational forces cannot exceed gravity in a stable star, however, and white dwarfs cannot rotate much faster than about a quarter-second. Thus, if very-short-period pulsars were found, white dwarfs could be ruled out entirely. Then Thomas Gold of Cornell University suggested the neutron-star version of the lighthouse model. He further noted that the objects might have strong magnetic fields and might emit high-energy charged particles; as a result they would tend to lose angular momentum and slow down. His predictions have turned out to be correct.

At the end of 1968 a pulsating radio source, later known as NP 0532, was discovered in the vicinity of the Crab Nebula by astronomers at the National Radio Astronomy Observatory with a period—one thirtieth of a second. Later work at the Arecibo Radio Observatory in Puerto Rico confirmed the result, showing that it was also gradually slowing down at a rate of 38 billionths of a second per day. The energy released in the slowing down process was found to be sufficient to keep the nebula glowing, thus another puzzle, the source of the Crab's energy was solved. Arguing the other way, it could now be asserted that stars of radii of the order of 10 km and masses approximately the mass of the sun—in other words, neutron stars—must exist, since the pulsar which supplies the energy of the Crab Nebula has exactly these properties. The fact that the Nebula is known to be the remnant of a supernova seen in A.D. 1054 by Chinese observers is also consistent with the neutron-star hypothesis.

It did not take long until the pulsar was identified optically. It turned out to be a very blue star, called the "south preceding star." It had been considered somewhat out of the ordinary, but the fact that it turned on and off thirty times per second had just not been noticed. With the help of a rotating shutter, operating like a stroboscope, its periodic flickering could now be demonstrated clearly. Other facts now began also to fall into place. As the star starts to contract, the magnetic lines of forces—effectively "frozen" into the stellar material—occupy smaller and smaller areas and as a result the magnetic field —compressed into these shrinking regions—increases immensely, reaching strengths more than billion times that of ordinary (magnetic) stars. The magnetic field in the vicinity of the rotating neutron star has the characteristic dipole shape, but farther out takes a spiral form. It is this field which is responsible for the emission of strong but low frequency (long wavelengths) radio waves. The supernova which was responsible for the Crab Nebula after explosion degenerated into the neutron star whose rotation—and consequent loss of energy—now keeps the nebulae shining.

At present there are no widely accepted theories for the physical origin of the pulses. Most theoretical models have adopted the lighthouse geometrical picture with the beam of light generated by charged particles streaming from the magnetic poles. The pulse width is taken as a measure of the beam width, which characteristically has a cone angle of about five degrees of arc. Charged particles can move much more easily along magnetic-field lines than across them, so that the dipole field can act as a collimator for the particle beams, thereby producing the "searchlight."

In 1971 a new kind of pulsar-like object was found by the UHURU satellite; these were strong *X-ray* (rather than radio) sources. Many such sources are now known, with pulsation periods usually much longer than the radio pulsars. The X-ray luminosities tend to be very large with the brighter ones 10,000 times the luminosity of the sun. They are usually found in binary systems, and often have extra intensity variations in addition to the "pulsations" resulting from the fact that during each revolution it is eclipsed by its companion. The X-ray source is a compact star, probably a rotating neutron star—although the rotation here is not important as an energy source—while its companion is a "normal" star with a mass at least 15 times that of the sun. The fact that these sources were found in binary sources and that their companions were observed to be losing mass provided the vital key. Recalling that each gram falling to the surface of a neutron star would liberate approximately $0.1 \, c^2 = 10^{20}$ ergs, it was clear that the neutron star could be fuelled by accretion, if even a small fraction of the matter leaving the companion star could be funneled to the surface. Somehow the surface X-ray luminosity is emitted in a beam which, as it sweeps past the observer, gives rise to the observed pulses.

The discovery of pulsars has opened new fields and illuminated old ones. An extraordinary new meeting ground of astrophysics, general relativity, and elementary particle physics has been found. It is still too early to know whether we have achieved a new understanding of nature, but the earliest attempts at comprehending pulsars have been so fruitful that optimism is hard to suppress.

QUASARS AND GRAVITATION

MARTIN J. REES

It is 15 years since quasars were discovered, but there has been disappointingly slow progress towards achieving a consensus about what they are. There is now, however, wider agreement that quasars are not *qualitatively* different from other forms of activity in galactic nuclei, and this has deflated the more bizarre ideas that were aired in the early days. Radio and optical astronomers have accumulated a larger (and more systematic) body of data, from which we can infer details of the structure and radiation mechanism. Things become more conjectural as we attempt to extend the chain of inference back towards the central "power-house." But this, of course, is the most interesting and fundamental aspect of the quasar phenomenon.

All entail a massive outpouring of energy from the nuclei of the galaxies, powered by something more exotic than stars, which gives rise to the most luminous objects yet recorded in the radio, optical, or X-ray bands. The data are only just beginning to fit into some kind of pattern, but the issues they raise seem of central importance for extra-galactic astronomy, and potentially for cosmology and gravitation theory as well.

Excerpts from the Halley Lecture, 1978. Read and approved by Professor Martin J. Rees, Institute of Astronomy, Cambridge, England.

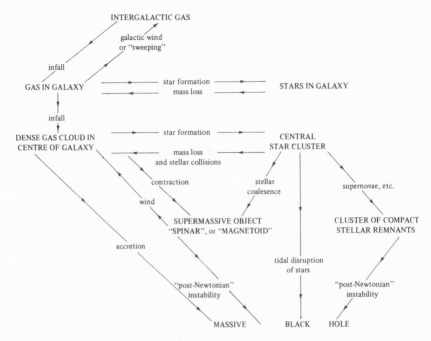

Fig. 1. "Flow diagram" indicating the processes whereby a massive black hole could form in a galactic nucleus. Quasars can be interpreted in terms of accretion of gas (or even entire stars) onto a black hole of 10^7–10^8 $M_{\odot}$; and some of the less violent phenomena observed in the nuclei of galaxies may represent "precursor" stages.

It is a tenable and widely accepted hypothesis that quasars are, in effect, optically hyperactive galactic nuclei, in which non-stellar light from the nucleus outshines the rest of the galaxy by a factor of up to a hundred or more. Quasars are thus detectable even when they are so far away that no trace of the surrounding galaxy could be seen.

As Eddington was the first to realise, a self-gravitating hot object exceeding a hundred solar masses or thereabouts is supported primarily by radiation pressure rather than gas pressure. This makes it rather unstable, and also means that it must contract to a smaller radius before getting hot enough to ignite nuclear fuel. This means that stable stars can exist only in a relatively small range of masses. Moreover any very large mass (more than a million solar masses, for instance) seems fated to undergo complete gravitational collapse before any nuclear energy is released at all. Detailed work confirms these general trends. Even though rotation may exert some stabilizing influence, a gravitating object exceeding a million solar masses is so fragile that it seems fated quickly to collapse. According to a theory of gravity such as general relativity it would turn into a black hole.

Some of the possibilities are sketched in the flow diagram, figure 1. The main message of this rather complicated diagram is this: once a large enough mass has become concentrated within a sufficiently small region, a runaway process leading to the eventual formation of a massive black hole seems almost unavoidable.

It is clear from this diagram that massive star clusters, massive objects, and accreting black holes, all of which have been proposed by different authors as models for active galactic nuclei, may represent successive stages in the evolution of a single system. Moreover, once a black hole has formed, it is a potentially more efficient power source than any conceivable pregenitor. So it seems plausible to interpret quasars, the most powerful cosmic phenomena, in terms of black hole accretion processes. Some of the precursor stages from which they evolve may yield an explanation of some less spectacular types of activity in galactic nuclei. The required inflow of material could be supplied by gas lost by stars in the body of the galaxy, provided that this material is not swept out by a galactic wind. Alternatively, the gas could be debris from collisions between stars in the nuclear regions, or could even be supplied by stars whose orbit takes them so close to the black hole that they are ripped apart by tidal forces.

Gravitation theory is plainly going to be a key ingredient in any satisfactory theory for quasars. It is one of the contexts where we cannot get by, as we can in most of astrophysics, with Newtonian gravitation. It is now over sixty years since the general theory of relativity was enunciated. Even though the "expanding Universe" solutions of Einstein's equations were already familiar in the 1930s, the prospects of discriminating between different cosmological theories were then dim. Relativity theory was then regarded as a rather stagnant topic, a glaring contrast with its present status as one of the liveliest frontiers of fundamental research. The renaissance in gravitational physics stems partly from the utilisation of new mathematical techniques, but it was also stimulated in the 1960s by the realisation that objects where relativistic effects are large may actually exist. In the short run, the most useful tests of gravitation theories may come from high precision experiments in the solar system. (Already these experiments are precise enough to exclude most rival theories and to confirm general relativity, at least in the so-called post-Newtonian approximation, with a precision of a few percent.) But to confirm the coefficient in the first term of a power series is not the same as vindicating the theory in the strong field limit: to do this one must look further afield, to possibly black holes and to the big bang itself.

Much of what I have said about the inevitability of gravitational collapse is insensitive to the detailed gravitational theory: the argument requires only that gravity should not, for instance, become repulsive in strong fields. The general arguments that accretion provides efficient mechanisms for generating non-thermal power are also qualitatively insensitive to gravitation theory. General relativity does however tell us *quantitatively* what black holes are like.

One of the key recent theoretical results has been the proof that black holes can form even when the collapse is not spherically symmetrical. Moreover, it seems that once a black hole forms it emits a burst of gravitational radiation, and quickly settles down to a standardised stationary state whose external gravitational field is characterised essentially by two parameters, mass and spin. This result is colloquially described as the theorem that "black holes have no hair."

To relativists, galactic nuclei signify the places where the space of our Universe gets punctured by the accumulation and collapse of large masses: collapse to standardised geometrical entities describable exactly by fairly simple equations. It would be exciting indeed if quasar observations led to some crucial diagnostic whereby, for instance, the radiation emitted by gas swirling inward towards a black hole has some measurable characteristic that directly indicates the form of the space time metric. Optimists may also of course hope that one might eventually detect bursts of gravitational radiation signalling the formation of massive black holes, but this would be feasible only if the collapse occurred in a peculiarly sudden way. The arguments in favour of black holes, and the prospect of making detailed relevant observations, seem less clear for quasars than for the putative stellar mass black holes identified with some X-ray sources, but it is perhaps the more massive holes which hold out the best long-term prospect for confronting observations with gravitation theory. This is because a black hole of stellar mass develops only after collapse to nuclear densities, with all the physical uncertainties entailed by high density physics; a black hole as massive as the one postulated in the giant elliptical galaxy M87 would, on the other hand, have formed before the mean density of its constituent material exceeded that of air. An experimenter falling into such an object would still have several hours, or even days, for leisured observation before being discomforted by tidal forces or imminent incorporation in the singularity.

GRAVITATIONAL COLLAPSE TO THE BLACK HOLE STATE
J. C. MILLER AND D. W. SCIAMA
Department of Astrophysics, University of Oxford

General relativity is *conceptually* very different from Newton's theory of gravity, which it superseded, but in almost all physically interesting situations the *predictions* of the two theories are almost identical. It is usually only under extreme circumstances that the differences become large. The study of black holes (regions from which light is prevented from escaping by a gravitational field) is one of the few areas where general relativity fully comes into its own. During the last fifteen years or so a great deal of effort has been devoted to determining the predicted properties and behaviour of these strange and exciting objects.

In order to create a black hole a quantity of matter must become compacted within a suitably small volume and this could happen in a number of ways:

    (i)   As a result of fluctuations in the early universe when densities were enormous.

   (ii)   By gravitational collapse at or after the end of normal evolution of some ordinary stars.

  (iii)   By gravitational collapse of supermassive stars, galactic nuclei or star clusters.

In this article we shall concentrate mainly on method (ii).

An ordinary star is at a much higher temperature than its surroundings and so it constantly radiates energy out into space. During most of its life, this energy is replaced by nuclear fusion reactions taking place in the interior but if central nuclear burning stops, the core contracts liberating gravitational potential energy.

Ordinary stars are able to support themselves against their own gravity basically because they are *hot*. A burned-out star with no prospect of liberating further energy by nuclear burning can only reach a stable equilibrium state if it is able to cool to the temperature of its surroundings. This temperature is very low and so pressure support in any final equilibrium state must come from non-thermal sources such as solid-state forces or quantum mechanical degeneracy. For a given rotation velocity there is a maximum mass which can be held up against its own gravity by non-thermal pressure. Under normal circumstances this critical value is probably less than three times the mass of the sun. Any star of higher mass than this (and there are very many of them) will have to lose all of the excess if it is to reach a final equilibrium state; otherwise it will continue to contract and will eventually become a black hole. In fact, there are many ways in which stars *do* lose mass but it seems almost inescapable that some of them will not lose sufficient. Even if a star *is* able to settle into a final equilibrium configuration it is still possible that it will subsequently accrete enough additional matter to bring it over the limit.

We now describe a collapse leading to formation of a black hole. This picture is a *theoretical prediction* based on the equations of general relativity and draws on the results of many pieces of research, some involving extensive numerical computations. Initially we restrict ourselves to a highly idealized non-rotating spherical model.

Consider first the collapse as seen by a distant observer. In the early stages he sees the infall velocity steadily increasing but then it reaches a maximum and decreases again, tending asymptotically to zero. The star appears to stabilize at a minimum radius, called the Schwarzschild radius. During the collapse, light emitted from the surface becomes progressively more red-shifted and, as the star approaches its Schwarzschild radius, the red-shift tends to infinity.

The picture of the collapse is very different for an observer standing on the surface of the star. To him the infall velocity appears to continue increasing. Nothing special happens as he passes the Schwarzschild radius but very shortly afterwards he experiences enormous tidal forces and is dragged into a space-time singularity where the density is formally infinite. In the late stages, pressure no longer helps to support the star but instead accelerates the collapse. Some portions of the matter then give *negative* contributions to the total energy.

When the star has collapsed inside its Schwarzschild radius, it is surrounded by a surface in space from within which it is impossible to communicate with the outside world. This surface (the boundary of a sphere whose radius is the Schwarzschild radius) is called the "event horizon" and the region within it is the black hold. Light rays and material objects can pass inwards through the event horizon but they cannot come out again. *Energy* can leave the environs of a black hole by various means but it cannot carry *information* from within the event horizon.

Up to this point we have been considering non-rotating models but real stars *do* rotate. In collapse of a rotating object one encounters the phenomenon that local space is "dragged round" by the matter. (Remember that in general relativity the structure of the space-time is dependent on the matter distribution.) Although no complete calculation has yet been carried out for collapse of a rotating star in general relativity we can use various known results to predict the probable nature of the collapse. The overall picture will be rather similar to that for a non-rotating model but the following additional features are expected:

(i)   Ellipticity of the star first increases but then reaches a maximum and decreases again. This is completely different from the behaviour predicted by Newtonian theory where ellipticity continues to increase and the star ends up as a disc.

(ii) In the late stages, rotation no longer tends to oppose collapse but instead accelerates it. (This is somewhat analogous to the behaviour of pressure.)

(iii) An "ergoregion" forms within which dragging is so strong that it is no longer possible for any object to remain at rest relative to infinity. In this region it is possible for an object to have binding energy greater than its rest mass (so that its net energy is negative). When the event horizon forms, the ergoregion extends outside it.

(iv) Gravitational radiation (which Einstein himself discussed) is emitted as a result of dynamical changes in shape. (This is not specifically connected with rotation; *any* collapsing object which is not spherically symmetric will normally emit gravitational radiation.)

The metric of a space-time containing a static, non-rotating black hole is that discovered by Schwarzschild in 1916 shortly after Einstein had first formulated general relativity. (This is the origin of the term "Schwarzschild radius.") However, it was not until 1963 that a metric was discovered (by Kerr) which was later shown to represent the space-time outside a stationary *rotating* black hole. These solutions are for the case of zero net electric charge. In principle a black hole may carry a charge (and the resulting metrics have been calculated) but, in practise, any net charge would probably be quickly neutralized. When a star has collapsed to form a black hole, an outside observer could still determine the total mass, angular momentum and charge but all more detailed information about composition and shape is lost.

In nature, collapse will be rather more complex than suggested by our idealized models although the overall picture and the results concerning the final state should remain unaltered. We will now consider in slightly more detail the case of a high mass star which has just exhausted all of the nuclear fuel in its core (i.e., all of the central material has been converted to elements having the most tightly bound nuclei). The core contracts and then collapses but this collapse phase is later abruptly halted by rising neutron gas pressure as the central core approaches the dimensions of a neutron star. A reflected shock wave forms which may blow off the outer parts of the star in a supernova explosion but, if it does not eject sufficient matter, the core will continue to accrete until it becomes too massive to exist in equilibrium. A second collapse phase towards the black hole state will then ensue. Any light or other electromagnetic radiation coming from the collapsing core will be very quickly scattered and absorbed by surrounding matter but gravitational waves are hardly affected at all because of their small coupling constant. They therefore give us our best opportunity to directly "see" the collapse. The emission of gravitational radiation is strongest when changes in shape are sudden and so, in the present case, one expects to see two main pulses: one at the bounce stage and another when the black hole is formed. This double pulse structure (with the radiation being predominantly at millisecond frequencies) seems to be characteristic of black hole formation in these circumstances. Further, more detailed structure can also be predicted.

Gravitational wave detectors are not yet sufficiently sensitive to pick up this radiation but experiments now being planned for the 1980s will quite probably reach the required sensitivity. If we then see pulse trains with the predicted distinctive structure mentioned above, the case will be overwhelmingly strong for saying that we are watching black holes being born.

VI. GRAVITATIONAL WAVES

Ever since Einstein showed that for weak gravitational fields (differing from flat space by small quantities) the field equations of general relativity have the form of wave equations, there has been speculation about the existence of gravitational waves. To illustrate this we reproduce only the first part of a paper by Einstein and Rosen leading to wavelike solutions of the field equations. There are several groups in the world which are conducting experiments in order to detect gravitational waves, but so far the only one who has claimed to have found them is the one in Maryland, headed by Joe Weber, the author of a descriptive article on Gravitational Waves. Even more discouraging is the perceptive analysis by Nathan Rosen who shows that a combination of advanced and retarded solutions may produce standing waves, but would not transmit energy by gravitational radiation.

ON GRAVITATIONAL WAVES

ALBERT EINSTEIN AND NATHAN ROSEN

ABSTRACT

The rigorous solution for cylindrical gravitational waves is given. For the convenience of the reader the theory of gravitational waves and their production, already known in principle, is given in the first part of this paper. After encountering relationships which cast doubt on the existence of *rigorous* solu-

From Journal of The Franklin Institute, 223 *(1937): 43. Due to its mathematical complexity only section I of the paper is reproduced. Reprinted by permission of Professor Nathan Rosen, the Estate of Albert Einstein, and the Franklin Institute.*

tions for undulatory gravitational fields, we investigate rigorously the case of cylindrical gravitational waves. It turns out that rigorous solutions exist and that the problem reduces to the usual cylindrical waves in euclidean space.

I. APPROXIMATE SOLUTION OF THE PROBLEM OF PLANE WAVES AND THE PRODUCTION OF GRAVITATIONAL WAVES

It is well known that the approximate method of integration of the gravitational equations of the general relativity theory leads to the existence of gravitational waves. The method used is as follows: We start with the equations

$$R_{\mu\nu} - \frac{1}{2}g_{\mu\nu}R = -T_{\mu\nu}. \tag{1}$$

We consider that the $g_{\mu\nu}$ are replaced by the expressions

$$g_{\mu\nu} = \delta_{\mu\nu} + \gamma_{\mu\nu},$$

where   (2)

$$\delta_{\mu\nu} = 1 \text{ if } \mu = \nu,$$
$$= 0 \text{ if } \mu \neq \nu,$$

provided we take the time coördinate imaginary, as was done by Minkowski. It is assumed that the $\gamma_{\mu\nu}$ are small, i.e., that the gravitational field is weak. In the equations the $\gamma_{\mu\nu}$ and their derivatives will occur in various powers. If the $\gamma_{\mu\nu}$ are everywhere sufficiently small compared to unity, one obtains a first-approximation solution of the equations by neglecting in (1) the higher powers of the $\gamma_{\mu\nu}$ (and their derivatives) compared with the lower ones. If one introduces further the $\bar{\gamma}_{\mu\nu}$ instead of the $\gamma_{\mu\nu}$ by the relations

$$\bar{\gamma}_{\mu\nu} = \gamma_{\mu\nu} - \frac{1}{2}\delta_{\mu\nu}\gamma_{aa},$$

then (1) assumes the form

$$\bar{\gamma}_{\mu\nu,\,aa} - \bar{\gamma}_{\mu\nu,\,av} - \bar{\gamma}_{\nu a,\,a\mu} + \bar{\gamma}_{aa,\,\mu\nu} = -2T_{\mu\nu}. \tag{3}$$

The specialization contained in (2) is conserved if one performs an infinitesimal transformation on the coördinates:

$$x_{\mu}' = x_{\mu} + \xi^{\mu}, \tag{4}$$

where the ξ^{μ} are infinitely small but otherwise arbitrary functions. One can therefore prescribe four of the $\bar{\gamma}_{\mu\nu}$ or four conditions which the $\gamma_{\mu\nu}$ must satisfy besides the equations (3); this amounts to a specialization of the coördinate system chosen to describe the field. We choose the coordinate system in the usual way by demanding that

$$\bar{\gamma}_{\mu a,\,a} = 0. \tag{5}$$

It is readily verified that these four conditions are compatible with the approximate gravitational equations provided the divergence $T_{\mu a,\,a}$ of $T_{\mu\nu}$ vanishes, which must be assumed according to the special theory of relativity.

It turns out however that these conditions do not completely fix the coördinate system. If $\gamma_{\mu\nu}$ are solutions of (2) and (5), then the $\gamma_{\mu\nu}{}'$ after a transformation of the type (4)

$$\gamma_{\mu\nu}{}' = \gamma_{\mu\nu} + \xi^{\mu},_{\nu} + \xi^{\nu},_{\mu} \tag{6}$$

are also solutions provided the ξ^{μ} satisfy the conditions

$$[\xi^{\mu},_{\nu} + \xi^{\nu},_{\mu} - \frac{1}{2}\delta_{\mu\nu}(\xi^{a},_{a} + \xi^{a},_{a})],_{\nu} = 0,$$

$$\xi^{\mu},_{aa} = 0. \tag{7}$$

If a γ-field can be made to vanish by the addition of terms like those in (6), i.e., by means of an infinitesimal transformation, then the gravitational field being described is only an apparent field.

With reference to (2), the gravitational equations for empty space can be written in the form

$$\left.\begin{aligned}\bar{\gamma}_{\mu\nu,\,aa} &= 0. \\ \gamma_{\mu a,\,a} &= 0.\end{aligned}\right\} \tag{8}$$

One obtains plane gravitational waves which move in the direction of the positive χ_1-axis by taking the $\bar{\gamma}_{\mu\nu}$ of the form $\varphi(x_1 + ix_4)\,(=\varphi(x_1 - t))$, where these $\bar{\gamma}_{\mu\nu}$ must further satisfy the conditions

$$\left.\begin{aligned}\bar{\gamma}_{11} + i\bar{\gamma}_{14} &= 0, \\ \bar{\gamma}_{41} + i\bar{\gamma}_{44} &= 0, \\ \bar{\gamma}_{21} + i\bar{\gamma}_{24} &= 0, \\ \bar{\gamma}_{31} + i\bar{\gamma}_{34} &= 0.\end{aligned}\right\} \tag{9}$$

One can accordingly subdivide the most general (progressing) plane gravitational waves into three types:

(a) pure longitudinal waves,

only $\bar{\gamma}_{11}, \bar{\gamma}_{14}, \bar{\gamma}_{44}$ different from zero,

(b) half longitudinal, half transverse waves,

only $\bar{\gamma}_{21}$ and $\bar{\gamma}_{24}$, or only $\bar{\gamma}_{31}$ and $\bar{\gamma}_{34}$ different from zero,

(c) pure transverse waves,

only $\bar{\gamma}_{22}, \bar{\gamma}_{23}, \bar{\gamma}_{33}$ are different from zero.

On the basis of the previous remarks it can next be shown that every wave of type *(a)* or of type *(b)* is an apparent field, that is, it can be obtained by an infinitesimal transformation from the euclidean field ($\bar{\gamma}_{\mu\nu} = \gamma_{\mu\nu} = 0$).

We carry out the proof in the example of a wave of type *(a)*. According to (9) one must set, if φ is a suitable function of the argument $x_1 + ix_4$,

$$\bar{\gamma}_{11} = \varphi, \quad \bar{\gamma}_{14} = i\varphi, \quad \bar{\gamma}_{44} = -\varphi,$$

hence also

$$\gamma_{11} = \varphi, \quad \gamma_{14} = i\varphi, \quad \gamma_{44} = -\varphi.$$

If one now chooses ξ^1 and ξ^4 (with $\xi^2 = \xi^3 = 0$) so that

$$\xi^{1.} = \chi(x_1 + ix_4), \quad \xi^4 = i\chi(x_1 + ix_4),$$

then one has

$$\xi^1{}_{,1} + \xi^1{}_{,1} = 2\chi', \quad \xi^1{}_{,4} + \xi^4{}_{,1} = 2i\chi', \quad \xi^4{}_{,4} + \xi^4{}_{,4} = -2\chi'.$$

These agree with the values given above for γ_{11}, γ_{14}, γ_{44} if one chooses $\chi' = \frac{1}{2}\varphi$. Hence it is shown that these waves are apparent. An analogous proof can be carried out for the waves of type *(b)*.

Furthermore we wish to show that also type *(c)* contains apparent fields, namely, those in which $\bar{\gamma}_{22} = \bar{\gamma}_{33} \neq 0$, $\bar{\gamma}_{23} = 0$. The corresponding $\gamma_{\mu\nu}$ are $\gamma_{11} = \gamma_{44} \neq 0$, all others vanishing. Such a wave can be obtained by taking $\xi^1 = \chi$, $\xi^4 = -i_\chi$, i.e. by an infinitesimal transformation from the euclidean space. Accordingly there remain as real waves only the two pure transverse types, the non-vanishing components of which are

$$\gamma_{22} = -\gamma_{33}, \tag{c_1}$$

or

$$\gamma_{23}. \tag{c_2}$$

It follows however from the transformation law for tensors that these two types can be transformed into each other by a spatial rotation of the coördinate system about the x_1-axis through the angle $\pi/4$. They represent merely the decomposition into components of the pure transverse wave (the only one which has a real significance). Type c_1 is characterized by the fact that its components do not change under the transformations

$$x_2' = -x_2, \quad x_1' = x_1, \quad x_3' = x_3, \quad x_4' = x_4,$$

or

$$x_3' = -x_3, \quad x_1' = x_1, \quad x_2' = x_2, \quad x_4' = x_4.$$

in contrast to c_2, i.e. c_1 is symmetrical with respect to the x_1–x_2-plane and the x_1–x_3-plane.

We now investigate the generation of waves as it follows from the approximate (linearized) gravitational equations. The system of the equations to be integrated is

$$\left. \begin{array}{c} \bar{\gamma}_{\mu\nu,\,aa} = -2T_{\mu\nu}, \\[2mm] \bar{\gamma}_{\mu a,\,a} = 0. \end{array} \right\} \tag{10}$$

Let us suppose that a physical system described by $T_{\mu\nu}$ is found in the neighborhood of the origin of coördinates. The γ-field is then determined mathematically in a similar way to that in which an electromagnetic field is determined through an electrical current system. The usual solution is the one given by retarded potentials

$$\bar{\gamma}_{\mu\nu} = \frac{1}{2\pi} \int \frac{[T_{\mu\nu}]_{(t-r)}}{r} \, dv. \tag{11}$$

Here r signifies the spatial distance of the point in question from a volume-element, $t = x_4/\iota$, the time in question.

If one considers the material system as being in a volume having dimensions small compared to r_0, the distance of our point from the origin, and also small compared to the wavelengths of the radiation produced, then r can be replaced by r_0 and one obtains

$$\bar{\gamma}_{\mu\nu} = \frac{1}{2\pi r_0} \int [T_{\mu\nu}]_{(t-r_0)} \, dv,$$

or

$$\bar{\gamma}_{\mu\nu} = \frac{1}{2\pi r_0} \left[\int T_{\mu\nu} dv \right]_{(t-r_0)}. \tag{12}$$

The $\bar{\gamma}_{\mu\nu}$ are more and more closely approximated by a plane wave the greater one takes r_0. If one chooses the point in question in the neighborhood of the x_1-axis, the wave normal is parallel to the x_1 direction and only the components $\bar{\gamma}_{22}, \bar{\gamma}_{23}, \bar{\gamma}_{33}$ correspond to an actual gravitational wave according to the preceding. The corresponding integrals (12) for a system producing the wave and consisting of masses in motion relative to one another have directly no simple significance. We notice however that T_{44} denotes the (negatively taken) energy density which in the case of slow motion is practically equal to the mass density in the sense of ordinary mechanics. As will be shown, the above integrals can be expressed through this quantity. This can be done because of the existence of the energy-momentum equations of the physical system:

$$T_{\mu a, a} = 0. \tag{13}$$

If one multiplies the second of these with x_2 and the fourth with $\frac{1}{2}x_2^2$ and integrates over the whole system, one obtains two integral relations, which on being combined yield

$$\int T_{22} \, dv = \frac{1}{2} \frac{\partial^2}{\partial x_4{}^2} \int x_2{}^2 T_{44} \, dv. \tag{13a}$$

Analogously one obtains

$$\int T_{33} \, dv = \frac{1}{2} \frac{\partial^2}{\partial x_4{}^2} \int x_3{}^2 T_{44} \, dv,$$

$$\int T_{23} \, dv = \frac{1}{2} \frac{\partial^2}{\partial x_4{}^2} \int x_2 x_3 \, T_{44} \, dv.$$

One sees from this that the time-derivatives of the moments of inertia determine the emission of the gravitational waves, provided the whole method of application of the approximation-equations is really justified. In particular one also sees that the case of waves symmetrical with respect to the x_1-x_2 and x_1-x_3 planes could be realized by means of elastic oscillations of a material system which has the same symmetry properties. For example, one might have two equal masses which are joined by an elastic spring and oscillate toward each other in a direction parallel to the x_3-axis.

From consideration of energy relationship it has been concluded that such a system, in sending out gravitational waves, must send out energy which reacts by damping the motion. Nevertheless, one can think of the case of vibration free from damping if one imagines that, besides the waves emitted by the system, there is present a second concentric wave-field which is propagated inward and brings to the system as much energy as the outgoing waves remove. This leads to an undamped mechanical process which is imbedded in a system of standing waves.

Mathematically this is connected with the following considerations, clearly pointed out in past years by Ritz and Tetrode. The integration of the wave-equation

$$\square \varphi = -4\pi\rho$$

by the *retarded* potential

$$\varphi = \int \frac{[\rho]_{(t-r)}}{r} dv$$

is mathematically not the only possibility. One can also do it with

$$\varphi = \int \frac{[\rho]_{(t+r)}}{r} dv,$$

i.e. by means of the "advanced" potential, or by a mixture of the two, for example,

$$\varphi = \frac{1}{2} \int \frac{[\rho]_{(t+r)} + [\rho]_{(t-r)}}{r} dv.$$

The last possibility corresponds to the case without damping, in which a standing wave is present.

It is to be remarked that one can think of waves generated as described above which approximate plane waves as closely as desired. One can obtain them, for example, through a limit-process by considering the wave-source to be removed further and further from the point in question and at the same time the oscillating moment of inertia of the former increased in proportion.

GRAVITATIONAL WAVES

J. WEBER

University of California, Irvine, California, and University of Maryland, College Park, Maryland

Einstein predicted that changes in the gravitational field are propagated with the velocity of light, and that it is possible to transmit energy, momentum, and information in the form of gravitational waves. The general theory of relativity gives a very detailed description of the properties of such waves. These are absorbed by matter to a much smaller degree than other forms of radiation and this is important in applications to astronomy.

Certain events in astronomy may not be observable because light is either not emitted or is absorbed by dust clouds. These events might be observed through detection of gravitational waves. Thus the gravitational wave astronomy is a new window through which to view the universe.

Einstein's unification of physics and geometry described gravitation as space time curvature. Suppose we have a region of space free of gravitation. Euclidean geometry is valid. A triangle (Figure 1) made up of light rays has the sum of its angles equal to 180 degrees. In the presence of a mass such as the sun (Figure 2) the light rays are bent by gravitational attraction. The space is "curved" and the sum of the angles exceeds 180 degrees. A gravitational

Research supported in part by NASA Grant #NSG 7196-S1 and in part by National Science Foundation Grant # PHY 77-14818.

wave propagates the space time curvature. Thus if a wave is propagated from left to right as in Figure 3, some regions of space are "convex" and a half wavelength away at the same time the regions are "concave."

Figure 1.   Triangle made of light rays in Euclidean (Gravitation Free) Space.

Figure 2.   Triangle made of light rays in space curved by the gravitational field of the sun.

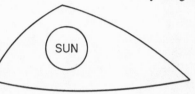

Figure 3.   Regions of space alternating from convex to concave in path of gravitational wave.

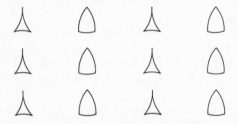

For the gravitational waves emitted by the closest double stars, with periods of a few hours, the curvature is extremely small. The sum of the angles differs from the Euclidean value by 10^{-40} radians. Such a small change is very difficult to measure.

In 1958 I was able to prove, using Einstein's equations that a gravitational wave would change the dimensions of an extended body. There are also small changes in distance of separated bodies caused by the gravitational waves. These changes in dimensions are caused by forces similar to those which the moon exerts on earth to give tides. Measurement of the changes in dimensions gives an accurate and direct measurement of the space-time curvature. These changes in dimensions are very much larger than the effects on the angles of a light ray triangle.

Figure 4 shows a gravitational radiation antenna. It is an aluminum cylinder having a mass of about 1½ tons. It is carefully suspended and isolated from earth vibrations by means of acoustic filters, and well shielded from electromagnetic disturbances. The very small changes in length induced by gravitational waves are converted to electrical signals by means of piezoelectric

Figure 4.
University of Maryland
kilohertz gravitational
frequency radiation antenna.

crystals bonded to the cylinder. The electrical signals are amplified by low noise electronics and eventually analyzed by a computer. The electronics can observe changes in length of the cylinder much smaller than the size of an atomic nucleus. The antenna operates at the relatively high frequency of 1660 Hertz, for detection of gravitational waves which might be expected from collapsing stars.

The Maryland group has observed coincident signals on widely separated antennas. These observations are not yet confirmed and are controversial.

SEARCH FOR RADIATION AT LOW FREQUENCIES

For very low frequencies, the earth and moon may be employed as elastic solid antennas. The earth may have oscillations excited at a frequency of one cycle every fifty-four minutes, and higher overtone frequencies. The moon may have oscillations excited at a frequency of one cycle every twenty minutes, and higher overtones. Einstein's general relativity theory predicts that only certain overtones will be excited by gravitational radiation. The Maryland group observed the surface acceleration of the earth for a number of years, and also observed the surface acceleration of the moon making use of equipment emplaced by the Apollo 17 astronauts. These observations have thus far produced no evidence that either earth or moon is excited by gravitational waves.

Research programs are in progress at many laboratories throughout the world to develop more sensitive antennas. Some of these will operate at very low temperatures, to reduce the heat induced internal motions. Exotic materials such as single crystals of sapphire and silicon may replace the aluminum cylinder. Attempts are also in progress to employ the gravitational wave induced changes in distance between mirrors of an interfermeter, for detection. By these means it is hoped to observe gravitational radiation from astronomical sources as far as the Virgo Cluster of galaxies.

IS THERE GRAVITATIONAL RADIATION?

NATHAN ROSEN
Faculty of Physics, Technion, Haifa, Israel

The Einstein field equations for the gravitational field of an oscillating source in the linear weak-field approximation have retarded-potential solutions which describe waves propagating outwardly from the source.[1] There also exist advanced-potential solutions which describe waves propagating into the source.[1] It is generally assumed that the solutions of the first kind are the correct ones and that they describe the emission of gravitational radiation by the source. However this assumption involves an asymmetry with respect to the sign of the time (that is, between past and future) which is not present in the field equations.

An analogous situation exists in the electromagnetic theory. Here we know that retarded-potential solutions give agreement with observation. However, in view of the time symmetry of the electromagnetic field equations, it is natural to take as the fundamental solution the time-symmetric one (½ retarded potential + ½ advanced potential). This was done by Wheeler and Feynman[2] for the case of a point-charge source. They showed that one nevertheless obtains the retarded-potential solution (and also the radiation-reaction force acting on the source) provided that one assumes that the source is surrounded by sufficient matter so that the outgoing field of the source is completely absorbed. What happens is that, when the surrounding matter absorbs the retarded part of the field emitted by the source, it generates a field, the advanced part of which arrives at the source (near the moment of emission of the original field) and combines with the symmetric field to give the retarded one that is observed.

This approach seems to be quite satisfactory in the electromagnetic case, and it is appropriate to carry it over to the case of gravitation. Accordingly, one takes as the fundamental solution of the Einstein field equations the time-symmetric one (½ retarded + ½ advanced). However, the consequences of this are different from those in the electromagnetic case. The coupling between a proton and the gravitational field is very much smaller than that between the proton and the electromagnetic field ($Gm_p{}^2/e^2 \simeq 8 \times 10^{-37}$, where G is the gravitational constant). Therefore all the matter in the universe is not enough to absorb the outgoing gravitational field of an oscillating source. One finds, for example, in the case of an oscillating mass-quadrupole source in a

1. A. Einstein and N. Rosen: *J. Franklin Inst. 223* (1937): 43.
2. J. A. Wheeler and R. P. Feynman: *Rev. Mod. Phys. 17,* (1945): 157.

small cavity surrounded by a sphere of matter of uniform density ρ and radius R, that the ratio of the amplitude of the field generated by the matter (a few wavelengths away from the source) to that of the source itself is of the order of

$$\sigma = a/\nu,$$

where $a = G\rho R/c$, and ν is the frequency of the oscillation. Corresponding to what we know about the universe, let us take $\rho \sim 10^{-30}$ gm-cm^{-3}, $R \sim 10^{28}$ cm.
Then we get

$$a \sim 10^{-20} \ \sec^{-1},$$

so that, for any reasonable conditions, the field generated by the surrounding matter is unimportant compared to the field of the source. Hence the solution will remain essentially time symmetric and will not be converted into the retarded one, as in the electromagnetic case.

It appears therefore that one should describe the gravitational field of a given source by means of the time-symmetric solution of the field equations, and not the retarded one. This can have some far-reaching consequences. For example, a physical system undergoing periodic motion will be surrounded by a gravitational field in the form of standing waves and will not lose energy as gravitational radiation. One may go even further and conclude that there are no free periodic gravitational waves in nature and hence that no gravitational quanta, or gravitons, exist.

The idea of using only the time-symmetric solution can be extended from the weak-field case to the general case. For a strong source, this can be accomplished by appropriate boundary conditions at a large distance, where the field is weak.

VII. TOWARD A UNIFIED FIELD THEORY

For the last thirty years of his life Einstein endeavored to find a unified field theory, a generalization of his field equations which would—as a first step —bring electromagnetism into the framework of general relativity. As he points out so eloquently in his brief essay, general covariance must be demanded from all physical laws from the start, and no Lorentz invariant system built into a general relativistic scheme will ever be able to produce a unified theory. The result of his investigations are described in an article written for *Scientific American,* and as he points out there are many difficulties, and only experience can tell if the aim has been achieved.

For many years no significant advance has been made, and it was only with the "discovery" of supersymmetry that there appeared the possibility of combining gravitation with other interactions. Stanley Deser, one of the originators of supergravity, describes for us here what it is and how it may lead to the fulfillment of Einstein's program. Gauge theories were first introduced by Hermann Weyl in order to unify electromagnetism with gravitation. Recently, these have taken on a geometrical look. Yuval Ne'eman discusses these ideas, which also include supergravity, and may lead to a geometrization and unification of physics.

A somewhat more pessimistic note is sounded by Christian Møller who feels that so far none of these endeavors have led to a theory which in beauty, cogency, and inherent power of conviction can compete with Einstein's original masterpiece.

A GENERALIZATION OF THE EQUATIONS OF GRAVITATION

Ever since the formulation of the theory of general relativity the physicists have endeavoured incessantly to devise a satisfactory theory of the unified field.

Boni Nell et al., A Bibliographical Checklist and Index of the Published Writing of A. Einstein *(New York: Pageant Press, 1960). Reproduced by permission of the Estate of Albert Einstein.*

Although these endeavours have not been successful until now, we cannot lose sight of that goal for the simple reason that it is difficult to convince ourselves that a subsequent synthesis of such a successful special theory to a unified totality should prove impossible.

On this point there exists nearly general agreement. On the other hand, very few colleagues will agree with me if I advocate this view: The attempt to create a theoretical basis for the whole of physics has to start from the relativistic theory of gravitation. Because judging from the present state of physics gravitation seems to be something like a second order effect which can be neglected for the present compared to the other forces which appear decisive practically alone for the structure of matter and radiation. In connection with this reasoning, however, one forgets a fundamental point. The theory of gravitation surely demonstrated reliably that the laws of nature are covariant under all continuous coordinate transformations. Therefore it will have to be demanded from the start that the laws possess covariance. A Lorentz invariant system of equations built into a general relativistic schema will never be able to produce a unified theory. One will therefore already from the beginning have to take this group (or perhaps an even more general one) as the basis.

ON THE GENERALIZED THEORY OF GRAVITATION

The editors of *Scientific American* have asked me to write about my recent work which has just been published. It is a mathematical investigation concerning the foundations of field physics.

Some readers may be puzzled: didn't we learn all about the foundations of physics when we were still at school? The answer is "yes" or "no," depending on the interpretation. We have become acquainted with concepts and general relations that enable us to comprehend an immense range of experiences and make them accessible to mathematical treatment. In a certain sense these concepts and relations are probably even final. This is true, for example, of the laws of light refraction, of the relations of classical thermodynamics as far as it is based on the concepts of pressure, volume, temperature, heat, and work, and of the hypothesis of the non-existence of a perpetual motion machine.

What, then, impels us to devise theory after theory? Why do we devise theories at all? The answer to the latter question is simply: because we enjoy "comprehending," i.e., reducing phenomena by the process of logic to some-

From Scientific American *182, no. 4 (April 1950). Also in* Ideas and Opinions *(New York: Crown Publishers, copyright 1954). Reprinted by permission of the Estate of Albert Einstein.*

thing already known or (apparently) evident. New theories are first of all necessary when we encounter new facts which cannot be "explained" by existing theories. But this motivation for setting up new theories is, so to speak, trivial, imposed from without. There is another, more subtle motive of no less importance. This is the striving toward unification and simplification of the premises of the theory as a whole (i.e., Mach's principle of economy, interpreted as a logical principle).

There exists a passion for comprehension, just as there exists a passion for music. That passion is rather common in children, but gets lost in most people later on. Without this passion, there would be neither mathematics nor natural science. Time and again the passion for understanding has led to the illusion that man is able to comprehend the objective world rationally, by pure thought, without any empirical foundations—in short, by metaphysics. I believe that every true theorist is a kind of tamed metaphysicist, no matter how pure a "positivist" he may fancy himself. The metaphysicist believes that the logically simple is also the real. The tamed metaphysicist believes that not all that is logically simple is embodied in experienced reality, but that the totality of all sensory experience can be "comprehended" on the basis of a conceptual system built on premises of great simplicity. The skeptic will say that this is a "miracle creed." Admittedly so, but it is a miracle creed which has been borne out to an amazing extent by the development of science.

The rise of atomism is a good example. How may Leucippus have conceived this bold idea? When water freezes and becomes ice—apparently something entirely different from water—why is it that the thawing of the ice forms something which seems indistinguishable from the original water? Leucippus is puzzled and looks for an "explanation." He is driven to the conclusion that in these transitions the "essence" of the thing has not changed at all. Maybe the thing consists of immutable particles and the change is only a change in their spatial arrangement. Could it not be that the same is true of all material objects which emerge again and again with nearly identical qualities?

This idea is not entirely lost during the long hibernation of Occidental thought. Two thousand years after Leucippus, Bernoulli wonders why gas exerts pressure on the walls of a container. Should this be "explained" by mutual repulsion of the parts of the gas, in the sense of Newtonian mechanics? This hypothesis appears absurd, for the gas pressure depends on the temperature, all other things being equal. To assume that the Newtonian forces of interaction depend on temperature is contrary to the spirit of Newtonian mechanics. Since Bernoulli is aware of the concept of atomism, he is bound to conclude that the atoms or (molecules) collide with the walls of the container and in doing so exert pressure. After all, one has to assume that atoms are in motion; how else can one account for the varying temperature of gases?

A simple mechanical consideration shows that this pressure depends only on the kinetic energy of the particles and on their density in space. This should have led the physicists of that age to the conclusion that heat consists in random motion of the atoms. Had they taken this consideration as seriously as it deserved to be taken, the development of the theory of heat—in particular the discovery of the equivalence of heat and mechanical energy—would have been considerably facilitated.

This example is meant to illustrate two things. The theoretical idea (atomism in this case) does not arise apart from and independent of experience; nor can it be derived from experience by a purely logical procedure. It is produced by a creative act. Once a theoretical idea has been acquired, one does well to hold fast to it until it leads to an untenable conclusion.

As for my latest theoretical work, I do not feel justified in giving a detailed account of it before a wide group of readers interested in science. That should be done only with theories which have been adequately confirmed by experience. So far it is primarily the simplicity of its premises and its intimate connection with what is already known (viz., the laws of the pure gravitational field) that speak in favor of the theory to be discussed here. It may, however, be of interest to a wide group of readers to become acquainted with the train of thought which can lead to endeavors of such an extremely speculative nature. Moreover, it will be shown what kinds of difficulties are encountered and in what sense they have been overcome.

In Newtonian physics the elementary theoretical concept on which the theoretical description of material bodies is based is the material point, or particle. Thus matter is considered *a priori* to be discontinuous. This makes it necessary to consider the action of material points on one another as "action at a distance." Since the latter concept seems quite contrary to everyday experience, it is only natural that the contemporaries of Newton—and indeed Newton himself—found it difficult to accept. Owing to the almost miraculous success of the Newtonian system, however, the succeeding generations of physicists became used to the idea of action at a distance. Any doubt was buried for a long time to come.

But when, in the second half of the nineteenth century, the laws of electrodynamics became known, it turned out that these laws could not be satisfactorily incorporated into the Newtonian system. It is fascinating to muse: Would Faraday have discovered the law of electromagnetic induction if he had received a regular college education? Unencumbered by the traditional way of thinking, he felt that the introduction of the "field" as an independent element of reality helped him to coordinate the experimental facts. It was Maxwell who fully comprehended the significance of the field concept; he made the fundamental discovery that the laws of electrodynamics found their natural expression in the differential equations for the electric and magnetic fields. These equations implied the existence of waves, whose properties corresponded to those of light as far as they were known at that time.

This incorporation of optics into the theory of electromagnetism represents one of the greatest triumphs in the striving toward unification of the foundations of physics; Maxwell achieved this unification by purely theoretical arguments, long before it was corroborated by Hertz's experimental work. The new insight made it possible to dispense with the hypothesis of action at a distance, at least in the realm of electromagnetic phenomena; the intermediary field now appeared as the only carrier of electromagnetic interaction between bodies, and the field's behavior was completely determined by contiguous processes, expressed by differential equations.

Now a question arose: Since the field exists even in a vacuum, should one conceive of the field as a state of a "carrier," or should it rather be endowed with an independent existence not reducible to anything else? In other words, is there an "ether" which carries the field; the ether being considered in the undulatory state, for example, when it carries light waves?

The question has a natural answer: Because one cannot dispense with the field concept, it is preferable not to introduce in addition a carrier with hypothetical properties. However, the pathfinders who first recognized the indispensability of the field concept were still too strongly imbued with the mechanistic tradition of thought to accept unhesitatingly this simple point of view. But in the course of the following decades this view imperceptibly took hold.

The introduction of the field as an elementary concept gave rise to an inconsistency of the theory as a whole. Maxwell's theory, although adequately describing the behavior of electrically charged particles in their interaction with one another, does not explain the behavior of electrical densities, i.e., it does not provide a theory of the particles themselves. They must therefore be treated as mass points on the basis of the old theory. The combination of the idea of a continuous field with that of material points discontinuous in space appears inconsistent. A consistent field theory requires continuity of all elements of the theory, not only in time but also in space, and in all points of space. Hence the material particle has no place as a fundamental concept in a field theory. Thus even apart from the fact that gravitation is not included, Maxwell's electrodynamics cannot be considered a complete theory.

Maxwell's equations for empty space remain unchanged if the spatial coordinates and the time are subjected to a particular kind of linear transformations—the Lorentz transformations ("covariance" with respect to Lorentz transformations). Covariance also holds, of course, for a transformation which is composed of two or more such transformations; this is called the "group" property of Lorentz transformations.

Maxwell's equations imply the "Lorentz group," but the Lorentz group does not imply Maxwell's equations. The Lorentz group may indeed be defined independently of Maxwell's equations as a group of linear transformations which leave a particular value of the velocity—the velocity of light—invariant. These transformations hold for the transition from one "inertial system" to another which is in uniform motion relative to the first. The most conspicuous novel property of this transformation group is that it does away with the absolute character of the concept of simultaneity of events distant from each other in space. On this account it is to be expected that all equations of physics are covariant with respect to Lorentz transformations *(special theory of relativity)*. Thus it came about that Maxwell's equations led to a heuristic principle valid far beyond the range of the applicability or even validity of the equations themselves.

Special relativity has this in common with Newtonian mechanics: The laws of both theories are supposed to hold only with respect to certain coordinate systems: those known as "inertial systems." An inertial system is a system in a state of motion such that "force-free" material points within it are not accelerated with respect to the coordinate system. However, this definition is empty if there is no independent means for recognizing the absence of forces. But such a means of recognition does not exist if gravitation is considered as a "field."

Let *A* be a system uniformly accelerated with respect to an "inertial system" *I*. Material points, not accelerated with respect to *I*, are accelerated with respect to *A*, the acceleration of all the points being equal in magnitude and direction. They behave as if a gravitational field exists with respect to *A*, for it is a characteristic property of the gravitational field that the acceleration is independent of the particular nature of the body. There is no reason to exclude the possibility of interpreting this behavior as the effect of a "true" gravitational field *(principle of equivalence)*. This interpretation implies that *A* is an "inertial system," even though it is accelerated with respect to another inertial system. (It is essential for this argument that the introduction of independent gravitational fields is considered justified even though no masses generating the field are defined. Therefore, to Newton such an argument would not have appeared convincing.) Thus the concepts of inertial system, the law of inertia and the law of motion are deprived of their concrete meaning—not only in classical mechanics but also in special relativity. Moreover, following up this train of thought, it turns out that with respect to *A* time cannot be measured by identical clocks; indeed, even the immediate physical significance of coordinate differences is generally lost. In view of all these difficulties, should one not try, after all, to hold on to the concept of the inertial system, relinquishing the attempt to explain the fundamental character of the gravitational phenomena which manifest themselves in the Newtonian system as the equivalence of inert and gravitational mass? Those who trust in the comprehensibility of nature must answer: No.

This is the gist of the principle of equivalence: In order to account for the equality of inert and gravitational mass within the theory it is necessary to admit non-linear transformations of the four coordinates. That is, the group of Lorentz transformations and hence the set of the "permissible" coordinate systems has to be extended.

What group of coordinate transformations can then be substituted for the group of Lorentz transformations? Mathematics suggests an answer which is based on the fundamental investigations of Gauss and Riemann: namely, that the appropriate substitute is the group of all continuous (analytical) transformations of the coordinates. Under these transformations the only thing that remains invariant is the fact that neighboring points have nearly the same coordinates; the coordinate system expresses only the topological order of the points in space (including its four-dimensional character). The equations expressing the laws of nature must be covariant with respect to all continuous transformations of the coordinates. This is the principle of *general relativity*.

The procedure just described overcomes a deficiency in the foundations of mechanics which had already been noticed by Newton and was criticized by Leibnitz and, two centuries later, by Mach: inertia resists acceleration, but acceleration relative to what? Within the frame of classical mechanics the only answer is: inertia resists acceleration *relative to space*. This is a physical property of space—space acts on objects, but objects do not act on space. Such is probably the deeper meaning of Newton's assertion *spatium est absolutum* (space is absolute). But the idea disturbed some, in particular Leibnitz, who did not ascribe an independent existence to space but considered it merely a property of "things" (contiguity of physical objects). Had his justified doubts won out at that time, it hardly would have been a boon to physics, for the empirical and theoretical foundations necessary to follow up his idea were not available in the seventeenth century.

According to general relativity, the concept of space detached from any physical content does not exist. The physical reality of space is represented by a field whose components are continuous functions of four independent variables—the coordinates of space and time. It is just this particular kind of dependence that expresses the spatial character of physical reality.

Since the theory of general relativity implies the representation of physical reality by a *continuous* field, the concept of particles or material points cannot play a fundamental part, nor can the concept of motion. The particle can only appear as a limited region in space in which the field strength or the energy density is particularly high.

A relativistic theory has to answer two questions: (1) What is the mathematical character of the field? (2) What equations hold for this field? Concerning the first question: From the mathematical point of view the field is essentially characterized by the way its components transform if a coordinate transformation is applied. Concerning the second question: The equations must determine the field *to a sufficient extent* while satisfying the postulates of general relativity. Whether or not this requirement can be satisfied depends on the choice of the field-type.

The attempt to comprehend the correlations among the empirical data on the basis of such a highly abstract program may at first appear almost hopeless. The procedure amounts, in fact, to putting the question: What most simple property can be required from what most simple object (field) while preserving the principle of general relativity? Viewed from the standpoint of formal logic, the dual character of the question appears calamitous, quite apart from the vagueness of the concept "simple." Moreover, from the standpoint of physics there is nothing to warrant the assumption that a theory which is "logically simple" should also be "true."

Yet every theory is speculative. When the basic concepts of a theory are comparatively "close to experience" (e.g., the concepts of force, pressure, mass), its speculative character is not so easily discernible. If, however, a theory is such as to require the application of complicated logical processes in order to reach conclusions from the premises that can be confronted with observation, everybody becomes conscious of the speculative nature of the theory. In such a case an almost irresistible feeling of aversion arises in people who are inexperienced in epistemological analysis and who are unaware of the precarious nature of theoretical thinking in those fields with which they are familiar.

On the other hand, it must be conceded that a theory has an important advantage if its basic concepts and fundamental hypotheses are "close to experience," and greater confidence in such a theory is certainly justified. There is less danger of going completely astray, particularly since it takes so much less time and effort to disprove such theories by experience. Yet more and more, as the depth of our knowledge increases, we must give up this advantage in our quest for logical simplicity and uniformity in the foundations of physical theory. It has to be admitted that general relativity has gone further than previous physical theories in relinquishing "closeness to experience" of fundamental concepts in order to attain logical simplicity. This holds already for the theory of gravitation, and it is even more true of the new generalization, which is an attempt to comprise the properties of the total field. In the generalized theory the procedure of deriving from the premises of the theory conclusions that can be confronted with empirical data is so difficult that so far no such result has been obtained. In favor of this theory are, at this point, its logical simplicity and its "rigidity." Rigidity means here that the theory is either true or false, but not modifiable.

The greatest inner difficulty impeding the development of the theory of relativity is the dual nature of the problem, indicated by the two questions we have asked. This duality is the reason why the development of the theory has taken place in two steps so widely separated in time. The first of these steps, the theory of gravitation, is based on the principle of equivalence discussed above and rests on the following consideration: According to the theory of special relativity, light has a constant velocity of propagation. If a light ray in a vacuum starts from a point, designated by the coordinates x_1, x_2 and x_3 in a three dimensional coordinate system, at the time x_4, it spreads as a spherical wave and reaches a neighboring point $(x_1 + dx_1, x_2 + dx_2, x_3 + dx_3)$ at the time $x_4 + dx_4$. Introducing the velocity of light, c, we write the expression:

$$\sqrt{dx_1{}^2 + dx_2{}^2 + dx_3{}^2} = cdx_4$$

This can also be written in the form:

$$dx_1^2 + dx_2^2 + dx_3^2 - c^2 dx_4^2 = 0$$

This expression represents an objective relation between neighboring space-time points in four dimensions, and it holds for all inertial systems, provided the coordinate transformations are restricted to those of special relativity. The relation loses this form, however, if arbitrary continuous transformations of the coordinates are admitted in accordance with the principle of general relativity. The relation then assumes the more general form:

$$\sum_{ik} g_{ik} \, dx_i \, dx_k = 0$$

The g_{ik} are certain functions of the coordinates which transform in a definite way if a continuous coordinate transformation is applied. According to the principle of equivalence, these g_{ik} functions describe a particular kind of gravitational field: a field which can be obtained by transformation of "field-free" space. The g_{ik} satisfy a particular law of transformation. Mathematically speaking, they are the components of a "tensor" with a property of symmetry which is preserved in all transformations; the symmetrical property is expressed as follows:

$$g_{ik} = g_{ki}$$

The idea suggests itself: May we not ascribe objective meaning to such a symmetrical tensor, even though the field *cannot* be obtained from the empty space of special relativity by a mere coordinate transformation? Although we cannot expect that such a symmetrical tensor will describe the most general field, it may well describe the particular case of the "pure gravitational field." Thus it is evident what kind of field, at least for a special case, general relativity has to postulate: a symmetrical tensor field.

Hence only the second question is left: What kind of general covariant field law can be postulated for a symmetrical tensor field?

This question has not been difficult to answer in our time, since the necessary mathematical conceptions were already at hand in the form of the metric theory of surfaces, created a century ago by Gauss and extended by Riemann to manifolds of an arbitrary number of dimensions. The result of this purely formal investigation has been amazing in many respects. The differential equations which can be postulated as field law for g_{ik} cannot be of lower than second order, i.e., they must at least contain the second derivatives of the g_{ik} with respect to the coordinates. Assuming that no higher than second derivatives appear in the field law, *it is mathematically determined by the principle of general relativity.* The system of equations can be written in the form:

$$R_{ik} = 0$$

The R_{ik} transform in the same manner as the g_{ik}, i.e., they too form a symmetrical tensor.

These differential equations completely replace the Newtonian theory of the motion of celestial bodies provided the masses are represented as singularities of the field. In order words, they contain the law of force as well as the law of motion while eliminating "inertial systems."

The fact that the masses appear as singularities indicates that these masses themselves cannot be explained by symmetrical g_{ik} fields, or "gravitational fields." Not even the fact that only *positive* gravitating masses exist can be deduced from this theory. Evidently a complete relativistic field theory must be based on a field of more complex nature, that is, a generalization of the symmetrical tensor field.

Before considering such a generalization, two remarks pertaining to gravitational theory are essential for the explanation to follow.

The first observation is that the principle of general relativity imposes exceedingly strong restrictions on the theoretical possibilities. Without this restrictive principle it would be practically impossible for anybody to hit on the gravitational equations, not even by using the principle of special relativity, even though one knows that the field has to be described by a symmetrical tensor. No amount of collection of facts could lead to these equations unless the principle of general relativity were used. This is the reason why all attempts to obtain a deeper knowledge of the foundations of physics seem doomed to me unless the basic concepts are in accordance with general relativity from the beginning. This situation makes it difficult to use our empirical knowledge, however comprehensive, in looking for the fundamental concepts and relations of physics, and it forces us to apply free speculation to a much greater extent than is presently assumed by most physicists. I do not see any reason to assume that the heuristic significance of the principle of general relativity is restricted to gravitation and that the rest of physics can be dealt with separately on the basis of special relativity, with the hope that later on the whole may be fitted consistently into a general relativistic scheme. I do not think that such an attitude, although historically understandable, can be objectively justified. The comparative smallness of what we know today as gravitational effects is not a conclusive reason for ignoring the principle of general relativity in theoretical investigations of a fundamental character. In other words, I do not believe that it is justifiable to ask: what would physics look like without gravitation?

The second point we must note is that the equations of gravitation are ten differential equations for the ten components of the symmetrical tensor g_{ik}. In the case of a non-general relativistic theory, a system is ordinarily not overdetermined if the number of equations is equal to the number of unknown functions. The manifold of solutions is such that within the general solution a certain number of functions of three variables can be chosen arbitrarily. For a general relativistic theory this cannot be expected as a matter of course. Free choice with respect to the coordinate system implies that out of the ten functions of a solution, or components of the field, four can be made to assume prescribed values by a suitable choice of the coordinate system. In other words, the principle of general relativity implies that the number of functions to be determined by differential equations is not 10 but 10–4=6. For these six functions only six independent differential equations may be postulated. Only six out of the ten differential equations of the gravitational field ought to be independent of each other, while the remaining four must be connected to those six by means of four relations (identities). And indeed there exist among the left-hand sides, R_{ik}, of the ten gravitational equations four identities— "Bianchi's identities"—which assure their "compatibility."

In a case like this—when the number of field variables is equal to the number of differential equations—compatibility is always assured if the equations can be obtained from a variational principle. This is indeed the case for the gravitational equations.

However, the ten differential equations cannot be entirely replaced by six. The system of equations is indeed "overdetermined," but due to the existence of the identities it is overdetermined in such a way that its compatibility is not lost, i.e., the manifold of solutions is not critically restricted. The fact that the equations of gravitation imply the law of motion for the masses is intimately connected with this (permissible) overdetermination.

After this preparation it is now easy to understand the nature of the present investigation without entering into the details of its mathematics. The problem is to set up a relativistic theory for the total field. The most important clue to its solution is that there exists already the solution for the special case of the pure gravitational field. The theory we are looking for must therefore be a generalization of the theory of the gravitational field. The first question is: What is the natural generalization of the symmetrical tensor field?

This question cannot be answered by itself, but only in connection with the other question: What generalization of the field is going to provide the most natural theoretical system? The answer on which the theory under discussion is based is that the symmetrical tensor field must be replaced by a non-symmetrical one. This means that the condition $g_{ik} = g_{ki}$ for the field components must be dropped. In that case the field has sixteen instead of ten independent components.

There remains the task of setting up the relativistic differential equations for a non-symmetrical tensor field. In the attempt to solve this problem one meets with a difficulty which does not arise in the case of the symmetrical field. The principle of general relativity does not suffice to determine completely the field equations, mainly because the transformation law of the symmetrical part of the field alone does not involve the components of the antisymmetrical part or *vice versa*. Probably this is the reason why this kind of generalization of the field has hardly ever been tried before. The combination of the two parts of the field can only be shown to be a natural procedure if in the formalism of the theory only the total field plays a role, and not the symmetrical and antisymmetrical parts separately.

It turned out that this requirement can indeed be satisfied in a natural way. But even this requirement, together with the principle of general relativity, is still not sufficient to determine uniquely the field equations. Let us remember that the system of equations must satisfy a further condition: the equations must be compatible. It has been mentioned above that this condition is satisfied if the equations can be derived from a variational principle.

This has indeed been achieved, although not in so natural a way as in the case of the symmetrical field. It has been disturbing to find that it can be achieved in two different ways. These variational principles furnished two systems of equations—let us denote them by E_1 and E_2—which were different from each other (although only slightly so), each of them exhibiting specific imperfections. Consequently even the condition of compatibility was insufficient to determine the system of equations uniquely.

It was, in fact, the formal defects of the systems E_1 and E_2 that indicated a possible way out. There exists a third system of equations, E_3, which is free of the formal defects of the systems E_1 and E_2 and represents a combination of them in the sense that every solution of E_3 is a solution of E_1 as well as of E_2. This suggests that E_3 may be the system we have been looking for. Why not postulate E_3, then, as the system of equations? Such a procedure is not justified without further analysis, since the compatibility of E_1 and that of E_2 do not imply compatibility of the stronger system E_3, where the number of equations exceeds the number of field components by four.

An independent consideration shows that irrespective of the question of compatibility the stronger system, E_3, is the only really natural generalization of the equations of gravitation.

But E_3 is not a compatible system in the same sense as are the systems E_1 and E_2, whose compatibility is assured by a sufficient number of identities, which means that every field that satisfies the equations for a definite value of the time has a continuous extension representing a solution in four-dimensional space. The system E_3, however, is not extensible in the same way. Using the language of classical mechanics, we might say: in the case of the system E_3 the "initial condition" cannot be freely chosen. What really matters is the answer to the question: Is the manifold of solutions for the system E_3 as extensive as must be required for a physical theory? This purely mathematical problem is as yet unsolved.

The skeptic will say: "It may well be true that this system of equations is reasonable from a logical standpoint. But this does not prove that it corresponds to nature." You are right, dear skeptic. Experience alone can decide on truth. Yet we have achieved something if we have succeeded in formulating a meaningful and precise question. Affirmation or refutation will not be easy, in spite of an abundance of known empirical facts. The derivation, from the equations, of conclusions which can be confronted with experience will require painstaking efforts and probably new mathematical methods.

FROM EINSTEIN'S GRAVITY TO SUPERGRAVITY

S. DESER

Department of Physics, Brandeis University, Waltham, Massachusetts

One of Einstein's great dreams was the unification of gravity with the other basic force of nature, electromagnetism. However, with the discovery that the other interactions at the nuclear and subnuclear level were not reducible to electromagnetism, and with the proliferation in the number of "elementary" particles, it was realized that the program of unification would be even more complex than Einstein had expected. At the same time, another problem of equal magnitude arose, that of reconciling in a satisfactory way the two basic pillars of physics, general relativity (the large-scale structure of spacetime) and quantum theory (the physics of very small distances) became apparent. Although Einstein had been the creator of the first and one of the founders of the second of these pillars, he was never happy with the latter and so never pursued that goal at all. In recent years, physicists have made some progress in both directions and come to realize that they are probably two aspects of the same underlying problem. One such very new, attractive but highly speculative attempt at unification and reconciliation is called supergravity; we shall briefly sketch its properties here.

To unify the graviton, the basic unit of general relativity viewed as a quantum system, with other known basic particles is a formidable task not only because there are so many of the latter, but because some of them, called fermions (which include the basic building-blocks of matter such as protons or, at a deeper level, quarks) are fundamentally different from gravitons and cannot even be understood except at the quantum level. Supergravity overcomes this obstacle in a way very similar to the way Dirac's immensely successful theory of the electron had explained (50 years earlier) the latter as a kind of quantum square root of an ordinary (non-quantum) particle. It associates to the graviton its "square root particle" which is also a fermion and is indissolubly part of the description of gravity at the quantum level. The resulting system includes Einstein theory as a special case, but is considerably richer in content. Conceptually, it has some revolutionary consequences, particularly the fact that space-time is so thoroughly unified with the new fermionic field that it is no longer an invariant system by itself.

The original supergravity described above was discovered in 1976 by Freedman, Van Nieuwenhuizen and Ferrara and by Zumino and the author. It has been extended since then to embrace a great many other systems, including electromagnetism itself and in this sense provides a realization of Einstein's original dream which is quite different from his unsuccessful classical ideas. Whether it is realistic enough to agree with nature is not yet clear. As to the reconciliation of gravity with quantum theory, there too supergravity

Supported in part by NSF Grant PHY-76-07299-A01.

has provided some encouraging indications with respect to the difficulties originally encountered by Einstein's theory in this respect (we refer here to the mathematical problems, the so called divergences, which beset quantum gravity). However, it is not clear either whether there is sufficient improvement to make a fully satisfactory quantum theory of supergravity. This exciting and rapidly developing field faces many challenges, therefore.

The above description is but another indication of the fruitfulness of Einstein's deep insights into nature, even when they seemed to fail completely. The challenges he raised still inspire our investigations into the next generation of physical phenomena.

GRAVITATION, GEOMETRY AND A GRAND UNIFICATION— THE PROMISE OF GAUGE THEORIES

YUVAL NE'EMAN

The Wolfson Chair Extraordinary, Tel Aviv University, Tel Aviv, Israel

GENERAL COVARIANCE OR A GAUGE?

In introducing General Relativity, one often stresses General Covariance as one of the key ingredients of the theory. Although the technical difficulties of achieving the World-Tensor systematics occupied some of the best geometricians of the Nineteenth Century, the physical content is nil. In the eyes of a Twentieth Century physicist, how could the laws of Physics ever have been thought to depend upon a coordinate relabelling (except for singular coordinate systems)? In fact, Twentieth Century mathematicians after Darboux and Cartan also came to regard General Covariance as self-evident, and introduced "anholonomic" systems defined by local frames and supporting a more informative active set of transformations.

That the laws of Physics should be the same whether they are expressed in Cartesian or Polar coordinates thus seems to us self-evident. But that they should be the same for any reference frame, including non-inertial ones, took ten years to discover, even for an Einstein. Explaining his theory in 1916, it is this issue which he emphasizes. He compares the observations of a physicist sitting in a "chest" in outer space which is being propelled by a "being" . . . with those of a physicist at rest with respect to that "being." This is the "postulate of impotence" (in the words of Whittaker) which he is after, the symmetry or invariance principle. There is no preferred reference frame—that is the "impotence" here, and this is just Invariance under (orbital) locally dependent Lorentz transformations (mostly time-dependent in this example of an acceleration).

The electron spin had not yet been discovered in 1916. Thus, the only known Lorentz-transformations were the orbital (or external) ones. Such transformations can be formally "absorbed" by a relabelling of the coordinate axes; a "passive" coordinate transformation. Indeed, general coordinate transformations can do much more "on paper," without touching the real world. Since the formalism of the Nineteenth Century Tensor Calculus was anyhow invariant under these relabellings, the physical transformations between inertial and non-inertial frames were considered as well taken care of with no further action.

With the discovery of Intrinsic Spin, this was insufficient. The geometry of Darboux and Cartan had to be invoked, with local frames of reference and a postulate of Invariance under Local Lorentz transformations enacted on the frames. This was already Lorentz gauge invariance, introduced in 1928 by H. Weyl and by Fock and Ivanenko. Weyl had pioneered the gauge approach back in 1919, when he had suggested a postulate of physical dilation invariance. This was a clear jump over and above the passive symmetry of the General Covariance group, which could always have accommodated a passive scale invariance anyhow. Unfortunately, the physical implications appeared to contradict the experimental situation, and dilation gauge invariance was abandoned. Incidentally, experiments since 1968 strongly indicate effects of dilation invariance *in the small,* within a proton or neutron, for instance, and our new theories try to account for that feature.

H. Weyl had started the idea to accommodate electromagnetism. Realizing this was not the answer, he invented the next gauge theory in 1929, this time the local invariance of the quantum phase in electromagnetism. This hit the jackpot and our present view of electric charge and the electromagnetic field is entirely based on this idea. It was generalized in 1954 by C. N. Yang and R. L. Mills for a Non-Abelian "internal" gauge group such as Isospin and in 1961 by M. Gell-Mann, A. Salam and J. C. Ward and by myself to SU(3). This meant that the dynamics of hadrons (particles such as nucleons and mesons, interacting through the Strong Nuclear Force) were assumed to be invariant under different choices of the SU(3) axes at different points in space time, or under active replacements changing the local SU(3) orientation: e.g., transforming $C^{14} \rightarrow N^{14}$ or $N^{14} \rightarrow O^{14}$ nuclei by replacing two neutrons by two protons each time (or, more fundamentally two "d" quarks by two "u" quarks at each step). Indeed, the nuclear levels stay the same, up to the weaker electromagnetic corrections.

The work of Yang and Mills made R. Utiyama, D. Sciama and T. W. Kibble try the gauge approach again in Gravity in 1955–1961. The result was that some gauging of the Lorentz group we mentioned in connection to Spin, and is known as the Einstein-Cartan theory. It adds an additional gravitational interaction at the Quantum level, with incredibly small physical effects except in very highest densities which might have existed at the origin of the present cosmological expansion. However, together with further clarifications by A. Trautman, P. v. der Heyde and F. W. Hehl, we can now regard General Relativity as embodying a physical gauge theory, that of the Poincaré group (with translations replaced by parallel transport). General Relativity indeed arises as a result of requiring local invariance of a frame under the transformations of Special Relativity. This fits Einstein's physical argument better than his own "overkill" handling of that issue, influenced as it was by General Relativity's emergence before the discovery of intrinsic Spin.

THE GEOMETRIZATION AND UNIFICATION PROGRAMS

There were two other considerations in Einstein's work which now seem to point to the Gauge approach. First, there was the Geometrization of Physics. He achieved it in General Relativity, but the entire development of the other interactions—Electromagnetic, Weak and Strong—appeared to point away from this superb elegance. Between 1928 and 1948, Electromagnetism became the first complete Relativistic Quantum Field Theory, with no geometrical features. The Weak Interactions, in a Unified Theory with Electromagnetism, and at least one part of the Strong Interactions (Quantum Chromodynamics) also appear to be describable in terms of such a Relativistic Quantum Field Theory. However, they are all Gauge theories, and between 1962 and 1974 the Weyl and Yang-Mills theories have taken on a clear geometric look. These theories are specific examples of Principal Fiber Bundles and some Associated Vector Bundles, a class of Manifolds which happen to have also attracted the attention of Differential Geometrists in the same period. The latest results in the Yang-Mills theories have been derived with the Geometrical machinery. Suddenly, Geometry is again the best description.

To deal with the Gauge theories of Gravitation, T. Regge and I, have had to develop a more general geometrical construct, the Group Manifold. This is as if one would adjoin at any point in Space-time the six dimensions of Lorentz parameters, i.e., the Euler angles and velocities. Under certain conditions, this Manifold undergoes Fibration, and we can disconnect these extra dimensions.

The new approach also serves to study two new extensions of Gravitation, in which the Poincaré group is replaced by a larger group. One such extension is Supergravity and its own Extensions.

In Special Relativity, Yu. A. Golfand and E. P. Likhtman discovered in 1971 a possible additional Quantum Symmetry of Space-time, now known as Supersymmetry, and developed mostly by J. Wess, B. Zumino, A. Salam and J. Strathdee. The new generators are spinors, and they transform a boson state into a fermion and vice versa. Gauging supersymmetry, D. Freedman, P. van Nieuwenhuizen and S. Ferrara constructed Supergravity, a gravitational theory in which there is a spinor-tetrad (anticommuting) frame (and a spin 3/2 field) aside from the usual vector-tetrad (spin 2). The theory, whose derivation was simplified by S. Deser and B. Zumino, can be extended to include several such spinor frames, one for each internal degree of freedom. It then reproduces a theory in which Gravitation has been merged with Electromagnetism or other interactions. The structure is self-consistent though there are as yet difficulties in identifying it with the physical world (one has to break the symmetry in order to have an electric coupling which will not be as weak as Newton's constant, etc. . . .). Looking back at Einstein's last Unified Field

Theory which allowed an antisymmetric piece in the metric, we note that this is exactly what is happening in Supergravity, where the spinors do introduce a small antisymmetric admixture.

There are other approaches to Gauging supersymmetry, but their main role is to study the background manifold, superspace, which is in fact a piece of that Group Manifold we mentioned.

Another extension of the Poincaré gauge consists in Gauging the Affine Group. This would imply invariance under shear stresses, with non-metricity and preservation of a 4-volume instead of a metric. We know this is not true in macroscopic space-time. However, there are many indications that we have collected in the micro-world inside hadrons which appear to fit such a picture exactly. With F. W. Hehl, Dj. Sijacki and others, we are gradually managing to go beyond General Relativity through the Affine Gauge. In this new picture, Gravity provides an additional short-range component which may be responsible for much of the strongest part of the Strong Interaction, the confinement of quarks inside hadrons.

In these last two years, leading to Einstein's Centenary, two of his greatest and most distant visions—Geometrization and Unification—suddenly appear much closer to our scientific frontier.

FROM EINSTEIN ONWARDS

C. MØLLER

Nordisk Institut for Teoretisk Atomfysik, Nordita, Kopenhagen, Danmark

Einstein's classical theory of general relativity and gravitation from 1915 was soon adopted by the majority of physicists, in spite of the difficulties in performing sufficiently accurate experimental tests at that time. The generality and simplicity of its basic ideas gave the theory an inherent power of conviction which explains this remarkable fact. Today, more than half a century later, the advanced experimental techniques have permitted accurate tests and verifications of all specific predictions of the theory, and it can now confidently be said that Einstein's classical theory gives the most reliable description of the gravitational phenomena, at least inside the solar system where the fields are comparatively weak.

At the same time more recent investigations have revealed alarming consequences which indicate that Einstein's theory, like all other theories, has a limited domain of applicability. In Einstein's classical theory the gravitational field is described by the metric tensor, the latter being a physical quantity which in principle can be measured by means of standard measuring sticks and standard clocks. From its definition it follows that the metric tensor satisfies certain inequalities; for instance the determinant of the metric tensor is always negative in a physical space-time.

According to Einstein's theory the metric tensor is connected with the matter tensor by Einstein's famous field equations. Now it turns out that the solutions of these equations in the case of sufficiently large and massive cosmic systems show properties that are incompatible with their definition as metrical quantities. This means that a system of matter plus gravitational field, which starts in a well-defined physical state where the above mentioned inequality conditions are satisfied, after a finite time may run into an entirely unphysical state, where these conditions are violated and where the notions of space and time lose their physical meaning.

This catastrophe occurs when the solutions of the field equations contain singularities, in the vicinity of which the gravitational field becomes "very strong," by which is meant a situation that is far from the situation inside the solar system. In accordance with Einstein's own expressed view we conclude that the theory breaks down in the case of very strong gravitational fields. Under these circumstances it seems imperative to investigate the possibility of constructing a theory of gravitation for macroscopic matter that is free of singularities and at the same time retains all the satisfactory features of Einstein's classical theory. First of all the new theory must give the same results as the classical theory in the case of weak fields up to the second order of approximation. But we have to require more than that; for there can be no question of returning to the ideas prevailing in physics in the pre-relativistic era. A number of the principles on which Einstein based his work must be regarded as irrevocable.

In the first place the principle of general relativity will be a headstone also in the new theory and the metric tensor must everywhere satisfy the inequality conditions mentioned above. Another fundamental feature of the classical theory which in my opinion should be retained is the "fusion of gravity and mechanics." This means that also the new gravitational field equations should have the property that the equations of motion of the matter are consequences of the field equations, the latter being non-linear particle differential equations in the gravitational field variables of not higher than the second order. Finally, Einstein's principle of equivalence, according to which the action of the gravitational field on matter can be locally transformed away by introducing suitable space-time coordinates, seems to me to be an indispensable tool in the attempt to develope a new theory of gravitation. If one now further would assume that the gravitational field is exhaustively described by the metric tensor alone then one would inevitably come back to Einstein's theory of 1915, and a generalization of this theory seems to be possible only if this assumption is abandoned.

In the course of time a large number of physicists have made attempts to generalize Einstein's classical theory from widely different points of view: Einstein himself spent the last thirty years of his life in such attempts. However, none of all these endeavours, which have been continued up to the present day, have so far led to a theory which in beauty, cogency, and inherent power of conviction can compete with Einstein's masterpiece from 1915.

VIII. GRAVITATION
AND THE UNIVERSE

One of the great contributions of general relativity to the understanding of the universe was the founding of relativistic cosmology. Einstein had shown that Newtonian theory was not in agreement with the idea of a uniform distribution of matter in the universe. The problem that he had set for himself was to see whether such a distribution of the fixed stars, as suggested by experience, and the absence of anything like a center of gravity of the total amount of matter could be reconciled with the general theory of relativity. Although he limited himself to static solutions—not in agreement with the idea of an expanding universe as suggested later—the concept of a finite but yet unbounded universe is the cornerstone of relativistic cosmology.

Hubble's velocity distance relation, briefly described here, led to a theory of an expanding universe developed by A. Friedmann. The concept and history of Relativistic Cosmology is lucidly discussed in the article by W. Rindler. A reprint of an article by the late Oscar Klein reviews some of the basis of general relativity and tries to show that relativistic cosmology is not in conformity with the basic postulate of the equivalence principle. Difficulties with the time scale led to "Steady State Cosmology," and we were fortunate in having one of its originators, Fred Hoyle, discuss it. In the meantime those difficulties were shown to be caused by wrong distance measurements and the Friedmann universe theory was reinstated. It achieved further credence by the discovery of the residual cosmic black-body radiation. Its connection to the "Big Bang" and relativity is discussed here by Ralph A. Alpher and Robert Herman, coauthors (with George Gamow) of the big-bang universe theory. The observational difficulties in pinning down two parameters, which could differentiate between different world models, are recounted in an excerpt of an article by Alan Sandage. This part is concluded by a review of cosmology during the last sixty years by the eminent cosmologist William H. McCrea.

COSMOLOGICAL DIFFICULTIES OF NEWTON'S THEORY

Apart from the difficulty discussed in Section XXI,* there is a second fundamental difficulty attending classical celestial mechanics, which, to the best of my knowledge, was first discussed in detail by the astronomer Seeliger. If we ponder over the question as to how the universe, considered as a whole, is to be regarded, the first answer that suggests itself to us is surely this: As regards space (and time) the universe is infinite. There are stars everywhere, so that the density of matter, although very variable in detail, is nevertheless on the average everywhere the same. In other words: However far we might travel through space, we should find everywhere an attenuated swarm of fixed stars of approximately the same kind and density.

This view is not in harmony with the theory of Newton. The latter theory rather requires that the universe should have a kind of centre in which the density of the stars is a maximum, and that as we proceed outwards from this centre the group-density of the stars should diminish, until finally, at great distances, it is succeeded by an infinite region of emptiness. The stellar universe ought to be a finite island in the infinite ocean of space.[1]

This conception is in itself not very satisfactory. It is still less satisfactory because it leads to the result that the light emitted by the stars and also individual stars of the stellar system are perpetually passing out into infinite space, never to return, and without ever again coming into interaction with other objects of nature. Such a finite material universe would be destined to become gradually but systematically impoverished.

In order to escape this dilemma, Seeliger suggested a modification of Newton's law, in which he assumes that for great distances the force of attraction between two masses diminishes more rapidly than would result from the inverse square law. In this way it is possible for the mean density of matter to be constant everywhere, even to infinity, without infinitely large gravitational fields being produced. We thus free ourselves from the distasteful conception that the material universe ought to possess something of the nature of a centre. Of course we purchase our emancipation from the fundamental difficulties mentioned, at the cost of a modification and complication of Newton's law which has neither empirical nor theoretical foundation. We can

From Albert Einstein, Relativity, *trans. Robert W. Lawson (New York: Crown Publishers, © 1961), Chapter XXX. Reprinted by permission of the Estate of Albert Einstein.*
*[See Part II, Mechanics and Relativity, in this book.]

1. *Proof*—According to the theory of Newton, the number of "lines of force" which come from infinity and terminate in a mass m is proportional to the mass m. If, on the average, the mass density ρ_0 is constant throughout the universe, then a sphere of volume V will enclose the average mass $\rho_0 V$. Thus the number of lines of force passing through the surface F of the sphere into its interior is proportional to $\rho_0 V$. For unit area of the surface of the sphere the number of lines of force which enters the sphere is thus proportional to $\rho_0 \frac{V}{F}$ or to $\rho_0 R$. Hence the intensity of the field at the surface would ultimately become infinite with increasing radius R of the sphere, which is impossible.

imagine innumerable laws which would serve the same purpose, without our being able to state a reason why one of them is to be preferred to the others; for any one of these laws would be founded just as little on more general theoretical principles as is the law of Newton.

A UNIVERSE—FINITE AND YET "UNBOUNDED"

But speculations on the structure of the universe also move in quite another direction. The development of non-Euclidian geometry led to the recognition of the fact, that we can cast doubt on the *infiniteness* of our space without coming into conflict with the laws of thought or with experience (Riemann, Helmholtz). These questions have already been treated in detail and with unsurpassable lucidity by Helmholtz and Poincaré, whereas I can only touch on them briefly here.

In the first place, we imagine an existence in two-dimensional space. Flat beings with flat implements, and in particular flat rigid measuring-rods, are free to move in a *plane*. For them nothing exists outside of this plane: that which they observe to happen to themselves and to their flat "things" is the all-inclusive reality of their plane. In particular, the constructions of plane Euclidean geometry can be carried out by means of the rods, *e.g.* the lattice construction, considered in Section XXIV.* In contrast to ours, the universe of these beings is two-dimensional; but, like ours, it extends to infinity. In their universe there is room for an infinite number of identical squares made up of rods, *i.e.* its volume (surface) is infinite. If these beings say their universe is "plane," there is sense in the statement, because they mean that they can perform the constructions of plane Euclidean geometry with their rods. In this connection the individual rods always represent the same distance, independently of their position.

Let us consider now a second two-dimensional existence, but this time on a spherical surface instead of on a plane. The flat beings with their measuring-rods and other objects fit exactly on this surface and they are unable to leave it. Their whole universe of observation extends exclusively over the surface of the sphere. Are these beings able to regard the geometry of their universe as being plane geometry and their rods withal as the realisation of "distance"? They cannot do this. For if they attempt to realise a straight line, they will obtain a curve, which we "three-dimensional beings" designate as a great circle, *i.e.* a self-contained line of definite finite length, which can be measured up by means of a measuring-rod. Similarly, this universe has a finite area that can be compared with the area of a square constructed with rods. The great charm resulting from this consideration lies in the recognition of the fact that

From Albert Einstein, Relativity, *trans. Robert W. Lawson (New York: Crown Publishers, © 1961), Chapter XXXI. Reprinted by permission of the Estate of Albert Einstein.*
*[See Part II, Euclidean and Non-Euclidean Continuum, in this book.]

the universe of these beings is finite and yet has no limits.

But the spherical-surface beings do not need to go on a world-tour in order to perceive that they are not living in a Euclidean universe. They can convince themselves of this on every part of their "world," provided they do not use too small a piece of it. Starting from a point, they draw "straight lines" (arcs of circles as judged in three-dimensional space) of equal length in all directions. They will call the line joining the free ends of these lines a "circle." For a plane surface, the ratio of the circumference of a circle to its diameter, both lengths being measured with the same rod, is, according to Euclidean geometry of the plane, equal to a constant value π, which is independent of the diameter of the circle. On their spherical surface our flat beings would find for this ratio the value

$$\pi \, \frac{\sin \left(\dfrac{r}{R} \right)}{\left(\dfrac{r}{R} \right)},$$

i.e. a smaller value than π, the difference being the more considerable, the greater is the radius of the circle in comparison with the radius R of the "world-sphere." By means of this relation the spherical beings can determine the radius of their universe ("world"), even when only a relatively small part of their world-sphere is available for their measurements. But if this part is very small indeed, they will no longer be able to demonstrate that they are on a spherical "world" and not on a Euclidean plane, for a small part of a spherical surface differs only slightly from a piece of a plane of the same size.

Thus if the spherical-surface beings are living on a planet of which the solar system occupies only a negligibly small part of the spherical universe, they have no means of determining whether they are living in a finite or in an infinite universe, because the "piece of universe" to which they have access is in both cases practically plane, or Euclidean. It follows directly from this discussion, that for our sphere-beings the circumference of a circle first increases with the radius until the "circumference of the universe" is reached, and that it thenceforward gradually decreases to zero for still further increasing values of the radius. During this process the area of the circle continues to increase more and more, until finally it becomes equal to the total area of the whole "world-sphere."

Perhaps the reader will wonder why we have placed our "beings" on a sphere rather than on another closed surface. But this choice has its justification in the fact that, of all closed surfaces, the sphere is unique in possessing the property that all points on it are equivalent. I admit that the ratio of the circumference c of a circle to its radius r depends on r, but for a given value of r it is the same for all points of the "world-sphere"; in other words, the "world-sphere" is a "surface of constant curvature."

To this two-dimensional sphere-universe there is a three-dimensional analogy, namely, the three-dimensional spherical space which was discovered by Riemann. Its points are likewise all equivalent. It possesses a finite volume, which is determined by its "radius" $(2\pi^2 R^3)$. Is it possible to imagine a spherical space? To imagine a space means nothing else than that we imagine an epitome of our "space" experience, i.e. of experience that we can have in the movement of "rigid" bodies. In this sense we *can* imagine a spherical space.

Suppose we draw lines or stretch strings in all directions from a point, and mark off from each of these the distance r with a measuring-rod. All the free end-points of these lengths lie on a spherical surface. We can specially measure up the area (F) of this surface by means of a square made up of measuring-rods. If the universe is Euclidean, then $F = 4\pi r^2$; if it is spherical, then F is always less than $4\pi r^2$. With increasing values of r, F increases from zero up to a maximum value which is determined by the "world-radius," but for still further increasing values of r, the area gradually diminishes to zero. At first, the straight lines which radiate from the starting point diverge farther and farther from one another, but later they approach each other, and finally they run together again at a "counter-point" to the starting point. Under such conditions they have traversed the whole spherical space. It is easily seen that the three-dimensional spherical space is quite analogous to the two-dimensional spherical surface. It is finite (i.e. of finite volume), and has no bounds.

It may be mentioned that there is yet another kind of curved space: "elliptical space." It can be regarded as a curved space in which the two "counter-points" are identical (indistinguishable from each other). An elliptical universe can thus be considered to some extent as a curved universe possessing central symmetry.

It follows from what has been said, that closed spaces without limits are conceivable. From amongst these, the spherical space (and the elliptical) excels in its simplicity, since all points on it are equivalent. As a result of this discussion, a most interesting question arises for astronomers and physicists, and that is whether the universe in which we live is infinite, or whether it is finite in the manner of the spherical universe. Our experience is far from being sufficient to enable us to answer this question. But the general theory of relativity permits of our answering it with a moderate degree of certainty, and in this connection the difficulty mentioned in Section XXX* finds its solution.

THE VELOCITY-DISTANCE RELATION

E. HUBBLE

When a ray of light passes through a glass prism (or other suitable device) the various colors of which the light is composed are spread out in an ordered sequence called a spectrum. The rainbow is, of course, a familiar example. The

*See previous article, "Cosmological Difficulties of Newton's Theory," in this book.
Excerpt from E. Hubble, The Realm of the Nebulae (New Haven: Yale University Press, 1936). Reprinted by permission of the publisher.

sequence never varies. The spectrum may be long or short, depending on the apparatus employed, but the order of the colors remains unchanged. Position in the spectrum is measured roughly by colors, and more precisely by wavelengths, for each color represents light of a particular wave-length. From the short waves of the violet, they steadily lengthen to the long waves of the red.

The spectrum of a light source shows the particular colors or wavelengths which are radiated, together with their relative abundance (or intensity), and thus gives information concerning the nature and the physical condition of the light source. An incandescent solid radiates all colors, and the spectrum is *continuous* from violet to red (and beyond in either direction). An incandescent gas radiates only a few isolated colors and the pattern, called an *emission* spectrum, is characteristic for any particular gas.

A third type, called an *absorption* spectrum and of special interest for astronomical research, is produced when an incandescent solid (or equivalent source), giving a continuous spectrum, is surrounded by a cooler gas. The gas absorbs from the continuous spectrum just those colors which the gas would radiate if it were itself incandescent. The result is a spectrum with a continuous background interrupted by dark spaces called absorption lines. The pattern of dark absorption lines indicates the particular gas or gases that are responsible for the absorption.

The sun and the stars give absorption spectra and many of the known elements have been identified in their atmospheres. Hydrogen, iron, and calcium produce very strong lines in the solar spectrum, the most conspicuous being a pair of calcium lines in the violet, known as H and K.

The nebulae in general show absorption spectra similar to the solar spectrum, as would be expected for systems of stars among which the solar type predominated. The spectra are necessarily short—the light is too faint to be spread over long spectra—but the H and K lines of calcium are readily identified and, in addition, the G-band of iron and a few hydrogen lines can generally be distinguished.

Nebular spectra are peculiar in that the lines are not in the usual positions found in nearby light sources. They are displaced toward the red of their normal position, as indicated by suitable comparison spectra. The displacements, called red-shifts, increase, on the average, with the apparent faintness of the nebula that is observed. Since apparent faintness measures distance, it follows that red-shifts increase with distance. Detailed investigation shows that the relation is linear.

Small microscopic shifts, either to the red or to the violet, have long been known in the spectra of astronomical bodies other than nebulae. These displacements are confidently interpreted as the results of motion in the line of sight—radial velocities of recession (red-shifts) or of approach (violet-shifts). The same interpretation is frequently applied to the red-shifts in nebular spectra and has led to the term "velocity-distance" relation for the observed relation between red-shifts and apparent faintness. On this assumption, the nebulae are supposed to be rushing away from our region of space, with velocities that increase directly with distance.

THE STRUCTURE OF SPACE

Since the publication of the first edition of this little book, our knowledge about the structure of space in the large ("cosmological problem") has had an important development, which ought to be mentioned even in a popular presentation of the subject.

My original considerations on the subject were based on two hypotheses:

(1) There exists an average density of matter in the whole of space which is everywhere the same and different from zero.
(2) The magnitude ("radius") of space is independent of time.

Both these hypotheses proved to be consistent, according to the general theory of relativity, but only after a hypothetical term was added to the field equations, a term which was not required by the theory as such nor did it seem natural from a theoretical point of view ("cosmological term of the field equations").

Hypothesis (2) appeared unavoidable to me at the time, since I thought that one would get into bottomless speculations if one departed from it.

However, already in the 'twenties, the Russian mathematician Friedmann showed that a different hypothesis was natural from a purely theoretical point of view. He realized that it was possible to preserve hypothesis (1) without introducing the less natural cosmological term into the field equations of gravitation, if one was ready to drop hypothesis (2). Namely, the original field equations admit a solution in which the "world radius" depends on time (expanding space). In that sense one can say, according to Friedmann, that the theory demands an expansion of space.

A few years later Hubble showed, by a special investigation of the extragalactic nebulae ("milky ways"), that the spectral lines emitted showed a red shift which increased regularly with the distance of the nebulae. This can be interpreted in regard to our present knowledge only in the sense of Doppler's principle, as an expansive motion of the system of stars in the large—as required, according to Friedmann, by the field equations of gravitation. Hubble's discovery can, therefore, be considered to some extent as a confirmation of the theory.

There does arise, however, a strange difficulty. The interpretation of the galactic line-shift discovered by Hubble as an expansion (which can hardly be doubted from a theoretical point of view), leads to an origin of this expansion which lies "only" about 10^9 years ago, while physical astronomy makes it

From Albert Einstein, Relativity, *trans. by Robert W. Lawson (New York: Crown Publishers, © 1961), Appendix IV. Reprinted by permission of the Estate of Albert Einstein.*

appear likely that the development of individual stars and systems of stars takes considerably longer. It is in no way known how this incongruity is to be overcome.[1]

I further want to remark that the theory of expanding space, together with the empirical data of astronomy, permit no decision to be reached about the finite or infinite character of (three-dimensional) space, while the original "static" hypothesis of space yielded the closure (finiteness) of space.

RELATIVISTIC COSMOLOGY

WOLFGANG RINDLER

University of Texas at Dallas, Richardson, Texas

Einstein's theory of gravity, namely general relativity, and especially his "Cosmological Considerations" paper of 1917, triggered and sustained the entire development of modern cosmology. His two great contributions to this subject were (i) to provide it with a consistent dynamics, i.e., a theory of how the universe moves under its own gravity, and (ii) to entertain the serious possibility that the universe is curved (and thus possibly finite). It seemed natural to Einstein to assume that the universe should be homogeneous and isotropic, i.e., that no location and no direction at any location is preferred. He also assumed—with all other scientists in 1917—that the universe is static. These assumptions led him uniquely to his hyperspherical universe, the three-dimensional analogue of a spherical surface. In it, if you fired a bullet straight ahead, it would ultimately hit you in the back; and if you blew up a balloon, and you had enough balloon and enough breath, the balloon would attain a maximum surface area, flip around, contract, and finally enclose you. (Consider the analogy of "blowing up circles" on a sphere.) Ironically, Einstein had to tamper with his original law of gravitation, much as Seeliger tampered with Newton's inverse square law, to make possible a static universe. The so-called "cosmological constant" λ that Einstein inserted for this purpose into his field equations has the effect (when positive) of a repulsion: take it away, and Einstein's universe would collapse under its own gravity.

In 1922 Friedmann, by one of those revolutionary insights otherwise more typical of Einstein, asked himself what would happen if one dropped one's insistence on the staticness of the universe, and thereby discovered a wealth of new models. In fact, Friedmann's set of models (completed by another paper in 1924) is still that which modern cosmologists use, both in their theories and in their interpretation of the data. But the regret that Einstein expressed—

1. Although the difficulty mentioned by Einstein gave rise to much speculation, including a new theory of cosmology, the "Steady State Theory," it turned out to be unfounded. The distance measurements necessary to calculate the age were found to be wrong by at least a factor of two, and after the correct data were used, the "origin" of the expansion was seen to have occurred about 10^{10} years ago, well beyond the age of individual stars. G.E.T.

namely that now our universe could be any one of a number of possible universes—is still valid, though it has been a chief concern of cosmologists in the intervening half-century to narrow down that choice. (Other concerns, more tractable, were the genesis of the chemical elements, the evolution of stars and galaxies, etc.)

The age difficulty mentioned by Einstein has by now evaporated. At fault were the early estimates of cosmic distances. The presently accepted value of the expansion rate is only about one-tenth of Hubble's original value, and so the time scale of all Friedmann models has increased tenfold. This allows them to accommodate the ages of the stars and galaxies (11–18 billion years) as estimated by geological and other means. In fact, the closeness of this accommodation in itself reinforces the theory.

Friedmann allowed both λ and the space curvature to take any values, and used Einstein's field equations to determine the resulting motion. Thus among his models there are not only flat and hyperspherical ones, but also negatively curved ones (analogous to a saddle rather than a sphere). With any of the three curvatures, the expansion can either go on forever, or just for a certain period and then change to contraction, depending on λ and on the energy of what we would now call the "big bang." For almost all Friedmann models have a sudden explosive beginning when the matter was infinitely concentrated. Only one model starts its expansion from a quasi-static Einstein universe, and one from a contracting state. Without the cosmological constant, i.e., with $\lambda = 0$, just three universes are possible: a flat and a negatively curved one, both expanding forever; and a hyperspherical one that expands from a big bang to maximum volume, halts, and then recontracts to an inverse big bang. As Banesh Hoffmann has said, Einstein eventually regarded this last as the adult version of his brainchild of 1917. For he came to detest and renounce his cosmological constant as an unnecessary and unaesthetic complication. Not all modern cosmologists would agree: the mathematical complication is slight, and to them it seems more satisfactory to let the observations determine whether or not the constant is zero—something quite feasible in principle.

Where do we stand today? The most important cosmological data in recent times have been collected by the radio astronomers, and none has had more impact than the discovery in 1965 of the 3°K blackbody microwave radiation that seems to fill the universe quite uniformly. It strongly suggests two things: (i) a hot big-bang origin of the universe, of which it is the well-understood (and in fact earlier predicted) remnant; and (ii) the isotropy of the universe from our vantage point, to a much higher degree than is evident optically or from observations of radio galaxies. Now, we would hardly expect to inhabit a special location in the universe, so isotropy probably holds everywhere. But then homogeneity follows: for if location A differed from location B, this would show up as a lack of isotropy at location C, midway between A and B. Since the Friedmann models are the most general homogeneous and istropic models within general relativity, and since most of them have a big bang, our faith in their applicability is greatly strengthened.

But we still don't know which among them applies to *our* universe. The cumulative evidence seems to point to a universe with negative curvature, and thus, assuming the simplest topology, with infinite volume. But there is no certainty, nor can we even guess the sign of λ. (Though we can restrict its range to about $\pm 10^{-56}$ cm^{-2}.) In the past, cosmologists have looked to the most distant galaxies (including quasars) for further clues. For example, by counting galaxies in depth, and measuring departures from the Euclidean relation between distance and volume, curvature information could be gained. By observing the redshift (expansion rate) to second order, information could be gained on whether the universe is accelerating or decelerating, and thus on λ. But unfortunately all such observations are beset by a grave difficulty: the unknown changes of brightness that a galaxy undergoes in time. We don't know how bright a really distant galaxy was billions of years ago when it emitted the light or radio signals whereby we now observe it. Thus our main method of judging galactic distances—by comparing a galaxy's intrinsic with its apparent brightness—becomes more and more uncertain the farther we probe, and this critically affects whatever cosmological conclusions could be drawn.

It has therefore been suggested that ultimately our most reliable data will come from *local* observations. If we could accurately determine the present average density of matter in the universe (and for this we need not look too far), and if, for example, we could arrive at an accurate estimate for its present age (by a combination of theory and local observation), then, in conjunction with our fairly accurate knowledge of its present expansion rate, this would fix the model uniquely. It is, perhaps, not unrealistic to expect that before this century is out we shall have our answer.

ON THE FOUNDATIONS OF GENERAL RELATIVITY THEORY AND THE COSMOLOGICAL PROBLEM

O. KLEIN

ABSTRACT

It is shown in some detail how Einstein's cosmological attempt was based on considerations strangely deviating from his essential foundation of general relativity theory—the principle of equivalence—by means of which the mathematical formalism of the theory obtains its physical interpretation. By means of a comparison between the cosmological solutions and the ordinary solutions of general relativity corresponding to a finite system embedded in an approximately empty region it is concluded that there are hardly any a priori arguments in favour of relativistic cosmology.

From Arkiv für Fysik *39, no. 11 (1968). Reprinted by permission of the Estate of Oscar Klein and publishers.*

1. INTRODUCTION

There is hardly any disagreement among physicists as to the success of general relativity theory, when applied to large-scale phenomena such as planetary motion, deflection of light-rays and change of frequency of spectral lines in gravitational fields; that in these respects it represents an important progress as compared with Newtonian mechanics and gravitational theory. This unanimity ceases, however, as soon as its foundations are brought under discussion, i.e. the significance of the equivalence of inertial forces and gravitational fields, the meaning of general covariance and the relevance of Mach's criticism of Newton's absolute space and his ideas about the origin of inertia. This again has led to very different views as to the range of applicability of the theory and its possible later development. Thus, some of the leading quantum-field and elementary particle physicists regard general relativity theory as purely macroscopical and gravitation not only as the weakest but also the least understood of elementary interactions. At the other extreme are those followers of Einstein himself who consider the gravitational field equations for the matter-free case as the very fundament of the theory and the first step towards a vast generalization embracing—without or with the quantum postulate—the whole of physics and cosmology.

Between these two extremes there are naturally many shades, and most of those physicists and mathematicians, who are actively engaged on the further development of the theory, do not take any of the extreme positions as to its meaning and range. To many of these the following attempt to steer between the extremes may seem almost trivial, while to others it may appear doubtful or even wrong. Its aim—like that of some earlier papers of the writer [1]—is to show that the real foundations on which Einstein developed general relativity theory—in some respects to be distinguished from what he himself meant them to be—will, when closely examined, remove the basis for the mentioned discrepancy and at the same time be shown to disagree with the ideas which led him to relativistic cosmology.

2. EINSTEIN'S WAY TO GENERAL RELATIVITY

In his first publications towards general relativity (1907 [2] and 1911 [3]) Einstein laid already the foundation of what was later called the *principle of equivalence,* thereby giving what is certainly the most original and probably the most far-reaching contribution since Newton to the problem of gravitation. It is well-known how he—starting from the hitherto uninterpreted experimental fact that all bodies suffer the same acceleration in a given gravitational field—compared two frames of reference, K and K', the former at rest in a homogeneous gravitational field, the latter being uniformly accelerated in a region, where gravitation is negligible, and, assuming the acceleration of K' equal to that suffered by a body falling freely in $K,$ put forward the claim that these frames are equivalent, not only mechanically—as they are according to Newtonian mechanics—but with respect to any physical agency. Also the important predictions as to the action of gravitation on light—later further developed in his general relativity theory and verified by observations—are well-known.

It is therefore astonishing that in the first full account of his general relativity theory, given in a paper in 1916 [4], he should regard Mach's idea about inertia as the principal reason for a generalization of special relativity to arbitrary motions. Then, as a further argument for such a generalization he introduces the equivalence point of view, but with an interesting shift of the stress. Thus, while in the 1911 paper he compared a case of ordinary gravitation with a case of inertial force, using their equivalence from a mechanical point of view as a basis for the hypothesis of their general equivalence, he now uses the same empirical background as an argument for the assumption that a frame of reference in non-uniform motion with respect to an inertial frame of reference may also be regarded as being at rest in a gravitational field. The same conclusion he had already drawn from Mach's idea, according to which the inertial force may be regarded as due to the non-uniform motion of the centre of gravity of the universe with respect to the frame of reference under consideration.

He draws now the important conclusion that the field equations for the gravitational field must be satisfied by the inertial forces due to arbitrary non-uniform motion with respect to an inertial frame of reference. From there the step is only small to his assumption that these questions must be covariant under general coordinate transformations. We shall return to this point below.

In the meantime it is interesting to notice the early influence on Einstein of Mach's epistemological criticism of the foundations of mechanics. He stresses this in the fascinating biographical notes, which with characteristic self-irony he called his obituary (published in the volume Albert Einstein Philosopher–Scientist [5], which appeared at the occasion of his 70th birthday). Later on in the same article he introduces the account of his way from special to general relativity by the following remark: "Also to Mach's question: 'how can it be that inertial systems are physically distinguished above all other coordinate systems?' this theory (special relativity theory) offers no answer" [5] p. 63. His own answer is clearly that they are not distinguished, because *no gravitational field* is but a special case of gravitational fields.

It will be seen that the question of the relative importance of the two arguments, that of Mach (we call it M) and the equivalence argument (E) can only be decided by looking at their respective roles in the actual development of the theory—both being used in support of his claim of general covariance of the laws of physics. There is, however, the immediate difference between them that, while M is based on general epistemological considerations, E has an experimental fact as its background. For this purpose we shall now give a short summary of the content of the 1916 paper and thereafter try to answer the above question.

Thus, after the introductory considerations about the two arguments, the paper contains a detailed account of the mathematical formulation of the theory including the law of motion of a particle in a given gravitational field and the equations for the gravitational field itself, which replace the Poisson equation of Newtonian theory, and further, the covariant form of Maxwell's electromagnetic equations, supposed to be valid in any gravitational field. It is then shown, that for weak gravitational fields and small velocities the new theory goes over into the Newtonian theory, and, finally, the striking results of the precise prediction of the deflection of light rays in the sun's gravitational field and the explanation of the secular rotation of the orbit of the planet Mercury are presented.

The last section of the introductory part of Einstein's 1916 paper begins with the following words: "Es kommt mir in dieser Abhandlung nicht darauf an die allgemeine Relativitätstheorie als ein möglichst einfaches System mit einem Minimum von Axiomen darzustellen. Sondern es ist mein Hauptziel diese Theorie so zu entwickeln, dass der Leser die psychologische Natürlich-keit des eingeschlagenen Weges empfindet und dass die zugrundegelegten Voraussetzungen durch die Erfahrung möglichst gesichert erscheinen. In die-sem Sinne sei nun die Voraussetzung eingeführt:

Für unendlich kleine vierdimensionale Gebiete ist die Relativitätstheorie im engeren Sinne bei passender Koordinatenwahl zutreffend" [4] p. 87.

After this he introduces the ten g_{ik} as the coefficients of the quadratic form

$$ds^2 = g_{ik}\,dx^i dx^k \tag{1}$$

which results when the general coordinates x^1, x^2, x^3, x^4, used for the map-ping of a finite space-time region, are regarded as functions of the cartesian space coordinates x, y, z and the time t of the local inertial frame of reference —i.e. the frame in which special relativity is valid—in the immediate neigh-bourhood of the point under consideration; ds^2, as expressed in the latter coordinates, is the fundamental Minkowskian invariant. Now, the assumption here used by Einstein is just that extension of his original equivalence consider-ations which has later been called Einstein's principle of equivalence.

It follows from the above quotation that the coordinates x, y, z, t of the local inertial frame are measurable in the usual way by means of good measur-ing rods and clocks at rest in this frame, while the general coordinates are in most cases not directly measurable. This is mentioned in the paper and strongly stressed in later publications, especially in the little book The Meaning of Relativity first published in 1921 [6]. That the g_{ik}, or rather their first coordinate derivatives, describe the gravitational field is concluded from the behaviour of a free mass point—which obeys the law of inertia in the local frame—the equations in the gravitational case following by a direct translation of this law to the general frame. This is shown in detail in a later section, after the development of the mathematical tools, where the equations of motion are explicitly given. In a similar way the equations for the electromagnetic field in the presence of gravitation, including the energy-momentum tensor, are derived. As will be seen, all this is directly based on the equivalence principle, which again is a direct generalization of the considerations of the 1911 paper.

Looking now at Einstein's derivation of the gravitational field equations we see that the role of the equivalence principle comes somewhat into the background as compared with the points of view of covariance and simplicity most strongly stressed by himself. Still it plays no unimportant role, though less direct than in the problems just mentioned. In the first place the g_{ik} themselves are, as we saw, defined by means of this principle, which is also the case with the claim that the inertial forces satisfy the field equations in the matter-free case which was used by Einstein as a guidance in his search for the field equations. In fact, since the g_{ik} belonging to these forces satisfy the equations

$$R_{ik} \cdot {}_{lm} = 0 \qquad (2)$$

where $R_{ik \cdot lm}$ are the twenty components of the well-known Riemann-Christoffel tensor formed from the g_{ik} and their first and second coordinate derivatives, the latter appearing linearly, it follows that the contracted two-indices tensor R_{ik}, formed by linear combinations of the $R_{ik \cdot lm}$ components, vanishes for such g_{ik}. Making now the further claim—suggested by the simplicity argument and further supported by the Laplace equation for the gravitational potential—that the equations should be linear in the second derivatives, there is no other two-indices tensor than a linear combination of R_{ik} and Rg_{ik}, where R is the scalar obtained by contraction of R_{ik}. In this way, using moreover the energy-momentum tensor T_{ik} as the natural generalization of the density standing at the right-hand side of the Poisson equation together with the property of this tensor of having a vanishing vector divergence, he arrived finally at his famous field equations

$$R_{ik} - \frac{1}{2} g_{ik} R = -\kappa T_{ik} . \qquad (3)$$

Since in the limit of small velocities of the matter to which the T_{ik} tensor belongs and of weak gravitational fields, the equation for the coefficient g_{44} takes the same form as the Poisson equation, the other equations playing a negligible role, he could fix the value of the constant κ as

$$\kappa = \frac{8\pi\gamma}{c^4} , \qquad (4)$$

where γ is the ordinary gravitational constant and c the vacuum velocity of light.

In the following we shall analyze the different assumptions behind Einstein's theory somewhat more closely, but already the above review shows that, while the equivalence argument plays an important role, the Mach argument plays no other role than of giving an epistemological background to the equivalence argument for general covariance. That this is so, is very strongly corroborated by the way general relativity theory is presented in Pauli's excellent book, which appeared in 1921 [7], the same year as the book by Einstein mentioned

THE COSMOLOGICAL PROBLEM   273

above. Although he follows Einstein's own arguments very closely in his connected and easily readable presentation of the subject, not only does he give them a more definite form but also changes their order. Thus, the whole theory is developed from the equivalence point of view, the equivalence principle being defined in the following way: "Es gibt für ein unendlich kleines Weltgebiet (d.h. ein so kleines Weltgebiet, dass die örtliche und zeitliche Variation der Schwere in ihm vernachlässigt werden kann) stets ein solches Koordinatensystem $K_0(X_1, X_2, X_3, X_4)$, in welchem ein Einfluss der Schwere weder auf die Bewegung von Massenpunkten noch auf irgendwelche anderen physikalischen Vorgänge vorhanden ist" [7] p. 705. Although Pauli follows Einstein also with respect to the Mach argument, this is not mentioned before the actual theory and its ordinary applications have been established, and then only in connection with the questions that led Einstein to his cosmological attempt. To this we shall come back below.

3. EINSTEIN'S WAY TO COSMOLOGY

Already a year after the paper reviewed in the last section Einstein published his famous closed-world solution, which gave the start to relativistic cosmology. His reasons for this attempt towards a description of the average situation of the universe are given in the paper and repeated in the book mentioned above but are again more distinctly presented in Pauli's book, which we shall follow here. He first discusses the approximate solution of Einstein's equations discovered a short time before by H. Thirring [8], where the gravitational field produced by a hollow rotating material sphere is shown to be similar to the inertial forces in a rotating frame of reference but extremely weak when the mass of the sphere is small enough to permit the perturbation method used in the calculation. To make the solution definite Thirring had to use the ordinary boundary condition $g_{ik} \rightarrow$ to their normal values at infinity, the g_{ik} of the solution deviating very little from the normal values. This solution was taken to mean a first step towards the fulfillment of Mach's idea about inertia and was somewhat generalized by Einstein in his book, where he writes: "We must see in them a strong support for Mach's ideas as to the relativity of all inertial actions. If we think these ideas consistently through to the end we must expect the *whole* inertia, that is, the *whole* $g_{\mu\nu}$-field, to be determined by the matter of the universe, and not mainly by the boundary conditions at infinity" [6], p. 103.

The first point which Pauli discusses in this connection concerns just the boundary conditions at infinity. Following Einstein—in his cosmological paper —he considers them as going against the spirit of the postulate of covariance, although not logically inconsistent with it. Against them he puts now the claim just quoted from Einstein, which he also regards as the natural expression within general relativity theory of Mach's idea about inertia, Mach's principle, as Einstein had called it at an earlier occasion, and he concludes: "Insbesondere ist zu fordern, dass die Trägheit der Materie durch die umgebenden

Massen allein bestimmt ist, also verschwinden soll, wenn alle übrigen Massen entfernt werden, weil es vom relativistischen Standpunkt aus keinen Sinn hat, von einem Widerstand gegen *absolute* Beschleunigungen zu sprechen (Relativität der Trägheit)" [7] pp. 744–745. He then reviews Einstein's arguments for the addition of the term—λg_{ik} to the left side of the gravitational field equations, λ being the so-called cosmological constant of dimension length^{-2}. Thereafter he shows that the modified equations are satisfied by Einstein's closed world solution of constant mass density proportional to λ^{-1}. Since the space in this solution is finite and unlimited the boundary conditions at infinity are avoided. Also with the cosmological term there is no longer a solution to the gravitational field equations in the absence of matter with constant values of the g_{ik} other than zero. Regarding this as an argument in favour of the Mach principle, Pauli writes: "*In einem völlig leeren Raum gibt es überhaupt kein G-Feld* (g_{ik}-field); weder eine Lichtfortpflanzung, noch die Existenz von Mass-Stäben und Uhren wären dann möglich. Damit hängt zusammen, dass auch das Postulat der Relativität der Trägheit befriedigt ist" [7] pp. 747–748. A little before, however, he expressed himself more cautiously: "Auch das Mach'sche Prinzip scheint durch die Feldgleichungen befriedigt zu sein, obwohl ein allgemeiner Beweis dafür noch nicht erbracht ist" [7] p. 747.

It should be mentioned that the λ-term, by means of which he obtained his closed solution, where boundary conditions at infinity were avoided and which gave him the hope of satisfying the Mach principle, was suggested to Einstein by another kind of difficulties, namely the impossibility in Newtonian gravitational theory to have a material universe of finite temperature embedded in an infinite empty space or, alternatively, an infinite universe of finite average density. These difficulties had been much discussed before the advent of relativity theory and many astronomers had accepted an idea, which seems to have been first proposed by Charlier [9], namely a hierarchical ordering of matter in analogy with what is the case with the known stellar systems, such that the average density goes towards zero, when the order goes towards infinity. Einstein seems not to have considered this possibility. We shall come back to this question below. However, Einstein himself abandoned later the λ-term in favour of Friedmann's expanding solutions of the original field equations, where the density is finite and which obtained what seemed a striking verification by Hubble's discovery of the general expansion of the system of the galaxies.

Here a few words should be said about Einstein's later attempts towards a further generalization of his gravitational field theory. The aim of these attempts was to found a unified field theory embracing both the electromagnetic field and matter, of which the matter-free gravitational field equations were to form a special case. That, thereby, he regarded the equivalence principle of only secondary importance is evident from the way he came to look on his original derivation of the equations of motion for a mass-point in a gravitational field. Thus in the appendix added to his little book in 1950 he wrote:

"This constitutes a hypothetic translation of Galileo's law of inertia to the ease of the existence of 'genuine' gravitational fields. It has been shown that this law of motion—generalized to the case of arbitrarily large gravitating masses —can be derived from the field equations of empty space alone. According to this derivation the law of motion is implied by the condition that the field be singular nowhere outside its generating mass points" [6] pp. 109–110. This program of Einstein may be summarized in the following way: Mach's principle → general covariance → gravitational field equations without matter → unified field theory.

4. SOME FURTHER COMMENTS ON THE PRINCIPLES OF EQUIVALENCE AND COVARIANCE

As we have seen, the actual achievements of general relativity theory as a branch of physics are: a) formulation of the laws of mechanics and electromagnetism in the case of an arbitrary gravitational field, and b) the differential equations for the gravitational field itself. Thereby the derivation of the generalized mechanical and electromagnetic laws, including the expression for the energy-momentum tensor appearing at the right-hand side of the gravitational field equations depends, as we have seen, entirely on the equivalence principle. In both cases there are strong reasons for believing that general relativity represents a real and important progress in comparison with the corresponding classical laws.

As regards the generalized space-time geometry of general relativity theory—formally a four-dimensional Riemannian geometry of hyperbolic character—it seems to me that it has been somewhat overemphasized, since it is directly based on the coordination of space and time characteristic of special relativity. In this respect the analogy, often stressed, with Gaussian geometry of curved surfaces is really striking. Just as Gaussian geometry is based on Euclidean geometry being valid in the infinitesimal, similarly the space-time geometry of general relativity is based on that of special relativity. For Gaussian geometry this implies that the concept of length is based on that of Euclidean geometry in the sense that the length of any line on a curved surface is defined as the limit of the sum of its elements at first regarded as finite and measured in the tangent plane by means of a rigid measuring rod. In the same way the concepts of space and time in general relativity theory depend on measurements in locally inertial frames by means of ordinary measuring tools. This has been strongly stressed by Einstein himself [6] p. 63, and other places.

Because space-time measurements are at the bottom of quantitative physics these considerations show that the *very physical interpretation* of the mathematical formalism of general relativity theory is directly based on the equivalence principle. In fact, the statement that the laws of special relativity form the background for those valid in the presence of gravitational fields— i.e. are valid in the infinitesimal when a locally inertial frame of reference is used—would be meaningless without this assumption.

Here an often raised objection against the principle of equivalence should be mentioned, namely that the connection between a tensor equation of special relativity and the corresponding generally covariant equation is not unambiguous, because a tensor containing the curvature components, which vanish in the quasi-Euclidean case, might always be added. Such an ambiguity is avoided, however, by including in the principle the assumption that the laws of physics can always be so formulated that no coordinate derivatives of the g_{ik} of higher order than the first appear in the basic equations. As is well-known this claim is fulfilled by the mechanical and electromagnetic laws, the only cases where general relativity theory has been tested. It would therefore seem natural to consider this claim—or an equivalent one, when quantum theory is introduced—as a heuristic guide in the further development of the theory.

It must not be forgotten, however, that the left-hand side of the equations for the gravitational field itself cannot be derived from the equivalence principle, when taken in its immediate sense, there being no corresponding equations in the specially relativistic case, when the gravitational field is absent. In view of the fundamental role of this principle the possibility suggests itself that, when quantum theory is introduced, these equations may follow from an action principle based on an integral, the integrand of which permits the removal of the gravitational field at any given space-time point. This would mean that formally the appearance of gravitational fields with non-vanishing curvature tensor would be an outcome of quantum theory, implying a certain connection between observation according to the principle of equivalence and Bohr's fundamental principle of observation in quantum theory, according to which quantum effects must be negligible in the description of the tools of measurement.

Let us, as a somewhat closer illustration of the role of the equivalence principle in measurements, consider the determination of the properties of an isolated system, for instance its mass. In the first place it must be remembered that the concept *isolated system* is an idealization never to be rigorously realized. It means that external influences are practically removed, among them gravitational effects due to other sources than the system itself. The latter purpose is fulfilled in a frame of reference falling freely in the external gravitational field, when this field is practically homogeneous over the dimensions of the system and constant in time during the measurement. Thus, the conditions in the measurement frame are just those required for the validity, at distances from the system large compared with its linear dimensions, of the external Schwarzschild solution. Hence the mass of the system is defined and in principle measurable, and thus also its total energy. Of course the practical measurability of a mass by its gravitational effects is limited by their weakness when it is not very large as compared with atomic masses. With these again—measured in the usual way by their resistance against acceleration—the effects of the earth's gravitational field are negligible, a frame of reference at rest with respect to the earth being practically inertial.

Just as the practical boundary conditions according to the above consider-ations are a direct consequence of the practical isolation of the system it follows that the boundary conditions at infinity are but an idealization more or less valid according to the problem—just as in classical physics—which has noth-ing to do with cosmology. Taking the solar system as an example, the frame of reference is one which is at rest with respect to its centre of gravity and hence freely falling in the galactic gravitational field surrounding it. That this is a very good approximation for the validity of the Schwarzschild solution outside of the system—but not too near to it—follows from its small linear dimensions as compared with the distance to the nearest stars. As is seen, the frame of reference is just the Newtonian one, i.e. almost exactly the Copernican one, which is therefore the natural one from the point of view of general relativity theory.

As a further example of the role of the equivalence principle in the interpretation of general relativity theory we shall consider the much discussed clock paradox. Thus, from the passengers' point of view the duration of a return voyage in a space-ship is given by the sum of the time intervals measured in the subsequent inertial rest-frames of the ship. This is clearly the same as the integral over the proper-time differential from the beginning to the end of the voyage, which is just Einstein's original statement.

The discussion is sometimes confused by introduction of the possible influence of the gravitational field appearing during the periods of acceleration and retardation on different processes inside the ship, such as the physiological ageing of the passengers. This, however, has no relevance to the problem of the clock paradox as is shown by the following example. We assume that the space-ship, after having left the earth, moves with a constant acceleration directed from floor to roof and equal to g here on earth. Only when the acceleration changes direction, which happens twice during the voyage, there is a short interval of weight-lessness, during which floor and roof are inter-changed. Finally the ship lands on earth. In the numerical example treated in the appendix the duration of the voyage is 12 years as judged by the passengers. Although they have lived under practically normal conditions in the space-ship the result as to ageing is sufficiently startling, the duration of the voyage having been 40 years as judged from the earth. Thus a passenger starting at the age of 28 years would be 40 years at its end, and hence of the same age as his son born just before the start.[1]

It is of course true that strong gravitational fields may have important physiological effects and may even kill the passengers. But this is clearly quite unconnected with the time change due to relativity. It should also be remarked that in the above example time could be measured with high precision inside the ship by means of an atomic clock, the influence of the weak gravitation

1. See Appendix I.

being quite negligible during the short time of 12 years.

Returning to Einstein's question, why the inertial frames are physically distinguished above all other coordinate frames, its answer according to the afore-said is clearly—and quite in the line of Einstein's own original ideas—*because they give the physical meaning of the mathematical formalism of general relativity theory.* It follows that his considerations, mentioned above, about the Mach idea are in fact incompatible with his own principle of equivalence. Also in his closed solution the mass of any physical system would have to be defined by means of a local inertial frame and not through the global character of the solution. Nor has the Thirring solution anything to do with the masses of particles inside the hollow sphere, giving simply an interesting addition to the gravitational field reigning there. Another thing is that in a future quantum theory the masses of elementary particles may have an indirect connection with gravitation, such a theory being probably also a generalized gravitational theory.

While, as already mentioned, the situation in relativity theory presents a close analogy to Gaussian geometry of curved surfaces the bearing of this analogy must not be exaggerated as is sometimes done, when it is assumed that only invariants under general coordinate transformations have physical significance. In fact, the very starting point for Einstein's equivalence considerations was that a coordinate transformation leading to a frame of reference accelerated with respect to an inertial frame will, when practically realized, mean the appearance of a gravitational field, which is certainly a change of the physical situation. In the geometrical case such non-invariant quantities as the gravitational field hardly possess any comparable interest.

Before leaving the subject of the relation of Mach's idea of inertia to the principle of equivalence we shall return to Pauli's statement quoted above—giving the essence of this idea—that a resistance against acceleration with respect to *absolute space* is devoid of physical meaning. This statement, however, which sounds like good common sense, is based on a priori assumption on what the expression *absolute space* ought to mean, while for Newton it had the empirical background of defining a frame of reference in which the laws of mechanics are valid. In replacing *absolute space* by the concept of *inertial frame of reference,* a frame in which the laws of special relativity are valid, its empirical background has become immensely strengthened, while at the same time it has obtained a much deeper content in forming the very basis for Einstein's general theory of gravitation. Moreover, its essential importance has obtained strong support from the development of quantum field theory, through which the concepts of *empty space* and *matter* have been shown to be related in a way quite unknown to classical physics, on which Mach's idea was based. On the other hand the other idea—which Mach rejected—means already a certain approach to present ideas about empty space.

Coming now to the question of the role of general covariance in the establishment of Einstein's theory—which like the equivalence principle has

THE COSMOLOGICAL PROBLEM   279

given rise to much controversy—these two viewpoints as is shown by the above review of Einstein's actual way of developing his theory are closely connected. In fact, no natural limit seems to present itself to the coordinate transformations implied in the principle of equivalence, by means of which gravitational fields are introduced or removed. Mathematically this is expressed by the general possibility of introducing a locally geodesic coordinate frame at any point in an arbitrary Riemannian geometry.

Sometimes the opinion is expressed that general covariance has no more physical meaning than the introduction of curvilinear coordinates into field equations of classical physics. This is not correct, however, because in contrast to classical field theory the metric coefficients—the g_{ik}—which in general relativity theory replace the gravitational potential of classical theory, are themselves field quantities satisfying covariant equations. Thus, as long as they are not specified numerically, all the equations of the theory are identical in the old and the new coordinates. In this respect the situation is just like that of the classical electromagnetic equations under a Lorentz-transformation. Hence, the group of general coordinate transformations *is* a symmetry of the mathematical formalism of general relativity theory.

Still those physicists are right who declare that general relativity is not a symmetry of nature in the ordinary sense of the word. This is because the inertial frames required to give a physical meaning to the formalism break the covariance of the theory, while a Lorentz transformation, in contrast to this, concerns directly observable physical quantities. It would be interesting to know whether the broken symmetries occurring in elementary particle theory might in some generalized way be connected with the situation in general relativity theory, the word generalized referring to some yet unknown formal generalization of the principle of equivalence. A certain indication of such a possibility may perhaps be seen in the five-dimensional representation of electromagnetism, which, however, would need some deep-going modification.

5. CONCLUDING REMARKS ON EINSTEIN'S COSMOLOGY ARGUMENTS

An important consequence of the view taken in the former section—that the equivalence principle forms the basis for the physical interpretation of the mathematical formalism of general relativity theory—is, as we saw, that the mass of an isolated system, be it an elementary particle or a stellar system etc., is determined with respect to an external inertial frame either by means of its gravitational effects or its resistance to non-gravitational forces. This is in direct contrast not only to the Mach principle but also to the more cautious view that the true inertial frames are those which are not accelerated with respect to a frame determined by the fixed stars. Thus, for instance, a frame of reference fixed to a satellite moving around the earth, although strongly accelerated with respect to the fixed stars, is practically weightless, particles and other bodies inside the satellite behaving according to the laws of special relativity theory. This, of course, corresponds quite to Einstein's original considerations. It is interesting that Newton, to whom these facts, as far as classical mechanics is concerned, were certainly familiar, did not notice this essential relativity displayed by his concept of "absolute space." But also to us, who through the development of quantum theory and special relativity theory have been forced to acquaint ourselves to strange deviations from our customary way of regarding physical phenomena, the full significance of the principle of equivalence—despite its nearness to well-known experience—is hard to grasp. On the other hand, Mach's explanation of inertia, although without any empirical basis whatever, appears so natural—even almost obvious—that we find it difficult to reject it, in spite of its incompatibility with the equivalence principle.

Our conclusion is that the Mach principle, being contradictory to the empirically based foundation of general relativity theory, cannot give support to relativistic cosmology.

Regarding the boundary conditions at infinity as an argument for cosmology, we have also seen that according to the principle of equivalence they belong to the idealization "isolated system" and, moreover, for a *practically* isolated system, the infinity is also *practical*, having no connection with the cosmological problem.

As regards the difficulty of the finite average density in an infinite universe, the idea of Charlier takes on an interesting aspect in general relativity theory. Let us assume that a system of a certain hierarchical order, approximated by a sphere of radius R (strictly the radial coordinate in the Schwarzschild frame) has the mass M.[1] Then the condition for practical isolation is

$$\frac{2\gamma M}{c^2 R} < 1. \qquad (5)$$

It follows that the gravitational acceleration at its surface is approximately equal to $\gamma M/R^2$ and at an inside point of radial coordinate r approximately equal to $(\gamma M/R^2) \cdot (r/R)$. But according to (5) this is smaller than $(c^2/2R) \cdot (r/R)$. With R equal to a lightyear (10^{18} cm), which is several powers of ten smaller than the linear dimensions of our galaxy, c^2/R is about equal to the gravitational acceleration at the surface of the earth.

Since the adaptation of a successful theory ought to start from those features which have the strongest empirical background the above would show that relativistic cosmology in the sense of describing the behaviour of the system of galaxies by means of a solution of the Friedmann-Lemaître type possesses a very small a priori probability in comparison with a theory of the Charlier type, satisfying the inequality (5), i.e. considering the system of galaxies as the first example of a regular, although extremely big type of stellar system.

1. See Appendix II.

On the other hand, the so-called fireball radiation, predicted on relativistic cosmology by Dicke, and the helium content of certain stars, predicted by Gamow *et al.*, are now regarded as strong a posteriori support of relativistic cosmology. They are certainly a challenge to those, who like the present writer are trying to replace cosmology by a theory more in conformity with the lines of ordinary physics.

ACKNOWLEDGEMENTS

An essential part of this paper was written during a stay at Nordita, Copenhagen, and I wish to express my warmest thanks to its staff, especially to Dr. Stefan Rozental, for their kind help.

APPENDIX I

The statements in the text are derived in the following way, which is closely related to Möller's representation of a constant homogeneous gravitational field in general relativity theory. Let g be the acceleration or retardation of the ship with respect to the inertial frame $K(t)$ in which the ship is at rest at time t. This time is measured in the ship, reckoned from the start of the voyage and given by the sum of the infinitesimal time-elements dt measured in the successive inertial rest-frames $K(t)$ of the ship. Let $v(t)$ be the velocity of the ship with respect to the frame K_0. Then

$$v(t + dt) = \frac{v(t) + gdt}{1 + \frac{gv(t)dt}{c^2}} = v(t) + \left(1 - \frac{v(t)^2}{c^2}\right)gdt$$

from which follows (with $v(0) = 0$)

$$v(t) = c \, \mathrm{tgh}\frac{gt}{c}. \tag{1}$$

Let now z be the coordinate along the line of the motion in the frame $K(t)$ reckoned from an origin fixed to the ship and z_0 the corresponding coordinate in K_0, the time in K_0 being t_0, while $K(0)$ coincides K_0 at the start. Then a Lorentz transformation from K_0 to $K(t)$ may be expressed in the following way

$$dt_0 = \frac{dt + \frac{v(t)}{c^2}dz}{\sqrt{1 - \frac{v(t)^2}{c^2}}}, \quad dz_0 = \frac{dz + v(t)dt}{\sqrt{1 - \frac{v(t)^2}{c^2}}}, \tag{2}$$

where dt_0, dz_0 and dt, dz are time and coordinate differences of two infinitesimally near events in K_0 and $K(t)$ respectively. Let now both events take place at the origin of $K(t)$. Then

$$dt_0 = \frac{dt}{\sqrt{1 - \frac{v(t)^2}{c^2}}} = \cosh\frac{gt}{c} \, dt, \quad dz_0 = \frac{v(t)dt}{\sqrt{1 - \frac{v(t)^2}{c^2}}} = c \sinh\frac{gt}{c} \, dt,$$

and, hence

$$t_0 = \frac{c}{g} \sinh \frac{gt}{c}, \quad z_0 = \frac{c^2}{g} \left(\cosh \frac{gt}{c} - 1 \right). \tag{3}$$

For small t-values the expression for z_0 gives, as it ought to, the classical expression

$$z_0 = \frac{1}{2} g t^2.$$

Applying the above to the roundtrip mentioned in the text we shall use the year as the unit of time and the lightyear as the unit of length. Thus we have $c = 1$. Moreover, we shall put $g = 1$ corresponding to 950 cm sec^{-2}, very close to the g-value here on earth. We divide now the voyage in four parts of equal duration, $t = 3$ years. In the first part the acceleration is directed away from the solar system, in the second and third it is towards the solar system and in the fourth again away from it. From (3) we get now for the total time $t_0 = 4 \sinh 3$, i.e., approximately 40 years, and for the largest distance reached 2 (cosh 3–1), i.e. about 18 lightyears, the duration as judged from the space-ship being only 12 years.

APPENDIX II

The question whether the Schwarzschild limit—where the inequality (5) is replaced by an equality—can be surpassed is still open. Under very general conditions for the equation of state of the matter forming the system a static solution of the Einstein equations satisfying the boundary condition at infinity requires the validity of (5). Moreover, a contracting solution of this kind will approach the limit asymptotically, reaching it in no finite time as judged from the external frame of reference, the velocity of the boundary approaching thereby that of light. Due to this the time as measured by a clock placed at the boundary will be finite. On the other hand, for the same reason, there will be no real mathematical connection, when the limit is surpassed, between the inner and outer frame of reference.

Thus, it would seem that the Schwarzschild limit marks a division line between such solutions of the relativistic equations which can be formed in a natural way as subdivisions of a larger and less dense system—such as stars and galaxies—and the cosmological solutions, the main characteristic of which is the lack of boundary conditions. Considering this as a—still tentative— claim to be fulfilled by the laws of physics, it may require a certain modification of Einstein's equations. As mentioned above these equations have a weaker support from the principle of equivalence than the rest of his theory. Their modification may therefore not be unexpected. On the other hand, more realistic assumptions about the properties and distribution of matter than have been made in the models so far studied may already diminish the possibility of approaching the Schwarzschild limit.

REFERENCES

1. Klein, O., Mach's principles and cosmology in their relation to general relativity. Recent Developments in General Relativity, p. 293. Pergamon Press, 1962.
   Klein, O., Some general aspects of Einstein's theory of relativity. Astrophysica Norvegica, IX, p. 161 (1964).
   Klein, O., Boundary conditions and general relativity. Preludes in theoretical Physics, p. 23. North Holland, 1966.

2. Einstein, A., Relativitätsprinzip und die aus demselben gezogenen Folgerungen. Jahrbuch der Radioaktivität, *4*, 411 (1907).

3. Einstein, A., Einfluss der Schwerkraft auf die Ausbreitung des Lichtes. Ann. der Phys. ser 4, *35*, 898 (1911).

4. Einstein, A., Die Grundlage der allgemeinen Relativitätstheorie, Ann. der Phys. Ser. 4, *49*, 769 (1916) (quotations from Lorentz-Einstein-Minkowski, Teubner 1922, pp. 81–124).

5. Einstein, A., Albert Einstein, Philosopher—Physicist, The Library of Living Philosophers, Evanston, Illinois, 1949.

6. Einstein, A., The Meaning of Relativity, Princeton University Press, 1921 (quotations from third edition, Princeton University Press, 1950).

7. Pauli, W., Relativitätstheorie, Teubner, 1921. (Sonderabdruck aus der Encyclopädie der mathematischen Wissenschaften.)

8. Thirring, H., Über die Wirkung ferner rotierender Massen in der Einsteinschen Relativitätstheorie, Phys. Ztschr. *19*, 33 (1918).

9. Charlier, C. V. L., Wie eine unendliche Welt aufgebaut sein kann. Arkiv f. Mat. Astr. o. Fys. *4*, 24 (1908).
   Charlier, C. V. L., How an infinite world may be built up. Arkiv f. Mat. Astr. o. Fys. *16*, 22 (1921).

THE STEADY-STATE COSMOLOGY

FRED HOYLE

The steady-state cosmology can be obtained, using the usual techniques of general relativity, without difficulty. One begins by considering a suitably differentiable scalar function of position, $C(x)$. To the usual action function of general relativity one then adds two terms, of the forms:

$$\sum_{\text{particles}} \int C_i \, dx^i, \quad \int C_i \, C^i \sqrt{-g} \, d^4x, \tag{1}$$

where $C_i = \partial C/\partial x^i$. The first of these terms contributes to the action only when the world lines of particles have "ends"—that is to say, when particles are created or destroyed. Although these are thus two terms added to the action, only one coupling constant appears, since an apparent second constant can always be observed into C itself. The effect of these terms in the action is to add a tensor of the form

$$(\text{constant}) \times (C_i \, C_k - \tfrac{1}{2} g_{ik} \, C_\varrho \, C^\varrho) \tag{2}$$

to the usual energy-momentum tensor of the Einstein theory. The field equations now have the de Sitter metric

$$ds^2 = dt^2 - \exp(2Ht) \, [dx^2 + dy^2 + dz^2] \tag{3}$$

as a solution, with a *non-zero* mass density ρ given by $8\pi\rho = 3 \, H^2$, and with H a constant that is related in a simple way to the constant in (2). Moreover, it can be shown that *all* approximately homogeneous and isotropic solutions of the field equations tend asymptotically to (3). This is the steady-state model.

It has proved difficult, although not strictly impossible, to incorporate the microwave background discovered in 1965 by Penzias and Wilson into the steady-state model. For this reason the model is not nowadays considered to be a viable representation of the universe. Yet it is the only model which seeks to describe the creation of matter explicitly, through the field C. The so-called "big-bang" models currently in vogue, which follow lines first discussed in 1922 by Friedmann, are placed in a curiously equivocal position with regard to the creation of matter. On the one hand, the Friedmann models require creation of matter, but they cannot describe it in mathematical terms—an attempt to do so simply leads to the steady-state model. Seemingly one must take one or other of two positions:

1. The creation of matter falls outside of laws that can be stated in mathematical form,
2. Matter was never created.

An attempt to follow (2) leads to the view that the so-called "origin" of the universe, the initial moment of the Friedmann models, was not a true origin, but was a conformal singularity of the type discussed by the author in *Astr. J., 196,* 661 (1975). In such a theory the universe has a piecewise character, with the Einstein theory being fully applicable [without the addition (2)] in each piece, but with additional conditions being necessary in order to describe continuity from one piece to another. In this form of the theory the "origin" of the universe is not a true origin. It is a portion of the boundary of the piece in which we happen to live.

EINSTEIN, BIG-BANG COSMOLOGY, AND THE RESIDUAL COSMIC BLACK-BODY RADIATION

RALPH A. ALPHER AND ROBERT HERMAN

The general theory of relativity formulated by Einstein (1) in 1916 provided the modern basis for modelling the universe as a whole. In 1917 Einstein (2) was the first to apply his own theory of gravitation to cosmological modelling as he attempted to describe the then popular view of a static universe. During the next thirty years a number of relativists developed the cosmological implications of Einstein's theory in a variety of models that exhibit expansion, contraction, or oscillation. These non-static models gained credence with the discovery by Hubble (3) that the extra-galactic nebulae were receding from one another and that the universe was in fact expanding.

The expansion of the universe provides rather strong evidence that the universe is evolving and suggested that in the past there existed a much more highly compressed state than is now the case. In fact the most straightforward extrapolation into the past of the present expansion would imply a singular event or "big bang" at which time the universe began to evolve.

In 1946 George Gamow (4) proposed that the conditions in the early stages of an evolving big-bang universe may well have been sufficiently extreme, i.e., very hot and very dense, to make nuclear transformations possible among the elementary constituents of the matter present. This suggestion, augmented by his view that one might build up the observed relative abundances of the chemical elements by some kind of neutron coagulation process during this period of nuclear transformation, was in response to the difficulties of understanding the relative abundances on any other basis known at that time.

These ideas were developed by Alpher and Herman (5), working with Gamow, through a series of successively improved calculations the first of which became known as the α-β-γ theory (6). In the course of this work, which combined for the first time the microphysics of nuclear matter and the macrophysics of the cosmos, it became possible to specify numerically, and over the years with increased precision, the physical conditions required to synthesize the elements from those basic constituents which existed in the primordial universe during the first few minutes after the big bang. The magnitude of two quantities, namely, the temperature and the density of matter, implied an early universe filled with black-body radiation characterized by a very high temperature and containing on a mass basis but a trace of matter.

With such a view of the early universe and with a relativistic cosmological model consistent with that view, Alpher and Herman were led to the conclusion that relatively early in the history of the expansion, sufficient cooling

Ralph A. Alpher, General Electric Research and Development Center, Schenectady, N.Y.
Robert Herman, General Motors Research Laboratories, Warren, Mich.

286   GRAVITATION AND THE UNIVERSE

occurred so that matter and radiation decoupled, and that the dynamics and cooling of the universe from then to the present has been controlled by matter rather than by radiation. Moreover they proposed that there should now be permeating the universe a residual black-body radiation characterized by a very low temperature—a vestige of the original big-bang—a residue of the early very high temperature radiation which has been red-shifted by the universal expansion. On the basis of the estimate current in 1948 of the amount of matter in the universe at present, and the amount of matter required in the early universe for nucleosynthesis, they were able to calculate the temperature characterizing this radiation to be about 5 degrees above absolute zero (7), in contrast to the temperature of ~15 billion degrees one second after the big bang. Since Hubble's results suggested that the universe was expanding isotropically, i.e., uniformly in all directions, and since all indications are that the distribution of matter in the universe is homogeneous when considered on a sufficiently large scale, one may characterize the big-bang universe as a basically homogeneous isotropic cosmological model. Therefore the residual black-body radiation permeating the universe should be as isotropic as was the distribution of matter in the universe when the all-pervasive radiation last interacted with that matter.

The so-called black-body radiation in the universe early or late is completely specified by a single quantity, namely, the temperature. Black-body radiation is ubiquitous in our everyday experience since to a first approximation all bodies above the absolute zero of temperature "glow" and, to the extent that they are nonreflective, emit radiation which is essentially black-body in character. (A precise definition is not required in this general discussion, although to be sure the above description is that of a gray body.) The energy in black-body radiation covers the entire frequency spectrum, but a very large fraction of the total energy emitted by a black body at a given temperature lies at and near a wavelength corresponding to the maximum of a sharply peaked spectral energy distribution. Moreover, this peak lies at shorter wavelengths the higher the temperature of the radiation. The wavelength of the maximum of the energy distribution for 5 degree black-body radiation, which corresponds to the original prediction by Alpher and Herman, is about 0.6 millimeter, which for the early (~1 second) 15 billion degree radiation the wavelength maximum would have been about 2×10^{-4} nanometers, i.e., gamma-ray wavelengths.

In 1965, seventeen years after the necessity of a relict black-body radiation was suggested by Alpher and Herman, Penzias and Wilson (8) observed an isotropic radiation at a wavelength of 7.35 centimeters, whose intensity, were the radiation sampled black body in origin, corresponded to a temperature of about 3.5 degrees absolute. This observation was interpreted by Dicke, Peebles, Roll and Wilkinson (9) and by Penzias and Wilson (8) as corresponding to a residual black-body radiation of cosmic origin. Since the original observation, more than thirty additional observations have been made at a variety of wavelengths, including wavelengths close to the peak of the spectral energy distribution, confirming that the spectral energy distribution is in fact black-body in character and corresponds to a temperature of 2.8 degrees absolute. The original prediction of 5 degrees reduces to the somewhat lower observed value when one takes into consideration the more accurate current estimates of the early and present densities of matter in the universe.

In the early efforts by Alpher, Gamow and Herman to understand the formation of the chemical elements, it was proposed that the primeval universe was the single locale for the synthesis of them all. However, it quickly became evident that forming elements in the early universe is a reasonable supposition only for the very lightest elements, namely, helium and deuterium. In 1957 Burbidge, Fowler and Hoyle (10) showed that the relative abundances of the elements could be understood as resulting from nuclear transformations in stellar interiors with subsequent distribution through the mechanisms of stellar explosions. However, this description as well as more recent work with various improvements have failed to provide a suitable explanation for the stellar synthesis of the elements helium and deuterium.

The fact that the primordial synthesis of helium and deuterium in correct abundances relative to hydrogen is readily understood in the big-bang cosmo-logical model (11) is now offered together with the observation of the universal expansion and the existence of a residual black-body radiation as evidence for the correctness of the big-bang model. This model is now taken by many scientific workers to be the standard or canonical model of the universe.

It should be noted that this canonical model is completely specified when one knows the rate of expansion of the universe, i.e., the Hubble constant, and the appropriate densities of matter and radiation.

More specifically, one can then calculate the radius of curvature of the universe which distinguishes among the three basic variants of the canonical model, i.e., open or ever-expanding, flat or of Newtonian character, or closed and oscillatory.

In the years since the observation of the cosmic black-body radiation there has been a great deal of interest in using the high degree of isotropy of this radiation as an observational probe. To the extent that departures from iso-tropy can be detected one is able to probe departures from homogeneity in the distribution of matter when matter and radiation decoupled during the rela-tively early stages of the expansion, or to detect interactions between the radiation and regions of dense hot gas in the universe. The already observed limits on the anisotropy suggest that the universe was so highly homogeneous when matter and radiation last interacted on a cosmic scale as to place severe limitations on theories of galactic formation resulting from the growth of fluctuations at early times in the expansion. Moreover, current observations of the angular dependence of the anisotropy suggest that our galaxy exhibits a small but measurable motion in a specific direction with respect to this early distribution of matter at the time of last matter-radiation interaction. In a certain sense this distribution of matter at the time of last interaction constitutes an absolute frame of reference. In addition, the existence of the cosmic black-body radiation and its very high isotropy have been exploited in the detection of gases in galactic clusters, in the study of the origin and propagation of cosmic rays and will no doubt find application in many other ways in future astrophysical inquiry.

The all pervading residual cosmic black-body radiation, which can be understood only in a cosmological framework stemming from Einstein's pioneering theory of general relativity and gravitation, is now perhaps one of the most accurately known physical parameters describing our universe.

During the early 1950's when the scientific community was rather skeptical of the reality of the type of considerations being discussed in this essay, e.g., see Weinberg (12). Alpher, Follin. and Herman (13) undertook an examination of the detailed physical phenomena involving particle and radiation interactions at the most fundamental level understood at that time, building on some earlier work by Hayashi (14). This work (13) which involved the extremely hot and dense state existing during the first few minutes after the big bang appears now to have provided the first modern framework for the study of the physics of this earliest epoch.

With the ever increasing credibility of the canonical cosmological model of the universe, many scientists are turning their attention to this very early state of the universe as an arena worthy of serious study (12)—an arena in which one is faced with some of the most penetrating and fundamental of questions concerning the limits and validity of quantum mechanics and relativity theory as one probes ever closer to what now can only be characterized as the "initial singularity."

REFERENCES

1. A. Einstein, Ann. der Phys. *49*, 769 (1916).

2. A. Einstein, Preuss. Akad. Wiss. Berlin, *6*, 142 (1917).

3. E. Hubble, Proc. Nat. Acad. Sci., *15*, 168 (1929).

4. George Gamow, Phys. Rev. *70*, 572 (1946).

5. For a more complete discussion of this point as well as other matters in this essay, and for a much more extensive bibliography, the reader is invited to peruse R. A. Alpher and R. Herman, Proc. Amer. Phil. Soc. *119*, 325 (1975).

6. R. A. Alpher, H. Bethe, and G. Gamow, Phys. Rev. *73*, 803 (1948).

7. R. A. Alpher and R. Herman, Nature, *162*, 774 (1948) and Phys. Rev. *75*, 1089 (1949).

8. A. A. Penzias and R. W. Wilson, Astrophys. Jour. *142*, 419 (1965).

9. R. H. Dicke, P. J. E. Peebles, P. G. Roll, and D. T. Wilkinson, Astrophys. Jour. *142*, 414 (1965).

10. E. M. Burbidge, G. R. Burbidge, W. A. Fowler and F. Hoyle, Rev. Mod. Phys. *29,* 547 (1957).

11. D. N. Schramm and R. V. Wagoner, Ann. Rev. Nucl. Sci. *27,* 37 (Annual Reviews, Inc. 1977).

12. S. Weinberg, *The First Three Minutes,* (Basic Books, Inc., New York, 1977).

13. R. A. Alpher, J. W. Follin, Jr., and R. Herman, Phys. Rev. *92,* 1347 (1953).

14. C. Hayashi, Progr. Theoret, Phys. (Japan) *5,* 224 (1950).

A SEARCH FOR TWO NUMBERS

ALLAN R. SANDAGE

Hale Observatories, Pasadena, California

As recently as the 1950's about all that observational cosmology had succeeded in establishing was that galaxies exist and the universe expands. But beginning in the 1960's a flood of new discoveries has enriched our picture of the universe and has begun to provide a basis on which to distinguish between competing cosmological models. There has been a 30-year effort now drawing to a close, to get precise measurements of two parameters that will provide a crucial test for cosmological models. The two key numbers are the rate of expansion *(the Hubble constant H_0)* and the *deceleration* in the expansion (q_0). The hope is that current research, by determining the extra-galactic distance scale for nearby galaxies and searching for exceedingly distant clusters where the redshift is large, will measure both of these numbers to a precision of 15%.

New discoveries of the 1960's, spurred by the sophistication of new instruments and ideas, include:

• Black-body radiation predicted by George Gamow, Ralph A. Alpher and Robert Herman and left over from the big-bang "creation" event

• Isotropic extragalactic x-ray and γ-ray background flux

• Quasars with redshifts greater than 2, which imply recession velocities greater than 80% of the speed of light

• Absorption lines in quasar optical spectra resulting perhaps from an intergalactic medium or from the passage of radiation through clusters of galaxies

• Evidence that the helium abundance is about 30% by mass in all primeval matter.

These discoveries relate directly to the two major classes of cosmological

From Allan R. Sandage, "A Search for Two Numbers," Physics Today, February 1970, pp. 34–35. Reprinted by permission of the American Institute of Physics.

models: In the big-bang models of A. Friedmann, Sir Arthur S. Eddington, Georges Lemaître, and Gamow, the expansion began from a singularity in space and time, emerging from that state a finite time ago amidst conditions of extreme density and pressure. On the other hand, the steady-state universe of Hermann Bondi, Thomas Gold, and Fred Hoyle had no beginning and no end, but rather continuously remakes itself according to a fixed and immutable pattern.

If the residual 3 K background flux discovered by Arno A. Penzias and Robert W. Wilson,[1] and studied with vigor by the Princeton group[2] is indeed degraded fireball radiation, then a big-bang origin would seem possible. Gamow, Rodger Taylor, Hoyle, and James Peebles emphasized that a similar conclusion follows if the pristine helium abundance is indeed 30%, because so much helium apparently can only be made in the primeval physical conditions immediately after a Friedmann-type singular state. Must we then take the big bang seriously?

Perhaps, but especially if we could establish that the time scale when all this might have happened agrees with other related events such as the age of the chemical elements and the age of the oldest stars. Unfortunately there is still incomplete knowledge of all parameters required to date accurately the oldest stars as well as lack of precise values for H_0, and q_0, but current research is working in this direction.

COSMOLOGY SIXTY YEARS ON

WILLIAM H. McCREA

Astronomy Centre, University of Sussex, Fulmer, Brighton, England

EINSTEIN AND MODERN COSMOLOGY

A characteristic of Einstein's great papers was that, although each abounded in original ideas, he produced it as though it was just what anybody must want to know about at that particular time. Having produced such a paper, in almost no time he would produce another on a totally different topic, again with the same air of inevitability.

In 1916 Einstein published his main paper on the foundations of general relativity, universally recognised as one of the very greatest achievements of any single mind. The dozen or so papers which followed in the next year included the two on the quantum theory of radiation that, by introducing the notion of transition probabilities, effectively set the aim of all future quantum theory. Then,[1] still in 1917, quite unheralded, came "Cosmological considerations on the general theory of relativity."

Although at the time astronomy was indeed beginning to feel its way in

1. A. A. Penzias, R. W. Wilson, *Astrophys. J. 142*, 419 (1965).
2. R. B. Partridge, *American Scientist 57*, 37 (1969).

the first quantitative steps to the edge of the Galaxy and beyond, this had no influence upon Einstein. Also, although the problem of gravitation in the universe in the large went back to Newton, it happened to be of no recent topical concern at the time when Einstein wrote. Indeed his paper made no reference to any other work except some by de Sitter on a rather technical point. From other evidence, we know that while still a student Einstein's thoughts had been directed to the large-scale behaviour of the universe by his reading of Mach, which had caused him, in particular, to wonder about the origin of inertia. But he did not mention even this in "Cosmological considerations." The paper was, in fact, the invention of modern cosmology.

GENERAL RELATIVITY AND THE UNIVERSE

The basic consideration, which was not fully clear even to Einstein at the time, is that it is impossible to do general relativity without doing cosmology. In Newtonian physics and in special relativity we study physical systems that are immersed in given infinite space time, but upon which they have no effect. In dealing with any such system, we must therefore prescribe boundary conditions. In general relativity, on the other hand, matter and its spatial and temporal relationships are features of a single entity, which may be called a *space-time* or a *geometry* (with a topology included). Any physical system studied in general relativity is describable completely only by the specification of the whole geometry, that is an entire universe—a cosmology, in fact.

Einstein did not fully appreciate this profound change which he himself had wrought in the formulation of mathematical physics, partly because no one could all at once make the complete transformation of concepts required. In any case, it was evident from the outset that classical concepts and procedures would continue to be used in most of physics. But it was also because to the end Einstein clung to the concept of a field-theory expressed by means of differential equations, and the solution of differential equations does require boundary conditions, and these, as indicated, are conceptually foreign to Einstein's own general relativity.

In "Cosmological considerations," he presented his famous closed static model universe—the first entire universe built in strict conformity with a physical theory. What pleased Einstein most was its demonstration by an actual example that general relativity can produce a whole system free of contradiction. As he[2] confessed in a letter (9 March 1917) to his friend Michele Besso, he had hitherto been uneasy lest 'the infinite' should conceal an irresolvable contradiction. For, at the time, the only other system built according to the theory was the Schwarzschild space-time, and this did rest on the assumption that a certain behaviour at infinity could be postulated without inconsistency. We must therefore admit that in 1917 Einstein's interest was in seeing that general relativity met a certain technical requirement, and not in discovering anything new about the astronomical universe. In the latter regard, he merely remarked that if the actual universe corresponds to his reasoning, then the model may be a rough representation of it. But, he expressly refrained from discussing the astronomical evidence. ⌡

COSMICAL CONSTANT

Even to get so far, however, Einstein—obviously without enthusiasm— had had to pay the price of introducing what he called *cosmical terms,* multiplied by a *cosmical constant* Λ, into his relations between the material and geometrical properties of the model. He was justified in claiming that this did not alter the general mathematical character of these relations, but, by bringing in any disposable constant, it affected the conceptual basis of the theory. The step had so much influence upon the subsequent history of the subject, that it has to be recalled even in the briefest sketch of that history.

At the time Einstein reconciled himself to the step because without Λ he could get no model, while with Λ he could get an apparently unique model, and one that did admit a Mach interpretation. Nevertheless he lost most of the satisfaction when de Sitter very soon discovered a different model apparently meeting the same general requirements as his own. This robbed Einstein's model of its uniqueness, and in some ways a theory that allowed the whole universe to behave in two totally different ways seemed at first to be worse than any theory that made no claim to say how the whole universe should behave. Moreover, the form of de Sitter's model was such that it reacted against the Mach interpretation.

EXPANDING UNIVERSE

One of the most inspired advances[3] in thought about the physical universe was that made by A. Friedmann in 1922 when he dared to contemplate the possibility of a model universe that is not static in the large. The idea that the universe might be changing cannot have been new, but the idea that cosmic change might be significantly treated by quite simple mathematics called for intellectual courage. Friedmann worked strictly in accordance with Einstein's general relativity—including the formal retention of the Λ-terms—and sought the simplest cosmological models that the theory would admit without the restriction to being unchanging in time. In fact he obtained the models of the expanding universe that are in use to this day. He resolved the embarrassment regarding the Einstein and de Sitter models by showing that in effect a model could start as an Einstein universe and end as a de Sitter universe. What was more important, his models were acceptable with the Λ-terms discarded. Einstein quickly withdrew a criticism he voiced of Friedmann's first paper, but then he and others fell silent on the subject until long after Friedmann's death in 1925. Meanwhile G. Lemaître, in ignorance of Friedmann's work, produced remarkably similar results in 1927. However, unlike Friedmann and Einstein, Lemaître appreciated the possible connexion with astronomical discoveries of the apparent recession of spiral nebulae, to which L. Silberstein and A. S. Eddington following W. de Sitter had already called attention. Indeed, it seems that Lemaître was the first to write of the expansion of the actual astronomical universe. Nevertheless, his work too was ignored until Eddington rediscovered it in 1930 in particular as showing that the Einstein model universe is unstable. Eddington forthwith arranged for the re-publication of Lemaître's paper in an English translation.[4]

Something like Hubble's law of the recession of the galaxies had for several years been foreshadowed by observations made by V. M. Slipher coupled with predictions following from de Sitter's cosmological model. E. B. Hubble and M. L. Humason started publishing their more extensive observations in 1929, and it was then not long before the expansion of the universe came to be generally regarded as an established empirical phenomenon—although there have all along been some sceptics. In Europe, the connexion with theory was through Eddington to Lemaître; in America, it was rather through H. P. Robertson and R. C. Tolman to Friedmann, both lines naturally going back to Einstein and de Sitter. Either way, it was evident that possibly the greatest of all astronomical discoveries had been predicted by general relativity.

NEW ERA

The time around 1930 thus became a great watershed in scientific history. Hitherto general relativity had yielded only minute new observable phenomena in return for revolutionary concepts of the physical world, and Einstein himself had started leading it into an arid quest for a unified field-theory. Suddenly, instead of merely those scarcely measurable phenomena, standard general relativity was found to have predicted the largest-scale effect ever observed by man. It was the salvation of general relativity. In more recent times the study of black holes—also a prediction of standard general relativity—has revitalized the subject, but with the difference that no black hole has yet been known to be observed, while the predicted expansion of the universe was observed around 1930 and has been observed ever more extensively since then.

The way things happened was fortunate for the subject. For the theory came to observers' notice mainly through Eddington's demonstration that the only static model (Einstein's) is unstable. Therefore they could say to anyone who doubted the obvious interpretation of the observations: Theory tells us that a static universe is impossible; the interpretation of the observations is that it is not static; so everything fits together in a beautifully simple manner!

Because of the occasion of the present publication, we ask how Einstein figured in this development. He spent the winter of 1930–1931 in California where he came in close touch with Hubble and his colleagues. In the face of the observations, he declared that he had abandoned his static cosmological model. On his return to Germany, he wrote[5] enthusiastically to Besso about the observational results, saying that they followed naturally from relativity theory without the cosmical constant. He went on to mention the "snag" that they implied a start of the expansion 10^{10} or 10^{11} years ago, and he said the situation was very exciting.

There are several points of historical interest. The last sentence of "Cosmological considerations" had been "That $\Box \Lambda \Box$ term is necessary only for the purpose of making possible a quasi-static distribution of matter, as required by the fact of the small velocities of the stars." As soon as Einstein saw that the requirement was no longer imposed by observation, he was only too relieved to drop the term. But Einstein was then one of the first to be impressed by the difficulty of the short time-scale admitted by the estimated rate of expansion of the universe. Had the inferred age of the universe actually been in the range he quoted to Besso, there need have been no problem. However, the estimates of the Hubble constant that were current until about the 1960s did lead to much shorter times; the age about 2×10^{10} years from more recent estimates is acceptable. Then in 1932 Einstein wrote a short note with de Sitter on the simplest of all the expanding universe models, which is still used as a standard for comparison. In 1946 he published[6] a third edition of his small book *The meaning of relativity*, with an appendix on "The cosmological problem" which he described as "nothing but an exposition of Friedmann's idea." He mentioned Hubble, but not Lemaître or Eddington or anyone else. It was not long after this that Bondi and Gold, and Hoyle published in 1948 their ideas about continual creation and steady-state cosmology, which had been instigated by the age problem just mentioned.[7] So far as one knows, Einstein never referred to these ideas in writing, but in 1954 he told A. Vibert Douglas that he disliked[8] them, and that he felt the necessity for a 'beginning.'

All in all, one gains the conviction that however much Einstein's theories may have contributed to the understanding of the astronomical universe, he himself never had a consuming interest in this particular outcome of his work.

FURTHER OBSERVATIONS

After the early work on cosmological models there was little more of interest to be done on the kinematic-gravitational aspects. Further progress would have to be on the more physical side, and this would require new observations. These came slowly, and each new discovery came as a surprise.

About 1952, W. Baade began to revise the distance scale of the universe; A. R. Sandage and others have continued the work ever since. As already mentioned, the results imply an age of the universe about 2×10^{10} years. Perhaps the most impressive feature of cosmology is that this empirical age agrees so well with ages inferred from astrophysical studies. More than anything, it has caused astronomers to give serious consideration to the notion of a *big bang* at such a time in the past.

From about 1955 it appeared that astronomers can see further away in distance, and so further back in time, in radio frequencies than in any others. Moreover, they were able to make significant *source-counts*, even if the early attempts were hard to interpret. Their first consequence was to demonstrate that the universe is not in a steady state.

From about 1964 it became almost certain that the observed cosmic abundance of helium was effectively established at an early stage of the universe before the existence of galaxies and stars.

The serendipitous discovery by A. Penzias and R. W. Wilson in 1965 of the 3°K microwave background radiation proved to be comparable in importance to the original discovery of the expansion of the universe. G. Gamow and his colleagues had predicted the phenomenon many years earlier. It is naturally interpreted as a relic of an even earlier stage of the universe than that of helium-formation. If so, it has suffered an enormous Hubble redshift, and so it is the most tangible evidence of the *hot* big bang.

As to the redshift itself, supposing the standard doppler interpretation to be valid, it had long seemed strange that much larger values were not being found. Then quasars were first discovered in 1963, and soon afterwards some of these were found to show almost incredibly large redshifts. Some astronomers still question this 'cosmological' character. Another unforeseen development, however, is likely to decide the matter quite soon. If certain changes in some quasars (so-called *superluminal* effects) that have been studied since about 1970 by 'very long baseline interferometry' at centimetre radio wavelengths can be explained, they will almost certainly lead to entirely new distance determinations. These can be expected to settle a number of doubts and controversies. It is almost certain that in the quasars of largest redshift astronomers see back to the youngest known bodies of galactic character, but whether they will prove to be young enough to afford clues as to their mode of origin nobody can yet tell.

There are also negative surprises. One is that astronomy from space vehicles has not yet had much direct effect upon cosmology—no doubt it will at any moment bring its own surprises in this field. Another is that while the passage from macrophysics to microphysics brings all the surprises of the quantum world, the passage from laboratory physics to cosmic physics has in itself brought no surprises at all.

HISTORY OF THE UNIVERSE

Described in simple terms the model universe[9] commonly considered to-day starts with a hot big bang; thereafter it obeys all the known laws of physics including those of general relativity. At each cosmic epoch it is homogeneous and isotropic in the large, and there is no cosmic electromagnetic field. There was a stage in the first one-hundredth of a second when most of the energy was in the form of particles like protons and their anti-particles. These proceed to annihilate each other in pairs. There is a relatively slight imbalance so that when the annihilation has gone as far as possible some protons survive and are those that compose all the atomic nuclei of the present universe. The energy is there mostly in the form of electrons and neutrinos, and their antiparticles, and photons. But soon the neutrinos decouple from the rest, while the electrons and positrons annihilate in pairs, leaving an imbalance of electrons to match that of the protons, so that most of the energy has gone into photons. This is the *radiation era,* starting about 10 seconds after the big bang. At the end of 3 or 4 minutes, about 25 percent by mass of the protons have gone to form alpha particles (helium nuclei), and this mixture, with perhaps traces of deuterium and a few other light nuclei, remains as the raw material for galaxy formation. After about 10^5 years, at a redshift of about 1000 if we could look back that far, when the temperature had fallen to about 3000°K, two things happened, and the circumstances—if true—that they did so at about the same time is either a profound but not yet understood property of the universe, or else an astonishing coincidence. The universe passes from being radiation-dominated to being matter-dominated, and the universe becomes transparent to most of the radiation present, i.e. the radiation and the matter become decoupled. Together these mean that the immediately ensuing epoch should be in the whole history of the universe that most favorable for the formation of condensations in the material destined to be the galaxies we observe. The central problem of astronomy at the present time is that of the origin of these condensations. But it may at any rate be claimed to be a major advance to have this much insight into the conditions under which they were formed.

The model implies that the time between the big bang and the emergence of the galaxies was only a small fraction of the past life of the universe, and that since then the smoothed out contents of the universe may be treated as pressure-free matter, as in the simplest Friedmann models. Moreover it was only after the galaxies had reached something approaching their present form that there was anything at all for astronomers to observe—apart from the unexciting background radiation. So the model renders it a self-consistent exercise for astronomers to seek to match the observed universe with a simple Friedmann model.

This is only a rough sketch of big-bang cosmology. In the first place, it should suffice to justify a claim that the coherence of the account, and its broad consistence with observation, make it almost unthinkable that it can be utterly mistaken. That being so, it is intended as a basis for a brief statement of the problems of the subject in its present state.[10]

PROBLEMS OF RELATIVISTIC COSMOLOGY

In recent years R. Penrose, S. W. Hawking and colleagues have proved some deep theorems about singularities in relativity theory.[11] They show that every space-time in the sense of the second section above, that admits a plausible physical interpretation, must possess at least one mathematical singularity. In the present context, this means that if our thinking about the universe is along the general lines of general relativity we are bound to find that it involves some 'bang' or 'bangs.' From this viewpoint, a Friedmann model with a unique big bang is the simplest one possible. If we wish, we may call the singularity in this model the 'creation' of the universe. We may then regard such a model as one extreme possibility where everything in the universe comes from a single event of creation. We should then regard a universe with continual creation as contemplated in, say, a steady-state model as the opposite extreme where every fundamental particle comes from a different singular event. Clearly the question arises as to whether we study the Friedmann model for no reason other than its being the simplest, or whether we study it because of some fundamental but as yet unknown reason for postulating no more than one singularity.

Closely related to this problem is that of the homogeneity and isotropy of the model. Again, do we postulate these for simplicity, or because of some physical grounds? A few years ago some cosmologists claimed to show that, were isotropy not postulated, at the outset, processes of radioactive and neutrino viscosity would rapidly bring about a close approach to isotropy. There is now some doubt as to the efficiency of the processes, but they afford some ground for concluding that the assumption about isotropy is not wholly arbitrary.

Whatever may be the epistemological approach, a practical problem in cosmology is to discover whether any particular Friedmann model fits the observations without contradiction. Apart from a scale-factor there is a 2-parameter family of such models, and so the exercise is to find whether all the observations enable us to evaluate the two parameters and whether all methods give the same answer.

In spite of the apparent success of the general concept, the attempts to fit a particular model are remarkably unsuccessful. As is well known, some of the models expand forever, while the rest, taken literally, would expand and collapse, expand and collapse . . . forever. There is no clear indication even as to which of these two general categories best fits the evidence.

There are some obvious difficulties. No one knows whether the matter seen in luminous galaxies is the bulk of the matter in the universe, or only a small part of it—there is some evidence for the existence of considerable 'missing mass.' Again, as remarked, when astronomers look into the distance they look also into the past; therefore they can interpret their observations only if they know about the manner in which the objects observed evolve in time.

Bound up with the search for a Friedmann model are other questions as to whether some of the more elementary physical assumptions ought to be modified. For instance, the prescription in the last section leads to a model that is finally all matter and no antimatter. Is this what we want, and if so why did the original mixture of matter and antimatter lead to a universe in which there are some 10^8 to 10^9 times as many photons as protons, and not some totally different ratio?

Another of the assumptions was that of homogeneity in the early stages of the model. Were the homogeneity ever perfect, then the model contains nothing that could ever cause it to become non-homogeneous. Since the actual universe, composed of galaxies and clusters of galaxies, is exceedingly non-homogeneous, we infer that it never was truly homogeneous. But in that case it is meaningless to ask what caused the first inhomogeneities in the universe. This paradox is still unresolved.

As stated, these are all problems for standard theory.

PROBLEMS BEYOND STANDARD THEORY

Some workers explore the possibility of theories that are in some fashion more extended than standard general relativity. For example, F. Hoyle and J. V. Narlikar suggest there should be a formulation[12] in which the laws of physics are what is called 'conformally invariant,' which is a constraint not imposed in standard general relativity. This seems not yet to lead to a precise modification of relativistic cosmology, although in a qualitative manner it is claimed to admit a more extended structure than a Friedmann model. It is claimed also to avoid singularities; but it is not obvious that *any* theory could be expected to hold good with no breakdown anywhere. Perhaps not basically far removed from such ideas are others, due particularly to P. A. M. Dirac, that seek to employ a gravitation 'constant' that is not constant but varies at least with cosmic time. This can scarcely be said to have afforded fresh insight.

The physical world, as represented by any of the cosmological models mentioned, is what it is because certain dimensionless universal constants, e.g. the ratio of the masses of the proton and the electron have the particular values that experiment finds them to have. Some physicists have cherished the hope that a meta-theory will be discovered that will show how in some sense these pure numbers *have* to take these values. It is generally supposed to be a consequence that the uniquely experienced universe is the only consistently conceivable universe. In particular, Eddington claimed to have made significant progress in constructing such a theory. However, Einstein was unsympathetic, and when Besso asked him if he would get somebody in his group to prepare a resumé of Eddington's *Fundamental Theory,* Einstein was uncompromising in declining.[13] All he would do was doubtfully to concede that there might be something valid in Eddington's line of thought.

Nowadays a few physicists speculate in an alternative fashion. In some sense of the word 'exist,' they suggest that an unbounded variety of universes exist, in which these universal constants take a multitude of values. However, we observe a unique universe because, on this view, only in a single one do the laws of physics and chemistry and all else conspire to allow creatures like us to come into being to do the observing.

It is hard to see that such a view as a whole is helpful, but it has one implication that is of significance. The only meaning we can usefully assign to 'laws of physics' applied to the universe in the large is that they are the means by which we, the observers, make some sense of *our* experience of the physical universe. Since we can have no experience of, for instance, the early stages of a big bang, maybe we are compelled to admit that we cannot make precise sense of it. We may tentatively surmise that two features of our experience, which have kept appearing in this account, may be associated with this interpretation. One is the circumstance that astronomers have not succeeded in selecting one particular Friedmann model that best fits all the observations; it may have to be admitted that we shall never be able to order our knowledge of the whole universe to the degree of precision required. The other is that owing to the difficulty of applying any observational check, the homogeneity and isotropy of the early universe must be subject to a degree of uncertainty that is reflected in the 'humpiness and lumpiness' of the contents of the universe when they do become observable. This would be some approach to resolution of the paradox mentioned in the previous section.

The notions of the present section have not yet been given standardized formulations.

REFERENCES

1. H. A. Lorentz, A. Einstein, H. Minkowski and H. Weyl, *The principle of relativity*, Methuen, London, 1923, also Dover Publications pp. 175–188.

2. P. Speziali, Albert Einstein—Michele Besso, Correspondence 1903–1955, Hermann, Paris, 1972, p. 102.

3. A. Friedman, Über die Krümmung des Raumes, *Z. Physik* 10 347–386 (1922), Über die Möglichkeit einer Welt mit konstanter negativer Krümmung des Raumes, *Z. Physik 21* 326 (1924).

4. G. Lemaître, A homogeneous universe of constant mass and increasing radius accounting for the radial velocity of extra-galactic nebulae, *Mgn. Not. Roy. Astr. Soc. 91* 483–490 (1931).

5. Ref. 2 p. 268.

6. A. Einstein, *The meaning of relativity*, third edition, Methuen, London, 1946.

7. See, for example, H. Bondi, *Cosmology*, Cambridge University Press, 1952, and later editions.

8. A. V. Douglas, Forty minutes with Einstein, *J. R. Astron. Soc. Cam. 50* 99–102 (1956).

9. See, in particular, S. Weinberg, *The first three minutes*, Deutsch, London, 1977.

10. M. Rowan-Robinson, *Cosmology*, Clarendon Press, Oxford, 1977.

11. S. W. Hawking and G. F. R. Ellis, *The large scale structure of space-time*, Cambridge University Press, 1973.

12. F. Hoyle and J. V. Narlikar, *Action at a distance in physics and cosmology*, Freeman, San Francisco, 1974.

13. Ref. 2, p. 500.

IX. CONCLUSION

It is not simple to find a suitable ending or summary to a collection of reprints and articles as in this book. We have been fortunate in that Professor Peter Bergmann, a former assistant of Einstein's, agreed to write an article on future developments. That article and the article Relativity and the Problem of Space (an appendix of Einstein's book) appear here in the concluding part.

RELATIVITY AND THE PROBLEM OF SPACE[1]

It is characteristic of Newtonian physics that it has to ascribe independent and real existence to space and time as well as to matter, for in Newton's law of motion the idea of acceleration appears. But in this theory, acceleration can only denote "acceleration with respect to space." Newton's space must thus be thought of as "at rest," or at least as "unaccelerated," in order that one can consider the acceleration, which appears in the law of motion, as being a magnitude with any meaning. Much the same holds with time, which of course likewise enters into the concept of acceleration. Newton himself and his most critical contemporaries felt it to be disturbing that one had to ascribe physical reality both to space itself as well as to its state of motion; but there was at that time no other alternative, if one wished to ascribe to mechanics a clear meaning.

It is indeed an exacting requirement to have to ascribe physical reality to space in general, and especially to empty space. Time and again since remotest times philosophers have resisted such a presumption. Descartes argued somewhat on these lines: space is identical with extension, but extension is connected with bodies; thus there is no space without bodies and hence no empty space. The weakness of this argument lies primarily in what follows. It is certainly true that the concept extension owes its origin to our experiences of

From Albert Einstein, Relativity, *trans. Robert W. Lawson (New York: Crown Publishers, © 1961), Appendix V. Reprinted by permission of the Estate of Albert Einstein.*

1. As with the original translation of this book in 1920, my old friend Emeritus Professor S. R. Milner, F. R. S., has again given me the benefit of his unique experience in this field, by reading the translation of this new appendix and making numerous suggestions for improvement. I am deeply grateful to him and to Professor A. G. Walker of the Mathematics Department of Liverpool University, who also read this appendix and offered various helpful suggestions. R.W.L.

laying out or bringing into contact solid bodies. But from this it cannot be concluded that the concept of extension may not be justified in cases which have not themselves given rise to the formation of this concept. Such an enlargement of concepts can be justified indirectly by its value for the comprehension of empirical results. The assertion that extension is confined to bodies is therefore of itself certainly unfounded. We shall see later, however, that the general theory of relativity confirms Descartes' conception in a roundabout way. What brought Descartes to his remarkably attractive view was certainly the feeling that, without compelling necessity, one ought not to ascribe reality to a thing like space, which is not capable of being "directly experienced."[1]

The psychological origin of the idea of space, or of the necessity for it, is far from being so obvious as it may appear to be on the basis of our customary habit of thought. The old geometers deal with conceptual objects (straight line, point, surface), but not really with space as such, as was done later in analytical geometry. The idea of space, however, is suggested by certain primitive experiences. Suppose that a box has been constructed. Objects can be arranged in a certain way inside the box, so that it becomes full. The possibility of such arrangements is a property of the material object "box," something that is given with the box, the "space enclosed" by the box. This is something which is different for different boxes, something that is thought quite naturally as being independent of whether or not, at any moment, there are any objects at all in the box. When there are no objects in the box, its space appears to be "empty."

So far, our concept of space has been associated with the box. It turns out, however, that the storage possibilities that make up the box-space are independent of the thickness of the walls of the box. Cannot this thickness be reduced to zero, without the "space" being lost as a result? The naturalness of such a limiting process is obvious, and now there remains for our thought the space without the box, a self-evident thing, yet it appears to be so unreal if we forget the origin of this concept. One can understand that it was repugnant to Descartes to consider space as independent of material objects, a thing that might exist without matter.[2] (At the same time, this does not prevent him from treating space as a fundamental concept in his analytical geometry.) The drawing of attention to the vacuum in a mercury barometer has certainly disarmed the last of the Cartesians. But it is not to be denied that, even at this primitive stage, something unsatisfactory clings to the concept of space, or to space thought of as an independent real thing.

The ways in which bodies can be packed into space (e.g. the box) are the

1. This expression is to be taken *cum grano salis.*
2. Kant's attempt to remove the embarrassment by denial of the objectivity of space can, however, hardly be taken seriously. The possibilities of packing inherent in the inside space of a box are objective in the same sense as the box itself, and as the objects which can be packed inside it.

subject of three-dimensional Euclidean geometry, whose axiomatic structure readily deceives us into forgetting that it refers to realisable situations.

If now the concept of space is formed in the manner outlined above, and following on from experience about the "filling" of the box, then this space is primarily a *bounded* space. This limitation does not appear to be essential, however, for apparently a larger box can always be introduced to enclose the smaller one. In this way space appears as something unbounded.

I shall not consider here how the concepts of the three-dimensional and the Euclidean nature of space can be traced back to relatively primitive experiences. Rather, I shall consider first of all from other points of view the rôle of the concept of space in the development of physical thought.

When a smaller box *s* is situated, relatively at rest, inside the hollow space of a larger box *S*, then the hollow space of *s* is a part of the hollow space of *S*, and the same "space," which contains both of them, belongs to each of the boxes. When *s* is in motion with respect to *S*, however, the concept is less simple. One is then inclined to think that *s* encloses always the same space, but a variable part of the space *S*. It then becomes necessary to apportion to each box its particular space, not thought of as bounded, and to assume that these two spaces are in motion with respect to each other.

Before one has become aware of this complication, space appears as an unbounded medium or container in which material objects swim around. But it must now be remembered that there is an infinite number of spaces, which are in motion with respect to each other. The concept of space as something existing objectively and independent of things belongs to pre-scientific thought, but not so the idea of the existence of an infinite number of spaces in motion relatively to each other. This latter idea is indeed logically unavoidable, but is far from having played a considerable rôle even in scientific thought.

But what about the psychological origin of the concept of time? This concept is undoubtedly associated with the fact of "calling to mind," as well as with the differentiation between sense experiences and the recollection of these. Of itself it is doubtful whether the differentiation between sense experience and recollection (or simple re-presentation) is something psychologically directly given to us. Everyone has experienced that he has been in doubt whether he has actually experienced something with his senses or has simply dreamt about it. Probably the ability to discriminate between these alternatives first comes about as the result of an activity of the mind creating order.

An experience is associated with a "recollection," and it is considered as being "earlier" in comparison with "present experiences." This is a conceptual ordering principle for recollected experiences, and the possibility of its accomplishment gives rise to the subjective concept of time, *i.e.* that concept of time which refers to the arrangement of the experiences of the individual.

What do we mean by rendering objective the concept of time? Let us consider an example. A person *A* ("I") has the experience "it is lightning." At the same time the person *A* also experiences such a behaviour of the person

B as brings the behaviour of B into relation with his own experience "it is lightning." Thus it comes about that A associates with B the experience "it is lightning." For the person A the idea arises that other persons also participate in the experience "it is lightning." "It is lightning" is now no longer interpreted as an exclusively personal experience, but as an experience of other persons (or eventually only as a "potential experience"). In this way arises the interpretation that "it is lightning," which originally entered into the consciousness as an "experience," is now also interpreted as an (objective) "event." It is just the sum total of all events that we mean when we speak of the "real external world."

We have seen that we feel ourselves impelled to ascribe a temporal arrangement to our experiences, somewhat as follows. If β is later than α and γ later than β, then γ is also later than α ("sequence of experiences"). Now what is the position in this respect with the "events" which we have associated with the experiences? At first sight it seems obvious to assume that a temporal arrangement of events exists which agrees with the temporal arrangement of the experiences. In general, and unconsciously this was done, until sceptical doubts made themselves felt.[1] In order to arrive at the idea of an objective world, an additional constructive concept still is necessary: the event is localised not only in time, but also in space.

In the previous paragraphs we have attempted to describe how the concepts space, time and event can be put psychologically into relation with experiences. Considered logically, they are free creations of the human intelligence, tools of thought, which are to serve the purpose of bringing experiences into relation with each other, so that in this way they can be better surveyed. The attempt to become conscious of the empirical sources of these fundamental concepts should show to what extent we are actually bound to these concepts. In this way we become aware of our freedom, of which, in case of necessity, it is always a difficult matter to make sensible use.

We still have something essential to add to this sketch concerning the psychological origin of the concepts space-time-event (we will call them more briefly "space-like," in contrast to concepts from the psychological sphere). We have linked up the concept of space with experiences using boxes and the arrangement of material objects in them. Thus this formation of concepts already presupposes the concept of material objects (e.g. "boxes"). In the same way persons, who had to be introduced for the formation of an objective concept of time, also play the rôle of material objects in this connection. It appears to me, therefore, that the formation of the concept of the material object must precede our concepts of time and space.

All these space-like concepts already belong to pre-scientific thought,

1. For example, the order of experiences in time obtained by acoustical means can differ from the temporal order gained visually, so that one cannot simply identify the time sequence of events with the time sequence of experiences.

along with concepts like pain, goal, purpose, etc. from the field of psychology. Now it is characteristic of thought in physics, as of thought in natural science generally, that it endeavours in principle to make do with "space-like" concepts *alone,* and strives to express with their aid all relations having the form of laws. The physicist seeks to reduce colours and tones to vibrations, the physiologist thought and pain to nerve processes, in such a way that the psychical element as such is eliminated from the causal nexus of existence, and thus nowhere occurs as an independent link in the causal associations. It is no doubt this attitude, which considers the comprehension of all relations by the exclusive use of only "space-like" concepts as being possible in principle, that is at the present time understood by the term "materialism" (since "matter" has lost its rôle as a fundamental concept).

Why is it necessary to drag down the Olympian fields of Plato the fundamental ideas of thought in natural science, and to attempt to reveal their earthly lineage? Answer: In order to free these ideas from the taboo attached to them, and thus to achieve greater freedom in the formation of ideas or concepts. It is to the immortal credit of D. Hume and E. Mach that they, above all others, introduced this critical conception.

Science has taken over from pre-scientific thought the concepts space, time, and material object (with the important special case "solid body"), and has modified them and rendered them more precise. Its first significant accomplishment was the development of Euclidean geometry, whose axiomatic formulation must not be allowed to blind us to its empirical origin (the possibilities of laying out or juxtaposing solid bodies). In particular, the three-dimensional nature of space as well as its Euclidean character are of empirical origin (it can be wholly filled by like constituted "cubes").

The subtlety of the concept of space was enhanced by the discovery that there exist no completely rigid bodies. All bodies are elastically deformable and alter in volume with change in temperature. The structures, whose possible congruences are to be described by Euclidean geometry, cannot therefore be represented apart from physical concepts. But since physics after all must make use of geometry in the establishment of its concepts, the empirical content of geometry can be stated and tested only in the framework of the whole of physics.

In this connection atomistics must also be borne in mind, and its conception of finite divisibility; for spaces of sub-atomic extension cannot be measured up. Atomistics also compels us to give up, in principle, the idea of sharply and statically defined bounding surfaces of solid bodies. Strictly speaking, there are no *precise* laws, even in the macro-region, for the possible configurations of solid bodies touching each other.

In spite of this, no one thought of giving up the concept of space, for it appeared indispensable in the eminently satisfactory whole system of natural science. Mach, in the nineteenth century, was the only one who thought seriously of an elimination of the concept of space, in that he sought to replace it by the notion of the totality of the instantaneous distances between all material points. (He made this attempt in order to arrive at a satisfactory understanding of inertia.)

THE FIELD

In Newtonian mechanics, space and time play a dual rôle. First, they play the part of carrier or frame for things that happen in physics, in reference to which events are described by the space co-ordinates and the time. In principle, matter is thought of as consisting of "material points," the motions of which constitute physical happening. When matter is thought of as being continuous, this is done as it were provisionally in those cases where one does not wish to or cannot describe the discrete structure. In this case small parts (elements of volume) of the matter are treated similarly to material points, at least in so far as we are concerned merely with motions and not with occurrences which, at the moment, it is not possible or serves no useful purpose to attribute to motions (*e.g.* temperature changes, chemical processes). The second rôle of space and time was that of being an "inertial system." From all conceivable systems of reference, inertial systems were considered to be advantageous in that, with respect to them, the law of inertia claimed validity.

In this, the essential thing is that "physical reality," thought of as being independent of the subjects experiencing it, was conceived as consisting, at least in principle, of space and time on one hand, and of permanently existing material points, moving with respect to space and time, on the other. The idea of the independent existence of space and time can be expressed drastically in this way: If matter were to disappear, space and time alone would remain behind (as a kind of stage for physical happening).

The surmounting of this standpoint resulted from a development which, in the first place, appeared to have nothing to do with the problem of space-time, namely, the appearance of the *concept of field* and its final claim to replace, in principle, the idea of a particle (material point). In the framework of classical physics, the concept of field appeared as an auxiliary concept, in cases in which matter was treated as a continuum. For example, in the consideration of the heat conduction in a solid body, the state of the body is described by giving the temperature at every point of the body for every definite time. Mathematically, this means that the temperature T is represented as a mathematical expression (function) of the space co-ordinates and the time t (temperature field). The law of heat conduction is represented as a local relation (differential equation), which embraces all special cases of the conduction of heat. The temperature is here a simple example of the concept of field. This is a quantity (or a complex of quantities), which is a function of the co-ordinates and the time. Another example is the description of the motion of a liquid. At every point there exists at any time a velocity, which is quantitatively described by its three "components" with respect to the axes of a co-ordinate system (vector). The components of the velocity at a point (field components), here also, are functions of the co-ordinates (x, y, z) and the time (t).

It is characteristic of the fields mentioned that they occur only within a ponderable mass; they serve only to describe a state of this matter. In accordance with the historical development of the field concept, where no matter was available there could also exist no field. But in the first quarter of the nineteenth century it was shown that the phenomena of the interference and motion of light could be explained with astonishing clearness when light was regarded as a wave-field, completely analogous to the mechanical vibration field in an elastic solid body. It was thus felt necessary to introduce a field that could also exist in "empty space" in the absence of ponderable matter.

This state of affairs created a paradoxical situation, because, in accordance with its origin, the field concept appeared to be restricted to the description of states in the inside of a ponderable body. This seemed to be all the more certain, inasmuch as the conviction was held that every field is to be regarded as a state capable of mechanical interpretation, and this presupposed the presence of matter. One thus felt compelled, even in the space which had hitherto been regarded as empty, to assume everywhere the existence of a form of matter, which was called "aether."

The emancipation of the field concept from the assumption of its association with a mechanical carrier finds a place among the psychologically most interesting events in the development of physical thought. During the second half of the nineteenth century, in connection with the researches of Faraday and Maxwell, it became more and more clear that the description of electro-magnetic processes in terms of field was vastly superior to a treatment on the basis of the mechanical concepts of material points. By the introduction of the field concept in electrodynamics, Maxwell succeeded in predicting the existence of electromagnetic waves, the essential identity of which with light waves could not be doubted, because of the equality of their velocity of propagation. As a result of this, optics was, in principle, absorbed by electrodynamics. *One* psychological effect of this immense success was that the field concept, as opposed to the mechanistic framework of classical physics, gradually won greater independence.

Nevertheless, it was at first taken for granted that electromagnetic fields had to be interpreted as states of the aether, and it was zealously sought to explain these states as mechanical ones. But as these efforts always met with frustration, science gradually became accustomed to the idea of renouncing such a mechanical interpretation. Nevertheless, the conviction still remained that electromagnetic fields must be states of the aether, and this was the position at the turn of the century.

The aether-theory brought with it the question: How does the aether behave from the mechanical point of view with respect to ponderable bodies? Does it take part in the motions of the bodies, or do its parts remain at rest relatively to each other? Many ingenious experiments were undertaken to decide this question. The following important facts should be mentioned in this connection: the "aberration" of the fixed stars in consequence of the annual motion of the earth, and the "Doppler effect," *i.e.* the influence of the relative motion of the fixed stars on the frequency of the light reaching us from them, for known frequencies of emission. The results of all these facts and experiments, except for one, the Michelson-Morley experiment, were explained by H. A. Lorentz on the assumption that the aether does not take part in the motions of ponderable bodies, and that the parts of the aether have no relative motions at all with respect to each other. Thus the aether appeared, as it were, as the embodiment of a space absolutely at rest. But the investigation of Lorentz accomplished still more. It explained all the electromagnetic and optical processes within ponderable bodies known at that time, on the assumption that the influence of ponderable matter on the electric field—and conversely—is due solely to the fact that the constituent particles of matter carry electrical charges, which share the motion of the particles. Concerning the experiment of Michelson and Morley, H. A. Lorentz showed that the result obtained at least does not contradict the theory of an aether at rest.

In spite of all these beautiful successes the state of the theory was not yet wholly satisfactory, and for the following reasons. Classical mechanics, of which it could not be doubted that it holds with a close degree of approximation, teaches the equivalence of all inertial systems or inertial "spaces" for the formulation of natural laws, *i.e.* the invariance of natural laws with respect to the transition from one inertial system to another. Electromagnetic and optical *experiments* taught the same thing with considerable accuracy. But the foundation of electromagnetic *theory* taught that a particular inertial system must be given preference, namely that of the luminiferous aether at rest. This view of the theoretical foundation was much too unsatisfactory. Was there no modification that, like classical mechanics, would uphold the equivalence of inertial systems (special principle of relativity)?

The answer to this question is the special theory of relativity. This takes over from the theory of Maxwell-Lorentz the assumption of the constancy of the velocity of light in empty space. In order to bring this into harmony with the equivalence of inertial systems (special principle of relativity), the idea of the absolute character of simultaneity must be given up; in addition, the Lorentz transformations for the time and the space co-ordinates follow for the transition from one inertial system to another. The whole content of the special theory of relativity is included in the postulate: The laws of Nature are invariant with respect to the Lorentz transformations. The important thing of this requirement lies in the fact that it limits the possible natural laws in a definite manner.

What is the position of the special theory of relativity in regard to the problem of space? In the first place we must guard against the opinion that the four-dimensionality of reality has been newly introduced for the first time by this theory. Even in classical physics the event is localised by four numbers, three spatial co-ordinates and a time co-ordinate; the totality of physical "events" is thus thought of as being embedded in a four-dimensional continuous manifold. But on the basis of classical mechanics this four-dimensional continuum breaks up objectively into the one-dimensional time and into three-dimensional spatial sections, only the latter of which contain simultaneous events. This resolution is the same for all inertial systems. The simultaneity of two definite events with reference to one inertial system involves the simultaneity of these events in reference to all inertial systems. This is what is meant when we say that the time of classical mechanics is absolute. According to the special theory of relativity it is otherwise. The sum total of events which are simultaneous with a selected event exist, it is true, in relation to a particular inertial system, but no longer independently of the choice of the inertial system. The four-dimensional continuum is now no longer resolvable objectively into sections, all of which contain simultaneous events; "now" loses for the spatially extended world its objective meaning. It is because of this that space and time must be regarded as a four-dimensional continuum that is objectively unresolvable, if it is desired to express the purport of objective relations without unnecessary conventional arbitrariness.

Since the special theory of relativity revealed the physical equivalence of all inertial systems, it proved the untenability of the hypothesis of an aether at rest. It was therefore necessary to renounce the idea that the electromagnetic field is to be regarded as a state of a material carrier. The field thus becomes an irreducible element of physical description, irreducible in the same sense as the concept of matter in the theory of Newton.

Up to now we have directed our attention to finding in what respect the concepts of space and time were *modified* by the special theory of relativity. Let us now focus our attention on those elements which this theory has taken over from classical mechanics. Here also, natural laws claim validity only when an inertial system is taken as the basis of space-time description. The principle of inertia and the principle of the constancy of the velocity of light are valid only with respect to an *inertial system*. The field-laws also can claim to have a meaning and validity only in regard to inertial systems. Thus, as in classical mechanics, space is here also an independent component in the representation of physical reality. If we imagine matter and field to be removed, inertial-space or, more accurately, this space together with the associated time remains behind. The four-dimensional structure (Minkowski-space) is thought of as being the carrier of matter and of the field. Inertial spaces, with their associated times, are only privileged four-dimensional co-ordinate systems, that are linked together by the linear Lorentz transformations. Since there exist in this four-dimensional structure no longer any sections which represent "now" objectively, the concepts of happening and becoming are indeed not completely suspended, but yet complicated. It appears therefore more natural to think of physical reality as a four-dimensional existence, instead of, as hitherto, the *evolution* of a three-dimensional existence.

This rigid four-dimensional space of the special theory of relativity is to some extent a four-dimensional analogue of H. A. Lorentz's rigid three-dimensional aether. For this theory also the following statement is valid: The description of physical states postulates space as being initially given and as existing independently. Thus even this theory does not dispel Descartes' uneasiness concerning the independent, or indeed, the *a priori* existence of "empty space." The real aim of the elementary discussion given here is to show to what extent these doubts are overcome by the general theory of relativity.

THE CONCEPT OF SPACE IN THE GENERAL THEORY OF RELATIVITY

This theory arose primarily from the endeavour to understand the equality of inertial and gravitational mass. We start out from an inertial system S_1, whose space is, from the physical point of view, empty. In other words, there exists in the part of space contemplated neither matter (in the usual sense) nor a field (in the sense of the special theory of relativity). With reference to S_1 let there be a second system of reference S_2 in uniform acceleration. Then S_2 is thus not an inertial system. With respect to S_2 every test mass would move with an acceleration, which is independent of its physical and chemical nature. Relative to S_2, therefore, there exists a state which, at least to a first approximation, cannot be distinguished from a gravitational field. The following concept is thus compatible with the observable facts: S_2 is also equivalent to an "inertial system"; but with respect to S_2 a (homogeneous) gravitational field is present (about the origin of which one does not worry in this connection). Thus when the gravitational field is included in the framework of the consideration, the inertial system loses its objective significance, assuming that this "principle of equivalence" can be extended to any relative motion whatsoever of the systems of reference. If it is possible to base a consistent theory on these fundamental ideas, it will satisfy of itself the fact of the equality of inertial and gravitational mass, which is strongly confirmed empirically.

Considered four-dimensionally, a non-linear transformation of the four co-ordinates corresponds to the transition from S_1 to S_2. The question now arises: What kind of non-linear transformations are to be permitted, or, how is the Lorentz transformation to be generalised? In order to answer this question, the following consideration is decisive.

We ascribe to the inertial system of the earlier theory this property: Differences in co-ordinates are measured by stationary "rigid" measuring rods, and differences in time by clocks at rest. The first assumption is supplemented by another, namely, that for the relative laying out and fitting together of measuring rods at rest, the theorems on "lengths" in Euclidean geometry hold. From the results of the special theory of relativity it is then concluded, by elementary considerations, that this direct physical interpretation of the co-ordinates is lost for systems of reference (S_2) accelerated relatively to inertial systems (S_1). But if this is the case, the co-ordinates now express only the order or rank of the "contiguity" and hence also the dimensional grade of the space, but do not express any of its metrical properties. We are thus led to extend the transformations to arbitrary continuous transformations.[1] This implies the general principle of relativity: Natural laws must be covariant with respect to arbitrary continuous transformations of the co-ordinates. This requirement (combined with that of the greatest possible logical simplicity of the laws) limits the natural laws concerned incomparably more strongly than the special principle of relativity.

This train of ideas is based essentially on the field as an independent concept. For the conditions prevailing with respect to S_2 are interpreted as a gravitational field, without the question of the existence of masses which produce this field being raised. By virtue of this train of ideas it can also be grasped why the laws of the pure gravitational field are more directly linked with the idea of general relativity than the laws for fields of a general kind (when, for instance, an electromagnetic field is present). We have, namely, good ground for the assumption that the "field-free" Minkowski-space represents a special case possible in natural law, in fact, the simplest conceivable special case. With respect to its metrical character, such a space is characterised by the fact that $dx_1^2 + dx_2^2 + dx_3^2$ is the square of the spatial separation, measured with a unit gauge, of two infinitesimally neighbouring points of a three-dimensional "space-like" cross section (Pythagorean theorem), whereas dx_4 is the temporal separation, measured with a suitable time gauge, of two events with common (x_1, x_2, x_3). All this simply means that an objective metrical significance is attached to the quantity

$$ds^2 = dx_1{}^2 + dx_2{}^2 + dx_3{}^2 - dx_4{}^2 \qquad (1)$$

as is readily shown with the aid of the Lorentz transformations. Mathematically, this fact corresponds to the condition that ds^2 is invariant with respect to Lorentz transformations.

If now, in the sense of the general principle of relativity, this space (cf. eq. (I)) is subjected to an arbitrary continuous transformation of the co-ordinates, then the objectively significant quantity ds is expressed in the new system of co-ordinates by the relation

$$ds^2 = g_{ik} dx_i dx_k \ldots \qquad (1a)$$

which has to be summed up over the indices i and k for all combinations 11, 12, ... up to 44. The terms g_{ik} now are not constants, but functions of the co-ordinates, which are determined by the arbitrarily chosen transformation. Nevertheless, the terms g_{ik} are not arbitrary functions of the new co-ordinates, but just functions of such a kind that the form $(1a)$ can be transformed back

---

1. This inexact mode of expression will perhaps suffice here.

again into the form (1) by a continuous transformation of the four co-ordinates. In order that this may be possible, the functions g_{ik} must satisfy certain general covariant equations of condition, which were derived by B. Riemann more than half a century before the formulation of the general theory of relativity ("Riemann condition"). According to the principle of equivalence, (1a) describes in general covariant form a gravitational field of a special kind, when the functions g_{ik} satisfy the Riemann condition.

It follows that the law for the pure gravitational field of a general kind must be satisfied when the Riemann condition is satisfied; but it must be weaker or less restricting than the Riemann condition. In this way the field law of pure gravitation is practically completely determined, a result which will not be justified in greater detail here.

We are now in a position to see how far the transition to the general theory of relativity modifies the concept of space. In accordance with classical mechanics and according to the special theory of relativity, space (space-time) has an existence independent of matter or field. In order to be able to describe at all that which fills up space and is dependent on the co-ordinates, space-time or the inertial system with its metrical properties must be thought of at once as existing, for otherwise the description of "that which fills up space" would have no meaning.[1] On the basis of the general theory of relativity, on the other hand, space as opposed to "what fills space," which is dependent on the co-ordinates, has no separate existence. Thus a pure gravitational field might have been described in terms of the g_{ik} (as functions of the co-ordinates), by solution of the gravitational equations. If we imagine the gravitational field, i.e. the functions g_{ik}, to be removed, there does not remain a space of the type (1), but absolutely *nothing*, and also no "topological space." For the functions g_{ik} describe not only the field, but at the same time also the topological and metrical structural properties of the manifold. A space of the type (1), judged from the standpoint of the general theory of relativity, is not a space without field, but a special case of the g_{ik} field, for which—for the co-ordinate system used, which in itself has no objective significance—the functions g_{ik} have values that do not depend on the co-ordinates. There is no such thing as an empty space, i.e. a space without field. Space-time does not claim existence on its own, but only as a structural quality of the field.

Thus Descartes was not so far from the truth when he believed he must exclude the existence of an empty space. The notion indeed appears absurd, as long as physical reality is seen exclusively in ponderable bodies. It requires the idea of the field as the representative of reality, in combination with the general principle of relativity, to show the true kernel of Descartes' idea; there exists no space "empty of field."

1. If we consider that which fills space (e.g. the field) to be removed, there still remains the metric space in accordance with (1), which would also determine the inertial behaviour of a test body introduced into it.

GENERALISED THEORY OF GRAVITATION

The theory of the pure gravitational field on the basis of the general theory of relativity is therefore readily obtainable, because we may be confident that the "field-free" Minkowski space with its metric in conformity with (1) must satisfy the general laws of field. From this special case the law of gravitation follows by a generalisation which is practically free from arbitrariness. The further development of the theory is not so unequivocally determined by the general principle of relativity; it has been attempted in various directions during the last few decades. It is common to all these attempts to conceive physical reality as a field, and moreover, one which is a generalisation of the gravitational field, and in which the field law is a generalisation of the law for the pure gravitational field. After long probing I believe that I have now found[1] the most natural form for this generalisation, but I have not yet been able to find out whether this generalised law can stand up against the facts of experience.

The question of the particular field law is secondary in the preceding general considerations. At the present time, the main question is whether a field theory of the kind here contemplated can lead to the goal at all. By this is meant a theory which describes exhaustively physical reality, including four-dimensional space, by a field. The present-day generation of physicists is inclined to answer this question in the negative. In conformity with the present form of the quantum theory, it believes that the state of a system cannot be specified directly, but only in an indirect way by a statement of the statistics of the results of measurement attainable on the system. The conviction prevails that the experimentally assured duality of nature (corpuscular and wave structure) can be realised only by such a weakening of the concept of reality. I think that such a far-reaching theoretical renunciation is not for the present justified by our actual knowledge, and that one should not desist from pursuing to the end the path of the relativistic field theory.

FUTURE DEVELOPMENTS

PETER G. BERGMANN

Syracuse University

The general theory of relativity can be judged as a physical theory according to several distinct points of view. Like any other physical theory, it must be capable of explaining the observed facts. As a theory of gravitation, general relativity has passed this test better than any rival theory. Wherever the

1. The generalisation can be characterised in the following way. In accordance with its derivation from empty "Minkowski space," the pure gravitational field of the functions g_{ik} has the property of symmetry given by $g_{ik}=g_{ki}$ ($g_{12}=g_{21}$, etc.). The generalised field is of the same kind, but without this property of symmetry. The derivation of the field law is completely analogous to that of the special case of pure gravitation.

predictions of general relativity differ from those of other theories of gravitation, the observational evidence has favored general relativity.

A second criterion for judging a physical theory is its intellectual and philosophical appeal. Albert Einstein's own evaluation has been to the effect that general relativity has succeeded in overcoming the deficiencies of the notion of inertial frames of reference as a distinguished class of frames, but that general relativity suffers from the dichotomy that the gravitational field appears as fundamentally distinct from all other kinds of physical fields. Attempts to overcome that dichotomy are usually referred to as unitary field theories. Many unitary field theories have been devised by Einstein himself, but other physicists and mathematicians have worked on these approaches as well.

General relativity has been conceived basically as a "classical theory," that is to say without regard to the quantum nature of atomic and subatomic processes. Many physicists have attempted to reconcile the foundations of general relativity with those of quantum theory, so far without complete success.

Whereas general relativity has been the outgrowth of a critical analysis of the physical measurements that underlie our assumptions concerning the metric properties of space and time, there has been no corresponding analysis of the ultimate structure of the elements of space-time themselves, of the so-called world points.

Finally, there is some question at the cosmological level whether ultimately our notions of space-time symmetry may not have to be revised. Depending on the importance that one attaches to these various points of view, one will visualize future developments.

From an experimental-observational point of view, there exists at present no significant reason for anticipating a change in the theory of the gravitational field. Quite the contrary. What one would rather look forward to is for gravitational waves and for other relativistic phenomena to play an increasing role in the exploration of the universe. Once gravitational wave detectors have been improved to the extent that the gravitational waves that are undoubtedly associated with many major astrophysical processes can be observed, the tremendous penetrating power of gravitational waves will render them a powerful tool for the investigation of stellar interiors. The vast area that is presently known as "relativistic astrophysics" will continue to expand and to help us unravel the mysteries of the universe at large.

Practically from 1916 onwards, Albert Einstein devoted an increasing part of his research efforts to the construction of unitary field theories. Whereas both the special and the general theories of relativity were the result of critical analyses of physically observed facts, aided, to be sure, by his unbelievable creative power, the search for unitary field theories was essentially a synthetic effort, guided entirely by considerations of esthetic and philosophical appeal. Einstein himself was fully aware of this situation, and he regretted it. He felt, though, that one should not simply wait to see whether other areas of physics would furnish substantive leads, and he continued in a direction that so far has proven itself refractory.

In recent years elementary particle physics has progressed to the extent where it looks as if we were approaching a stage that might be called a "periodic table for elementary particles." Just like the periodic table of chemical elements, the classification schemes conceived for elementary particles suggest the existence of even more basic constituents, which have been given such names as quarks, gluons, etc. What may be even more significant, the manner in which these constituents appear to combine to form the particles observed in high-energy laboratories indicates the likelihood of symmetries that are independent of those known in general relativity and electrodynamics. "Supergravity" is but one class of attempts to build these symmetries into a new unitary field theory, which is also intended to ameliorate the problem of taking account of the quantum character of nature.

General relativity, unitary field theories, and even quantum field theories have one thing in common: They all assume that space and time represent a four-dimensional *manifold*. The term manifold is highly technical. It refers to structures of arbitrary dimensionality whose elements, the points, can be identified by clusters of real numbers, their coordinate values, and so that points lie close together if their respective coordinate values differ but slightly. The possibility of at least local coordinate systems is essential to the notion of manifold.

In reality we cannot grasp an element of space-time by itself, but only in terms of "what happens there and then." Any "event" is, however, extended both in space and in time. Once we descend to the level of interactions between elementary particles, there are severe limitations to the ultimate resolution of spatial and temporal separations, which might not be overcome even by future technological improvements. Many physicists consider it likely that eventually the concept of manifold will have to be abandoned, or at least modified, to do justice to the properties of the real world about us.

Both the special and the general theories of relativity are based on the proposition that all members of a large class of frames of reference are equivalent when it comes to the formulation of the basic laws of nature. In the special theory that class is composed of all inertial frames of reference, in the general theory of relativity the class of equivalent frames of reference includes all systems of spatial coordinates and time-marking instruments that satisfy minimum requirements of continuity. Up to now these classes of equivalent frames have been confirmed by every conceivable experiment. As nearly as one can tell, two relativistically moving particles of specified types will interact with each other in a manner that depends only on the distance between them, on their relative velocity, and on the relative orientations of their respective spins.

On the cosmological scale we know that the average movements of galaxies determine local states of rest with considerable accuracy. Typical velocities of neighboring galaxies are of the order of a few hundred km sec^{-1}, that is to say, one ten-thousandth of the speed of light. One-hundredth of one percent then is the maximum scatter of galactic movements about the "local" streaming velocity of matter. It is not unlikely that our failure to perceive an influence of the galactic matter on the outcome of laboratory experiments stems from limitations of our instrumentation, and that sufficiently precise observations would show such an influence. This is not to suggest that physics will ever return to the time before Einstein. Relativistic physics as we know it describes the behavior of high-energy particles so much better than pre-relativistic physics, that there can be no question as to which is more adequate. Rather, the suggestion is that a time may come when we must go beyond our present level of understanding. No one knows what that future physics might look like, though many have tried to guess.

Whatever directions physical theorizing may take in the years to come, the manner in which theorists will conduct their search will forever bear the stamp of the genius of Albert Einstein.

APPENDIXES

APPENDIX 1

THEORY OF THE GRAVITATIONAL FIELD

§ 13. Equations of Motion of a Material Point in the Gravitational Field. Expression for the Field-components of Gravitation

A freely movable body not subjected to external forces moves, according to the special theory of relativity, in a straight line and uniformly. This is also the case, according to the general theory of relativity, for a part of four-dimensional space in which the system of co-ordinates K_0, may be, and is, so chosen that they have the special constant values given in (4).

If we consider precisely this movement from any chosen

From "Die Grundlage der allgemeinen Relativitätstheorie," Annalen d r Physik *49 (1916): 769–822, section C. Trans. in* "The Principle of Relativity" *papers by H. A. Lorentz, A. Einstein, H. Minkowski, and H. Weyl; trans. by W. Perrett and G. B. Jeffery (New York: Dover, 1923). Reprinted by permission of the Estate of Albert Einstein.*

system of co-ordinates K_1, the body, observed from K_1, moves, according to the considerations in § 2, in a gravitational field. The law of motion with respect to K_1 results without difficulty from the following consideration. With respect to K_0 the law of motion corresponds to a four-dimensional straight line, i.e. to a geodetic line. Now since the geodetic line is defined independently of the system of reference, its equations will also be the equation of motion of the material point with respect to K_1. If we set

$$\Gamma^\tau_{\mu\nu} = - \{\mu\nu, \tau\} \qquad . \qquad . \qquad . \quad (45)$$

the equation of the motion of the point with respect to K_1, becomes

$$\frac{d^2 x_\tau}{ds^2} = \Gamma_{\mu\nu}{}^\tau \frac{dx_\mu}{ds} \frac{dx_\nu}{ds} \qquad . \qquad . \qquad . \quad (46)$$

We now make the assumption, which readily suggests itself, that this covariant system of equations also defines the motion of the point in the gravitational field in the case when there is no system of reference K_0, with respect to which the special theory of relativity holds good in a finite region. We have all the more justification for this assumption as (46) contains only *first* derivatives of the $g_{\mu\nu}$, between which even in the special case of the existence of K_0, no relations subsist.*

If the $\Gamma^\tau_{\mu\nu}$ vanish, then the point moves uniformly in a straight line. These quantities therefore condition the deviation of the motion from uniformity. They are the components of the gravitational field.

§ 14. The Field Equations of Gravitation in the Absence of Matter

We make a distinction hereafter between " gravitational field " and " matter " in this way, that we denote everything but the gravitational field as " matter." Our use of the word therefore includes not only matter in the ordinary sense, but the electromagnetic field as well.

Our next task is to find the field equations of gravitation in the absence of matter. Here we again apply the method employed in the preceding paragraph in formulating the equations of motion of the material point. A special case in

---

* It is only between the second (and first) derivatives that the relations $B^\rho_{\mu\sigma\tau} = 0$ subsist.

which the required equations must in any case be satisfied is that of the special theory of relativity, in which the $g_{\mu\nu}$ have certain constant values. Let this be the case in a certain finite space in relation to a definite system of co-ordinates K_0. Relatively to this system all the components of the Riemann tensor $B_{\mu\sigma\tau}^{\rho}$, defined in (43), vanish. For the space under consideration they then vanish, also in any other system of co-ordinates.

Thus the required equations of the matter-free gravitational field must in any case be satisfied if all $B_{\mu\sigma\tau}^{\rho}$ vanish. But this condition goes too far. For it is clear that, e.g., the gravitational field generated by a material point in its environment certainly cannot be "transformed away" by any choice of the system of co-ordinates, i.e. it cannot be transformed to the case of constant $g_{\mu\nu}$.

This prompts us to require for the matter-free gravitational field that the symmetrical tensor $G_{\mu\nu}$, derived from the tensor $B_{\mu\nu\tau}^{\rho}$, shall vanish. Thus we obtain ten equations for the ten quantities $g_{\mu\nu}$, which are satisfied in the special case of the vanishing of all $B_{\mu\nu\tau}^{\rho}$. With the choice which we have made of a system of co-ordinates, and taking (44) into consideration, the equations for the matter-free field are

$$\left.\begin{array}{r}\dfrac{\partial \Gamma_{\mu\nu}^{\alpha}}{\partial x_{\alpha}} + \Gamma_{\mu\beta}^{\alpha}\Gamma_{\nu\alpha}^{\beta} = 0 \\[2ex] \sqrt{-g} = 1 \end{array}\right\} \qquad . \quad . \quad . \quad (47)$$

It must be pointed out that there is only a minimum of arbitrariness in the choice of these equations. For besides $G_{\mu\nu}$ there is no tensor of second rank which is formed from the $g_{\mu\nu}$ and its derivatives, contains no derivations higher than second, and is linear in these derivatives.*

These equations, which proceed, by the method of pure mathematics, from the requirement of the general theory of relativity, give us, in combination with the equations of motion (46), to a first approximation Newton's law of attraction, and to a second approximation the explanation of the motion of the perihelion of the planet Mercury discovered by Leverrier (as it remains after corrections for perturbation

---

* Properly speaking, this can be affirmed only of the tensor

$$G_{\mu\nu} + \lambda g_{\mu\nu}g^{\alpha\beta}G_{\alpha\beta},$$

where λ is a constant. If, however, we set this tensor $= 0$, we come back again to the equations $G_{\mu\nu} = 0$.

have been made). These facts must, in my opinion, be taken as a convincing proof of the correctness of the theory.

§ 15. The Hamiltonian Function for the Gravitational Field. Laws of Momentum and Energy

To show that the field equations correspond to the laws of momentum and energy, it is most convenient to write them in the following Hamiltonian form :—

$$\left. \begin{array}{c} \delta \int H d\tau = 0 \\[2mm] H = g^{\mu\nu} \, \Gamma^{\alpha}_{\mu\beta} \, \Gamma^{\beta}_{\nu\alpha} \\[2mm] \sqrt{-g} = 1 \end{array} \right\} \qquad . \qquad . \qquad . \qquad (47a)$$

where, on the boundary of the finite four-dimensional region of integration which we have in view, the variations vanish.

We first have to show that the form (47a) is equivalent to the equations (47). For this purpose we regard H as a function of the $g^{\mu\nu}$ and the $g^{\mu\nu}_{\sigma}$ $(= \partial g^{\mu\nu}/\partial x_{\sigma})$.

Then in the first place

$$\delta H = \Gamma^{\alpha}_{\mu\beta} \Gamma^{\beta}_{\nu\alpha} \, \delta g^{\mu\nu} + 2 g^{\mu\nu} \Gamma^{\alpha}_{\mu\beta} \, \delta \Gamma^{\beta}_{\nu\alpha}$$

$$= - \Gamma^{\alpha}_{\mu\beta} \Gamma^{\beta}_{\nu\alpha} \, \delta g^{\mu\nu} + 2 \Gamma^{\alpha}_{\mu\beta} \, \delta (g^{\mu\nu} \Gamma^{\beta}_{\nu\alpha}).$$

But

$$\delta \left(g^{\mu\nu} \Gamma^{\beta}_{\nu\alpha} \right) = - \tfrac{1}{2} \delta \left[g^{\mu\nu} g^{\beta\lambda} \left(\frac{\partial g_{\nu\lambda}}{\partial x_{\alpha}} + \frac{\partial g_{\alpha\lambda}}{\partial x_{\nu}} - \frac{\partial g_{\alpha\nu}}{\partial x_{\lambda}} \right) \right].$$

The terms arising from the last two terms in round brackets are of different sign, and result from each other (since the denomination of the summation indices is immaterial) through interchange of the indices μ and β. They cancel each other in the expression for δH, because they are multiplied by the quantity $\Gamma^{\alpha}_{\mu\beta}$, which is symmetrical with respect to the indices μ and β. Thus there remains only the first term in round brackets to be considered, so that, taking (31) into account, we obtain

$$\delta H = - \Gamma^{\alpha}_{\mu\beta} \Gamma^{\beta}_{\nu\alpha} \delta g^{\mu\nu} + \Gamma^{\alpha}_{\mu\beta} \delta g^{\mu\beta}_{\alpha}.$$

Thus

$$\left. \begin{array}{c} \dfrac{\partial H}{\partial g^{\mu\nu}} = - \Gamma^{\alpha}_{\mu\beta} \Gamma^{\beta}_{\nu\alpha} \\[4mm] \dfrac{\partial H}{\partial g^{\mu\nu}_{\sigma}} = \Gamma^{\sigma}_{\mu\nu} \end{array} \right\} \qquad . \qquad . \qquad . \qquad (48)$$

Carrying out the variation in (47a), we get in the first place

$$\frac{\partial}{\partial x_{\alpha}} \left(\frac{\partial H}{\partial g^{\mu\nu}_{\alpha}} \right) - \frac{\partial H}{\partial g^{\mu\nu}} = 0, \qquad . \qquad . \qquad . \qquad (47b)$$

which, on account of (48), agrees with (47), as was to be proved.

If we multiply (47b) by $g^{\mu\nu}_\sigma$, then because

$$\frac{\partial g^{\mu\nu}_\sigma}{\partial x_a} = \frac{\partial g^{\mu\nu}_a}{\partial x_\sigma}$$

and, consequently,

$$g^{\mu\nu}_\sigma \frac{\partial}{\partial x_a}\left(\frac{\partial H}{\partial g^{\mu\nu}_a}\right) = \frac{\partial}{\partial x_a}\left(g^{\mu\nu}_\sigma \frac{\partial H}{\partial g^{\mu\nu}_a}\right) - \frac{\partial H}{\partial g^{\mu\nu}_a}\frac{\partial g^{\mu\nu}_a}{\partial x_\sigma},$$

we obtain the equation

$$\frac{\partial}{\partial x_a}\left(g^{\mu\nu}_\sigma \frac{\partial H}{\partial g^{\mu\nu}_a}\right) - \frac{\partial H}{\partial x_\sigma} = 0$$

or *

$$\left.\begin{array}{c} \dfrac{\partial t^a_\sigma}{\partial x_a} = 0 \\[2mm] - 2\kappa t^a_\sigma = g^{\mu\nu}_\sigma \dfrac{\partial H}{\partial g^{\mu\nu}_a} - \delta^a_\sigma H \end{array}\right\} \qquad . \qquad . \qquad . \quad (49)$$

where, on account of (48), the second equation of (47), and (34)

$$\kappa t^a_\sigma = \tfrac{1}{2}\delta^a_\sigma g^{\mu\nu}\Gamma^\lambda_{\mu\beta}\Gamma^\beta_{\nu\lambda} - g^{\mu\nu}\Gamma^a_{\mu\beta}\Gamma^\beta_{\nu\sigma} \qquad . \qquad . \quad (50)$$

It is to be noticed that t^a_σ is not a tensor; on the other hand (49) applies to all systems of co-ordinates for which $\sqrt{-g} = 1$. This equation expresses the law of conservation of momentum and of energy for the gravitational field. Actually the integration of this equation over a three-dimensional volume V yields the four equations

$$\frac{d}{dx_4}\int t^4_\sigma dV = \int (lt^1_\sigma + mt^2_\sigma + nt^3_\sigma)dS. \qquad . \quad (49a)$$

where l, m, n denote the direction-cosines of direction of the inward drawn normal at the element dS of the bounding surface (in the sense of Euclidean geometry). We recognize in this the expression of the laws of conservation in their usual form. The quantities t^a_σ we call the " energy components " of the gravitational field.

I will now give equations (47) in a third form, which is particularly useful for a vivid grasp of our subject. By multiplication of the field equations (47) by $g^{\nu\sigma}$ these are obtained in the " mixed " form. Note that

---

* The reason for the introduction of the factor $- 2\kappa$ will be apparent later.

$$g^{v\sigma}\frac{\partial \Gamma^a_{\mu\nu}}{\partial x_a} = \frac{\partial}{\partial x_a}\left(g^{v\sigma}\Gamma^a_{\mu\nu}\right) - \frac{\partial g^{v\sigma}}{\partial x_a}\Gamma^a_{\mu\nu},$$

which quantity, by reason of (34), is equal to

$$\frac{\partial}{\partial x_a}\left(g^{v\sigma}\Gamma^a_{\mu\nu}\right) - g^{v\beta}\Gamma^\sigma_{a\beta}\Gamma^a_{\mu\nu} - g^{\sigma\beta}\Gamma^v_{\beta a}\Gamma^a_{\mu\nu},$$

or (with different symbols for the summation indices)

$$\frac{\partial}{\partial x_a}\left(g^{\sigma\beta}\Gamma^a_{\mu\beta}\right) - g^{\gamma\delta}\Gamma^\sigma_{\gamma\beta}\Gamma^\beta_{\delta\mu} - g^{v\sigma}\Gamma^a_{\mu\beta}\Gamma^\beta_{va}.$$

The third term of this expression cancels with the one arising from the second term of the field equations (47); using
relation (50), the second term may be written

$$\kappa(t^\sigma_\mu - \tfrac{1}{2}\delta^\sigma_\mu t),$$

where $t = t^a_a$. Thus instead of equations (47) we obtain

$$\left.\begin{array}{c} \dfrac{\partial}{\partial x_a}\left(g^{\sigma\beta}\Gamma^a_{\mu\beta}\right) = -\kappa(t^\sigma_\mu - \tfrac{1}{2}\delta^\sigma_\mu t) \\[2mm] \sqrt{-g} = 1 \end{array}\right\} \quad . \quad . \quad (51)$$

§ 16. The General Form of the Field Equations of Gravitation

The field equations for matter-free space formulated in
§ 15 are to be compared with the field equation

$$\nabla^2\phi = 0$$

of Newton's theory. We require the equation corresponding
to Poisson's equation

$$\nabla^2\phi = 4\pi\kappa\rho,$$

where ρ denotes the density of matter.

The special theory of relativity has led to the conclusion
that inert mass is nothing more or less than energy, which
finds its complete mathematical expression in a symmetrical
tensor of second rank, the energy-tensor. Thus in the
general theory of relativity we must introduce a corresponding energy-tensor of matter T^a_σ, which, like the energy-components t_σ [equations (49) and (50)] of the gravitational field,
will have mixed character, but will pertain to a symmetrical
covariant tensor.*

The system of equation (51) shows how this energy-tensor
(corresponding to the density ρ in Poisson's equation) is to
be introduced into the field equations of gravitation. For if

---

* $g_{a\tau}T^a_\sigma = T_{\sigma\tau}$ and $g^{\sigma\beta}T^a_\sigma = T^{a\beta}$ are to be symmetrical tensors.

we consider a complete system (e.g. the solar system), the total mass of the system, and therefore its total gravitating action as well, will depend on the total energy of the system, and therefore on the ponderable energy together with the gravitational energy. This will allow itself to be expressed by introducing into (51), in place of the energy-components of the gravitational field alone, the sums $t^\sigma_\mu + T^\sigma_\mu$ of the energy-components of matter and of gravitational field. Thus instead of (51) we obtain the tensor equation

$$\frac{\partial}{\partial x_a}(g^{\sigma\beta}T^a_{\mu\beta}) = -\kappa[(t^\sigma_\mu + T^\sigma_\mu) - \tfrac{1}{2}\delta^\sigma_\mu(t + T)], \left.\begin{array}{c} \\ \\ \end{array}\right\} \quad (52)$$

$$\sqrt{-g} = 1$$

where we have set $T = T^\mu_\mu$ (Laue's scalar). These are the required general field equations of gravitation in mixed form. Working back from these, we have in place of (47)

$$\frac{\partial}{\partial x_a}\Gamma^a_{\mu\nu} + \Gamma^a_{\mu\beta}\Gamma^\beta_{\nu a} = -\kappa(T_{\mu\nu} - \tfrac{1}{2}g_{\mu\nu}T), \left.\begin{array}{c} \\ \\ \end{array}\right\} \quad (53)$$

$$\sqrt{-g} = 1$$

It must be admitted that this introduction of the energy-tensor of matter is not justified by the relativity postulate alone. For this reason we have here deduced it from the requirement that the energy of the gravitational field shall act gravitatively in the same way as any other kind of energy. But the strongest reason for the choice of these equations lies in their consequence, that the equations of conservation of momentum and energy, corresponding exactly to equations (49) and (49a), hold good for the components of the total energy. This will be shown in § 17.

§ 17. The Laws of Conservation in the General Case

Equation (52) may readily be transformed so that the second term on the right-hand side vanishes. Contract (52) with respect to the indices μ and σ, and after multiplying the resulting equation by $\tfrac{1}{2}\delta^\sigma_\mu$, subtract it from equation (52). This gives

$$\frac{\partial}{\partial x_a}(g^{\sigma\beta}\Gamma^a_{\mu\beta} - \tfrac{1}{2}\delta^\sigma_\mu g^{\lambda\beta}\Gamma^a_{\lambda\beta}) = -\kappa(t^\sigma_\mu + T^\sigma_\mu). \quad (52a)$$

On this equation we perform the operation $\partial/\partial x_\sigma$. We have

$$\frac{\partial^2}{\partial x_a \partial x_\sigma}\left(g^\sigma\Gamma^a_{\ \beta\mu}\right) = -\tfrac{1}{2}\frac{\partial^2}{\partial x_a \partial x_\sigma}\left[g^{\sigma\beta}g^{a\lambda}\left(\frac{\partial g_{\mu\lambda}}{\partial x_\beta} + \frac{\partial g_{\beta\lambda}}{\partial x_\mu} - \frac{\partial g_{\mu\beta}}{\partial x_\lambda}\right)\right].$$

The first and third terms of the round brackets yield contributions which cancel one another, as may be seen by interchanging, in the contribution of the third term, the summation indices a and σ on the one hand, and β and λ on the other. The second term may be re-modelled by (31), so that we have

$$\frac{\partial^2}{\partial x_a \partial x_\sigma}\left(g^{\sigma\beta}\Gamma^\alpha_{\mu\beta}\right) = \tfrac{1}{2}\frac{\partial^3 g^{\alpha\beta}}{\partial x_a \partial x_\beta \partial x_\mu} \qquad . \qquad . \quad (54)$$

The second term on the left-hand side of (52a) yields in the first place

$$- \tfrac{1}{2}\frac{\partial^2}{\partial x_a \partial x_\mu}\left(g^{\lambda\beta}\Gamma^\alpha_{\lambda\beta}\right)$$

or

$$\tfrac{1}{4}\frac{\partial^2}{\partial x_a \partial x_\mu}\left[g^{\lambda\beta}g^{a\delta}\left(\frac{\partial g_{\delta\lambda}}{\partial x_\beta} + \frac{\partial g_{\delta\beta}}{\partial x_\lambda} - \frac{\partial g_{\lambda\beta}}{\partial x_\delta}\right)\right].$$

With the choice of co-ordinates which we have made, the term deriving from the last term in round brackets disappears by reason of (29). The other two may be combined, and together, by (31), they give

$$- \tfrac{1}{2}\frac{\partial^3 g^{\alpha\beta}}{\partial x_a \partial x_\beta \partial x_\mu},$$

so that in consideration of (54), we have the identity

$$\frac{\partial^2}{\partial x_a \partial x_\sigma}\left(g^{\rho\beta}\Gamma_{\mu\beta} - \tfrac{1}{2}\delta^\sigma_\mu g^{\lambda\beta}\Gamma^\alpha_{\lambda\beta}\right) \equiv 0 \qquad . \qquad . \quad (55)$$

From (55) and (52a), it follows that

$$\frac{\partial(t^\sigma_\mu + T^\sigma_\mu)}{\partial x_\sigma} = 0. \qquad . \qquad . \qquad . \quad (56)$$

Thus it results from our field equations of gravitation that the laws of conservation of momentum and energy are satisfied. This may be seen most easily from the consideration which leads to equation (49a); except that here, instead of the energy components t^σ of the gravitational field, we have to introduce the totality of the energy components of matter and gravitational field.

§ 18. The Laws of Momentum and Energy for Matter, as a Consequence of the Field Equations

Multiplying (53) by $\partial g^{\mu\nu}/\partial x_\sigma$, we obtain, by the method adopted in § 15, in view of the vanishing of

$$g_{\mu\nu}\frac{\partial g^{\mu\nu}}{\partial x_\sigma},$$

the equation

$$\frac{\partial t^a_\sigma}{\partial x_a} + \tfrac{1}{2}\frac{\partial g^{\mu\nu}}{\partial x_\sigma}T_{\mu\nu} = 0,$$

or, in view of (56),

$$\frac{\partial T^{\alpha}_{\sigma}}{\partial x_{\alpha}} + \tfrac{1}{2}\frac{\partial g^{\mu\nu}}{\partial x_{\sigma}}T_{\mu\nu} = 0 \qquad . \qquad . \qquad . \qquad (57)$$

Comparison with (41b) shows that with the choice of system of co-ordinates which we have made, this equation predicates nothing more or less than the vanishing of divergence of the material energy-tensor. Physically, the occurrence of the second term on the left-hand side shows that laws of conservation of momentum and energy do not apply in the strict sense for matter alone, or else that they apply only when the $g^{\mu\nu}$ are constant, i.e. when the field intensities of gravitation vanish. This second term is an expression for momentum, and for energy, as transferred per unit of volume and time from the gravitational field to matter. This is brought out still more clearly by re-writing (57) in the sense of (41) as

$$\frac{\partial T^{\alpha}_{\sigma}}{\partial x_{\alpha}} = -\Gamma^{\beta}_{\alpha\sigma}T^{\alpha}_{\beta} \qquad . \qquad . \qquad . \qquad (57a)$$

The right side expresses the energetic effect of the gravitational field on matter.

Thus the field equations of gravitation contain four conditions which govern the course of material phenomena. They give the equations of material phenomena completely, if the latter is capable of being characterized by four differential equations independent of one another.*

* On this question cf. H. Hilbert, Nachr. d. K. Gesellsch. d. Wiss. zu Göttingen, Math.-phys. Klasse, 1915, p. 3.

APPENDIX 2

THE "COSMOLOGICAL PROBLEM"[1]

We observe that the systems of stars, as seen by us, are spaced with approximately the same density in all directions. Thereby we are moved to the assumption that the *spatial* isotropy of the system would hold for all observers, for every place and every time of an observer who is at rest as compared with surrounding matter. On the other hand we no longer make the assumption that

From Albert Einstein, The Meaning of Relativity *(Princeton: Princeton University Press),* © *1950, Appendix for the second edition. Reprinted by permission of the Estate of Albert Einstein.*
[1]The following is essentially an exposition of Friedmann's idea, A. Friedmann, Zeitschr. für Physik, 10, *(1922): 377–386.*

the average density of matter, for an observer who is at rest relative to neighboring matter, is constant with respect to time. With this we drop the assumption that the expression of the metric field is independent of time.

We now have to find a mathematical form for the condition that the universe, *spatially speaking,* is isotropic everywhere. Through every point *P* of (four-dimensional) space there is the path of a particle (which in the following will be called "geodesic" for short). Let *P* and *Q* be two infinitesimally near points of such a geodesic. We shall then have to demand that the expression of the field shall be invariant relative to any rotation of the coordinate system keeping *P* and *Q* fixed. This will be valid for any element of any geodesic.*

The condition of the above invariance implies that the entire geodesic lies on the axis of rotation and that its points remain invariant under rotation of the coordinate system. This means that the solution shall be invariant with respect to all rotations of the coordinate system around the triple infinity of geodesics.

For the sake of brevity I will not go into the deductive derivation of the solution of this problem. It seems intuitively evident, however, for the three-dimensional space that a metric which is invariant under rotations around a double infinity of lines will be essentially of the type of central symmetry (by suitable choice of coordinates), where the axes of rotations are the radial straight lines, which by reasons of symmetry are geodesics. The surfaces of constant radius are then surfaces of constant (positive) curvature which are everywhere perpendicular to the (radial) geodesics. Hence we obtain in invariant language:

There exists a family of surfaces orthogonal to the geodesics. Each of these surfaces is a surface of constant curvature. The segments of these geodesics contained between any two surfaces of the family are equal.

Remark. The case which has thus been obtained intuitively is not the general one in so far as the surfaces of the family could be of constant negative curvature or Euclidean (zero curvature).

The four-dimensional case which interests us is entirely analogous. Furthermore there is no essential difference when the metric space is of index of inertia 1; only that one has to choose the radial directions as timelike and correspondingly the directions in the surfaces of the family as spacelike. The axes of the local light cones of all points lie on the radial lines.

CHOICE OF COORDINATES

Instead of the four coordinates for which the spatial isotropy of the universe is most clearly apparent, we now choose different coordinates which are more convenient from the point of view of physical interpretation.

*This condition not only limits the metric, but it necessitates that for every geodesic there exists a system of coordinates such that relative to this system the invariance under rotation around this geodesic is valid.

As timelike lines on which x_1, x_2, x_3 are constant and x_4 alone variable we choose the particle geodesics which in the central symmetric form are the straight lines through the center. Let x_4 further equal the metric distance from the center. In such coordinates the metric is of the form:

(2)
$$\begin{cases} ds^2 = dx_4{}^2 - d\sigma^2 \\ d\sigma^2 = \gamma_{ik} dx_i dx_k \quad (i, k = 1, 2, 3) \end{cases}$$

$d\sigma^2$ is the metric on one of the spherical hypersurfaces. The γ_{ik} which belong to different hypersurfaces will then (because of the central symmetry) be the same form on all hypersurfaces except for a positive factor which depends on x_4 alone:

(2a)
$$\gamma_{ik} = \underset{0}{\gamma_{ik}} G^2$$

where the γ_0 depend on x_1, x_2, x_3 only, and G is a function of x_4 alone. We have then:

(2b)
$$d\sigma^2 = \underset{0}{\gamma_{ik}} dx_i dx_k \quad (i, k = 1, 2, 3)$$

is a definite metric of constant curvature in three dimensions, the same for every G.

Such a metric is characterized by the equations:

(2c)
$$\underset{0}{R_{iklm}} - B(\underset{0}{\gamma_{il}}\underset{0}{\gamma_{km}} - \underset{0}{\gamma_{im}}\underset{0}{\gamma_{kl}}) = 0$$

We can choose the coordinate system (x_1, x_2, x_3) so that the line element becomes conformally Euclidean:

(2d)
$$d\sigma^2 = A^2(dx_1{}^2 + dx_2{}^2 + dx_3{}^2) \quad \text{i.e.} \ \underset{0}{\gamma_{ik}} = A^2 \delta_{ik}$$

where A shall be a positive function of $r(r = x_1{}^2 + x_2{}^2 + x_3{}^2)$ alone. By substitution into the equations, we get for A the two equations:

(3)
$$\begin{cases} -\frac{1}{r}\left(\frac{A'}{Ar}\right)' + \left(\frac{A'}{Ar}\right)^2 = 0 \\ -\frac{2A'}{Ar} - \left(\frac{A'}{A}\right)^2 - BA^2 = 0 \end{cases}$$

The first equation is satisfied by:

(3a)
$$A = \frac{c_1}{c_2 + c_3 r^2}$$

where the constants are arbitrary for the time being. The second equation then yields:

(3b)
$$B = 4\frac{c_2 c_3}{c_1^2}$$

About the constants c we get the following: If for $r = 0$, A shall be positive, then c_1 and c_2 must have the same sign. Since a change of sign of all three constants does not change A, we can make c_1 and c_2 both positive. We can also make c_2 equal to 1. Furthermore, since a positive factor can always be incorporated into the G^2, we can also make c_1 equal to 1 without loss of generality. Hence we can set:

(3c)
$$A = \frac{1}{1 + cr^2} \; ; B = 4c$$

There are now three cases:

$c > 0$ (spherical space)
$c < 0$ (pseudospherical space)
$c = 0$ (Euclidean space)

By a similarity transformation of coordinates ($x_1' = ax_i$, where a is constant), we can further get in the first case $c = 1/4$, in the second case $c = -1/4$.

For the three cases we then have respectively:

(3d)
$$\begin{cases} A = \dfrac{1}{1 - \dfrac{r^2}{4}} \; ; B = + 1 \\[3em] A = \dfrac{1}{1 - \dfrac{r^2}{4}} \; ; B = - 1 \\[3em] A = 1 \; ; B = 0 \end{cases}$$

In the spherical case the "circumference" of the unit space

$$(G = 1) \text{ is} \int_{\infty}^{\infty} \frac{dr}{1 + \dfrac{r^2}{4}} = 2\pi \text{ the "radius" of the unit}$$

space is 1. In all three cases the function G of time is a measure for the change with time of the distance of two points of matter (measured on a spatial section). In the spherical case, G is the radius of space at the time x_4.

Summary. The hypothesis of *spatial* isotropy of our idealized universe leads to the metric:

(2)
$$ds^2 = dx_4^2 - G^2 A^2 (dx_1^2 + dx_2^2 + dx_3^2)$$

where G depends on x_4 alone, A on r ($= x_1^2 + x_2^2 + x_3^2$) alone, where:

(3)
$$A = \frac{1}{1 + \frac{z}{4} r^2}$$

and the different cases are characterized by $z = 1$, $z = -1$, and $z = 0$ respectively.

THE FIELD EQUATIONS

We must now further satisfy the field equations of gravitation, that is to say the field equations without the "cosmologic member" which had been introduced previously *ad hoc:*

(4)
$$(R_{ik} - \tfrac{1}{2} g_{ik} R) + \kappa T_{ik} = 0$$

By substitution of the expression for the metric, which was based on the assumption of spatial isotropy, we get after calculation:

$$R_{ik} - \tfrac{1}{2} g_{ik} R = \left(\frac{z}{G^2} + \frac{G'^2}{G^2} + 2 \frac{G''}{G} \right) GA\delta_{ik} \qquad (i,\, k = 1,\, 2,\, 3)$$

(4a)
$$R_{44} - \tfrac{1}{2} g_{44} R = -3 \left(\frac{z}{G^2} + \frac{G'^2}{G^2} \right)$$

$$R_{i4} - \tfrac{1}{2} g_{i4} R = 0 \qquad (i = 1,\, 2,\, 3)$$

Further we have for T_{ik}, the energy tensor of matter, for "dust":

(4b)
$$T^{ik} = \rho \frac{dx_i}{ds} \frac{dx_k}{ds}$$

The geodesics, along which the matter moves, are the lines along which x_4 alone varies; on them $dx_4 = ds$. We have:

(4c)
$$T^{44} = \rho$$

the only component different from zero. By lowering of the indices we get as the only non-vanishing component of T_{ik}:

(4d)
$$T_{44} = \rho$$

Considering this, the field equations are:

(5)
$$\begin{cases} \dfrac{z}{G^2} + \dfrac{G'^2}{G^2} + 2\dfrac{G''}{G} = 0 \\[2ex] \dfrac{z}{G^2} + \dfrac{G'^2}{G^2} - \dfrac{1}{3}\kappa\rho = 0 \end{cases}$$

$\dfrac{z}{G^2}$ is the curvature in the spatial section $x_4 = \text{const.}$ Since G is in all cases

a relative measure for the metric distance of two material particles as function

of time, $\dfrac{G'}{G}$ expresses Hubble's expansion. A drops out of the equations, as

it has to if there shall be solutions of the equations of gravity of the required symmetrical type. By subtraction of both equations we get:

(5a)
$$\frac{G''}{G} + \frac{1}{6}\kappa\rho = 0$$

Since G and ρ must be everywhere positive, G'' is everywhere negative for nonvanishing ρ. $G(x_4)$ can thus have no minimum nor a point of inflection; further there is no solution for which G is constant.

THE SPECIAL CASE OF VANISHING SPATIAL CURVATURE ($z = 0$)

The simplest special case for non-vanishing density ρ is the case $z = 0$,

where the sections $x_4 = \text{const}$ are not curved. If we set $\dfrac{G'}{G} = h,$ the field

equations in this case are:

(5b)
$$\begin{cases} 2h' + 3h^2 = 0 \\ \quad\;\; 3h^2 = \kappa\rho \end{cases}$$

The relation between Hubble's expansion h and the average density ρ, which is given in the second equation, is comparable to some extent with experience, at least as far as the order of magnitude is concerned. The expansion is given as 432 km/sec for the distance of 10^6 parsec. If we express this in the system of measures used by us (cm—as unit length; unit of time—that of motion of light of one cm) we get:

$$h = \frac{432 \cdot 10^5}{3.25 \cdot 10^6 \cdot 364 \cdot 24 \cdot 60 \cdot 60} \cdot \left(\frac{1}{3 \cdot 10^{10}}\right)^2 = 4.71 \cdot 10^{-28}.$$

Since further $\kappa = 1.86 \; 10^{-27}$, the second equation of (5b) yields:

$$\rho = \frac{3h^2}{\kappa} = 3.5 \cdot 10^{-28} \; \text{g./cm.}^3 .$$

This value corresponds, according to the order of magnitude, somewhat with the estimates given by astronomers (on the basis of the masses and parallaxes of visible stars and systems of stars). I quote here as example G. C. McVittie (Proceedings of the Physical Society of London, vol. 51, 1939, p. 537): "The average density is certainly not greater than 10^{-27} g./cm.^{3} and is more probably of the order 10^{-29} g./cm.^{3}"

Owing to the great difficulty of determining this magnitude I consider this for the time being a satisfactory correspondence. Since the quantity h is determined with greater accuracy than ρ, it is probably not an exaggeration to assert that the determination of the structure of observable space is tied up with the more precise determination of ρ. Because, due to the second equation of (5), the space curvature is given in the general case as:

(5c) $$zG^{-2} = \frac{1}{3} \kappa\rho - h^2 .$$

Hence, if the right side of the equation is positive, the space is of positive constant curvature and therefor finite; its magnitude can be determined with the same accuracy as this difference. If the right side is negative, the space is infinite. At present ρ is not sufficiently determined to enable us to deduce from this relation a non-vanishing mean curvature of space (the section $x_4 = $ const).

In case we neglect spatial curvature, the first equation of (5c) becomes, after suitable choice of the initial point of x_4:

(6) $$h = \frac{2}{3} \cdot \frac{1}{x_4}$$

This equation has a singularity for $x_4 = 0$, so that such a space has either a negative expansion and the time is limited from above by the value $x_4 = 0$, or it has a positive expansion and begins to exist for $x_4 = 0$. The latter case corresponds to what we find realized in nature.

From the measured value of h we get for the time of existence of the world up to now $1.5 \cdot 10^9$ years. This age is about the same as that which one has obtained from the disintegration of uranium for the firm crust of the earth. This is a paradoxical result, which for more than one reason has aroused doubts as to the validity of the theory.

The question arises: Can the present difficulty, which arose under the assumption of a practically negligible spatial curvature, be eliminated by the introduction of a suitable spatial curvature? Here the first equation of (5), which determines the time-dependence of G, will be of use.

SOLUTION OF THE EQUATIONS IN THE CASE OF NON-VANISHING SPATIAL CURVATURE

If one considers a spatial curvature of the spatial section ($x_4 =$ const), one has the equations:

(5)
$$zG^{-2} + \left(2\frac{G''}{G} + \left(\frac{G'}{G}\right)^2\right) = 0$$
$$zG^{-2} + \left(\frac{G'}{G}\right)^2 - \frac{1}{3}\kappa\rho = 0$$

The curvature is positive for $z = +1$, negative for $z = -1$. The first of these equations is integrable. We first write it in the form:

(5d) $$z + 2GG'' + G'^2 = 0.$$

If we consider $x_4 (= t)$ as a function of G, we have:

$$G' = \frac{1}{t'}, G'' = \left(\frac{1}{t'}\right)'\frac{1}{t'}.$$

If we write $u(G)$ for $\frac{1}{t'}$, we get:

(5e) $$z + 2Guu' + u^2 = 0$$

or

(5f) $$z + (Gu^2)' = 0.$$

From this we get by simple integration:

(5g) $$zG + Gu^2 = G_0$$

or, since we set

$$u = \frac{1}{\dfrac{dt}{dG}} = \frac{dG}{dt}:$$

(5h) $$\left(\frac{dG}{dt}\right)^2 = \frac{G_0 - zG}{G}$$

where G_0 is a constant. This constant cannot be negative, as we see if we differentiate (5h) and consider that G'' is negative because of (5a).

(a) Space with positive curvature

    G remains in the interval $0 \leq G \leq G_0$. G is given quantitatively by a sketch like the following:

(1)

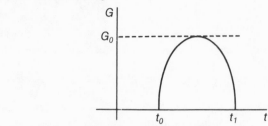

The radius G rises from 0 to G_0 and then again drops continuously to 0. The spatial section is finite (spherical)

(5c)
$$\frac{1}{3} \kappa \rho - h^2 > 0$$

(b) Space with negative curvature

$$\left(\frac{dG}{dt} \right)^2 = \frac{G_0 + G}{G}.$$

G increases with t from $G = 0$ to $G = +\infty$ (or goes from $G = \infty$ to $G = 0$). Hence $\frac{dG}{dt}$ decreases monotonically from $+\infty$ to 1 as illustrated by the sketch:

(2)

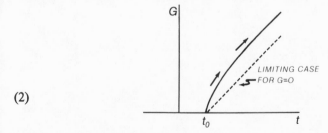

This is then a case of continued expansion with no contraction. The spatial section is infinite, and we have:

(5c)
$$\frac{1}{3} \kappa \rho - h^2 < 0 .$$

The case of plane spatial section, which was treated in the previous section, lies between these two cases, according to the equation:

$$(5h) \qquad \left(\frac{dG}{dt}\right)^2 = \frac{G_0}{G}.$$

Remark. The case of negative curvature contains as a limiting case that of vanishing ρ. For this case $(\frac{dG^2}{dt}) = 1$ (see sketch 2). This is the Euclidean case; since the calculations show that the curvature tensor vanishes.

The case of negative curvature with non-vanishing ρ approaches this limiting case more and more closely, so that with increasing time the structure of space will be less and less determined by the matter contained in it.

From this investigation of the case of non-vanishing curvature results the following. For every state of non-vanishing ("spatial") curvature, there exists, as in the case of vanishing curvature, an initial state in which $G = 0$ where the expansion starts. Hence this is a section at which the density is infinite and the field is singular. The introduction of such a new singularity seems problematical in itself.*

It appears, further, that the influence of the introduction of a spatial curvature on the time interval between the start of the expansion and the drop to a fixed value $h = \frac{G'}{G}$ is negligible in its order of magnitude. This time interval may be obtained by elementary calculations from $(5h)$, which we shall omit here. We restrict ourselves to the consideration of an expanding space with vanishing ρ. This, as mentioned before, is a special case of negative spatial curvature. The second equation of (5) yields (considering the reversal of sign of the first member):

$$G' = 1.$$

Hence (for suitable initial point for x_4)

$$G = x_4$$

$$(6a) \qquad h = \frac{G'}{G} = \frac{1}{x_4} \ldots$$

---

*However, the following should be noted: The present relativistic theory of gravitation is based on a separation of the concepts of "gravitational field" and of "matter." It may be plausible that the theory is for this reason inadequate for very high density of matter. It may well be the case that for a unified theory there would arise no singularity.

Hence this extreme case yields for the duration of the expansion the same result as the case of vanishing spatial curvature (see Eq. 6) except for a factor of order of magnitude 1.

The doubts mentioned in connection with Eq. 6, namely that this would give such a remarkably short duration for the development of the stars and systems of stars which are observable at present, cannot therefore be removed by the introduction of a spatial curvature.[†]

GLOSSARY–INDEX

This glossary can also serve as an index since the main parts in which the various terms appear are indicated whenever possible.

The following sources, in addition to various articles and relevant material, have been consulted:

The Basic Dictionary of Science. Edited by E. C. Graham. New York: Macmillan Co., 1965.

Chambers Dictionary of Science and Technology. Edited by T. C. Collocott. London: W. R. Chambers Ltd., 1971.

Glossary of Terms Frequently Used in Cosmology. H. H. Rogers. New York: American Institute of Physics, 1966.

Glossary of Terms Frequently Used in Relativistic Astrophysics. S. Sofia. New York: American Institute of Physics, 1967.

ABERRATION   An apparent (angular) displacement in a star's position caused by the earth's orbital motion and the finite speed of light. (Part IX)

ABUNDANCE relative (of elements)   The proportion of percentage of a particular element to the total as occurring in nature. (Part VIII)

AGE, the universe of   Usually refers to the Hubble Age of the universe, which is given by the reciprocal of the **HUBBLE CONSTANT.**[*] In general, however, the age of the universe depends also on the **COSMOLOGICAL CONSTANT** and the **DECELERATION PARAMETER.** (Parts II, VIII)

ALPHA PARTICLE   A particle identical in properties with the atom of Helium stripped of its electrons. (Part VIII)

α-β-γ THEORY   A theory, proposed by R. A. Alpher (α) and G. Gamow (γ) as well as R. Herman to explain the known abundance of elements. (The β stands for H. Bethe whose name was included in the title of the paper.) (Part VIII)

AMPLITUDE   Maximum value of a periodically varying quantity during a cycle. (Part V)

[†](However, see note following Part VIII.)

[*]NOTE: Bold-faced expressions within a definition are defined in the glossary—except that sometimes the order of words is interchanged; e.g., ELECTROMAGNETIC RADIATION may be found under RADIATION, ELECTROMAGNETIC.

ANGULAR MOMENTUM   A measure of the rotational motion of a **SYSTEM**. (Parts III, VIII)

ANNIHILATION   Spontaneous conversion of a particle and its **ANTI-PARTICLE** into **RADIATION**. (Part VIII)

ANISOTROPY   Properties depending on direction. (Part VIII)

ANTIMATTER   Matter composed of **ANTI-PARTICLES**. (Part VIII)

ANTI-PARTICLE   One having all the properties of the corresponding particle, but with an opposite charge. (However, neutral particles also have anti-particles from which they are undistinguishable.) (Part VIII)

ANTI-RELATIVISTIC COMPANY   A name Einstein used for a group of German "scientists" attacking relativity. (Part II)

APHELION   For an elliptic orbit about the sun, the point farthest from the sun.

APOLLO   The code name for the project that put a man on the moon. (Part III)

ASTRONOMICAL UNIT   The mean distance of the earth from the sun, approximately 93 million miles (150 million kilometers). (Part V)

AXIOM   An assumption, usually a basic postulate underlying a particular branch of mathematics or physical theory. (Parts II, III)

BACKGROUND RADIATION   Extraneous signals arising from any cause that might be confused with the required measurement. (Part VIII)

BARYON   One of the classes of elementary particles; includes all **FERMIONS** of mass equal to or greater than that of the proton.

BIANCHI COSMOLOGY   A **COSMOLOGY**, which unlike the **FRIEDMANN** cosmology, dispenses with the notion of **ISOTROPY** and considers homogeneous spaces. (Part VIII)

BIANCHI IDENTITIES   Identities among the derivatives of the **RIEMANN CUR-VATURE TENSOR**. (Part VIII)

BIG BANG   The original explosion that is assumed to have occurred at the beginning of the universe. (Parts V, VIII)

BIG BANG MODEL   A model of the universe that started with an **INITIAL SIN-GULARITY** (e.g. **FRIEDMANN UNIVERSE**). Part VIII

BINARY STARS   Two neighboring stars that revolve around their common center of gravity. The fainter of the two is called the companion. (Part V)

BLACKBODY   An idealized body that absorbs (or emits) perfectly all wavelengths of **ELECTROMAGNETIC RADIATION**. (Parts I, VIII)

BLACKBODY RADIATION   Electromagnetic radiation whose spectral intensity distribution is that of a **BLACKBODY** in accordance with **PLANCK'S LAW**. (Parts I, VIII)

BLACK HOLE   A gravitationally collapsed mass inside the **SCHWARZSCHILD RADIUS** from which no light beams can escape. (Parts III, V, VIII)

BOHR RADIUS   The radius of the smallest orbit of an electron in an atom, particularly hydrogen, according to the old **QUANTUM THEORY**. A convenient unit of length in atomic problems.

BOSE-EINSTEIN STATISTICS   The form of **QUANTUM STATISTICS** which has as one of its assumptions the conditions that any number of identical particles can be in a given **STATE** at the same time (*see also* **FERMI-DIRAC STATISTICS**). (Part I)

BOSON A fundamental particle described by the **BOSE-EINSTEIN STATISTICS** having angular momentum nh, where n is an integer and h **PLANCK'S CONSTANT.** (Part VIII)

BROWNIAN MOTION Small movement of light suspended bodies (such as colloids in solution) due to statistical **FLUCTUATION** in the bombardment of surrounding molecules in the medium. (Part I)

BOUNDARY CONDITIONS Conditions imposed on the **DIFFERENTIAL EQUATIONS** at the boundary of the distribution or region of interest. (Part VIII)

CENTRAL FORCE The pull responsible for keeping a particle in an orbit. (Part II)

CENTRIFUGAL FORCE The force or reaction a body experiences moving along a curved path against the constraint. The force divided by the mass gives the *centrifugal acceleration.* (Parts II, III)

CHARGE Quantity of unbalanced electricity in a body (particle, etc.). (Part I)

CLASSICAL MECHANICS Theories of mechanics based on concepts established before **RELATIVITY** and/or **QUANTUM MECHANICS.** (Part II)

COLLAPSED STAR *See* **BLACK HOLE.**

COLLOIDAL SOLUTION Small particles suspended in solution (*see* **BROWNIAN MOTION**). (Part I)

COMPLEMENTARITY The relationship between two contradictory pictures of matter—its description in terms of particles, and its description in terms of a continuum (**WAVES**). (Parts I, IX)

CONGRUENCE Quantities that in all relevant respects are equal. (Part II)

CONSERVATION LAWS Expressions of the fact that in any process in an isolated **SYSTEM,** the measure of certain quantities is the same at the end as at the beginning. (Part II)

CONSERVATION OF MATTER AND ENERGY The total amount of matter and energy in an object can neither be created nor destroyed, but can be transformed from one form to the other. (Part II)

CONSERVED QUANTITY A quantity that remains unchanged in the course of the evolution of a dynamical system. (Part II)

CONSTANT A quantity whose value is the same in all situations and at all times (*see also* **VARIABLE** and **PARAMETER**). (Part VIII)

CONSTANT OF THE MOTION A **DYNAMIC VARIABLE** whose value does not change as long as the **SYSTEM** is not disturbed; a **VARIABLE** subject to a **CONSERVATION LAW.** (Part II)

CONTINUOUS CREATION The spontaneous creation of matter out of nothing. (Part VIII)

CONTINUUM The aggregate of all points in a line, plane, space arrived at by passing continuously from one point to a neighboring one and repeating the process a (large) number of times. A line, straight or curved, is a *one-dimensional continuum;* a surface, flat or curved, is a *two-dimensional continuum.* Space is a *three-dimensional continuum,* and Einstein's space is a *four-dimensional continuum.* (Parts II, IV)

CONTINUUM, EUCLIDEAN   A **CONTINUUM** for which the path from one point to another is independent of the way it is reached (viz., first along the horizontal and then along the vertical axis, or vice versa). (Part II)

CONTINUUM, NON-EUCLIDEAN   A continuum for which **EUCLIDEAN GEOMETRY** does not hold. (Part II)

COORDINATES   A set of numbers serving to describe, according to some conventional rules, the location of a point or geometrical configuration. (Part II)

COORDINATES, CARTESIAN   System of **COORDINATES** in which the position of a point in a plane (or in space) is specified by its distances from two lines (or three planes respectively) orthogonal to each other. (Parts II, VII, IX)

COORDINATES, POLAR   System of **COORDINATES** in which the position of a point (or body) is specified by its distance from a fixed point, and the angles from fixed lines (or planes) through the fixed point. (Part VII)

COORDINATE SYSTEM   A **FRAME OF REFERENCE** with respect to which a point is given by its distances from fixed axes (or planes). (Part IV)

COORDINATE TRANSFORMATION   A **TRANSFORMATION** of coordinates from one **COORDINATE SYSTEM** to another. (Part VII)

CORIOLIS EFFECT   The acceleration that a body in motion experiences when observed in a rotating **FRAME OF REFERENCE**. (Parts II, III)

CORRESPONDENCE PRINCIPLE   The principle that requires that in the limit of large **QUANTUM NUMBERS** (i.e., for a large **SYSTEM**) the predictions of **QUANTUM MECHANICS** and classical physics always correspond. (Part I)

COSMIC BACKGROUND RADIATION   Isotropic (to better than one part in 1000) radiation first detected by *Penzias* and *Wilson*. It is interpreted as relict radiation from the **BIG BANG**. (Part VIII)

COSMIC TIME   The universal time measured by all observers moving with the **SUBSTRATUM**. (Parts II, VIII)

COSMOGONY   The science of the history of the **UNIVERSE**. **COSMOLOGY** includes **COSMOGONY**. (Part VIII)

COSMOLOGICAL CONSTANT   A (constant) term introduced by *Einstein* in his field equations in order to obtain a **STATIC COSMOLOGICAL MODEL** of the **UNIVERSE**. He later discarded it, but it is still used in more complicated models (such as the *Lemaître universe*). (Parts II, VIII)

COSMOLOGICAL DISTANCES   Distances implied by assuming the **HUBBLE LAW** between **RED SHIFT** and distance. (Part VIII)

COSMOLOGICAL MODEL   The result of theoretical calculation intended to represent the positions and motions of the material in the **UNIVERSE**. For the case of *relativistic cosmological models* they are derived from solutions to Einstein's field equations. (Parts II, VIII)

COSMOLOGICAL PRINCIPLE   The assumption that all observers everywhere in space moving with the **SUBSTRATUM** would at a given **COSMIC TIME** view the same large-scale picture of the **UNIVERSE** (*see also* **PERFECT COSMO-LOGICAL PRINCIPLE**). (Parts II, VIII)

COSMOLOGICAL PRINCIPLE, PERFECT   The assumption adopted by the **STEADY-STATE THEORY** that all observers everywhere in space and at all times would view the same large-scale picture of the **UNIVERSE**. (Part VIII)

COSMOLOGICAL PROBLEM   The study of the structure of space. In particular, it investigates the applicability of **GENERAL RELATIVITY** for a description of the **UNIVERSE**. (Parts II, VIII)

COSMOLOGICAL RED SHIFT   The **RED SHIFT** due to the expansion of the **UNIVERSE**. (Part VIII)

COSMOLOGY   The study of the origin, structure, and evolution of the **UNIVERSE**, and the basic physical laws governing its large scale behavior. (Parts II, VIII, Appendix)

COULOMB FORCES   Electrostatic attraction (or repulsion) between two charged particles. It is in magnitude directly proportionate to the product of the charges and inversely proportionate to the square of the distance between them. (Parts II, IV)

COUPLING CONSTANT   A measure of the strength of an **INTERACTION**. (Parts VII, VIII)

COVARIANCE   The properties of a set of relationships between mathematical or physical quantities if they remain unchanged after **TRANSFORMATION** to a different **COORDINATE SYSTEM**. (Part II)

COVARIANCE, GENERAL   The extension of **COVARIANCE** to general **COORDINATE TRANSFORMATIONS**. (Parts II, VII)

CRAB NEBULA   A **NEBULA,** so called because it vaguely resembles a crab in shape. It is believed to be the remnant of a supernova explosion, and known to contain a **PULSAR**. (Part V)

CURVATURE   Measures the rate of change (at a point) in the angle which the tangent makes with a fixed axis relative to the arc length. (Parts II, III)

CURVED SPACE   Cosmological theories may be formulated in spaces of positive, negative, or zero **CURVATURE**. Such spaces are called *elliptical, hyperbolic,* and *Euclidean,* respectively. (Appendix)

deBROGLIE WAVE   Assignable—according to deBroglie's hypothesis—to any particle in motion. (Part IV)

deBROGLIE WAVELENGTH   The wavelength of the **deBROGLIE WAVE**. It is equal to **PLANCK'S CONSTANT** divided by the (linear) momentum of the particle. (Part IV)

DECELERATION PARAMETER   Measures the rate of change of the rate of expansion of the universe. (Part VIII)

DEFLECTION of LIGHT   Amount of bending of light rays passing close to a massive body. (Parts II, III)

deSITTER UNIVERSE   An empty (expanding) **WORLD MODEL**. (Parts II, VIII)

DEUTERIUM   Isotope of element of hydrogen having one **NEUTRON** and one **PROTON** in its nucleus. (Part VIII)

DIFFERENTIAL EQUATION   An equation for determining a **FUNCTION**, involving the function as well as its rate of change. (Parts II, VIII, Appendix)

DIFFRACTION   The bending of light in passing a sharp edge or tiny aperture. (Part II)

DILATION INVARIANCE   **INVARIANCE** of quantities upon dilation, i.e., expansion or contraction. (Part VII)

DISPLACEMENT OF SPECTRAL LINES   Due to the motion of the source or difference in the **GRAVITATIONAL FIELD** the spectral lines characteristic of a particular atom are displaced from their proper position (*see also* **DOPPLER SHIFT, RED SHIFT**). (Parts II, III)

DOPPLER SHIFT   A shift in the wavelength of spectral lines emitted by a source due to relative motion between the source and the observer. (Parts III, VIII, IX)

ECCENTRICITY   The amount by which an elliptic orbit deviates from circularity. (Part III)

EINSTEIN A and B COEFFICIENTS   Probability for emission (A) and absorption (B) of a molecule exposed to radiation. (Part I)

EINSTEIN-BOSE STATISTICS   *See* **BOSE-EINSTEIN STATISTICS.**

EINSTEIN deSITTER MODEL   A homogeneous **WORLD MODEL** of finite density and zero **CURVATURE**. (Parts II, VIII)

EINSTEIN ROSEN BRIDGE   A transformation that eliminates the **SCHWARZSCHILD SINGULARITY** connecting the inside and outside of two spaces. (Part IV)

EINSTEIN UNIVERSE   A static, homogeneous isotropic **WORLD MODEL** characterized by a positive **COSMOLOGICAL CONSTANT** and a non-vanishing density. (Parts II, VIII)

ELECTROMAGNETIC FIELD   A portion of space, in which electric and magnetic forces exist. (Parts II, III)

ELECTROMAGNETIC WAVE   A wave produced by an oscillating charge that moves at the speed of light. (Parts II, VI)

ELECTRON   A negatively charged (fundamental) particle with a mass of about 9×10^{-28} grams. (Parts I, V)

ENERGY DENSITY   Energy per unit volume averaged for the whole distribution, or in a small region. (Parts II, VI)

EÖTVÖS EXPERIMENT   An experiment performed in 1909 by the Hungarian physicist Roland v. Eötvös to establish that the gravitational acceleration of a body does not depend on its composition; i.e., that **INERTIAL MASS** and **GRAVITATIONAL MASS** are exactly equal. (Parts II, III)

EQUATION OF STATE   A relation between the pressure, density, and temperature of a fluid. (Part V)

EQUIVALENCE, PRINCIPLE OF   One of the fundamental principles of **GENERAL RELATIVITY** which asserts that accelerated motion is equivalent to the presence of a **GRAVITATIONAL FIELD** and vice versa. It is based on the equivalence of **INERTIAL MASS** and **GRAVITATIONAL MASS**. (Parts II, III, VII, IX)

ESCAPE VELOCITY   The minimum velocity needed to overcome the gravitational attraction of a gravitationally bound **SYSTEM**. (Parts II, V)

ETHER   A supposed medium which fills all space and through which radiant energy of all kinds is propagated. (Parts II, VII, IX)

EUCLIDEAN GEOMETRY   A geometry based on the axioms of Euclid, such as parallel lines do not meet (except at infinity). (Parts I, II, IV, VI, IX)

EVENT   A "point" in four-dimensional space-time. (Part II)

FERMI-DIRAC STATISTICS   The form of **QUANTUM STATISTICS** which has as one of its assumptions the condition that no more than one of several identical particles can be in a given **STATE** at the same time (compare **BOSE-EINSTEIN STATISTICS**). (Part V)

FERMION   A particle whose **SPIN** is ½ plus an integer (including zero). (Parts III, V, VII) The name arises because fermions obey **FERMI-DIRAC STATISTICS**.

FIELD   A **DYNAMIC VARIABLE** which has, at any instant, values at every point in space. Also region of space through which a force operates (e.g., a magnet has a magnetic field around it). (Parts II, IX)

FIELD, ELECTROMAGNETIC   See **ELECTROMAGNETIC FIELD**.

FIELD EQUATIONS   Equations which relate to one of the fundamental fields. **GENERAL RELATIVITY** is called a **FIELD THEORY** because it describes the **GRAVITATIONAL FIELD**, and Einstein's equations of general relativity are called field equations. (Appendix)

FIELD, GRAVITATIONAL   See **GRAVITATIONAL FIELD**.

FIELD THEORY   A theory in which the action of particles and forces is described in terms of **FIELDS**. (Parts II, IV, IX)

FIELD THEORY, UNIFIED   See **UNIFIELD FIELD THEORY**.

FITZGERALD LORENTZ CONTRACTION   See **LORENTZ CONTRACTION**.

FLUCTUATION   Variation in the value of physical quantities. (Part VIII)

FRAME OF REFERENCE   A set of axes to which positions and motions in a **SYSTEM** can be referred. (Parts II, III)

FREQUENCY   The number of oscillations per second of any kind of wave. (Part I)

FRIEDMANN UNIVERSE   A homogeneous, isotropic **WORLD MODEL** of the universe involving non-static (i.e., expanding or contracting) solutions to Einstein's **FIELD EQUATIONS** (with zero **COSMOLOGICAL CONSTANT**) calculated by the Russian mathematician A. Friedmann in 1922. (Parts II, VIII, Appendix)

FUNCTION   A rule of dependence of one quantity on one or more other quantities (called *arguments* of the function), so that when the value of each of the arguments is specified, the value of the dependent quantity may be computed.

GALAXY   A system in space containing as many as 10^{13} stars, together with gas, dust, magnetic field, and energetic particles. (Part VIII)

GALAXY, THE   The name given to the belt of stars known as the Milky Way. It refers to the entire system of stars, etc. (a galaxy), of which the sun is a member. (Part VIII)

GALILEAN COORDINATES, SYSTEM OF   A system of coordinates of which the state of motion is such that Newton's first law of motion holds. (Parts II, III)

GAMMA RAYS   Electromagnetic **QUANTA** of high energy emitted after nuclear reactions or by radioactive atoms. (Part III)

GAS, DEGENERATE   A gas of **FERMIONS** most particles of which are in the lowest state. All available energy levels have been filled up to the so-called *Fermi level.* (Part V)

GAS, IDEAL   Also called *Perfect Gas.* A gas with molecules of negligible sizes and exerting no intermolecular attractive forces. The behavior of real gases becomes increasingly close to an ideal gas as the pressure is reduced. (Part V)

GAUSSIAN COORDINATES   Coordinates introduced by Carl Friedrich Gauss, a German mathematician, to describe curved surfaces. (Part II)

GEODESIC   The shortest distance between two points on a surface. In relativity it corresponds to that curve which makes the variation of the invariant distance a minimum. (Part II, Appendix)

GEODESIC NULL   The path of a light ray in curved space-time. (Parts II, IV)

GRAVITATION   The force of attraction between matter which varies inversely to the square of the distance between the attracting masses. (Part A11)

GRAVITATIONAL COLLAPSE   The sudden collapse of a massive star when the radiation pressure outward is no longer sufficient to balance the gravitational pressure inward (*see also* **BLACK HOLE**). (Parts IV, V)

GRAVITATIONAL CONSTANT   The constant of proportionality in the attraction between two unit masses a unit distance apart. (Parts II, V, VIII)

GRAVITATIONAL FIELD   **FIELD** produced by heavy masses that in turn acts upon **TEST PARTICLES** and other masses. (Part II, Appendix)

GRAVITATIONAL MASS   The property of matter that causes it to create a **GRAVITATIONAL FIELD** and attract other particles. (Parts II, III)

GRAVITATIONAL RADIATION   Energy emitted by (large) oscillating masses. (Part VI)

GRAVITATIONAL RADIUS   *See* **SCHWARZSCHILD RADIUS.**

GRAVITATIONAL RED SHIFT   A **RED SHIFT** of spectral lines due to the fact that atoms in a **GRAVITATIONAL FIELD** emit photons of larger wavelength, as time slows down in a gravitational field. (Part III)

GRAVITATIONAL WAVES   Waves moving at the speed of light generated by vibrating or accelerating masses. (Part VI)

GRAVITON   A (hypothetical) elementary particle associated with the gravitational **INTERACTION.** (Parts III, VI)

GROUP   Set of elements A, B, C, etc., such that: i) the "product" of any two elements is an element of the group. ii) $A(BC) = (AB)C$ where ( ) denotes the product. iii) there exists a unit element I such that $AI = IA = A$. iv) there exists an inverse A^{-1} to any element A, such that $A A^{-1} = A^{-1} A = I$. (Part VII)

GROUP ABELIAN   A group whose elements also commute, i.e., $AB = BA$. (Part VII)

GROUP AFFINE   The group of **AFFINE TRANSFORMATIONS.** (Part VI)

GROUP, GENERAL COVARIANCE   A group of general coordinate transformations. (Part VII)

GROUP LORENTZ   The group of **LORENTZ TRANSFORMATIONS.** (Part II)

GROUP POINCARÉ   The group of transformations in **RELATIVITY.** (Part VII)

GYROSCOPE   Spinning body whose axis of **SPIN** precesses as the result of external forces. (Part III)

HADRON   One of a class of elementary particles, including **MESONS, PROTONS,** and **NEUTRONS.** (Part VII)

HAMILTONIAN EQUATIONS   A system of linear **DIFFERENTIAL EQUATIONS** describing the equations of motion of a particle. (Part IV)

HERTZSPRUNG–RUSSELL DIAGRAM   A diagram showing the relationship between the absolute **MAGNITUDE** and **SPECTRAL TYPE** of stars. (Part V)

HOMOGENEITY   The quality of being uniform at all points. Note that homogeneity does not imply **ISOTROPY.** (Part VIII)

HUBBLE CONSTANT   The constant of proportionality in the relation between the recession velocities of galaxies and their distances from us. (Part VIII)

HUBBLE DIAGRAM   Plot of apparent **MAGNITUDE** of galaxies versus their **RED SHIFT.** (Part VIII)

HUBBLE LAW   The distance of galaxies from us is linearly related to their **RED SHIFT.** (Part VIII)

HYPERSURFACE   A "surface" in four-dimensional space. (Part IV, Appendix)

INERTIA   That property of matter, by virtue of which it persists in its state of rest or uniform motion in a straight line, unless some force changes that state (*see* **NEWTON'S LAWS**). (Part II)

INERTIAL FRAME   A frame of reference being at rest or moving with constant velocity. (Part II)

INERTIAL MASS   The property of matter which gives it **INERTIA.** (Parts II, III)

INERTIAL OBSERVER   An observer who moves in an **INERTIAL FRAME** of reference. (Part II)

INERTIAL SYSTEM   A system moving with constant velocity with respect to another inertial system or one at rest (*see also* **INERTIAL FRAME**). (Parts II, IV, VII, IX)

INITIAL SINGULARITY   A mathematical **SINGULARITY** at the beginning of expanding **WORLD MODELS** of the universe. It is believed to correspond to the **BIG BANG.** (Part VIII)

INTERACTIONS   There are four primary types of interactions in nature: *i) Strong interaction*—responsible for the force that holds the nucleus together. *ii) Electromagnetic interaction*—interaction of charged particles with electromagnetic fields. *iii) Weak interaction*—responsible for decay, i.e., disintegration of certain elementary particles. *iv) Gravitational interaction*—this is the weakest of the four types. It results in the mutual gravitational attraction of all objects.

INTERFERENCE   Alternate reinforcement and cancelation of two or more beams of **ELECTROMAGNETIC RADIATION** from the same source. (Part II)

INTERGALACTIC MEDIUM   The space between **GALAXIES** filled with gas, dust, or particles. (Part VIII)

INVARIANCE   The property ascribed to quantities which remain the same under transformations or other operations. (Parts VII, IX)

INVARIANT DISTANCE   A distance that remains unchanged under transformation of coordinates (*see also* **LINE ELEMENT**). (Part II)

INVERSE SQUARE LAW   A force law, or other phenomenon, where the force decreases inversely as the square of the (increasing) distance. (Part II)

ISOTROPY   The quality of having the same properties in all directions. Note that isotropy does not imply **HOMOGENEITY.** (Part VIII, Appendix)

KEPLERIAN ORBIT   The orbit of a (spherical) particle of finite mass around another (spherical) particle, also of finite mass. (Part III)

KINETIC ENERGY   Energy of motion. It is equal to the product of an object's mass and its velocity squared. (Parts I, VII)

KINETIC THEORY   The conception of gas molecules as elastic spheres whose bombardment of the walls of the containing vessel due to their thermal agitation causes the pressure exerted by the gas. (Parts I, II)

LASER RANGING   Using *laser* beams to gauge the distance from celestial objects. Laser stands for *L*ight *A*mplification by *S*timulated *E*mission of *R*adiation. (Part III)

LIGHT PRINCIPLE   The fact that the **LIGHT VELOCITY** is constant no matter whether the source or the observer, or both, are moving. (Part II)

LIGHT VELOCITY   The velocity or speed of light, usually denoted by c is equal to 186,000 miles (or 300,000 kilometers) per second. (Parts II, VI)

LIGHT-YEAR   The distance light travels in one year. It is approximately equal to six trillion miles. (Parts II, V)

LINE ELEMENT   The **INVARIANT DISTANCE** ds between two neighboring points. It is given by $ds^2 = g_{\mu\nu} \, dx^\mu \, dx^\nu$ ($\mu, \nu = 1$ to 4 and summed over) where $g_{\mu\nu}$ is the **METRIC TENSOR** and dx^μ the difference in the coordinate x^μ between the neighboring points (*see also* **METRIC**). (Parts II, IV, Appendix)

LINE ELEMENT, SPACE-LIKE ds^2 is negative. (Part IV)

LINE ELEMENT, TIME-LIKE ds^2 is positive. (Part IV)

LITTLE GREEN MEN   When **PULSARS** were first discovered, the regular signals seemed to indicate that they were sent by intelligent beings, referred to as Little Green Men. (Part V)

LONDON MOMENT   Forces arising from small perturbations of electron clouds of two atoms or molecules. (Part III)

LORENTZ CONTRACTION   An apparent contraction of moving rods and other objects along the direction of motion when viewed from an **INERTIAL OBSERVER** traveling at a velocity comparable to the speed of light. (Part II)

LORENTZ INVARIANT   Quantities that are invariant under a **LORENTZ TRANSFORMATION.** (Part II)

LORENTZ TRANSFORMATION   A transformation of coordinates that enables one to relate physical **PARAMETERS** describing an object when viewed in one frame of reference to those which are appropriate to an observer moving with a uniform velocity in that frame of reference. (Parts II, IV, VII)

LUMINOSITY   The measure of the amount of light emitted by an object (e.g., star). (Part V)

MACH'S PRINCIPLE   A statement, enunciated by Ernst Mach, to the effect that the **INERTIA** of an object is determined by all the rest of the mass in the universe. (Parts II, IV, VIII)

MANIFOLD   A mathematical concept used to describe the geometry of space-time. (Parts II, VII)

MASER   *M*icrowave *A*mplification by *S*timulated *E*mission of *R*adiation. A device employed in the detection of very weak signals of very low intrinsic noise. (Part III)

MAXWELL'S FIELD EQUATIONS   Equations governing the various electric and magnetic **FIELDS** in a vacuum or in a medium (*see also* **FIELD EQUATIONS**). (Part II)

MERCURY   Innermost planet of the solar system. (Parts III, IV, Appendix)

MESON   One of a series of unstable particles with masses between that of the electron and proton, considered as carrier of the nuclear field (force). (Part I)

METRIC   A differential expression of the **INVARIANT DISTANCE** or **LINE ELEMENT** in a generalized vector space. (Part II, Appendix)

METRIC TENSOR   *See* **TENSOR, METRIC.**

MICHELSON–MORLEY EXPERIMENT   An attempt to detect and measure the relative velocity of the earth with respect to the **ETHER.** No such motion was detected. (Parts II, IX)

MICROWAVE BACKGROUND RADIATION   Radiation believed to be left over from the **BIG BANG** (*see also* **COSMIC BACKGROUND RADIATION**). (Part VIII)

MINKOWSKI SPACE   A four-dimensional **SPACE-TIME** with a flat (i.e., Euclidean) geometry. (Parts II, IV)

NEBULA   Refers either to permanent cloudy patches of gas and dust in the Milky Way or various extragalactic stellar structures (**GALAXIES**). (Part VIII)

NEUTRINO   An uncharged particle with zero **REST MASS**, interacting weakly with matter. (Parts V, VIII)

NEUTRON   An uncharged particle (**FERMION**) of mass of the **PROTON**. It is stable within the nucleus, but free neutrons decay into protons, electrons, and neutrinos. (Parts V, VIII)

NEUTRON STAR   A star consisting mostly of neutrons moving at high velocity and under great pressure. It may be likened to a giant atomic nucleus held together by gravity. A typical neutron star may have a diameter of about 10 kilometers and a mass equivalent to that of the Sun. (Part V)

NEWTON'S LAWS OF MOTION
1. Every body remains in its state of rest or in uniform motion in a straight line unless it is compelled to change that state by forces impressed on it.
2. The alteration of motion is proportionate to the motive force impressed, and is made in the direction of the straight line in which that force is impressed.
3. To every action there is always an opposite and equal reaction; or the mutual actions of two bodies upon each other are always equal, and in the opposite direction. (Part II)

NEWTON'S LAW OF UNIVERSAL GRAVITATION   Every particle of matter attracts every other particle of matter with a force that is directly proportionate to their masses and inversely proportional to the square of the distance between them. (Part II)

NEWTONIAN MECHANICS   A mechanics based on **NEWTON'S LAWS OF MOTION.** (Part VII)

NOVA   A dark star whose light output is suddenly greatly increased, so that a new star (nova) seems to have appeared in the sky, and which after some time becomes dark as before (*see also* **SUPERNOVA**). (Part VIII)

OPACITY   The quality or state of a substance that compares its opaqueness with **ELECTROMAGNETIC RADIATION.**

ORBIT   The path described by one body (e.g., a planet) moving around another (e.g., the sun). Bodies obeying the **INVERSE SQUARE LAW** describe ellipses with the attracting object at one focus. (Parts II, III)

OSCILLATING SOURCE   Masses that oscillate or perhaps revolve around each other, resulting in the emission of **GRAVITATIONAL RADIATION**. (Part VI)

PARAMETER   An auxiliary independent variable available for arbitrary assignment of value.

PAULI EXCLUSION PRINCIPLE   A principle, due to W. Pauli, which states that no two **FERMIONS** may occupy the same **STATE**. (Part V)

PERIASTRON   The closest point in an orbit of a star revolving around another one in an elliptic orbit (viz., **BINARY STAR**). (Part III)

PERIASTRON SHIFT   Similar to the **PERIHELION MOTION** of planets there is a shift of the periastron. (Part III)

PERIHELION   In a planetary orbit, the point of closest approach to the sun. (Part III)

PERIHELION MOTION   The slow rotation of the major axis of a planet's orbit in the same direction as the revolution of the planet itself, due to gravitational interactions with other planets and/or other effects, such as those due to general relativity. (Part III)

PERIOD   The time of one complete cycle of vibrations, currents, etc. (Parts III, V)

PHASE SPACE   A fictitious space in which components of the linear momentum are taken as **COORDINATES** in addition to the space variables. (Part V)

PHOTOELECTRIC EFFECT   The freeing of electrons, and thus production of electric currents, for special substances by bombardment with light. (Part I)

PHOTON   The **QUANTUM** associated with the electromagnet field. (Part I)

PLANCK'S CONSTANT   A numerical constant, conventionally denoted by h, relating the frequency of a **PHOTON** to its **QUANTUM** of energy. (Part I)

PLANCK'S RADIATION LAW   The law giving the intensity of radiation from a **BLACK BODY** as a function of frequency or wave length at given temperature. (Part I)

PLASMA   An electrically neutral, ionized gas. (Part V)

POISSON'S EQUATION   A **DIFFERENTIAL EQUATION** for the potential distribution of matter (or electricity and magnetism). (Part II)

POLYTROPE   An **EQUATION OF STATE** of the form (pressure) = (constant) x (density)$^{1+1/n}$ where n, the *index* of the polytrope, is an integer.

PONDERABLE MATTER   Matter that has weight. (Parts II, IX)

POTENTIAL   A means of describing the interaction between two particles (or of one particle with its surroundings) by giving the interaction energy as a **FUNCTION** of the distance between the particles (or of the position of the particle). (Parts III, VI)

POTENTIAL, ADVANCED   A potential whose effect is felt in a shorter time than it would take the signal to travel. (Advanced potentials by themselves are not physical and can occur only in combination with **RETARDED POTENTIALS**). (Part VI)

POTENTIAL, RETARDED   A potential whose effect is felt in a longer time than it would take the signal to travel. (Part VI)

PRIMEVAL FIREBALL   The primeval (or primordial) "atom" containing all the mass of the universe, whose explosion was responsible according to the **BIG BANG** theory for the present expanding universe. (Part VIII)

PROTON   A positively charged particle (**FERMION**) that is the nucleus of the hydrogen atom, but also a constituent of the other atomic nuclei. (Parts V, VI, VIII)

PTOLEMAIC SYSTEM   The (ancient) system of the world designating the earth at rest and sun, planets, and stars as revolving around it. (Part II)

PULSAR   Rapidly pulsing **RADIO SOURCE** that is thought to be a rapidly spinning and magnetized **NEUTRON STAR.** (Part V)

QUANTUM   A discrete quantity of energy hν associated with a wave of frequency ν, where h is **PLANCK'S CONSTANT.** (Part I)

QUANTUM FIELD THEORY   The relativistically invariant version of **QUANTUM MECHANICS.** (Parts I, II, IX)

QUANTUM HYPOTHESIS   The hypothesis that energy is absorbed or transmitted in discrete quantities, **QUANTA.** (Part I)

QUANTUM MECHANICS   A theory or system developed to explain the quantized behavior of the **SYSTEM** of particles of the size of atoms or smaller. It differs from classical mechanics in that it gives only the probability or expectation value of various measurements on the system. (Parts II, IV)

QUANTUM NUMBERS   Integers or half integers specifying the values of certain **DYNAMIC VARIABLES** in **QUANTUM MECHANICS.** (Part I)

QUANTUM STATISTICS   A method of accounting for some properties of many-particle systems by relating them to the probabilities of the various **STATES** available to the component particles, taking their quantum mechanical behavior into account (*see also* **FERMI-DIRAC STATISTICS** and **BOSE-EINSTEIN STATISTICS**).

QUANTUM THEORY   An extension of classical dynamics, needed for an adequate description of the behavior of submicroscopic **SYSTEMS** (*see also* **QUANTUM MECHANICS**). Parts I, II, III, IX)

QUARK   Hypothetical particle, considered as the fundamental building stone of **MESONS** and nucleons, etc. (Part VII)

QUASAR   *Qua*si-*S*tella*r R*adio Source—an object with a dominant starlike component emitting an extremely large amount of energy and with an emission **LINE SPECTRUM** showing a large **RED SHIFT.** (Parts V, VIII)

RADAR TRACKING   The use of powerful radar transmitters and receivers to detect high-frequency waves (radar) reflected by celestial bodies, such as nearby planets in order to gauge their distances, velocites, and other properties. (Part III)

RADIATION   The emission of electromagnetic energy at any and all frequencies. (Parts I, VI)

RADIATION, ELECTROMAGNETIC   Radiation of energy involving electric and magnetic **FIELDS,** traveling at the speed of light. (Part II)

RADIATION, GRAVITATIONAL   *See* **GRAVITATIONAL RADIATION.**

RADIATION, THERMAL   The radiation emitted by a hot **BLACK BODY.** (Parts V, VIII)

RADIATION ERA   The early stage of the universe in which mostly only radiation was present. (Part VIII)

RADIATION LAW   *See* **PLANCK'S RADIATION LAW.**

RADIO ASTRONOMY   The detection, study, and interpretation of extraterrestrial **ELECTROMAGNETIC RADIATION.** (Part VIII)

RADIO SOURCE   A source of extraterrestrial radio radiation. (Part VIII)

RED SHIFT   The shift of spectral lines toward longer (i.e., redder) wave lengths, either because of a **DOPPLER SHIFT** or because of the **GRAVITATIONAL RED SHIFT,** or a combination of both. (Parts III, VIII)

RED SHIFT, GRAVITATIONAL   *See* **GRAVITATIONAL RED SHIFT.**

RELATIVISTIC EFFECTS   Effects or corrections due to **RELATIVITY.** (Part V)

RELATIVITY   The theory developed by Einstein to describe the relative motions of objects and observers, particularly when relative velocities approaching that of light and/or large masses are involved.

RELATIVITY, GENERAL   Takes up the point of view of systems whose motions relative to one another are not fixed and regular, and offers an important new outlook on **GRAVITATION.** (Parts II, V, VII, VIII)

RELATIVITY PRINCIPLE   A universal law of motion that states that the laws of mechanics are not affected by a uniform rectilinear motion of the system of coordinates to which they are referred. (Part II)

RELATIVITY PRINCIPLE, GENERAL   All systems of reference, K, K', etc., are equivalent in the description of natural phenomena, whatever may be their state of motion. (Parts II, VII)

RELATIVITY, SPECIAL   Gives an account of events from the point of view of two systems moving at a fixed and regular rate relative to one another. (Parts II, VII, IX)

REST MASS   The mass of a body at rest (derived consistently with Newton's second law of motion).

RIEMANN CURVATURE TENSOR   A **TENSOR** that determines the curvature of space-time in **RIEMANNIAN GEOMETRY.** Only if all its components vanish is the space flat (Euclidean). (Part II)

RIEMANNIAN GEOMETRY   A geometry that is based on the existence of a **LINE ELEMENT** or **METRIC.** (Parts I, II, IV)

RIEMANNIAN METRIC   A **METRIC** in V_4, a four-dimensional continuum (this is not the most general definition, however). (Part II)

RIEMANNIAN SPACE   A space, usually V_4, in which **RIEMANNIAN GEOME- TRY** is valid. (Part II)

RIGEL   A bright star in the constellation Orion. (Part III)

SCHWARZSCHILD RADIUS   A critical radius for any gravitating mass according to the general theory of relativity. If the mass is compressed inside the Schwarzschild radius the curvature of space will become so great that light will not be able to escape from the body to an external observer. Such light will become infinitely **RED-SHIFTED** as the body approaches the Schwarzschild radius. (*See also* **BLACK HOLE.**) (Parts II, IV, V, VIII)

SCHWARZSCHILD SINGULARITY   A mathematical singularity in the **SCHWARZSCHILD SOLUTION** if the radial distance is equal to the **SCHWARZSCHILD RADIUS.** (Parts II, IV)

SCHWARZSCHILD SOLUTION   A solution of the **FIELD EQUATIONS** in the case of the exterior region of a spherically symmetric distribution of matter found by K. Schwarzschild. (Parts II, IV)

SIMULTANEITY   Events that occur at precisely the same time but not at the same place, for a given observer. (Since such events are relative, what is simultaneous for one observer may not be to another one.) (Parts III, IV)

SINGULARITY   A point where space is so curved by matter that its radius is zero yet its density is infinite. (Parts II, VIII)

SIRIUS   Brightest known star in the constellation Canis Major. (Part III)

SIRIUS, COMPANION OF   A **WHITE DWARF** forming a binary system with Sirius. (Parts III, V)

SOLAR WIND   Ionized gas streaming from the sun into space. (Part V)

SOURCE COUNTS   Counts of **RADIO SOURCES** to determine their distribution in space. (Part VIII)

SOUTH PRECEDING STAR   A pulsating star in the **CRAB NEBULA** responsible for the energy radiated from the Crab (*See also* **PULSARS**). (Part V)

SPACE-TIME   The unification of space and time in a four-dimensional **CONTINUUM**. (Parts II, IV, VIII)

SPECTRAL CLASS   A classification of stars based primarily on their temperatures and chemical contents. (Part V)

SPECTRUM   Electromagnetic radiation arranged in accordance with its wavelengths in an orderly manner. It covers the whole family ranging from very long radio wavelengths through infrared, visible light, ultraviolet, X rays to gamma rays. (Parts V, VIII)

SPECTRUM ABSORPTION   The line absorbed by an atom from a **CONTINUOUS SPECTRUM** that would be present if the atom were to radiate energy. (Part VIII)

SPECTRUM, CONTINUOUS   A spectrum that contains all wavelengths. Such spectra are obtained from incandescent solids and liquids, and gases under high pressure. (Part VIII)

SPECTRUM, LINE   A spectrum in which only certain wavelengths are present, characteristic of the atom emitting the radiation, so that it takes the form of a number of clear-cut lines with space between them. (Part VIII)

SPIN   The property of a particle, such as the electron, in virtue of which it has a magnetic moment and mechanical moment (angular momentum). It is, however, independent of how the particle is moving. (Parts VII, III) In **QUANTUM MECHANICS** the spin is characterized by integral or half-integral **QUANTUM NUMBERS**.

SPIN ATTRACTION   The mutual attraction of two objects (particles) caused by the magnetic moment produced by their spin. (Part III)

SPINOR   A quantity describing **FIELDS,** usually of particles with half-integral spin (**FERMIONS**) with special transformation properties. (Part VII)

STATE   An atom or other **SYSTEM** is in a given state if its energy and other specified properties are momentarily fixed. (Part V)

STEADY STATE THEORY   A cosmological theory propounded by H. Bondi, T. Gold, and F. Hoyle, in which the universe has no beginning and no end and maintains the same mean density, in the face of its observed expansion by the continuous creation of matter. (Part VIII)

SUBSTRATUM   A simple model for the material content of the universe, in which all detail of local irregularities, such as galaxies, is suppressed by smearing it out over large volumes of space. More precisely, the matter in the universe is replaced by a homogeneous fluid of very low density. (Part VIII)

SUPERCONDUCTIVITY   The property possessed by many (but not all) metals at *very* low temperature of offering no resistance whatever to the passage of electric currents. (Part III)

SUPERGRAVITY   An attempt to adduce additional fields, describing **FERMIONS,** to gravity (general relativity). (Part VII)

SUPERNOVA   An exceptionally bright **NOVA,** in which a star ejects into space a major fraction of its mass, probably leading to the complete death of the star resulting in a **WHITE DWARF** or **NEUTRON STAR.** (Parts III, V)

SYSTEM   Any assemblage of particles, e.g., nucleus, atom, etc., whose properties are under consideration. (Parts II, V, VIII)

TENSOR   A mathematical entity specified by a set of components with respect to a **SYSTEM OF COORDINATES** such that the **TRANSFORMATION** that has to be applied to these components to obtain other components relating to a new system of coordinates is related to the transformation that had to be applied to the system of coordinates. (Parts II, VII)

TENSOR CALCULUS   A branch of mathematics that is concerned with the algebra and differential properties of **TENSORS.** (Parts I, IV, VII)

TENSOR CURVATURE   *See* **RIEMANN CURVATURE TENSOR.**

TENSOR, ENERGY MOMENTUM   A **TENSOR** whose components describe the distribution of energy and momentum of a distribution of matter and/or radiation. (Appendix)

TENSOR, METRIC   The fundamental **TENSOR** $g_{\mu\nu}$ ($\mu,\nu = 1$ to 4) in the **LINE ELEMENT** and Einstein's field equations that determines the **METRIC** of space-time. (Parts II, VII)

TENSOR, NONSYMMETRIC   A **TENSOR** whose value depends on the order of its indexes. It is *anti-symmetric* only if it changes sign upon interchange of any two of its indexes. (Part VII)

TENSOR, SYMMETRIC   A **TENSOR** whose value remains unchanged upon interchange of any two of its indexes. (The **METRIC TENSOR** is a symmetric tensor.) (Part II)

TEST PARTICLE   A particle that feels the effects of forces or fields, but that is too small to have any effect on these fields itself. (Part IX)

TETRAD   A set of four mutually orthogonal unit vectors at a point in space-time. (Part VII)

THERMODYNAMICS   The science of mathematical relations between heat and work and other forms of energy, and of general laws controlling changes in the heat of bodies and effects produced by heat. (Parts II, VII)

THERMODYNAMICS, SECOND LAW OF   It is impossible for heat to go by itself from a colder to a warmer body (without doing work on the system). (Part II)

3C CATALOG   The third Cambridge catalog of **RADIO SOURCE** positions. (Part III)

3C 273   One of the first discovered **QUASARS.** (Part III)

TIME DELAY (TEST)   A test of general relativity that is based on the time delay of a signal traveling through a gravitational field. (Part III)

TIME DILATION   The slowing down of time in a gravitational field; i.e., clocks tick slower, atoms vibrate slower, etc. (Part III)

TORSION BALANCE   A delicate instrument for measuring very small forces by their effect in moving a small rod suspended from its center from a thin wire. (Part III)

TRANSFER CONVECTIVE   The transfer of heat (or energy) by the motion of the particles themselves. (Part V)

TRANSFER RADIATIVE   The transfer of heat (or energy) by the radiation of energy. (Part V)

TRANSFORMATION   A process or rule for deriving a corresponding entity for a given mathematical entity (e.g., point, line, function, etc.). (Parts II, VII)

TRANSFORMATION, AFFINE   A transformation between two sets of variables in which each variable of either set is expressible as a linear combination of the variables of the other set. (Part VII)

TRANSFORMATION, COORDINATES   *See* **COORDINATE TRANSFORMA-TION.**

TRANSFORMATION, GALILEAN   A linear transformation of spatial variables leaving the time unchanged. (Part II)

TRANSFORMATION, LINEAR   A transformation between two sets of n variables represented by n equations in which the variables of both sets occur linearly. (Part IV)

TRANSFORMATION LORENTZ   *See* **LORENTZ TRANSFORMATION.**

TRANSIT   The transit (passing) of a celestial body across the field of view on the face of another celestial body. (Part III)

UHURU   The name of a space-satellite. Uhuru means freedom. (Part V)

ULTRAVIOLET   That range in the electromagnetic **SPECTRUM,** which lies in wavelengths just below the visible region. (Part I)

UNIFIED FIELD THEORY   A theory that attempts to unify gravitation (general relativity) with other fields—mostly electromagnetic fields. (Parts I, II, VII, VIII)

UNIVERSE   The total celestial cosmos. (Parts I, VIII)

UNIVERSE, CLOSED   A **WORLD MODEL** in which the expansion velocity of the original **BIG BANG** is less than the **ESCAPE VELOCITY** of the universe. In this model the rate of expansion will steadily decrease and come to a halt, and then the universe will start to contract. (Part VIII)

UNIVERSE, EXPANDING   The nature of the universe when the radial distance increases with the time. It is based on the observed recession of galaxies. (Parts III, VIII)

UNIVERSE, HOMOGENOUS   A universe in which the matter distribution is uniform, so that there is no center. (Part VIII)

UNIVERSE, ISOTROPIC   A universe that offers the same view (distribution) in all directions as seen by any observer. (Part VIII)

UNIVERSE, OPEN   A **WORLD MODEL** with a hyperbolic geometry, i.e., one in which the initial velocity of the particles in the **BIG BANG** exceeds the **ESCAPE VELOCITY** of the universe. (Part VIII)

UNIVERSE, OSCILLATING   A **WORLD MODEL** with a spherical geometry and in which the expansion curve is a cycloid. In this model the universe continuously undergoes successive cycles of expansion and contraction. (Part VIII)

UNIVERSE, STATIC   A universe whose radius of curvature is constant and independent of time, such as the **EINSTEIN UNIVERSE**. (Part VIII)

VARIABLE   A quantity whose value is not fixed, but may take any value (if *independent* variable) or one determined by a functional relationship (if *dependent* variable) in a given range. (Parts II, VIII)

VARIABLE, DYNAMIC   A variable that can be used in describing the behavior of the **SYSTEM** in question (e.g., position, momentum energy). (Part VII)

VELOCITY-DISTANCE RELATION   A relation between the velocity of recession of galaxies (as determined by the **DOPPLER SHIFT**) and the distance (*see also* **HUBBLE LAW**). (Part VIII)

VIKING   Code name of a spaceship that landed on Mars. (Part III)

VULCAN   A fictitious planet, which was supposed to exist between the sun and Mercury in order to explain that planet's **PERIHELION MOTION**. (Part III)

WAVE   A disburbance in the value of a **FIELD,** propagating itself through space. (Part VI)

WAVE MECHANICS   *See* **QUANTUM MECHANICS.**

WAVELENGTH   The distance between any point in a **WAVE** and the point having the same position in the wave before or after. (Part VIII)

WAVES, LONGITUDINAL   Waves that are propagated by motion of particles along the line of propagation. (Part VI)

WAVES, PLANE   Waves whose surfaces of propagation are plane surfaces. (Part VI)

WAVES, STANDING   Periodic waves having a fixed distribution in space, resulting from interference of progressive waves of the same frequency and kind traveling in opposite directions. (Part VI)

WAVES, TRANSVERSE   Waves that are propagated by oscillation of fields (or particles) moving at right angles to the line of propagation. (Part VI)

WELTANSCHAUUNG   A conception of the world; a philosophy of life. (Part I)

WHITE DWARFS   Small white stars of high density, having approximately the mass of the sun and size of the earth. The electrons of the atoms in the interior form a **DEGENERATE GAS.** White dwarfs are believed to be one of the last stages in a normal star's lifetime, the other two being a **NEUTRON STAR** and a **BLACK HOLE.** (Part V)

WHITE HOLE   The opposite of a **BLACK HOLE.** Matter flows into space rather than being pulled out of it. (Part V)

WORLD LINE   The trajectory of a particle (or light) in a four-dimensional **SPACE-TIME** diagram. Such a curve indicates not only the motion of the particle in space but also the development of that motion in time. (Parts II, VIII)

WORLD MODEL   A mathematical model of the universe (sometimes also called *cosmological model*). (Part VIII)

WORLD POINT   *See* **EVENT.** (Part II)

ZEEMAN EFFECT   The splitting of the lines of a **LINE SPECTRUM** into groups of lines, when the substance or body producing the lines is in a strong magnetic field. (Part III)

CONTRIBUTORS

R. A. Alpher	Einstein, Big Bang Cosmology, and the Residual Cosmic Black-Body Radiation (with R. Herman)
S. Arrhenius	Nobel Prize for Physics—1921 (reprint)
P. G. Bergmann	Future Developments
N. Bohr	Albert Einstein: 1879–1955 (reprint)
S. Chandrasekhar	Why Are the Stars as They Are?
G. M. Clemence	The Relativity Effect in Planetary Motions (reprint)
S. Deser	From Einstein's Gravity to Supergravity
B. S. DeWitt	Gravitational Deflection of Light. Solar Eclipse of 30 June 1973
R. H. Dicke	The Eötvös Experiment
A. S. Eddington	The Theory of Relativity and Its Influence on Scientific Thought
F. Everitt	Experimental Tests of General Relativity: Past, Present and Future